GW00832650

Eight Lessons in Love

Eight Lessons

A DOMESTIC

in Love

VIOLENCE READER

Mark Spilka

UNIVERSITY OF MISSOURI PRESS
Columbia and London

University of Missouri Press, Columbia, Missouri 65201
Printed and bound in the United States of America

5 4 3 2 1 01 00 99 98 97

Library of Congress Cataloging-in-Publication Data

Spilka, Mark.
Eight lessons in love : a domestic violence reader / Mark Spilka.
p. cm.
Includes bibliographical references and index.
ISBN 0-8262-1123-2 (alk. paper)
1. Short stories, American—History and criticism. 2. Short stories, English—History and criticism. 3. Family violence in literature. 4. Family violence—Fiction. 5. Short stories, American. 6. Short stories, English. I. Title.
PS374.F265S66 1997
813'.0108355—dc21 97-274
CIP

∞™ This paper meets the requirements of the American National Standard for Permanence of Paper for Printed Library Materials, Z39.48, 1984.

Text Design: Elizabeth K. Young
Jacket Design: Stephanie Foley
Typesetter: BOOKCOMP
Printer and binder: Thomson-Shore, Inc.
Typefaces: Times Roman, Bernhard Modern

For

Shelly Spilka, who helped me to pull this book and so much else together.

And for all those brave dedicated unsung members of the Rhode Island Coalition Against Domestic Violence.

Especially those friends, colleagues, and mentors—Anne Grant, Barbara Fuyat, Michael Grupp, Andy deLong, Jim McDonald, John Kotula, Michael Rudnick, Bobby Johnson, Ruth Horton, Gary French, Claude LaBrosse, Birkin James Diana, and Jim O'Donnell—who helped me to understand some of the more difficult problems of the field.

Contents

Acknowledgments

Because domestic violence is such a new and volatile subject, and because its fictional expressions are as yet uncharted, I am more than usually indebted to friends and colleagues for responding to my views and for helping me to develop and improve these essays. I owe thanks to Professor Deborah Allen Thomas of Villanova University for the chance to lecture there on domestic violence in *Janet's Repentance* in November 1995, and to the editors of *Novel: A Forum on Fiction,* especially Nancy Armstrong, for their helpful criticisms of the original manuscript. I am indebted also to Professor Lawrence Gamache of the University of Ottawa for the chance to address the international Lawrence conference there on domestic violence in "The White Stocking" in June 1993, and to publish that paper in the Ottawa conference anthology (1996), and to Professor Ellen Spolsky of Bar-Ilan University in Israel for the chance to repeat the lecture there in January 1994. I am indebted also to my colleague at Brown, Bob Scholes, for the foundational effect of his early work on Joyce on my examination of Joyce's "Counterparts," and for his friendly forbearance of our several ongoing ideological disagreements elsewhere. I owe thanks also to Professor Linda Wagner-Martin, then Vice-President of the Hemingway Society, for the chance to address the international Hemingway conference at the Kennedy Library in Boston on domestic violence in Hemingway's fiction in July 1990, and to the Portuguese Association for Anglo-American Studies for the chance to repeat the lecture at their conference in Porto, Portugal, in March 1992 and to publish it in their conference anthology (1993).

More recently, as a peripatetic proselytizer for these essays in the fall of 1996, I have been able to repeat and refine my Hemingway and George Eliot chapters, and to test condensed versions of my chapters on Ann Petry and Isaac Bashevis Singer, before assorted academic audiences. For these welcome opportunities, and for the extraordinary hospitality of my several hosts, I want to thank Grace Farrell at Butler University, David Hertz at Indiana University, Janice Harris and Caroline McCracken-Flesher at the University of Wyoming, Michael Johnson and Cheryl Lester at Kansas University, Bonnie Nelson at Kansas State, and Rabbi Jerome Gurland at Western New England College.

I want to thank also Gil Garcetti, Los Angeles County District Attorney, for his kind response to my essay "Ann Petry's Determinist Dilemma: Unchosen

Violence in 'Like a Winding Sheet' " at the end of the Simpson trial, and for his decision to place the essay on file with his Family Violence Division staff, and to thank also my younger colleague in Afro-American studies at Brown, Dorothy Denniston, for reading and responding to the essay. I am indebted to Professor Ed Jansen, my wife's colleague at Western New England College, for introducing me to John Cheever's "Torch Song" and other stories for my essay on that writer's work on domestic violence; and to my old friend Professor Emeritus Charles Shapiro of York College, CUNY, for arranging our brief visit many years back with the Cheevers. Finally I want to thank the several helpful preliminary readers of my essay on Isaac Bashevis Singer: my close friend and fellow emeritus at Brown, Edwin Honig; Rabbi Alan Flam at Brown and Rabbi Leslie Gutterman at Temple Beth El in Providence; Professor Janet Hadda at UCLA and (again) Professor Grace Farrell at Butler. I might add here that my wife, Shelly Shapira Regenbaum Spilka, has been the first reader of all but two of these essays, and my dearest and most supportive critic.

I owe thanks also to the following publishers for U.S., Canadian, and British permission rights: to Simon and Schuster and to the Hemingway Foreign Rights Trust, for permission to reprint and quote passages from "The Snows of Kilimanjaro" and to quote passages from *To Have and Have Not* by Ernest Hemingway; to Penguin USA and to Reed Consumer Books Ltd. for permission to reprint "The Murder" by John Steinbeck; to Russell and Volkening, Inc., for permission to reprint and quote passages from "Like a Winding Sheet" by Ann Petry; to Random House and Alfred Knopf and to Wylie, Aitken, and Stone Inc. for permission to reprint and quote passages from "Torch Song" by John Cheever; to Farrar, Straus and Giroux and to Jonathan Cape of Random House UK for permission to reprint and quote passages from "The Wife Killer: A Folk Tale" by Isaac Bashevis Singer and to quote passages from *The Family Moskat, Gimpel the Fool and Other Stories,* and *The Spinoza of Market Street* by Singer; to Lescher and Lescher Ltd, as well as Farrar, Straus and Giroux, for permission to quote passages from Singer's "The Witch"; and to Houghton Mifflin Company for permission to quote passages from Ann Petry's *The Street* and Susan Cheever's *Home before Dark.*

Last but hardly least, I want to express my personal as well as professional gratitude to Director Beverly Jarrett and Managing Editor Jane Lago of the University of Missouri Press for their inestimable help in making this book possible and presentable, and to Heidi Kuhn of the Brown University English Department secretarial staff, for her heroic resistance to the computer dybbuks who threatened the book's clear transmission as a pristine manuscript.

Eight Lessons in Love

A Personal Introduction

I. About My Title

The original prosaic title of this book—*Domestic Violence in Short Modern Fictions: A Critical Sampler*—offered a fair working description of its contents. The present grimly ironic title—*Eight Lessons in Love: A Domestic Violence Reader*—comes closer to the book's imaginative aims and depth. Indeed, the gist of this title—"lessons in love"—came to me in a happy dream, shortly after the manuscript was accepted for publication. The "lessons" I have since derived from it are twofold.

First, there are the lessons that batterers hope to teach to their supposedly beloved wives or children. In George Eliot's pioneering tale, *Janet's Repentance* (1858), for instance, the abusive male protagonist comes home drunk after a triumphant political rally and, when his wife fails to answer his peremptory call, becomes upset: "I'll teach you to keep me waiting in the dark," he tells her. "I'll beat you into your senses." Similarly, in James Joyce's "Counterparts" (1916), the decidedly less triumphant male protagonist comes home drunk after the day's humiliations and beats his son viciously for a kitchen mishap: "By God, I'll teach you to do that again. . . . I'll teach you to let the fire out." In Steinbeck's "The Murder" (1934), the male protagonist teaches his foreign wife an even grimmer lesson by shooting her sleeping lover and then bullwhipping her in the barn the next day, to the ultimate delight of the townspeople, who admire and approve his manly conduct, and to the more immediate satisfaction of his straying wife.

The message behind all such violent lessons is this: "I'll teach you who's boss in this household." As professionals in the field have observed, it is a drastic lesson in power and control. They have argued accordingly that domestic violence is not about love, as we now understand it, but about the need for men to reassert their threatened or lost command in marriage.

Actually such lessons occur in service of an older hierarchical form of love whereby men are still seen as lords and masters of their households and wives and children are seen as subservient and subordinate creatures. Eliot and Joyce are obviously critical of the demeaning and damaging implications of such love and want their readers to agree with them. But Steinbeck is intrigued by the lordful view; he wants to shock his readers into accepting the supposed wisdom of the older hierarchical arrangements, and even to accept their violent implications. All three writers are also responding, however, to our new and decidedly more democratic understanding of what love implies, that of a romantic marriage between equals. The conflict between these old and new forms of love seems to me crucial to the apparent increase in domestic violence in modern times. As Joyce's story indicates, it extends even to the relations between parents and children, for the violence done to the hapless Catholic son in that story was meant for his more formidable and less easily mastered mother, and this is frequently the case with domestic abuse of children: it is in varied ways an offshoot of conflict between adult partners as they cope with each other and the world.

Indeed, more broadly speaking, domestic violence of any kind is an offshoot of the wider conflicts of hierarchical power relations in modern industrial and supposedly democratic societies as they make their inevitable impress on family life. In Joyce's story the protagonist is a lowly Catholic clerk in a Dublin law office who is sharply reprimanded by his northern Irish and therefore probably Protestant boss, a servant himself of the new commercial spirit of early modern times; and the compensations this lowly clerk then seeks in comradely Irish pubs lead to further humiliations, erotic and athletic putdowns that help to turn him into his boss's domestic counterpart and to prime him for irrational and displaced revenge. Similarly, in Ann Petry's story of domestic violence between a young black couple, "Like a Winding Sheet" (1945), the protagonist is primed for irrational revenge by the racial and gender stresses of his nightshift work in a modern factory, where as a mere black male gofer he is humiliated by his white woman supervisor. In Isaac Bashevis Singer's pre- and post-holocaust stories of Jewish life in Warsaw and New York, moreover, the deadly consequences of ethnic hierarchies before, during, and after World War II are similarly reflected in the instabilities and sometimes violent irrationalities of Jewish family relations.

The paradoxical power hierarchies of modern democratic society, then, along with the conflict between hierarchical and democratic forms of love, contribute to the many stresses on modern marriage and to its emotional and sometimes physical disruptions. That "necessary conflict" between death-directed and life-directed options in marriage in D. H. Lawrence's fictions, on which I have often commented elsewhere, becomes increasingly a conflict involving the more physically abusive forms of domestic violence. This brings us to my second and more central purpose in changing my title to *Eight Lessons in Love.* As I will later indicate more fully, I want my readers to ponder the multiple meanings of the eight fictional treatments of domestic violence gathered in this book, and more particularly to take my own readings of these fictions as appraisals that may well yield lessons on the failures of love, the disruptions through violence of even the most intimate relations. Indeed, it was my own sense of the emotional violence of modern marriage, as expressed by the modern fictions I had been teaching for some thirty years at Brown, Michigan, Indiana, and elsewhere, and to a degree as I had experienced them myself, which led me to the volunteer work discussed below.

II. About Me

Between 1983 and 1992 I worked as a volunteer group counselor and grant writer for a social service organization called Brother to Brother, a Rhode Island agency (now defunct) for the rehabilitation of male batterers. Within a short time I also became a nonvoting member of the coordinating council for that agency. It was then that my previous professional training as a literary critic, journal editor, and teacher of literature began to converge with my avocational training. I began to ask myself literary questions, that is to say, about domestic violence. Why did Hemingway think a man could die well, in "The Snows of Kilimanjaro" (1934), by writing stories in his mind, yet still abuse his wife while dying? Why did Margaret Drabble, in *The Realms of Gold* (1975), admire the married lover of her unmarried archaeologist heroine for patiently beating his wife? And why did she insist that the wife provoked such beatings so as to complain to her lesbian lover? Why did Vladimir Nabokov make such a joking/poking/lyrical matter, in *Lolita* (1955), out of the abusive attempts of a grown male child molester to possess and love a twelve-year-old girl? And why, in his autobiographical fictions, did D. H. Lawrence avoid direct depictions of his own domestic violence?

When such questions began to multiply I decided to organize them into courses on domestic violence in modern fiction for my students at Brown University. Before my recent retirement, I was able to teach four or five such courses in which I applied to selected fictions the outlook on domestic violence I had absorbed from my volunteer work in the field. That is the radical outlook at work in the critical essays contained in this reader: an application of present wisdom about domestic violence to fictional attempts to cope with that theme in the fairly recent past. I shall discuss the terms of that outlook in a later section. For the time being let me present some relevant historical, social, and literary considerations about domestic violence; and let me briefly indicate also the specific nature of my eight critical readings of eight short modern fictions on that theme.

III. About Domestic Violence in Fiction

Domestic violence entered the field of fiction in the nineteenth century as an unarticulated and unfocused social problem. For Emily and Charlotte Brontë its sensational aspects could be foregrounded through exalted heroes like Heathcliff and Rochester whose brutalities were then rationalized as romantic excesses; for male writers including Dickens, Dostoyevsky, and Zola, those same brutalities could be accommodated and absorbed within some larger focus on religious, economic, or bureaucratic tyrannies or, in Dostoyevsky's case, through ideological wrestlings with the radical inhumanities of nihilism and socialism. But none of these writers could handle the problem straightforwardly, on its own narrowly domestic terms, as a legal felony, as a criminal abuse of personal rights, and therefore, in more broadly appropriate focus, as a damaging form of moral and legal irresponsibility, on the one hand, and of gender bias, on the other, at once the symptom and reflection of a collapsing family ethos.

These are the terms of modern discourse about domestic violence. They help us to understand and talk about it in ways unprecedented before the present decade. Indeed, it has taken some two centuries of cumulative effort even to begin to develop our current all-too-limited range of articulation and focus, and most of the crucial gains have been registered only recently, with the advent of the feminist movement of the 1970s and 1980s, when women's shelters and group counseling for male batterers first emerged and state laws began to be formulated and amended. The radical increase of media attention to domestic violence in the 1990s depended heavily, moreover, on these social and political advances. There was simply nothing like it in the way of public attention in previous decades, nor any precedent for it in the past two centuries.

Nothing, that is to say, except literary treatments of the theme and the kind of concerned awareness they would gradually foster, or help to foster. The contributions of fictional treatments to this gathering focus seem in this light considerable. These fictions have scarcely been straightforward, but the movement toward deeper and richer understandings of the theme has been fairly constant; and, particularly in modern times, through closer and more realistic attention to the sources of domestic conflict, it has proved enormously enlightening. For this reason a study of the difficulties and rewards of modern fictional treatments of domestic violence is decidedly worth making. The difficulties, as we shall see, are those endemic to the problem itself, to its denials and obfuscations over time, to its engagement with clashing claims and beliefs, and to its intersections with those larger systems already mentioned—religious, economic, bureaucratic, and political—by which domestic life is inevitably shaped and defined.

Although almost no writer has struggled altogether effectively with these difficulties, it seems safe to say that all serious writings on the theme have clarified and amplified its possible present meanings and their past entanglements. The rewards of dealing with such literary struggles are accordingly great: they steep us in the same complexities and contradictions, the same myths and realities, that exist outside fiction, and so help us to confront them; as an added and distinct advantage, they give us also breathing room and space for discussing these live and difficult problems without acrimony or contention; and finally, for serious students of literature, they indicate in the most graphic way possible how writers on domestic violence have always struggled to make imaginative sense of very real enormities.

IV. About This Book

The present *Domestic Violence Reader* has been designed with these rewards and advantages in mind. It consists of eight critical appraisals of eight short fictions, each of them followed by the work to which it alludes, and each alluding also to other texts by the same author, so that readers or students are free to pursue further each writer's development of such themes.

These paired readings and texts begin with a premodern example, George Eliot's early novella, *Janet's Repentance,* from *Scenes of Clerical Life* (1858), which I take to be the first really modern assessment of domestic violence as a serious social problem. Eliot's several difficulties and triumphs in handling this theme are instructive, moreover, in prefiguring the comparable difficulties faced by her more temporally modern successors and their comparable triumphs in overcoming them. She is the first woman writer, for instance, to work against the pressures of the patriarchal system on women who choose to expose its propensities for domestic violence—though as we shall see, she yields somewhat to those pressures even while boldly confronting them. Here is the first brave, bold, yet somewhat collusive attempt, then, to think through the implications of such violence for family relations, whether marital or parental. Not the least of its merits, moreover, is Eliot's connection of such disruptions with a wide range of social problems: from religious, social, and gender biases in the community to the alcoholism of both partners. Indeed, she gives us our first overall social view of the problem—our first "lesson" in the range and depth of its social and personal dimensions and of its hazards for women writers.

Our second example, D. H. Lawrence's "The White Stocking" (1914), is remarkable for its almost classic interpretation of the stages by which such incidents of domestic violence proceed and for its more particular account of their premarital origins and marital consequences. Lawrence was strongly influenced by Eliot, and in his first great autobiographical novel, *Sons and Lovers* (1913), he probably drew on her novella for similar scenes of domestic violence between a drunken husband and his battered wife. That more than half a century lies between Eliot's novella and his own early efforts is one further measure of the gradualness by which awareness of these problems has grown.

Lawrence's position as an early avatar of the sexual revolution, and the otherwise adventurous Eliot's inhibiting Victorian moorings, suggest how much an overall change in cultural awareness of intimate gender relations has been necessary for such literary advances to take place. One relevant indication of that change, for instance, is Lawrence's deliberate avoidance of the hazards of sentimentality by which Eliot's Victorian treatment of domestic conflict is sometimes hampered. Through these advantages he is able to give us a fuller and more "classic" lesson on how and why the problem begins in a specific instance and why it inevitably recurs—as we see all too sadly in his own lifelong struggles with it. Indeed, whatever his advantages, Lawrence plainly shares with Eliot a personal need to deal with the angers and frustrations roused by such conflict, whether in batterers or in victims, and it seems evident enough that he depends on and works from her impressive precedent.

Lawrence's tale take us into a white-collar household in the industrial British Midlands and involves direct relations with an amorous factory owner. Our third example, James Joyce's *Dubliners* (1914), takes us into a more mercantile urban scene and deals with a harshly demanding rather than an erotic boss; but that boss's power over his employees, and the detailed evidence of that power ladder as it works in an urban and mercantile society, is very much the conflictual "counterpart" of the drastic domestic consequences that we see, in this hierarchical tale, as the embittered protagonist, a lowly office clerk, returns home late at night, drunk and discouraged, and takes out his day's humiliations on his innocent son. This nice connection of child abuse with office putdowns on the socioeconomic ladder offers a model, then, of the direct workings of social inhumanities on family relations, and its extensions into the rivalrous night world of Irish barrooms continues the contributory theme of alcoholism that begins in Eliot's novella. Indeed, Joyce's more sophisticated lesson in the interconnections between power hierarchies and domestic violence begins with and improves upon Eliot's suggestive precedent.

Our fourth example, Hemingway's "The Snows of Kilimanjaro" (1934), exhibits at some length the egoistic satisfactions of verbal abuse and their psychic origins in the wasted life of the protagonist, a writer much like Hemingway who has traded his talent for the idle riches of a convenient marriage. Paradoxically, the tale also rewards this dying verbal abuser of his safari wife with a heavenward journey, presumably because he has fought against gangrenous death by writing his many unwritten stories in his mind as he reviews the lost opportunities for inscribing them. Hemingway's failure to figure into the moral arithmetic of this heavenward journey the abusive treatment of a supportive wife, or his possible willingness to write it off against the larger gains of manliness—those of a brave private death—helps to place this story as an unusually provocative example of the revived machismoism of the 1920s and 1930s, the widespread male reaction to disturbing problems of economic displacement and lost gender hegemony posed in the aftermath of World War I. A look at Hemingway's later attempts to avoid such warped lessons through fictions involving nonabusive deaths, such as *To Have and Have Not* (1937) and *For Whom the Bell Tolls* (1940), suggests that he was uncomfortable with his own earlier position and worked to overcome its gender bias and its limited view of manliness. Finally, with Hemingway as with Joyce, the relation of alcoholism to domestic violence is again all too relevant.

Our fifth author, John Steinbeck, is represented here by his early prizewinning tale "The Murder" (1934), valued in its day for hard-hitting realism, but now more sexist-seeming than Steinbeck could have imagined. Indeed, along with *Of Mice and Men* (1937) and other early tales, the story exemplifies an even more deep-rooted misogyny than we have yet witnessed, one more difficult to transcend and only challenged by his late ambitious struggle to get beyond the obsessive notion of a monstrously evil woman in *East of Eden* (1952). Thus Steinbeck's early attraction to the low threshold of anger frequently cultivated by misogynous men like the itinerant worker George Milton, the supposedly better and wiser half of the pairing of George and Lennie in *Of Mice and Men,* is reflected in "The Murder" by the easygoing husband's deliberate and controlled shooting of his foreign wife's sleeping lover, and even more deliberate bullwhipping of his unfaithful wife, after finding them in bed together on his unexpected return from one of his own adulterous jaunts into town. The blatant "lesson" of this harrowing tale—that a woman's fear of and respect for deadly male brutality is the only sure basis for marital happiness—now seems like an obvious explanation for its early popularity, only thinly disguised for early American readers by the story's western "frontier" setting and its invocation of Old World practices like wife beating as extreme and exotic rather than usual New World measures. The sad evidence in these early tales of Steinbeck's almost defiant preoccupation with "blameless murder" and "blameless wife-whipping," however uncomfortable to contemplate, is hard to ignore.

It seems worth noting also that my early examination of such cultivated sexist rages, in "Of George and Lennie and Curley's Wife: Sweet Violence in Steinbeck's Eden" (1974), would lead to my application to the other fictions here included—notably Lawrence's "The White Stocking" and Ann Petry's "Like a Winding Sheet"—of the Anger Iceberg Chart used by professional counselors to educate male batterers in the nature and consequences of their own cultivated rages: for in all these stories we see parallel fictional examples of just such "talking up" of hidden resentments and old unsettled scores into explosive violence, as opposed to "talking [them] down" as a step toward calm and respectful negotiations with equal partners.

Our sixth example, Ann Petry's "Like a Winding Sheet" (1945), takes us into the vexed public arena of racism and sexism and their clashing claims for attention and predominance. These virulent claims, which seem so prominent today in such media sensations as the O. J. Simpson murder trial, the Mike Tyson conviction for sexual assault, and the Supreme Court candidacy hearings of Clarence Thomas, go back past midcentury for African American observers, who have long been divided between the need to stand together as a community against white racism and the need to confront the internal disruptions of black sexism in and out of marriage. As early as 1938, for instance, black male reviewer Richard Wright could dismiss Zora Neale Hurston's *Their Eyes Were Watching God* for its supposed minstrel-show panderings to white expectations about black behavior without any acknowledgment of Hurston's running critique, in that pioneering novel, of male abusiveness in black marriages—and, needless to say, without much self-awareness of his own forthcoming justifications for sexist violence in *Native Son* (1940). At the same time, Hurston's divided feelings about her own critical boldness, and her strong personal investment in at least one of her black male characters, had led to a kind of collusive protection of that character (the otherwise charming and attractive Tea Cake) from responsibility for his own violent propensities in marriage.

This kind of communally induced self-division seems understandable enough in the works of black women writers, given the evident pressures of such clashing claims. It occurs in a number of Toni Morrison's novels in our own time, and it occurred also for Ann Petry in the 1940s and 1950s as she responded to the exemplary realism established by Wright and other black male contemporaries with her own more sophisticated and gender-conscious fictions. Her protection of the wife-battering hero of "Like a Winding Sheet" is inevitably intermixed with her indictment of the racism that largely drives him—like the hero of Joyce's "Counterparts"—to seek domestic revenge for public humiliations; but she is too sensitive to the sexist hazards faced by her own gender, in and out of marriage, not to record them with force and fidelity even as she tries to shield her black male protagonist from his own gender difficulties, his own misogynous leanings. At the end, however, she presents her male batterer as the hapless witness to his own uncontrolled rages, whatever their social or psychic origins, and therefore as the victim of his own unconscious choices. The result is a powerful lesson about conflicting racial and sexual claims in which the problem of male accountability for the brutal and possibly deadly abuse of the batterer's innocent wife is left unresolved.

Our seventh selection, John Cheever's "Torch Song" (1953), is at once an example of the widespread cultural demonization of women and of its misogynous origins, in this case in the author's well-documented reactions to his own homoerotic impulses. This powerful story is nominally about a cheerfully deadly woman, a falsely merciful *la belle dame sans merci* who is drawn toward weak or suffering men and sees them to their graves. Her progress is observed, however, by a male friend who almost becomes her final victim, but who manfully rebels against the prospect of his own untimely death. Through his manful reaction, moreover, we see that the abusiveness and often drug-related violence of her many previous victims was only a perverse form of rebellion against her cheerfully deadly wiles.

This final dubious implication, that all men who batter their female partners are really fighting against death, recalls the misogynous view of the 1920s and 1930s of women as castrating bitches, here updated to accommodate the grim ambience of suffering and death in World War II. Thus in "Torch Song" that larger wartime ambience is symbolically related to the morbid lusts of its oddly cheerful heroine. The frequent anthologization of this story further suggests the ongoing force of its mythic view of the female of the species as somehow deadlier than the male. Since the statistics of domestic violence prove quite otherwise, we may legitimately speculate that such views are projective, and that those who propose them are struggling somehow with their own hostilities, their own propensities for real or imagined violence. In Cheever's case the propensities were imagined, though he was himself an alcoholic, had frequent quarrels with his wife, betrayed her openly with other women—and secretly with other men. Only late in his life was he able to become more truly brave and turn openly to relations with other men.

The story seems to reflect an early homophobic stage in this progression, when he condemned himself for his secret urges. In this sense the hidden "illness" of the heroine's many lovers is homosexuality, the heroine herself represents the author's fear of open involvement with "ailing" men, and the rebellion of the male protagonist reflects the author's determination to become more "manly" and to avoid identification as an "ailing" man himself. The evidence from biographical sources that the heroine's cheerful manner and peculiarly pleasing voice were derived from Cheever's wife, Mary, further supports this speculative reading. The evidence from the author's journals and from his more obviously autobiographical fictions—*The Wapshot Chronicle* (1947); *Falconer* (1977)—confirms his struggles early and late with his own homoerotic urges.

The professional value of this tale as a lesson in homophobic projection seems obvious enough. Like Cheever, who early feared his own "unmanly" propensities, most batterers feel insecure about their masculinity; they tend to be homophobic as well as misogynous, and their fear of being mistaken for a homosexual is like their fear of becoming or being mistaken for a woman. It is part of the overall threat to their shaky and frequently challenged maleness, their ability to compete in a largely male-oriented world. They are, in a very real sense, victims of their own machismoism, their own rigid gender definitions, and sadly in search of scapegoats to punish for their several insecurities. When their control or possession of female partners is in any way threatened, their control of their own masculinity is also threatened; they may react violently against their partners—and project their own hostilities upon them. Unhappily, the professional problem of explaining homophobic reactions to homophobic men is still very much unsolved; if more effectively pursued, this difficult job could be one way to ease the self-induced and culturally fortified distress about maleness among batterers, and so help to break the cycle of domestic violence.

The subtitle of our final selection, Isaac Bashevis Singer's "The Wife Killer" (1957), is "A Folk Tale." As with many other tales by Singer, its locus is the Jewish section—the shtetl—of a Polish village called Turbin, circa 1900. Singer is famous as the chronicler of this lost world of traditional Jewish life. Most of his fictions about this world, originally written in Yiddish, have been translated into English by admirers and disciples, and they now constitute a major contribution to modern American fiction. Singer's modernity—his interest in sexual relations, in irrational behaviors, in the tensions between old and new generations and between traditional and enlightened beliefs—makes him an ideal transmitter of Old World views and practices into New World culture. He reminds us, in his oscillations between these worlds, of the survival into modern times of traditional assumptions about domestic relations, and of our own oscillations between these old and new assumptions.

Indeed, I have placed him as our final example because of his ongoing concern with the hierarchical view of marriage (as opposed to marriage between equal partners) that survives from the Gentile as well as the Jewish past and that continues to affect the annals of domestic violence. Singer's frequent concern, for instance, with the orthodox Jewish view of women as unclean, on the one hand, and frighteningly seductive, on the other, helps us to locate one of the religious origins of surviving hostile views of women as deadly, vain, deceitful, and demonic creatures—femmes fatale, *belle dames sans merci,* witches, bitches, sirens—which we have already seen in Cheever's and Steinbeck's authorial projections, and will see again in Singer's frequent demonizations of the legendary Lilith. When Dr. Yaretzky, the bachelor protagonist of Singer's "The Shadow of a Crib" (1962), tells us confidently that "deceit is as essential to women as violence is to men," he offers a convenient epitomization of the deadly basis for such demonizing projections.

Similarly, Singer's struggles with his own hostilities toward women, his attractions toward violence and withdrawal, toward "wife killers" and escape artists, offers a useful key to the male struggles in our time with abusive propensities; his partial resolution of those propensities, in such late fictions as "The Shadow of a Crib" and "The Witch" (1975), may serve as an interrelated solution for all such strugglers. Meanwhile his Old World protagonists, often sympathetically portrayed, have an extraordinarily New World penchant for either doing in or abandoning wives and sweethearts. And Singer himself, as the authorial dispatcher of vain wives and other sinful female characters, may be said to rival the Angel of Death whom George Eliot dispatches against the abusive male characters who mistreat her self-blaming, anger-repressing heroines.

Singer is in this respect and others an Attractive Oscillator, a master of ambivalent stances, of ways of using opposed positions to correct or criticize each other. His curious empathy, for instance, with the devils, imps, and demons who frequently narrate his tales suggests a convenient way to indulge the "devilish" or rebellious impulses of his youth while at the same time affirming his father's traditional moral and religious attitudes toward such "sinful" impulses. Indeed, he is famous for his preoccupation with demonology, which he explains as an index to the irrational and mysterious possibilities of life, whether in pre-holocaust Poland or post-holocaust America; but a different explanation for that obsessive interest may be found in his own early oscillations between faith and enlightenment, traditional religion and rational philosophy, and their respective family embodiments. Thus his cabalist father, his rational mother, and his enlightened older brother, the famous novelist Israel Joshua Singer, decidedly helped to shape these contradictory swings and oscillations and their demonic expressions. Joshua's forthright rebellion from the family and Isaac's much more passive rebellion may be usefully compared in this light as indices to their philosophical differences.

More important for our purposes is Joshua's forthright satire of an overly aggressive rabbi, the wife killer of his early novel *Yoshe Kalb* (1933), through which Isaac first learned about that interesting Jewish folk prohibition against marrying a man whose first three wives have died. Isaac's mixed and ultimately sympathetic view of Pelte the Wife Killer, whose fourth wife, Zlateh the Bitch, proves more commercially ruthless and more domestically abusive than he, then dies of her own fears of dying, should be compared as an essentially waffling comic treatment with Israel Joshua's hard-hitting satiric portrait of Rabbi Melech in *Yoshe Kalb,* his direct indictment of such former orthodox practices as forcing early arranged marriages on children, wearing out wives through frequent childbearing and interminable childrearing, shaving their hair and covering their shaven heads with wigs to curb their seductiveness and prevent infidelities, confining them to domestic and sexual servitude, refusing them the option of divorce, and replacing them like interchangeable parts when they finally die. Pelte is a milder and much more passive wife killer than Rabbi

Melech, a kind of Dostoyevskian buffoon, a Polish/Jewish Fyodor Karamazov, replete with zany fits and sulks and a yen for younger women. But at least he introduces us to the frequency of death in abusive domestic relations, and to the painful realization that the threat of death to battered or oppressed wives is inherent in such relations—not a minor statistic to be trivialized by defending lawyers, as in the recent Simpson trials, but an ongoing deadly reality that can affect the outcome of any abusively disrupted marriage.

To his credit, Singer is aware of these violent propensities, in himself and in his fictional heroes, but he is more obviously like the withholders and escapers in his fictions, the passively aggressive buffoons like Pelte and the charming but reluctant bachelors like Dr. Yaretzky. He is less inclined to actual violence than to delayed and roundabout withdrawal and retreat. In a sense he is the perennial secular yeshiva boy, the lifelong student of Torah and/or philosophy, who enjoys the male privilege of being supported by the community while he writes and studies—or who is supported, if he marries, by a devoted wife through her diligent labors inside and outside the home. Indeed, in 1940 Singer actually married such a wife, Anna Haimann Wasserman, who helped to support his writing for many years by continuing to work in Macy's sales department in New York. It was not until ten years later, when *The Family Moskat* appeared as the first of Singer's works to be translated into English, that he was able to support her as well as himself through his own writing. To such male privileges, moreover, we must also add artistic privileges, for Singer loved to induce from other women their stories about the Old World, or bizarre events in America, as material for his fictions, and his understanding wife not only approved of such helpful relations but also looked the other way when they blossomed into romantic interludes.

No wonder then that Singer became such as ardent advocate of the finer aspects of traditional or "hierarchical" marriage! With both male and artistic privileges working for him, he could afford to underplay those repressive aspects his brother confronted so bravely and directly. But then Joshua wasn't as interested as he was in salvaging the finer aspects of Old World tradition. At his best, moreover, Isaac too tried to sort out the destructive repressions as well as the saving restraints of their common heritage. It is in Isaac's fiction, for instance, that the problem of the old hierarchical view of marriage conjoins with the modern problem of male hostility to women; and it is through Isaac's struggle with that conjunction, particularly after his brother's untimely death in 1944, that we are able to take a long and careful look at its historic origins, at its murderously consequential lessons, and at the author's honest fictional attempts to come to terms with its troubling as well as its revealing impress on domestic relations.

This brings us to a principle we will touch upon again in the section ahead. In his fictions about domestic violence, and particularly in those in which he wrote about philosophical oscillators like himself—men torn between faith and doubt, such as Asa Hashel Bannet in *The Family Moskat,* Dr. Fischelson in "The Spinoza of Market Street" (1962), Dr. Yaretsky in "The Shadow of a Crib," Jacques Kohn in "A Friend of Kafka" (1970), Rabbi Nechemia in "Something Is There" (1970), Boris Lemkin's shadow/friend Harry in "The New Year Party" (1975), and Mark Meitels in "The Witch"—Singer was always his better self; he was always a better person in such writings than in his private life.

V. About My Outlook

Casual as well as careful readers of the previous section will have noticed my use of a number of professional terms employed by counselors in the domestic violence field: the Power Ladder; the Anger Iceberg Chart; batterers and victims; verbal, emotional, sexual, and physical forms of abuse; child abuse; racism and sexism; misogyny and machismoism; gender bias; female collusion; male accountability. Inevitably the employment of such terms involves a particular social, moral, and historical outlook on the problem of domestic violence that all readers may not share. The essays ahead, however, are governed by that outlook as applied to the fictions I have selected; and the approach I take to those fictions, written by various hands over a period of some 140 years, can be considered ethnocentric—that is to say, relevant to our own time, but not to all time—as well as biased in our time in favor of professional as opposed to public views. Indeed, by some observers it may be considered, in public terms, as a feminist or profeminist outlook, as opposed to a masculinist or even an antifeminist outlook, like that of popular commentators such as Rush Limbaugh when he speaks of "feminazis." Even within the feminist purview, there are factions who dislike the stress on victimization that this professional outlook inevitably entails, and some who even argue for the equally aggressive role of women in cases of domestic violence and for their equal physical strength. The subject is in these and other respects explosive, troubling, open to widely differing views.

I am going to argue, nonetheless, for a consensus view, as I see it, of the implications of domestic violence and for the value of the professional considerations I apply here as more sharable by thoughtful people from many walks of life than any other position. There is after all some consensus today, in state laws and in the drive for national laws, that domestic violence is a crime and can no longer be protected as a private practice occurring in domestic sanctuaries; and there is some consensus as well about the moral and social implications of domestic violence in the social sources from which those recent laws were drawn and are being drawn: namely, the women's shelter movement and the group counseling services that emerged in its wake for the rehabilitation of male batterers. I want to emphasize here, moreover, the collective nature and the collective wisdom of these sources for the defining of new laws: for these are the people who have been most directly concerned with the treatment of battered women and with the reeducation of their male batterers, and they have been working together on these problems for more than two decades.

Their collective outlook, moreover, is an informed and evolving outlook: it has been shaped as much by access to the cumulative knowledge of the past, obtained as much by widespread new research, as by present hands-on experience of immediate problems and practical resolutions; and it has proved useful also in shaping much of our present public knowledge of these problems. It is in these respects as close to a consensus outlook as we are likely to come in the near future and seems therefore a valuable tool for my purposes, which are to understand and assess recent literary versions of domestic violence—versions that are themselves part of our evolving and changing awareness. These are the justifications, at any rate, for my critical approach to this literary theme, the terms of which I would now like to expound.

The key terms to my approach are *female collusion* and *male accountability.* They suggest, on the one hand, the enormous pressures on women to accept their vulnerable positions, their openness to further battering, and to accede to their partners' views and ways, so as to protect themselves (and often their children) from even worse treatment; on the other hand, they indicate the total responsibility of male batterers for their own violent actions and the enormous difficulty in getting them to acknowledge and accept that responsibility. As that "other hand" suggests, the problem of domestic violence between heterosexual partners is seen by professionals in the field as strictly a male problem. This is itself an unpopular view, particularly among male batterers, who almost uniformly begin by insisting that their female partners are either altogether or equally to blame, that they provoke violence or "ask for it" as desired and expected punishment for bad behavior, or that they are themselves often aggressive and strike the first blow or blows. The professional answer to these views is that damaging domestic violence is known to be male-inflicted in 95 percent of all cases, for the good reason that most men are physically stronger than their partners and far more likely to inflict serious damage; that men are in any case literally responsible for their own violent behavior, whatever their partners do; and that the existence of a large number of women's shelters, and the virtual absence of such shelters for men, indicates fairly graphically where the real trouble lies. Finally, all counselors stress the irrefutable point that violence, no matter how or by whom it is provoked, is an unacceptable solution to family problems: its chief function is to ensure continued power and control over recalcitrant partners, to literally beat them into submission, which is at once a barbaric way to treat other human beings and an unconscionable way to solve marital disputes. It is now also a legal felony in some twenty or more states.

My critical strategy, at any rate, has been to transpose questions of accountability and collusion from actual male batterers and their female partners to authors and characters of fictions about domestic violence. The idea that authors, male or female, may be held accountable for their fictional treatments of such problems is, in an aesthetic sense, morally intrusive. It assumes that aesthetic creations have moral dimensions and moral consequences, and that their creators may in certain circumstances be held responsible for them. Such considerations have been recognized in legal cases involving obscenity or libel charges, for which publishers are also held responsible; and they have been applied in current cultural criticism to fictions that purportedly contain racist or sexist sentiments, often viewed as the publicly encoded prejudices of a given time and place. But they have not been applied to questions of honest or dishonest presentations of publicly volatile problems like domestic violence, particularly among male authors, or to questions of collusion with the perpetrators of such violence among women authors.

Perhaps that is because such questions are now considered unfashionable. They involve a positive as well as a negative sense of moral responsibility, an active sense, that is to say, of moral agency in authors that is now frequently denied them. If not altogether dead, like Old Testament versions of God, authors have been neutralized and diminished by many recent critics as the unconscious purveyors of the public codes that shape them and that also shape their language. Whatever the half-truths at work in those assumptions, I would now like to revive and complicate a more positive and active notion of moral function—that of the writer's better self—whereby most writers can be said to relate better to their own fictions than to other people, and to aspire to and generally be more honest in their creative efforts than in their private lives. The complicating corollary to this sanguine premise is, of course, that they get into moral trouble when they are forced to confront volatile and personally engaging issues like domestic violence. But this means that both their best and their worst selves are, on this issue at least, open to our inspection; it means their aspirations and their difficulties alike can give us a kind of moral purchase on their literary struggles; they can help us to see, for instance, how authors choose to present such charged and volatile materials, what they make of them, and what we in turn can make of them with the help of present wisdom. On these grounds, in any case, I think we are justified in viewing authors as themselves actively involved in the moral struggle to make sense of domestic violence, and that we in turn are justified in bringing both social and biographical information to bear on their murkier moral findings.

I hereby invite my readers to join with me in applying such assumptions to the problematic texts ahead. I want them to take seriously the existence of authors as moral agents, still alive and well themselves as responsible critics of society and, beyond that, still involved as much with the claims of individual consciousness, on themselves and their characters, as with the claims of the collective consciousness that are now almost exclusively stressed by many academic critics. One obvious advantage of my approach, in this light, is that it reintroduces the moral claims of individual consciousness into problems where the moral claims of collective consciousness now predominate. This is what has actually happened in the field of domestic violence, where the issue of male accountability is based on the legal assumption of personal responsibility for crimes and misdemeanors: men can be sent to jail for such felonies, and often are. To continue that principle into group counseling for male batterers is accordingly to extend it into the very heart of a collective problem: the gender bias against women as an oppressed class of supposedly subordinate and lesser creatures.

So too with the extension of moral responsibility into the creation of fictional versions of domestic violence. For authors also can be considered accountable in their treatments of such collective problems. With male authors there is the same necessity for honest acknowledgment of their personal stake in patriarchal privileges; with female authors there is the same need to avoid collusion with patriarchal demands. Indeed, our chief critical problem will be to assess the extent to which male authors overcome their patriarchal biases and achieve a self-critical stance on male accountability, and the contrasting extent to which women writers tend to collude with patriarchal pressures, either by protecting male characters who victimize female partners or by blaming those partners for their own victimization. Thus the problem for women authors is one of courage in confronting patriarchal pressures and presenting their female characters as victims of male violence; the problem for male authors is one of self-searching honesty in detecting and acknowledging their own complicity in creating such pressures and their own accountability for such violence.

For defiant women writers, however, the problem of professional courage is also a problem of professional survival. Like the battered women they depict, they must learn to take care of themselves, to protect themselves from the hazards of patriarchal disapproval in the same way that battered women must learn to protect themselves and their children, by whatever means they deem necessary, from the hazards of direct defiance of vengeful male partners. For this good reason we can't altogether blame women writers for protecting themselves—not at least in the same way we can blame male writers for being dishonest—we can only define and record their self-preservative strategies and perhaps question their self-awareness—their own honesties and dishonesties—in devising them.

This difference in our approach to male and female writers spills over into differences in our gender approach to characters and contributes to still another kind of aesthetic problem. We are accustomed to demanding of authors fair and credible treatment in their depiction of conflicts between characters: they must not weight such conflicts unfairly or unrealistically against one character or another: we must believe in what happens between them, and in the author's supposedly neutral or objective presentation of what happens. If the author favors one character over another, it may upset our credulity or arouse our distaste for unfair treatment. This is particularly true of domestic conflicts, where we tend to accept the folk adage that it takes two to tango or entangle, and where our own experience of mixed blame and censure confirms that adage. But as we have seen, the professional definition of domestic violence undermines such expectations: the general male advantage of greater physical strength, and the overwhelming cultural stress on male rights and privileges, makes it chiefly a problem of male perpetration and female victimization.

One obvious source of this cultural imbalance is the hierarchical view of marriage, already mentioned, by which men are routinely described as heads of households. I will deal elsewhere, notably in the Lawrence, Steinbeck, and Singer essays, with the clash between this view as it derives from biblical tradition and the modern view of marriage between equals that supposedly supersedes it. Whenever domestic violence intrudes, this supersession is demonstrably reversed: the man assumes physical control of his wife as his cultural privilege. To deal with this reversal in terms of moral and social equality is accordingly unfair and misleading. The civilized contract between equals has been savagely disrupted, and our moral perspectives must take that disruption into account. We must readjust our moral focus to accommodate the conflicting claims of individual and collective consciousness: we must admit that the balance of power has been changed, that the woman is no longer being treated as an equal individual but as a member of a controlled and subordinate class, and that her very life is now in jeopardy.

As that last thought suggests, the stakes in domestic violence are extraordinarily high: they are the life-or-death stakes, previously noted, that D. H. Lawrence posits as endemic to modern marriage. What better place to study that perilous condition than in fictional versions of the problem that reflect and contribute to our evolving awareness of its implications? It is for that good purpose that

I offer this critical sampling to interested readers. Here we can begin to look together at specific and dramatic ramifications of the problem.

VI. Additional Lessons

We can do so not only by reading the texts and critical glosses at hand. We can also begin to confirm their professional relevance by consulting specific items on the Domestic Violence Checklist at the back of the book. Further, we can begin to follow up some of those allusions, already mentioned, to other relevant fictions, long or short, by these and other authors: to Gwendolyn Harleth's troubled marriage, for example, in George Eliot's *Daniel Deronda* (1876); to the early marital quarrels of Paul Morel's parents in *Sons and Lovers;* to the Richard Gordon subplot in Hemingway's *To Have and Have Not* (1937); or to the stunning murder scene in Ann Petry's *The Street* (1946) and to her remarkable study of interracial and gender power conflicts in the deadly conclusion to *The Narrows* (1953). Similar and more expansive treatments of the racism versus sexism dilemma can be found in Zora Neale Hurston's *Their Eyes Were Watching God* (1937), Toni Morrison's *The Bluest Eye* (1970), and Alice Walker's *The Color Purple* (1982). Ambivalent treatments of another kind occur in Mary McCarthy's *The Group* (1963) and Margaret Drabble's *The Needle's Eye* (1972); downright sexist versions occur in Wright's *Native Son* (1940), Norman Mailer's *An American Dream* (1965), and Nabokov's *Lolita* (1955). In *The Collector* (1970) John Fowles offers a more straightforward and distinctly psychodynamic study of an extreme male obsession with power and control. Then there are foreign fictions in translation, such as Dostoyevsky's *Crime and Punishment* (1867), Zola's *Germinal* (1885), Kafka's *The Metamorphosis* (1915), Camus's *The Stranger* (1942), or Camilo José Cela's *The Family of Pascal Duarte* (1942), that will repay intensive study. Finally, there are some sophisticated recent texts, including Fannie Flagg's *Fried Green Tomatoes at the Whistle Stop Cafe* (1987), Jane Smiley's *A Thousand Acres* (1991), and Roddy Doyle's *The Woman Who Walked into Doors* (1996), that suggest we may be reaching a public range of shared awareness about domestic violence on which writers can rely. Now the rest of us can ponder and pursue that evolving awareness.

Domestic Violence in *Janet's Repentance*

GEORGE ELIOT'S BRAVE SUBTEXT

There is at present no literary history of the incidence of domestic violence in fiction. Although the subject now commands widespread public attention in England and America as a national social issue, its literary study has barely begun to surface. A number of feminist researches have appeared, and the theme has begun to receive attention in academic conference panels; but there is little focus as yet in published studies.

Perhaps that explains the curious neglect of George Eliot's pioneer treatment of the theme in *Janet's Repentance,* first published in serial form in *Blackwood's Edinburgh Magazine* in 1857, then republished the next year as the last of three novellas in *Scenes of Clerical Life.* Although Eliot's work has never lacked for critical attention, she has never received much credit for this modest early achievement, this surprisingly bold depiction of a troubling theme.

That she deserves such credit seems evident enough today. For most of her male contemporaries, whatever their open treatment of domestic murders and seductions, battering was largely an offstage event. Even among her sister novelists, male abusiveness and cruelty were more frequently romanticized and sensationalized, as with the Brontës, than directly presented and indicted. Eliot's precedent stands out, then, as the first extended treatment in British fiction of a long-neglected theme, one that has only recently become a veritable hot potato among modern feminist concerns.

I had better enter at this point my own male credentials for broaching such concerns. For some forty years I have been teaching and writing about novels by male and female authors. From 1983 until fairly recently I have also been a volunteer worker—first as a co-counselor, then as a grant writer—in the treatment of male batterers through group reeducation. From the latter experience I have learned a great deal about male accountability and its frequent denials, and about female collusion and its basis in patriarchal pressures, which has struck me as fruitful when applied to my own ongoing literary studies of violent heterosexual conflict. Both of these common gender reactions to violence have critical relevance, for instance, for Eliot's brave literary precedent, and I would accordingly like to place the question of their applicability on the table, and to ask men and women readers alike to suspend their understandable suspicions about male intrusions into women's fields. I know the risks of male egoism and will try to avoid them. I think it is important meanwhile that men as well as women should enter into the discussion and exploration of these troubling matters because we all have much at stake in learning to understand them. Indeed, we need all the help we can get, and since I believe that my own contribution should prove helpful, I hope you will excuse—or at least entertain—my male temerities.

Suppression, denial, disguise—these long-standing male responses to domestic violence contribute obviously to the meagerness of present literary studies. Even today, they help to explain the relative neglect of Eliot's bold precedent. Among Eliot's postmodern critics, for example, there is the characteristic male denial of patriarchal practices that feminists have often noted on other relevant grounds. Thus Thomas A. Noble, one of the more recent chroniclers of Eliot's *Scenes of Clerical Life,* spoke in 1965 about male brutality in *Janet's Repentance* without bothering to specify what form it takes; and David Lodge, in his introduction to the Penguin edition of *Scenes of Clerical Life,* spoke in 1973 about the heroine's controversial drinking problem without even mentioning that she's a battered wife.[1] Indeed, that critical issue might never have surfaced if Sandra Gilbert and Susan Gubar hadn't touched upon it tellingly in 1979 in *The Madwoman in the Attic,* and if Virginia B. Morris, in her feminist study of fictional Victorian women who kill their abusive partners, hadn't drawn more extensive attention to it in 1990. Thus, in *Double Jeopardy,* Morris credits Eliot with straightforward presentation of the wife in *Janet's Repentance* as a victim of battering, then goes on to praise Eliot's sympathetic and direct treatment of women who kill under similar circumstances—as with Hetty Sorel's response to impregnation and desertion in *Adam Bede* and Gwendolyn Harleth's to abusive treatment in *Daniel Deronda.*[2]

Appropriately enough, the problem of male denial and suppression begins with Eliot's editor and publisher, John Blackwood, who was troubled, among other things, by the battered wife's unsentimental beer and the husband's barefaced brutality in what he euphemistically called "a case but too common";

1. Noble, *George Eliot's* Scenes of Clerical Life, 88; Lodge, "Introduction," 29.

2. See Gilbert and Gubar, "George Eliot as the Angel of Destruction," 487–90; and Morris, *Double Jeopardy: Women Who Kill in Victorian Fiction,* 74–75. As Eliot's readers know, the responses Morris cites are through crimes of commission and omission: Hetty kills her illegitimate baby; Gwendolyn lets her abusive husband drown.

but when Eliot insisted she had softened the real facts and would withdraw the story rather than revise it further for his journal, he withdrew in turn his classist objections.[3] Yet Eliot herself may be responsible in large part for the tale's ongoing neglect. As her title suggests, she is in several ways drawn toward blaming the victim for her own predicament. By insisting on Janet's need for repentance, and by creating for her that old Victorian standby, the opportunity for self-sacrificial redemption, Eliot dims and weakens her own bold indictment of male abusiveness. Like those contemporary battered women who for various good reasons collude with and protect their oppressors, she colludes with her male or male-oriented readers and disappoints even her possible feminist admirers. As we shall see, this is one of the characteristic ways in which authors themselves, whether male or female, betray their own conflictual stake in such dilemmas. With male authors it is decidedly a question of accountability and its frequent disguises and denials, its dishonest suppressions; with women authors, it is—more protectively—a question of how they must take care of themselves in response to patriarchal pressures like those, for instance, applied by Eliot's male editor to her distasteful domestic subject. Indeed, Eliot's adoption of her male pseudonym, like the adoption of such pseudonyms by the Brontë sisters before her, can be seen as her first authorial response to the need for protection from male abuses of this kind.

But finally it was Eliot's personal concern with religious conflict as a major theme, and the roots of that concern in her protective needs, that chiefly obscured her bold approach to domestic violence. *Janet's Repentance* is preceded in *Scenes of Clerical Life,* for instance, by two other tales about clergymen heroes, *Amos Barton* and *Mr. Gilfil's Love-Story.* It follows them nominally in telling the story of a third clergyman, the Evangelical minister Mr. Tryan, through whom Eliot tries to do justice to the abandoned Evangelical convictions of her youth. But as the title indicates, that story is intertwined with and ultimately taken over by the subtext about Janet Dempster and her abusive husband, an unscrupulous lawyer who for his own ends exploits the local Anglican opposition in the small town of Milby to the Evangelical movement then sweeping England. Dempster claims publicly to uphold the local stress on good works against the Evangelical stress on faith alone as the true means of salvation. But his real interest is to obtain political power in Milby through manipulated acts of public violence, and that interest from the main religious plot translates readily into his concern with power and control through personal violence in the domestic subtext, which ultimately becomes the novella's chief concern. Meanwhile the convolutions

3. As quoted in Gordon S. Haight, *George Eliot: A Biography,* 234; see also Noble, *George Eliot's* Scenes, 47–50, 151, 154; Lodge, "Introduction," 29; Morris, *Double Jeopardy,* 75.

of the main religious controversy, whether for Eliot's past critics or for present readers, tend to minimize her more adventurous forays into domestic conflict and to obscure their boldness.

I

Thus the novel opens with four chapters of religious and communal exposition, set in taverns and parlors and along village streets, in which Eliot introduces her cast of village characters and provides a brief historical overview of their changing ways and beliefs. Through these leisurely means she also shows us, now directly, now obliquely, how lawyer Dempster sets up and leads a protest rally against the new Evangelical minister Mr. Tryan, stirs rowdy followers to attend it, and hits the punch bowl himself in celebration of his seeming triumph. It is only then, at the end of chapter 4, that Eliot sends her villainous character on his slow drunken way home to beat his wife. He arrives in a less than sanguine mood, having sharply dismissed the kindly bartender who tries to see him safely to his door:

> There was a large heavy knocker on the green door, and though Mr. Dempster carried a latch-key, he sometimes chose to use the knocker. He chose to do so now. The thunder resounded through Orchard Street, and, after a single minute, there was a second clap louder than the first. Another minute and still the door was not opened; whereupon Mr. Dempster, muttering, took out his latch-key, and, with less difficulty than might have been expected, thrust it into the door. When he opened the door the passage was dark.
>
> "Janet!" in the loudest rasping tone, was the next sound that rang through the house.
>
> "Janet!" again—before a slow step was heard on the stairs, and a distant light began to flicker on the wall of the passage.
>
> "Curse you! you creeping idiot! Come faster, can't you?"
>
> Yet another few seconds, and the figure of a tall woman, holding aslant a heavy-plated drawing-room candlestick, appeared at the turning of the passage that led to the broader entrance. . . . Her grandly-cut features . . . have premature lines about them telling that the years have been lengthened by sorrow, and the delicately-curved nostril, which seems made to quiver with the proud consciousness of power and beauty, must have quivered to the heart-piercing griefs which have given that worn look to the corners of the mouth. Her wide open black eyes have a strangely fixed, sightless gaze, as she pauses at the turning, and stands silent before her husband.
>
> "I'll teach you to keep me waiting in the dark, you pale staring fool!" advancing with his slow drunken step. "What, you've been drinking again, have you? I'll beat you into your senses."

> He laid his hand with a firm grip on her shoulder, turned her round, and pushed her slowly before him along the passage and through the dining-room door. . . .
>
> There was a portrait of Janet's mother, a gray-haired, dark-eyed old woman, in a neatly-fluted cap, hanging over the mantelpiece. Surely the aged eyes take on a look of anguish as they see Janet—not trembling, no! it would be better if she trembled—standing stupidly unmoved in her great beauty, while the heavy arm is lifted to strike her. The blow falls—another—and another. Surely the mother hears that cry—"O Robert! pity! pity!"[4]

I have quoted the passage at some length to catch the chief indications of Dempster's exercise of domestic power and control. Eliot is careful to show, for instance, that his knock on the door is a demand for special service. He seems quite able to open it for himself with his latchkey, but he wants Janet to relieve him of that necessity and to light his drunken way in the dark; for this, paradoxically, he requires her to be quick and sober. His demand for service implies, then, the superior male right to indulge his leisurely vices while others run to do his bidding. That right in turn implies his exertion of power over another that he can't exercise over himself: he beats Janet for his own failing, which she can't afford if she is to serve him properly in his superior state. His verbal abuses prepare us also for this violent display of power over a lesser creature and contrast tellingly with the narrator's moving description of the signs of Janet's suffering intelligence and hurt pride: for the imperial husband she is merely a "creeping idiot," a "pale staring fool" who has kept him waiting "in the dark," and whom he will now "teach" the punitive lesson of obedience to higher authority.

But that lesson will also be observed by the portrait on the wall of Janet's mother, for whom the narrator now speaks in an oddly effective form of sentimental intrusion. Thus the reader sees and hears Janet being beaten through the painted mother's animated senses. And in the next paragraph the empathetic author further intrudes with a maternal review of this abject daughter's early promise:

> Poor gray-haired woman! Was it for this you suffered a mother's pangs in your lone widowhood five-and-thirty years ago? Was it for this you kept the little worn morocco shoes that Janet had first run in, and kissed them day by day when she was away from you, a tall girl at school? Was it for this you looked proudly at her when she came back to you in her rich pale beauty, like a tall white arum that has just unfolded its grand pure curves to the sun? (225/63)

---

4. George Eliot, *Janet's Repentance,* 224–25/62–63. Further page references will be given in the text, with the first number referring to the edition listed in the bibliography and the second to the reprinting of the novella below. Note that the reprinting of the novella below is slightly abridged.

The intrusive and now plainly sentimental narrator turns next to the mother's actual room in the village, where she lies sleepless, praying, weeping, anticipating with dread this cruel night for her child. Then, pulling out the final sentimental stops, the narrator points to another picture over the mother's mantelpiece, "drawn in chalk by Janet long years ago," of "a head bowed beneath a cross, and wearing a crown of thorns" (225/63). This Christian martyr motif of present suffering, and perhaps of future redemption, is drawn, as it were, with Janet's borrowed childhood chalk.

Thus the main text and subtext meet, and Eliot bravely presents her domestic revelation through a mixture of direct reporting and sentimental, even melodramatic, intrusion. But the sentimentality and the melodrama are oddly functional; they do their well-placed work because in fiction we can indeed look inside our neighbors' doors and hearts and heads and see such unexpectedly grim things going on, in decided contrast to our imagined and unexamined expectations, here supported by the mother's and daughter's ventriloquized feelings.

There is, even so, a narrative anomaly in this early tale: as we later learn the narrator is a young man from this community who couldn't possibly know and directly see such things, nor without further self-definition even imagine them for us with this kind of "feminized" comprehension, in keeping with Eliot's famous doctrine of sympathy. Perhaps because she is still trying out her early disguised male identity, Eliot hasn't yet found the omniscient narrative stance that will characterize her more mature major fictions and solve such empathetic problems.

A second violent scene occurs in chapter 14. By this time the religious controversy has been settled and grimmer personal events are plainly pending. Dempster's mother has died. He has lost the battle to prevent Mr. Tryan from preaching, and he has also lost several clients in the process. His drinking has stepped up. The two town doctors are speculating as to whether he might break his neck in a driving accident in his horse-and-buggy or, failing that, fall prey to meningitis and delirium tremens. Janet's home misery increases accordingly, but when she speaks to her mother of God's and her husband's cruelties that somber lady tells her to submit to them and be thankful for the gift of life (271/97).

The impending crisis breaks on the night that Robert has asked Janet to prepare a dinner for four friends. He comes home drunk and in "an angry humor"; but Janet is determined to speak pleasantly:

> "Robert," she said gently, as she saw him seat himself in the dining-room in his dusty snuffy clothes, and take some documents out of his pocket, "will you not wash and change your dress? It will refresh you."
>
> "Leave me alone, will you?" said Dempster, in his most brutal tone.

> "Do change your coat and waistcoat, they are so dusty. I've laid all your things out ready."
>
> "O, you have, have you?" After a few minutes he rose very deliberately and walked up-stairs into his bedroom. Janet had often been scolded before for not laying out his clothes, and she thought now, not without some wonder, that this attention of hers had brought him to compliance.
>
> Presently he called out, "Janet!" and she went up-stairs.
>
> "Here! Take that!" he said, as soon as she reached the door, flinging at her the coat she had laid out. "Another time, leave me to do as I please, will you?"
>
> The coat, flung with great force, only brushed her shoulder, and fell some distance within the drawing-room, the door of which stood open just opposite. She hastily retreated as she saw the waistcoat coming, and one by one the clothes she had laid out were all flung into the drawing-room. (272–73/98–99)

Janet's back is up, and "for the first time in her life" she overcomes her humble and passive acceptance of his brutality. She leaves the clothes on the floor, thinking "they shall lie there until the visitors come, and he shall be ashamed of himself" (273/99). But Dempster has been demonstrating his "no-win" philosophy; it is control itself he favors, and his recent business failures add to this power game a familiar bit of scapegoating. Thus, when the guests come in and see the scattered clothes, Dempster only gives Janet "a devilish glance of concentrated hatred," calls a servant to remove the clothes, and delays his next move until midnight, when the guests finally leave (273/99). Then he rouses Janet and subverts her brief defiance with his own more drastic measures:

> "So you think you'll defy me, do you? We'll see how long that will last. Get up, madam; out of bed this instant!"
>
> In the close presence of the dreadful man—of this huge crushing force, armed with savage will—poor Janet's desperate defiance all forsook her, and her terrors came back. Trembling she got up, and stood helpless in her night-dress before her husband.
>
> He seized her with his heavy grasp by the shoulder, and pushed her before him.
>
> "I'll cool your hot spirit for you! I'll teach you to brave me!"
>
> Slowly he pushed her along before him, down stairs and through the passage, where a small oil-lamp was still flickering. What was he going to do to her? She thought every moment he was going to dash her before him on the ground. But she gave no scream—she only trembled.
>
> He pushed her on to the entrance, and held her firmly in his grasp while he lifted the latch of the door. Then he opened the door a little way, thrust her out, and slammed it behind her. (274/100)

At first Janet feels relieved at her deliverance—she had feared he meant to kill her for trying to teach *him,* for once, the lesson of shame. But her brief rebellion has been quashed; she has been expelled like Eve from her husband's dubious Eden for offending its self-appointed God. A half-century later D. H. Lawrence would follow and build upon this exemplary scene in describing Mrs. Morel's similar expulsion by her drunken husband in *Sons and Lovers,* as if honoring an effective precedent.

II

Eliot offers, then, a bold challenge to the hierarchical view of marriage and to the ramifications of its physical abuses. As no small part of that challenge, she also helps us to place it morally by showing selectively how various members of the community respond to the ongoing situation. In chapter 3, for instance, at a gossip session in Mrs. Linnet's parlor, there is a telling exchange between kindly Mrs. Pettifer, genial Miss Rebecca Linnet, and prim Miss Pratt on the disputed subject of Janet Dempster's character and conduct. The conversation has already ranged from the question of Mr. Tryan's linen to his political fate as a religious leader in the community; and since these women are all his staunch supporters and describe his villainous opponent Dempster as "Old Harry" in human form, they have also raised the question of Dempster's reckless drunken driving, the suffering he must have caused Janet's mother, and his bad marriage with Janet herself. They are all agreed on Dempster's wickedness and on Janet's early promise and present suffering; but they divide sharply on the question of Janet's misguided pride in backing her husband's view of Mr. Tryan:

> "Well, poor thing," said Mrs Pettifer, "you know she stands up for everything her husband says and does. She never will admit to anybody that he's not a good husband."
>
> "That is her pride," said Miss Pratt. "She married him in opposition to the advice of her best friends, and now she is not willing to admit that she was wrong. . . ."
>
> "Pride or no pride," said Mrs. Pettifer, "I shall always stand up for Janet Dempster. She sat up with me night after night when I had that attack of rheumatic fever six years ago. There's great excuses for her. When a woman can't think of her husband coming home without trembling, it's enough to make her drink something to blunt her feelings—and no children either, to keep her from it. You and me might do the same, if we were in her place."
>
> "Speak for yourself, Mrs. Pettifer," said Miss Pratt. "Under no circumstances can I imagine myself resorting to a practice so degrading. A woman should find support in her own strength of mind."
>
> "I think," said Rebecca, who considered Miss Pratt still very blind in spiritual things, notwithstanding her assumption of enlightenment, "she will find poor support if she trusts only to her own strength. She must seek aid elsewhere than in herself." (215–16/54–55)

The conversation is predictive as well as revealing; Janet will indeed look for help outside herself, once free of Dempster by exclusion. Meanwhile the community seems divided between finding "great excuses for her" and deploring her lack of inner strength—what we might now call her poor sense of agency or selfhood. Even gentle Mr. Tryan, though he talks at the end of chapter 3 about meeting Janet attending the poor, expresses great surprise about her conduct: "I have heard the worst account of her habits—that she is almost as bad as her husband" (219/158). At this point, in other words, he sees her as an abusive person who drinks. Like all too many others, he makes no distinction between the abuser and the abused.

As it turns out, that view is still highly vocal in Milby as late as chapter 13, where Mrs. Phipps finds Janet rather "strange" when Mrs. Crewe, the Anglican minister's wife, also finds excuses for her:

> To be sure, there were dreadful stories about the way Dempster used his wife; but in Mrs. Phipps's opinion, it was six of one and half-a-dozen of the other. Mrs. Dempster had never been like other women; she had always a flighty way with her, carrying parcels of snuff to old Mrs. Tooke, and going to drink tea with Mrs. Brinley, the carpenter's wife; and then never taking care of her clothes, always wearing the same things week-day or Sunday. A man has a poor look-out with a wife of that sort. Mr. Phipps, amiable and laconic, wondered how it was women were so fond of running each other down. (269/96)

Mrs. Phipps, taking a class-oriented view of Janet's "flighty ways"—her concern for the old and the poor, her careless dress—finds these aberrations sufficient cause for any suffering husband to beat his wife. Meanwhile Eliot herself, or her narrator, is not above giving a male observer, the amiable Mr. Phipps, the last word in what seems to be an appalling triumph of middle-class proprieties over sisterhood and selfhood.

As we learn much earlier, in chapter 7, those proprieties have already triumphed in the Dempster household itself, where Dempster's mother feels that what her son has needed all along is a meek wife like herself, "who would have borne him children, and been a deft, orderly housekeeper" (234/70). Instead, he apparently gets a proud wife like Janet whose failings as a housekeeper and cook and barren woman seem to the elder Mrs. Dempster to excuse her son's violence. With a better wife, she assumes, her son "might have been a good husband" (234/70). Thus she too blames the victim, though not without that interestingly oblique affirmation of Janet's active pride, her presently confounded form of selfhood.

In chapter 21, when Janet seemingly disappears, still another household denizen, Cook Betty, speaks out for a battered woman's right and need to run away:

> "I'd ha' overrun him long afore now, if it had been me. I wouldn't stan' bein' mauled as she is by no husband, not if he was the biggest lord i' the land. It's poor work bein' a wife at that price: I'd sooner be a cook wi'out perkises, an' hev roast, an' boil, an' fry, an' bake all to mind at once. She may well do as she does. I know I'm glad enough of a drop o' summat myself when I'm plagued." (296/119)

Betty's feisty lower-class views round out the social spectrum Eliot covers in the novel, adding the now familiar question of why the victim doesn't pack up and leave in the first place; yet Betty insists even more strongly, in the light of Janet's recent absence from home, that she is right to leave her mauling husband now, that marriage under those circumstances is "poor work" for a wife, and that drinking is an understandable response to it.

Considering this ongoing range of communal response to the wife-beating problem in the novel, and the dramatic rendition of that problem in two focal scenes, it seems almost impossible—at least from our present perspective—that past commentators of both sexes have paid it so little attention. The same spectrum of opinion seems evident enough today, and the more sympathetic characters discuss the problem with something like current perspicacity and realistic concern. Moreover, Eliot herself, in the person of her male narrator, comments directly and insightfully on the most pertinent issues. In chapter 13, for instance, she tells us exactly where she stands on Dempster's cruelty and his motives for it:

> But do not believe that it was anything either present or wanting in poor Janet that formed the motive of her husband's cruelty. Cruelty, like every other vice, requires no motive outside itself—it only requires opportunity. You do not suppose Dempster had any motive for drinking beyond the craving for drink; the presence of brandy was the only necessary condition. And an unloving, tyrannous, brutal man needs no motive to prompt his cruelty: he needs only the perpetual presence of a woman he can call his own. A whole park full of tame or timid-eyed animals to torment at his will would not serve him so well to glut his lust of torture; they could not *feel* as one woman does; they could not throw out the keen retort which whets the edge of hatred. (268/94)

The condition for male cruelty that Eliot seizes upon—the "presence of a woman he can call his own"—converts her apparent sense of cruelty as a kind of medieval vice or humour into the postmodern notion of possession as the condition for the "motiveless" desire for power and control. It is this notion that professionals in the domestic violence field posit as an end in itself, for male batterers, with its own set of gratifications. Eliot's references also to how a woman feels, and to her capacity for "the keen retort which whets the edge of hatred," keep alive the sense of agency, and direct her views also beyond the familiar modern notion of sadism as a psychological explanation of battering. It is necessary, in this light, for male batterers to possess and torture into submission, or failing that, to altogether dispossess, someone who has just proved to be their equal in intelligence and feeling—someone who has questioned their authority and so threatened their rightful access to power and control. This is what happens in the next chapter, when Janet braves her husband's wrath and is forced outside the home by his renewed show of power and control.[5]

III

But as the title and its attendant plot suggest, George Eliot does temporize with her harsh material. As already noted, she is in several ways drawn toward blaming Janet for her own predicament. After leaving Dempster, for instance, Janet looks instinctively to the Evangelical minister, Mr. Tryan, for help. Her first words are those of a self-convicted sinner: "I want to tell you how unhappy I am—how weak and wicked. I feel no strength to live or die." When she then asks him to help her, Mr. Tryan responds in kind: "Perhaps I can . . . for in speaking to me you are speaking to a fellow sinner who has needed just the comfort and help you are seeking" (286/110). Janet then describes how she began drinking in response to being abused and beaten by her husband, how the craving for drink demonically possessed her, and how God began to seem cruel to her for placing temptation in her way. Her "wickedness" lies, then, in turning her "demonic" possession by drink into self-hatred and blasphemy. Mr. Tryan in turn describes his own "evil passions" and how a friend led him to find not only forgiveness in God but also "that strength which enables us to conquer sin" (287/112). Thus the plot itself now seems to confirm that Janet's alcoholism is in itself a cause for guilt and shame, and that it will be cured only through religious regimen.

---

5. Eliot was more equivocal about Dempster's case in the original manuscript of the novella. In a long passage on the prevalence of drinking in Milby, she discusses Dempster as an exception to the rule: "Dempster's life, to be sure, was thought too flagrantly irregular; his drinking was out of all bounds, and he often abused his wife beyond what was reasonable. Still he was one of those valuable public characters in whom society has at all times tolerated an extra amount of private aberration; he was very well received in most houses, and there were several ladies rather proud of 'knowing how to manage Dempster', or of jocosely twitting him with being a sad husband" (Haight, *Biography,* 239; Noble, *George Eliot's* Scenes, 156). The ambiguous passage here, "and he often abused his wife beyond what was reasonable," may well be a mimicking of Milby's views, but it leaves Eliot's position in some doubt early in the novel. Its elimination in the published version accordingly strengthens her narrative stand. One would have liked, however, for those comments on Dempster's "valuable public character" to have remained, in the light of our own current equivocations about such "publicly valuable" batterers and killers.

It could be argued here that repentance and its religious cure are Eliot's version of the problem of female agency in response to male victimization, and certainly Janet does begin to act now to overcome her craving and recuperate well-being. But the method here prescribed has its shortcomings even on those positive grounds. Its obvious resemblance to contemporary methods of curing alcoholism, through the twelve steps recommended by Alcoholics Anonymous, may help to show this. As that argument runs, alcoholics are powerless alone; they too must learn to rely on a higher power, seek the help of fellow sinners, and acknowledge guilt or weakness. Although there is much to be said for this approach, and particularly for the group support available at AA meetings, recent feminist critics have raised the neglected problem of gender differences. Thus Charlotte Davis Kasl, writing in *Ms.,* makes the telling argument that these steps "were formulated by a white, middle-class male in the 1930s," that "they work to break down an overinflated ego, and put reliance on an all-powerful male God," and that most women suffer by contrast "from the lack of a healthy, aware ego." Consequently, such women "need to strengthen their sense of self by affirming their own inner wisdom."[6]

Kasl accordingly goes on to rewrite the twelve steps so as to put more stress on female empowerment and to remove the negative view of selfhood and of character defects usually attributed to women—the stress, for example, on their wrongs and shortcomings. By this argument, of course, Eliot is pushing a male view of Janet's shortcomings and their appropriate cure, a view that tends to undermine that sense of frustrated pride and self-regard Eliot has rightly and deftly stressed in describing Janet's suffering. Here is a telling instance, then, of that contradictory tension about which Gilbert and Gubar and Carol Christ have commented so incisively, by which George Eliot converts herself into a kind of avenging angel for her self-censuring and renunciatory heroines, who have successfully renounced their justifiable anger and resentment, but whose male abusers—as we shall see—are nonetheless punished by providential death.[7]

A second indication of this contradictory tension, and of Janet's ambivalent guiltiness in Eliot's eyes, occurs when she returns home to nurse Dempster in

6. "The Twelve-Step Controversy," 30.

7. See Gilbert and Gubar, "Angel of Destruction," esp. 491, where they speak of "the contradiction between feminine renunciation countenanced by the narrator and female (even feminist) vengeance exacted by the author." Here the authors follow Carol Christ's lead; in "Aggression and Providential Death in George Eliot's Fiction," she argues that Eliot uses renunciation to overcome anger and aggression in her heroines, then "uses Providence to enact the aggression that she does not allow her characters to enact" (134). Gilbert and Gubar try to show, further, "how all the heroines" are also "implicated in the author's violence," and how the male characters she punishes "specifically symbolize patriarchal power" ("Angel of Destruction," 491). Thus, they make a point of specifying, as Christ does not, that Dempster batters his wife and fears her plainly exhibited resentment.

his fatal illness, following the driving accident the town doctors had earlier predicted. Thus Eliot seems at first to be aware of the folly of Janet's previous impulse to return. While Janet is recuperating in secret at Mrs. Pettifer's house, for instance, after her expulsion by Dempster, she asks Mr. Tryan whether she "ought" to go back to her husband at some point. His reply is refreshing enough: "No, certainly not, at present. Something should be done to secure you from violence. Your mother, I think, should consult some confidential friend, some man of character and experience, who might mediate between you and your husband" (292/116). In the next chapter, Mrs. Raynor, Janet's mother, builds impressively on this possibility:

> "That was certainly good advice of Mr. Tryan's you told me of last night—that we should consult some one that may interfere for you with your husband; and I've been turning it over in my mind while I've been lying awake in the night. I think nobody will do so well as Mr. Benjamin Landor, for we must have a man that knows the law, and that Robert is rather afraid of. And perhaps he could bring about an agreement for you to live apart. Your husband's bound to maintain you, you know; and, if you liked, we could move away from Milby and live somewhere else." (295/118)

Plainly Eliot was anticipating here such modern strategies as women's shelters and men's counseling groups for male batterers; it seems heartening, too, that there were laws on the books in her time against wife beating and for financial support after separation. But Janet, sadly enough, and Eliot with her, seems to resist these happy propositions:

> "O, mother, we must do nothing yet; I must think about it a little longer. I have a different feeling this morning from what I had yesterday. Something seems to tell me that I must go back to Robert some time—after a little while. I loved him once better than all the world, and I have never had any children to love. There were things in me that were wrong, and I should like to make up for them if I can." (295/118)

Her mother's response to this impulse is again quite healthy: she fears that Janet might "take some premature step in relation to her husband, which might lead back to all the former troubles"; and she wisely thinks that Janet's morning hint about returning "showed a new eagerness for difficult duties," an urge that makes "the long-saddened sober mother tremble" (300/122).

Apparently Eliot trembles with her; but she also arranges for the plot to resolve the problem in favor of Janet's initial impulse. Thus Dempster's drunken accident follows hard upon Mrs. Raynor's tremblings, and though she and Mrs. Pettifer and Mr. Tryan agree on keeping the news from Janet, who has begun to doubt her own desire to return to Dempster, that restless spirit nevertheless leaves her shelter to help others and accidentally discovers what has happened. Seeing her husband, again as predicted, in the throes of delirium tremens, she at once decides to stay and help the nurses care for him. Armed now with her new religious faith in helping others and trusting herself to God, she hopes that his illness will alter him, or that she herself will be able to melt his cruelty and renew his love through her own loving attentions. Indeed, she recalls now "the too short years of love that went before . . . when they sat on the grass together, and he laid scarlet poppies on her black hair, and called her his gypsy queen" (311/132); and in the "tide of loving oblivion" that follows she hopes for a future of mutual "love and forgiveness" (312/133). Even when she knows he is dying she hopes for a redemptive moment of awakening—and she almost gets her moment when he comes to just before dying and tries to speak (314/135).

As the emphasis on mutual forgiveness suggests, Eliot winds up softening her indictment of Dempster's brutality and lessening, if not altogether equalizing, his degree of blame for it. She proceeds, of course, in keeping with her own sense of characterization as "a presentation of mixed human beings in such a way as to call forth tolerant judgment, pity and sympathy."[8] But that laudable and familiar novelistic aim seems joined here with an almost personal need to assume blame and guilt whenever reconciliation with an estranged loved one seems possible. The ongoing rejection by and estrangement from her beloved brother, which had reached a focal point during the composition of *Janet's Repentance,* helps to explain her personal stake in a protective repentance and redemption plot undercut by the husband's punitive death. By such ambiguous plotting devices she might simultaneously express, and so assuage, her mixed feelings of guilt, anguish, and resentment for the loss of her brother's approving love. This seems to me an obvious personal source of what Carol Christ has called her "deep preoccupation with and fear of [her own] aggression" and of her need to protect herself from that patriarchal fear.[9]

Eliot's softening of the indictment against Dempster in response to patriarchal pressures—in this case her brother's ongoing bourgeois disapproval of her character and conduct—calls to mind several instances of similar protective collusions by future women novelists—most notably, Zora Neale Hurston's transmogrification of Tea Cake's abusive treatment of Janie, in *Their Eyes Were*

8. Haight, *Biography,* 222.

9. See ibid., 226–33, and Christ, "Aggression," 139. It was at this point that Eliot wrote to her brother to announce her "marriage" to George Henry Lewes. When her brother coldly indicated through an intermediary his disapproval of her failure to inform him of such "intentions and prospects" and his inability to respond "in a Brotherly Spirit," she wrote back to the intermediary that she was in fact engaged in a common-law marriage: "Our marriage is not a legal one, but it is regarded by us both as a sacred bond" (Haight, *Biography,* 332). Her estrangement from her brother continued unabated for the next twenty-three years, until her legal marriage to John Cross in 1880 won his approval, some six months after Lewes's death and only six months before her own. She had good familial reasons, then, to fear the consequences of her own assertions and resentments.

Watching God, into an admirable model for less fortunate black men with tougher and darker-skinned wives. Hurston too was responding, in this novel, to an idealized relation with a similarly beloved if abusive man, her former suitor A.W.P; and like George Eliot, as Gilbert and Gubar see her, Hurston too would become an avenging angel and fictively punish her beloved "Tea Cake" with death.[10]

Such protective yieldings to patriarchal pressures, whether from love or disapproval or similar causes, can be found in works dealing with domestic violence by later women writers such as Ann Petry, Mary McCarthy, Margaret Drabble, and Tony Morrison and seem to constitute one of the more rueful female risks of dealing with that controversial theme. For male novelists the problem is, by contrast, one of honesty and self-correction in confronting their own personal responsibility for such abusive behaviors, for maintaining them through suppression, denial, and disguise, and all too often for defensive aggrandizements of their own "sufferings." If we consider, however, the frequent failure to achieve such honest self-corrections in fictions by such prominent writers as Lawrence, Hemingway, Nabokov, Steinbeck, Wright, and Mailer, we can see why current readers now look chiefly to women novelists, whatever their self-protective collusions, for the bravest and most direct presentations of domestic violence—for which Eliot and Hurston are the foremost pioneers.

IV

Eliot's example was in several ways more powerful than she knew. In her depiction of Dempster's delirium, for instance, she anticipated later views of male dichotomies and myths about women as demonized monsters and idealized angels and, in effect, foresaw their importance for misogynistic outlooks. Thus Dempster's delirious ravings are striking for what they reveal about his secret attitudes toward Janet and, one might add, all other women:

> "Let me go, let me go," he said in a loud, hoarse whisper; "she's coming. . . . she's cold. . . . she's dead. . . . she'll strangle me with her black hair. Ah!" he shrieked aloud, "her hair is all serpents. . . . they're black serpents. . . . they hiss. . . . they hiss. . . . let me go. . . . let me go. . . . she wants to drag me with her cold arms. . . . her arms are serpents. . . . they are great white serpents. . . . they'll twine round me. . . . she wants to drag me into the cold water. . . . her bosom is cold. . . . it is black. . . . it is all serpents. . . ." (307/129)

---

10. See Hurston, *Their Eyes Were Watching God,* 140–41, and *I Love Myself When I'm Laughing . . . And Then Again When I Am Looking Mean and Impressive: A Zora Neale Hurston Reader,* 75–79, where Hurston describes "the real love affair" of her life with the "perfect man," and where she acknowledges her effort to "embalm all the tenderness of my passion for him [through Janie's love for Tea Cake] in *Their Eyes Were Watching God.*"

A bit later it becomes evident that Dempster believes that Janet has drowned herself after being locked out of the house, and has now returned to seek revenge:

> "Dead. . . . is she dead? *She* did it, then. She buried herself in the iron chest. . . . she left her clothes out, though. . . . she isn't dead. . . . why do you pretend she's dead?. . . . she's coming. . . . she's coming out of the iron closet. . . . there are the black serpents. . . . stop her. . . . let me go. . . . stop her. . . . she wants to drag me away into the cold black water. . . . her bosom is black. . . . it is all serpents. . . . they are getting longer. . . . the great white serpents are getting longer. . . ." (308/130)

This sad evidence that he has all along demonized his wife as a serpentine threat to his life, a monstrous version of the biblical Eve, is endemic to his misogynistic outlook and is aptly completed here as he twice calls for the servant-wife Janet, the angel in the house, to save him as it were from the serpent-wife of his own invention. The woman as serpent and as servant, then, was already part of his outlook as he entered the marriage, and, in concert with his growing need for power and control, these icons have worked to overcome its promising beginnings. Like a true male chauvinist of any time, he has demonized the opposite sex and at the same time reduced it to domestic servitude. Against such hidden and overt odds, Janet never had a chance.

We may ask now if Eliot has in turn demonized Dempster beyond characterological redemption? Certainly, as Gilbert and Gubar argue, she has invoked the female goddess Nemesis to punish him for his abusive crimes, while at the same time revealing their demonic sexist origins. But at least her treatment of Mr. Tryan helps to counterbalance such extreme male villainy.[11] Outwardly, Mr. Tryan's story of his sinful seduction and abandonment of another woman, and of precipitating her melodramatic death on the streets, only confirms and supports the novella's dismal view of intimate male behavior; but the fact that Tryan holds himself accountable for such exploitative crimes, as Dempster surely does not, makes an inward and ongoing difference in how we judge him. Tryan struggles to overcome his sexist criminality and dedicates his life to making up as best he can for its disastrous outcome. He is the novella's responsible or reformed chauvinist, now asexual but otherwise a loving male, as opposed to the irresponsible and unloving chauvinist who batters Janet. These ostensibly true and false religious opponents are ultimately seen, moreover, as true and false lovers: for not only does Tryan serve as Janet's redeemer and

11. In "Angel of Destruction," 498–99, Gilbert and Gubar first demonstrate Dempster's "sickened imagination" at its demonic work, then invoke Nemesis as a punitive female power: "We are told . . . . about a female power that is definitively involved in causing Dempster's death: 'Nemesis is lame, but she is of colossal stature, like the gods; and sometimes . . . she stretches out her huge left arm and grasps her victim. The mighty hand is invisible, but the victim totters under the dire clutch' (chap. 13)."

Janet as his most devoted and loving disciple; they also kiss once before his death in a kind of spiritual pledge toward sexless marriage in heaven. As such sexlessness reminds us, the Dempsters' marriage is also significantly barren. In this decidedly Victorian text, as in later novels by Eliot where damaged or delayed loves are barren, the Victorian taboo on sexuality must also be taken into account as another underlying subtext.[12]

Janet, at any rate, is henceforth empowered to ease her guilt by helping others, and in that sense to help herself. She has also achieved motherhood by adoption, if not by sexual means, so that we leave her in old age surrounded by grandchildren (334/152). Meanwhile, she is no longer Dempster's nor anyone else's gypsy queen—that romantic emblem of early erotic promise has been purged from this text by alcohol, domestic violence, and religion. It would recur, of course, in *The Mill and the Floss,* where Maggie Tulliver's early flight to the gypsies prefigures her later sensual attraction to Stephen Guest; and it would figure in more sophisticated ways in *Middlemarch.* Lawrence would respond to it in his time, but he would also respond to its ambivalent suppressions and denials, as in his famous tale "Daughters of the Vicar."[13]

The suppression and denial of such sensual urgencies no longer surprises us; we are familiar with that Victorian problem to the point of arguing against its existence, as with Michel Foucault's counterinsistence that an obsessive sexual discourse then existed and with related arguments for the secret sexual freedoms of many if not most Victorians.[14] What is "surprising" about *Janet's Repentance,* in the light of present knowledge, is the absence of any helpful verbal discourse for defining and appraising domestic violence. In her correspondence with her publisher, for instance, neither Eliot nor Blackwood calls Dempster a batterer, nor describes his conduct as battering, nor speaks directly to that actuality. In the text itself none of the middle-class characters even says outright that Dempster beats his wife, and only a few hold him accountable. They are not as silent on that subject as Eliot's later male critics Thomas Noble, David Lodge, or Gordon Haight; indeed, they speak in lively ways all around it, and Eliot herself, as I have been arguing, converts her dramatic subtext on battering into her real concern, and finds effective ways of expressing every form of domestic abuse—

12. See, for example, Godfrey Cass's barren marriage to Nancy Lammeter in *Silas Marner,* after his illicit fathering of Little Eppie; and Maggie Tulliver's tainted love for Stephen Guest in *The Mill and the Floss,* undone ostensibly by her belated concern for her cousin Lucy and, more deeply, by her greater love for her brother Tom.

13. As other critics have noted, the Reverend Massy in "Daughters of the Vicar" derives his short stature and his clerical coldness from Eliot's hunchback Philip Wakem in *The Mill and the Floss* and the asexual heroes of her clerical stories.

14. See Foucault, *The History of Sexuality,* vol. 1, *An Introduction;* and Peter Gay, *The Bourgeois Experience: Victoria to Freud.*

verbal, physical, emotional, sexual, economic. She is the first British novelist, moreover, to give social as well as personal dimensions to the expression of that long-standing problem. But neither she nor her contemporaries nor, until recently, we postmodern sophisticates have had a vocabulary for discussing it. Indeed, it has taken over a century of sluggish progress to produce one and to reach our present stage of public awareness of the gravity of the social problem.

This missing public discourse may well be what Eliot herself reaches after in her 1860 letter to Blackwood urging that *Scenes of Clerical Life* "should have every chance of impressing the public with its existence," chiefly because "there are ideas presented in these stories about which I care a great deal, and am not sure I can ever embody again."[15] It is the brave beauty of *Janet's Repentance* that she does present such pioneering ideas so boldly and so confidently—in the face of patriarchal denials and of her own protective softenings—and with such prescient awareness of their more ample and unsoftened embodiments in our time.

15. Lodge, "Introduction," 32.

Janet's Repentance

by George Eliot

Chapter I

"No!" said lawyer Dempster, in a loud, rasping, oratorical tone, struggling against chronic huskiness, "as long as my Maker grants me power of voice and power of intellect, I will take every legal means to resist the introduction of demoralizing, methodistical doctrine into this parish; I will not supinely suffer an insult to be inflicted on our venerable pastor, who has given us sound instruction for half a century."

It was very warm everywhere that evening, but especially in the bar of the Red Lion at Milby, where Mr. Dempster was seated mixing his third glass of brandy-and-water. He was a tall and rather massive man, and the front half of his large surface was so well dredged with snuff, that the cat, having inadvertently come near him, had been seized with a severe fit of sneezing—an accident which, being cruelly misunderstood, had caused her to be driven contumeliously from the bar. Mr. Dempster habitually held his chin tucked in, and his head hanging forward, weighed down, perhaps, by a preponderant occiput and a bulging forehead, between which his closely-clipped coronal surface lay like a flat and new-mown table-land. The only other observable features were puffy cheeks and a protruding yet lipless mouth. Of his nose I can only say that it was snuffy, and as Mr. Dempster was never caught in the act of looking at anything in particular, it would have been difficult to swear to the color of his eyes.

"Well! I'll not stick at giving *myself* trouble to put down such hypocritical cant," said Mr. Tomlinson, the rich miller. "I know well enough what your Sunday-evening lectures are good for—for wenches to meet their sweethearts, and brew mischief. There's work enough with the servant-maids as it is—such as I never heard the like of in my mother's time, and it's all along o' your schooling and newfangled plans. Give me a servant as can nayther read nor write, I say, and doesn't know the year o' the Lord as she was born in. I should like to know what good those Sunday schools have done, now. Why, the boys used to go a birds'-nesting of a Sunday morning; and a capital thing, too—ask any farmer; and very pritty it was to see the strings o' heggs hanging up in poor people's houses. You'll not see 'em nowhere now."

"Pooh!" said Mr. Luke Byles, who piqued himself on his reading, and was in the habit of asking casual acquaintances if they knew anything of Hobbes; "it is right enough that the lower orders should be instructed. But this sectarianism within the Church ought to be put down. In point of fact, these Evangelicals are not Churchmen at all; they're no better than Presbyterians."

"Presbyterans? what are they?" inquired Mr. Tomlinson, who often said his father had given him "no eddication, and he didn't care who knowed it; he could buy up most o' th' eddicated men he'd ever come across."

"The Presbyterians," said Mr. Dempster, in rather a louder tone than before, holding that every appeal for information must naturally be addressed to him, "are a sect founded in the reign of Charles I., by a man named John Presbyter, who hatched all the brood of Dissenting vermin that crawl about in dirty alleys, and circumvent the lord of the manor in order to get a few yards of ground for their pigeon-house conventicles."

"No, no, Dempster," said Mr. Luke Byles, "you're out there. Presbyterianism is derived from the word presbyter, meaning an elder."

"Don't contradict *me,* sir!" stormed Dempster. "I say the word presbyterian is derived from John Presbyter, a miserable fanatic who wore a suit of leather, and went about from town to village, and from village to hamlet, inoculating the vulgar with the asinine virus of Dissent."

"Come, Byles, that seems a deal more liker," said Mr. Tomlinson, in a conciliatory tone, apparently of opinion that history was a process of ingenious guessing.

"It's not a question of likelihood; it's a known fact. I could fetch you my Encyclopaedia, and show it you this moment."

"I don't care a straw, sir, either for you or your Encyclopaedia," said Mr. Dempster; "a farrago of false information, of which you picked up an imperfect copy in a cargo of waste paper. Will you tell *me,* sir, that I don't know the origin of Presbyterianism? I, sir, a man known through the county, entrusted with the affairs of half a score parishes; while you, sir, are ignored by the very fleas that infest the miserable alley in which you were bred."

A loud and general laugh, with "You'd better let him alone, Byles"; "you'll not get the better of Dempster in a hurry," drowned the retort of the too well-informed Mr. Byles, who, white with rage, rose and walked out of the bar.

"A meddlesome, upstart, Jacobinical fellow, gentlemen," continued Mr. Dempster. "I was determined to be rid of him. What does he mean by thrusting himself into our company? A man with about as much principle as he has property, which, to my knowledge, is considerably less than none. An insolvent atheist, gentlemen. A deistical prater, fit to sit in the chimney-corner of a pot-house, and make blasphemous comments on the one greasy newspaper fingered by beer-swilling tinkers. I will not suffer in my company a man who speaks lightly of religion. The signature of a fellow like Byles would be a blot on our protest."

"And how do you get on with your signatures?" said Mr. Pilgrim, the doctor, who had presented his large top-booted person within the bar while Mr. Dempster was speaking. Mr. Pilgrim had just returned from one of his long day's rounds among the farmhouses, in the course of which he had sat down to two hearty meals that might have been mistaken for dinners, if he had not declared them to be "snaps"; and as each snap had been followed by a few glasses of "mixture," containing a less liberal proportion of water than the articles he himself labeled with that broadly generic name, he was in that condition which his groom indicated with poetic ambiguity, by saying that "master had been in the sunshine." Under these circumstances, after a hard day, in which he had really had no regular meal, it seemed a natural relaxation to step into the bar of the Red Lion, where, as it was Saturday evening, he should be sure to find Dempster, and hear the latest news about the protest against the evening lecture.

"Have you hooked Ben Landor yet?" he continued, as he took two chairs, one for his body, and the other for his right leg.

"No," said Mr. Budd, the churchwarden, shaking his head, "Ben Landor has a way of keeping himself neutral in everything, and he doesn't like to oppose his father. Old Landor is a regular Tryanite. But we haven't got your name yet, Pilgrim."

"Tut tut, Budd," said Mr. Dempster sarcastically, "you don't expect Pilgrim to sign? He's got a dozen Tryanite livers under his treatment. Nothing like cant and methodism for producing a superfluity of bile."

"O, I thought, as Pratt had declared himself a Tryanite, we should be sure to get Pilgrim on our side."

Mr. Pilgrim was not a man to sit quiet under a sarcasm, nature having endowed him with a considerable share of self-defensive wit. In his most sober moments he had an impediment in his speech, and as copious gin-and-water stimulated not the speech but the impediment, he had time to make his retort sufficiently bitter.

"Why, to tell you the truth, Budd," he spluttered, "there's a report all over the town that Deb Traunter swears you shall take her with you as one of the delegates, and they say there's to be a fine crowd at your door the morning you start, to see the row. Knowing your tenderness for that member of the fair sex, I thought you might find it impossible to deny her. I hang back a little from signing on that account, as Prendergast might not take the protest well if Deb Traunter went with you."

Mr. Budd was a small, sleek-headed bachelor of five-and-forty, whose scandalous life had long furnished his more moral neighbors with an after-dinner joke. He had no other striking characteristic, except that he was a currier of choleric temperament, so that you might wonder why he had been chosen as clergyman's churchwarden, if I did not tell you that he had recently been elected through Mr. Dempster's exertions, in order that his zeal against the threatened evening lecture might be backed by the dignity of office.

"Come, come, Pilgrim," said Mr. Tomlinson, covering Mr. Budd's retreat, "you know you like to wear the [town] crier's coat, green o' one side and red o' the other. You've been to hear Tryan preach at Paddiford Common—you know you have."

"To be sure I have; and a capital sermon too. It's a pity you were not there. It was addressed to those 'void of understanding.' "

"No, no, you'll never catch me there," returned Mr. Tomlinson, not in the least stung, "he preaches without book, they say, just like a Dissenter. It must be a rambling sort of a concern."

"That's not the worst," said Mr. Dempster, "he preaches against good works; says good works are not necessary to salvation—a sectarian, antinomian, anabaptist doctrine. Tell a man he is not to be saved by his works, and you open the floodgates of all immorality. You see it in all these canting innovators; they're all bad ones by the sly; smooth-faced, drawling, hypocritical fellows, who pretend ginger isn't hot in their mouths, and cry down all innocent pleasures; their hearts are all the blacker for their sanctimonious outsides. Haven't we been warned against those who make clean the outside of the cup and the platter? There's this Tryan, now, he goes about praying with old women, and singing with charity children; but what has he really got his eye on all the while? A domineering ambitious Jesuit, gentlemen; all he wants is to get his foot far enough into the parish to step into Crewe's shoes when the old gentleman dies. Depend upon it, whenever you see a man pretending to be better than his neighbors, that man has either some cunning end to serve, or his heart is rotten with spiritual pride."

As if to guarantee himself against this awful sin, Mr. Dempster seized the brandy bottle, and poured out a larger quantity than usual.

"Have you fixed on your third delegate yet?" said Mr. Pilgrim, whose taste was for detail rather than for dissertation.

"That's the man," answered Dempster, pointing to Mr. Tomlinson. "We start for Elmstoke Rectory on Tuesday morning; so, if you mean to give us your signature, you must make up your mind pretty quickly, Pilgrim."

Mr. Pilgrim did not in the least mean it, so he only said, "I shouldn't wonder if Tryan turns out too many for you, after all. He's got a well-oiled tongue of his own, and has perhaps talked over Prendergast into a determination to stand by him."

"Ve-ry little fear of that," said Dempster, in a confident tone. "I'll soon bring him round. Tryan has got his match. I've plenty of rods in pickle for Tryan."

At this moment Boots entered the bar, and put a letter into the lawyer's hands, saying, "There's Trower's man just come into the yard wi' a gig, sir, an' he's brought this here letter."

Mr. Dempster read the letter and said, "Tell him to turn the gig—I'll be with him in a minute. Here, run to Gruby's and get this snuff-box filled—quick!"

"Trower's worse, I suppose; eh, Dempster? Wants you to alter his will, eh?" said Mr. Pilgrim.

"Business—business—business—I don't know exactly what," answered the cautious Dempster, rising deliberately from his chair, thrusting on his low-crowned hat, and walking with a slow but not unsteady step out of the bar.

"I never see Dempster's equal; if I did I'll be shot," said Mr. Tomlinson, looking after the lawyer admiringly. "Why, he's drunk the best part of a bottle o' brandy since here we've been sitting, and I'll bet a guinea, when he's got to Trower's his head 'll be as clear as mine. He knows more about law when he's drunk than all the rest on 'em when they're sober."

"Aye, and other things too besides law," said Mr. Budd. "Did you notice how he took up Byles about the Presbyterians? Bless your heart, he knows everything, Dempster does. He studied very hard when he was a young man."

Chapter II

. . . [I]n spite of three assemblies and a charity ball in the winter, the occasional advent of a ventriloquist, or a company of itinerant players, some of whom were very highly thought of in London, and the annual three-days' fair in June, Milby might be considered dull by people of a hypochondriacal temperament, and perhaps this was one reason why many of the middle-aged inhabitants, male and female, often found it impossible to keep up their spirits without a very abundant supply of stimulants. It is true there were several substantial men who had a reputation for exceptional sobriety, so that Milby habits were really not as bad as possible; and no one is warranted in saying that old Mr. Crewe's flock could not have been worse without any clergyman at all.

The well-dressed parishioners generally were very regular church-goers, and to the younger ladies and gentlemen I am inclined to think that the Sunday morning service was the most exciting event of the week, for few places could present a more brilliant show of out-door toilettes than might be seen issuing from Milby church at one o'clock. There were the four tall Miss Pittmans, old Lawyer Pittman's daughters, with cannon curls surmounted by large hats, and long, drooping ostrich feathers of parrot green. There was Miss Phipps, with a crimson bonnet, very much tilted up behind, and a cockade of stiff feathers on the summit. There was Miss Landor, the belle of Milby, clad regally in purple and ermine, with a plume of feathers neither drooping nor erect, but maintaining a discreet medium. There were the three Miss Tomlinsons, who imitated Miss Landor, and also wore ermine and feathers; but their beauty was considered of a coarse order, and their square forms were quite unsuited to the round tippet which fell with such remarkable grace on Miss Landor's sloping shoulders. Looking at this plumed procession of ladies, you would have formed rather a high idea of Milby wealth; yet there was only one closed carriage in the place, and that was old Mr. Landor's, the banker, who, I think, never drove more than one horse. These sumptuously-attired ladies flashed past the vulgar eye in one-horse chaises, by no means of a superior build. . . .

Old lawyer Pittman had once been a very important person indeed, having in his earlier days managed the affairs of several gentlemen in those parts, who had subsequently been obliged to sell everything and leave the country, in which crisis Mr. Pittman accommodatingly stepped in as a purchaser of their estates, taking on himself the risk and trouble of a more leisurely sale; which, however, happened to turn out very much to his advantage. Such opportunities occur quite unexpectedly in the way of business. But I think Mr. Pittman must have been unlucky in his later speculations, for now, in his old age, he had not the reputation of being very rich; and though he rode slowly to his office in Milby every morning on an old white hackney, he had to resign the chief profits, as well as the active business of the firm, to his younger partner, Dempster. No one in Milby considered old Pittman a virtuous man, and the elder townspeople were not at all backward in narrating the least advantageous portions of his biography in a very round unvarnished manner. Yet I could never observe that they trusted him any the less, or liked him any the worse. Indeed, Pittman and Dempster were the popular lawyers of Milby and its neighborhood, and Mr. Benjamin Landor, whom no one had anything particular to say against, had a very meager business in comparison. Hardly a landholder, hardly a farmer, hardly a parish within ten miles of Milby, whose affairs were not under the legal guardianship of Pittman and Dempster, and I think the clients were proud of their lawyers' unscrupulousness, as the patrons of the [boxing ring] are proud of their champion's "condition." It was not, to be sure, the thing for ordinary life, but it was the thing to bet on in a lawyer. Dempster's talent in "bringing through" a client was a very common topic of conversation with the farmers, over an incidental glass of grog at the Red Lion. "He's a long-headed feller,

Dempster; why, it shows yer what a headpiece Dempster has, as he can drink a bottle o' brandy at a sittin', an' yit see further through a stone wall when he's done, than other folks 'll see through a glass winder." Even Mr. Jerome, chief member of the congregation at Salem Chapel, an elderly man of very strict life, was one of Dempster's clients, and had quite an exceptional indulgence for his attorney's foibles, perhaps attributing them to the inevitable incompatibility of law and gospel.

The standard of morality at Milby, you perceive, was not inconveniently high in those good old times, and an ingenuous vice or two was what every man expected of his neighbor. Old Mr. Crewe, the curate, for example, was allowed to enjoy his avarice in comfort, without fear of sarcastic parish demagogues; and his flock liked him all the better for having scraped together a large fortune out of his school and curacy, and the proceeds of the three thousand pounds he had with his little deaf wife. It was clear he must be a learned man, for he had once had a large private school in connection with the grammar school, and had even numbered a young nobleman or two among his pupils. The fact that he read nothing at all now, and that his mind seemed absorbed in the commonest matters, was doubtless due to his having exhausted the resources of erudition earlier in life. It is true he was not spoken of in terms of high respect, and old Crewe's stingy housekeeping was a frequent subject of jesting; but this was a good old-fashioned characteristic in a parson who had been part of Milby life for half a century: it was like the dents and disfigurements in an old family tankard, which no one would like to part with for a smart new piece of plate fresh from Birmingham. The parishioners saw no reason at all why it should be desirable to venerate the parson or any one else: they were much more comfortable to look down a little on their fellow-creatures.

Even the Dissent in Milby was then of a lax and indifferent kind. The doctrine of adult baptism, struggling under a heavy load of debt, had let off half its chapel area as a ribbon-shop; and Methodism was only to be detected, as you detect curious larvae, by diligent search in dirty corners. The Independents were the only Dissenters of whose existence Milby gentility was at all conscious, and it had a vague idea that the salient points of their creed were prayer without book, red brick, and hypocrisy. The Independent chapel, known as Salem, stood red and conspicuous in a broad street; more than one pewholder kept a brass-bound gig; and Mr. Jerome, a retired corn-factor, and the most eminent member of the congregation, was one of the richest men in the parish. But in spite of this apparent prosperity, together with the usual amount of extemporaneous preaching mitigated by furtive notes, Salem belied its name, and was not always the abode of peace. For some reason or other, it was unfortunate in the choice of its ministers. . . . These reverend gentlemen, one and all, gave it as their opinion that the Salem church members were among the least enlightened of the Lord's people, and that Milby was a low place, where they would have found it a severe lot to have their lines fall for any long period; though, to see the smart and crowded congregation assembled on occasion of the annual charity sermon, any one might have supposed that the minister of Salem had rather a brilliant position in the ranks of Dissent. . . . [M]any Church people there were of opinion that Dissent might be a weakness, but, after all, had no great harm in it. These lax Episcopalians were, I believe, chiefly tradespeople, who held that, inasmuch as Congregationalism consumed candles, it ought to be supported, and accordingly made a point of presenting themselves at Salem for the afternoon charity sermon, with the expectation of being asked to hold a plate. Mr. Pilgrim, too, was always there with his half-sovereign; for as there was no Dissenting doctor in Milby, Mr. Pilgrim looked with great tolerance on all shades of religious opinion that did not include a belief in cures by miracle.

On this point he had the concurrence of Mr. Pratt, the only other medical man of the same standing in Milby. Otherwise, it was remarkable how strongly these two clever men were contrasted. Pratt was middle-sized, insinuating, and silvery-voiced; Pilgrim was tall, heavy, rough-mannered, and spluttering. Both were considered to have great powers of conversation, but Pratt's anecdotes were of the fine old crusted quality to be procured only of Joe Miller; Pilgrim's had the full fruity flavor of the most recent scandal. Pratt elegantly referred all diseases to debility, and with a proper contempt for symptomatic treatment, went to the root of the matter with port wine and [quinine]; Pilgrim was persuaded that the evil principle in the human system was plethora, and he made war against it with cupping, blistering, and cathartics. They had both been long established in Milby, and as each had a sufficient practice, there was no very malignant rivalry between them; on the contrary, they had that sort of friendly contempt for each other which is always conducive to a good understanding between professional men; and when any new surgeon attempted, in an ill-advised hour, to settle himself in the town, it was strikingly demonstrated how slight and trivial are theoretic differences compared with the broad basis of common human feeling. There was the most perfect unanimity between Pratt and Pilgrim in the determination to drive away the obnoxious and too probably unqualified intruder as soon as possible. Whether the first wonderful cure he effected was on a patient of Pratt's or of Pilgrim's, one was as ready as the other to pull the interloper by the nose, and both alike directed their remarkable powers of conversation towards making the town too hot for him. But by their respective patients these two distinguished men were pitted against each other with great virulence. Mrs. Lowme could not conceal her amazement that Mrs. Phipps should trust her life in the hands of Pratt, who let her feed herself up to that degree, it was really shocking to hear how short her breath was; and Mrs. Phipps had no patience with Mrs. Lowme, living, as she did, on tea and broth, and looking as yellow as any crow-flower, and yet letting Pilgrim bleed and blister her and give her lowering medicine till her clothes hung on her like a scarecrow's. On the whole, perhaps, Mr. Pilgrim's reputation was at the higher pitch, and when any lady under Mr. Pratt's care was doing ill, she was half disposed to think that a little more "active treatment" might suit her better. But without very definite provocation no one would take so serious a step as to part with the family doctor, for in those remote days there were few varieties of human hatred more formidable than the medical. The doctor's estimate, even of a confiding patient, was apt to rise and fall with the entries in the daybook; and I have known Mr. Pilgrim discover the most unexpected virtues in a patient seized with a promising illness. At such times you might have been glad to perceive that there were some of Mr. Pilgrim's fellow-creatures of whom he entertained a high opinion, and that he was liable to the amiable weakness of a too admiring estimate. A good inflammation fired his enthusiasm, and a lingering dropsy dissolved him into charity. Doubtless this *crescendo* of benevolence was partly due to feelings not at all represented by the entries in the day-book; for in Mr. Pilgrim's heart, too, there was a latent store of tenderness and pity which flowed forth at the sight of suffering. Gradually, however, as his patients became convalescent, his view of their characters became more dispassionate; when they could relish mutton-chops, he began to admit that they had foibles, and by the time they had swallowed their last dose of tonic, he was alive to their most inexcusable faults. After this, the thermometer of his regard rested at the moderate point of friendly backbiting, which sufficed to make him agreeable in his morning visits to the amiable and worthy persons who were yet far from convalescent.

Pratt's patients were profoundly uninteresting to Pilgrim: their very diseases were despicable, and he would hardly have thought their bodies worth dissecting. But of all Pratt's patients, Mr. Jerome was the one on whom Mr. Pilgrim heaped the most unmitigated contempt. In spite of the surgeon's wise tolerance, Dissent became odious to him in the person of Mr. Jerome. Perhaps it was because that old gentleman, being rich, and having very large yearly bills for medical attendance on himself and his wife, nevertheless employed Pratt—neglected all the advantages of "active treatment," and paid away his money without getting his system lowered. On any other ground it is hard to explain a feeling of hostility to Mr. Jerome, who was an excellent old gentleman, expressing a great deal of goodwill towards his neighbors, not only in imperfect English, but in loans of money to the ostensibly rich, and in sacks of potatoes to the obviously poor. . . .

Such as the place was, the people there were entirely contented with it. They fancied life must be but a dull affair for that large portion of mankind who were necessarily shut out from an acquaintance with Milby families, and that it must be an advantage to London and Liverpool, that Milby gentlemen occasionally visited those places on business. But the inhabitants became more intensely conscious of the value they set upon all their advantages, when innovation made its appearance in the person of the Rev. Mr. Tryan, the new curate at the chapel-of-ease on Paddiford Common. It was soon notorious in Milby that Mr. Tryan held peculiar opinions; that he preached extempore; that he was founding a religious lending library in his remote corner of the parish; that he expounded the Scriptures in cottages; and that his preaching was attracting the Dissenters, and filling the very aisles of his church. The rumor sprang up that Evangelicalism had invaded Milby parish;—a murrain or blight all the more terrible, because its nature was but dimly conjectured. Perhaps Milby was one of the last spots to be reached by the wave of a new movement; and it was only now, when the tide was just on the turn, that the limpets there got a sprinkling. Mr. Tryan was the first Evangelical clergyman who had risen above the Milby horizon: hitherto that obnoxious adjective had been unknown to the townspeople of any gentility; and there were even many Dissenters who considered "evangelical" simply a sort of baptismal name to the magazine which circulated among the congregation of Salem Chapel. But now, at length, the disease had been imported, when the parishioners were expecting it as little as the innocent Red Indians expected small-pox. As long as Mr. Tryan's hearers were confined to Paddiford Common—which, by the by, was hardly recognizable as a common at all, but was a dismal district where you heard the rattle of the handloom, and breathed the smoke of coal-pits—the "canting parson" could be treated as a joke. Not so when a number of single ladies in the town appeared to be infected, and even one or two men of substantial property, with old Mr. Landor, the banker, at their head, seemed to be "giving in" to the new movement—when Mr. Tryan was known to be well received in several good houses, where he was in the habit of finishing the evening with exhortation and prayer. Evangelicalism was no longer a nuisance existing merely in by-corners, which any well-clad person could avoid; it was invading the very drawing-rooms, mingling itself with the comfortable fumes of port-wine and brandy, threatening to deaden with its murky breath all the splendor of the ostrich feathers, and to stifle Milby ingenuousness, not pretending to be better than its neighbors, with a cloud of cant and lugubrious hypocrisy. The alarm reached its climax when it was reported that Mr. Tryan was endeavoring to obtain authority from Mr. Prendergast, the nonresident rector, to establish a Sunday evening lecture in the parish church, on the ground that old Mr. Crewe did not preach the Gospel.

It now first appeared how surprisingly high a value Milby in general set on the ministrations of Mr. Crewe; how convinced it was that Mr. Crewe was the model of a parish priest, and his sermons the soundest and most edifying that had ever remained unheard by a church-going population. All allusions to his brown wig were suppressed, and by a rhetorical figure his name was associated with venerable gray hairs; the attempted intrusion of Mr. Tryan was an insult to a man deep in years and learning; moreover, it was an insolent effort to thrust himself forward in a parish where he was clearly distasteful to the superior portion of its inhabitants. The town was divided into two zealous parties, the Tryanites and anti-Tryanites; and by the exertions of the eloquent Dempster, the anti-Tryanite virulence was soon developed into an organized opposition. A protest against the meditated evening lecture was framed by that orthodox attorney, and after being numerously signed, was to be carried to Mr. Prendergast by three delegates representing the intellect, morality, and wealth of Milby. The intellect, you perceive, was to be personified in Mr. Dempster, the morality in Mr. Budd, and the wealth in Mr. Tomlinson; and the distinguished triad was to set out on its great mission, as we have seen, on the third day from that warm Saturday evening when the conversation recorded in the previous chapter took place in the bar of the Red Lion.

Chapter III

It was quite as warm on the following Thursday evening, when Mr. Dempster and his colleagues were to return from their mission to Elmstoke Rectory; but it was much pleasanter in Mrs. Linnet's parlor than in the bar of the Red Lion. Through the open window came the scent of mignonette and honeysuckle; the grass-plot in front of the house was shaded by a little plantation of Gueldres roses, syringas, and laburnums; the noise of looms and carts and unmelodious voices reached the ear simply as an agreeable murmur, for Mrs. Linnet's house was situated quite on the outskirts of Paddiford Common; and the only sound likely to disturb the serenity of the feminine party assembled there, was the occasional buzz of intrusive wasps, apparently mistaking each lady's head for a sugar-basin. No sugar-basin was visible in Mrs. Linnet's parlor, for the time of tea was not yet, and the round table was littered with books which the ladies were covering with black canvas as a reinforcement of the new Paddiford Lending Library. Miss Linnet, whose manuscript was the neatest type of zigzag, was seated at a small table apart, writing on green paper tickets, which were to be pasted on the covers. Miss Linnet had other accomplishments besides that of a neat manuscript, and an index to some of them might be found in the ornaments of the room. She had always combined a love of serious and poetical reading with her skill in fancywork, and the neatly-bound copies of Dryden's *Virgil,* Hannah More's *Sacred Dramas,* Falconer's *Shipwreck,* Mason *On Self-Knowledge,* Rasselas, and Burke *On the Sublime and Beautiful,* which were the chief ornaments of the book-case, were all inscribed with her name, and had been bought with her pocket-money when she was in her teens. It must have been at least fifteen years since the latest of those purchases, but Miss Linnet's skill in fancy-work appeared to have gone through more numerous phases than her literary taste; for the japanned boxes, the alum and sealing-wax baskets, the fan-dolls, the "transferred" landscapes on the fire-screens, and the recent bouquets of wax-flowers, showed a disparity in freshness which made them referable to widely different periods. Wax-flowers presuppose delicate fingers and robust patience, but there are still many points of mind and person which they leave vague and problematic; so I must tell you that Miss Linnet had dark ringlets, a sallow complexion, and an amiable disposition. As to her features, there was not much to criticize in them, for she had little nose, less lip, and no eyebrow; and as to her intellect, her friend Mrs. Pettifer often said: "She didn't know a more sensible person to talk to than Mary Linnet. There was no one she liked better to come and take a quiet cup of tea with her, and read a little of Klopstock's *Messiah.* Mary Linnet had often told her a great deal of her mind when they were sitting together: she said there were many things to bear in every condition of life, and nothing should induce her to marry without a prospect of happiness. Once, when Mrs. Pettifer admired her wax-flowers, she said, 'Ah, Mrs. Pettifer, think of the beauties of nature!' She always spoke very prettily, did Mary Linnet; very different, indeed, from Rebecca."

Miss Rebecca Linnet, indeed, was not a general favorite. While most people thought it a pity that a sensible woman like Mary had not found a good husband—and even her female friends said nothing more ill-natured of her, than that her face was like a piece of putty with two Scotch pebbles stuck in it—Rebecca was always spoken of sarcastically, and it was a customary kind of banter with young ladies to recommend her as a wife to any gentleman they happened to be flirting with—her fat, her finery, and her thick ankles, sufficing to give piquancy to the joke, notwithstanding the absence of novelty. Miss Rebecca, however, possessed the accomplishment of music, and her singing of "Oh no, we never mention her," and "The Soldier's Tear," was so desirable an accession to the pleasures of a tea-party, that no one cared to offend her, especially as Rebecca had a high spirit of her own, and in spite of her expansively rounded contour, had a particularly sharp tongue. Her reading had been more extensive than her sister's, embracing most of the fiction in Mr. Procter's circulating library, and nothing but an acquaintance with the course of her studies could afford a clue to the rapid transitions in her dress, which were suggested by the style of beauty, whether sentimental, sprightly, or severe, possessed by the heroine of the three volumes actually in perusal. A piece of lace, which drooped round the edge of her white bonnet one week, had been rejected by the next; and her cheeks, which, on Whitsunday, loomed through a Turnerian haze of net-work, were, on Trinity Sunday, seen reposing in distinct red outline on her shelving bust, like the sun on a fog-bank. The black velvet, meeting with a crystal clasp, which one evening encircled her head, had on another descended to her neck, and on a third to her wrist, suggesting to an active imagination, either a magical contraction of the ornament, or a fearful ratio of expansion in Miss Rebecca's person. With this constant application of art to dress, she could have had little time for fancy-work, even if she had not been destitute of her sister's taste for that delightful and truly feminine occupation. And here, at least, you perceive the justice of the Milby opinion as to the relative suitability of the two Miss Linnets for matrimony. When a man is happy enough to win the affections of a sweet girl, who can soothe his cares with *crochet,* and respond to all his most cherished ideas with beaded urn-rugs and chair-covers in German wool, he has, at least, a guarantee of domestic comfort, whatever trials may await him out of doors. What a resource it is under fatigue and irritation to have your drawing-room well supplied with small mats, which would always be ready if you ever wanted to set anything on them! And what styptic for a bleeding heart can equal copious squares of *crochet,* which are useful for slipping down the moment you touch them? How our fathers managed without *crochet* is the wonder; but I believe some small and feeble substitute existed in their time under the name of "tatting." Rebecca Linnet, however, had neglected tatting as well as other forms of fancy-work. At school, to be sure, she had spent a great deal of time in acquiring flower-painting, according to the ingenious method then fashionable, of applying the shapes of leaves and flowers cut out in cardboard, and scrubbing a brush over the surface thus conveniently marked out; but even the spill-cases and hand-screens which were her last half-year's performances in that way, were not considered eminently successful and had long been consigned to the retirement of the best bedroom. Thus, there was a good deal of family unlikeness between Rebecca and her sister, and I am afraid there was also a little family dislike; but Mary's disapproval had usually been kept imprisoned behind her thin lips, for Rebecca was not only of a headstrong disposition, but was her mother's pet; the old lady being herself stout, and preferring a more showy style of cap than she could prevail on her daughter Mary to make up for her.

But I have been describing Miss Rebecca as she was in former days only, for her appearance this evening, as she sits pasting on the green tickets, is in striking contrast with what it was three or four months ago. Her plain gray gingham dress and plain white collar could never have belonged to her wardrobe before that date; and though she is not reduced in size, and her brown hair will do nothing but hang in crisp ringlets down her large cheeks, there is a change in her air and expression which seems to shed a softened light over her person, and make her look like a peony in the shade, instead of the same flower flaunting in a [flower bed] in the hot sunlight.

No one could deny that Evangelicalism had wrought a change for the better in Rebecca Linnet's person—not even Miss Pratt, the thin, stiff lady in spectacles, seated opposite to her, who always had a peculiar repulsion for "females with a gross habit of body." Miss Pratt was an old maid; but that is a no more definite description than if I had said she was in the autumn of life. Was it autumn when the orchards are fragrant with apples, or autumn when the oaks are brown, or autumn when the last yellow leaves are fluttering in the chill breeze? The young ladies in Milby would have told you that the Miss Linnets were old maids; but the Miss Linnets were to Miss Pratt what the apple-scented September is to the bare, nipping days of late November. The Miss Linnets were in that temperate zone of old-maidism, when a woman will not say but that if a man of suitable years and character were to offer himself, she might be induced to tread the remainder of life's vale in company with him; Miss Pratt was in that arctic region where a woman is confident that at no time of life would she have consented to give up her liberty, and that she has never seen the man whom she would engage to honor and obey. If the Miss Linnets were old maids, they were old maids with natural ringlets and embonpoint, not to say obesity; Miss Pratt was an old maid with a cap, a braided "front," a backbone and appendages. Miss Pratt was the one blue-stocking of Milby, possessing, she said, no less than five hundred volumes, competent, as her brother the doctor often observed, to conduct a conversation on any topic whatever, and occasionally dabbling a little in authorship, though it was understood that she had never put forth the full powers of her mind in print. Her *Letters to a Young Man on his Entrance into Life,* and *De Courcy, or the Rash Promise, a Tale for Youth,* were mere trifles which she had been induced to publish because they were calculated for popular utility, but they were nothing to what she had for years had by her in manuscript. Her latest production had been Six Stanzas, addressed to the Rev. Edgar Tryan, printed on glazed paper with a neat border, and beginning, "Forward, young wrestler for the truth!"

Miss Pratt having kept her brother's house during his long widowhood, his daughter, Miss Eliza, had had the advantage of being educated by her aunt, and thus of imbibing a very strong antipathy to all that remarkable woman's tastes and opinions. The silent handsome girl of two-and-twenty, who is covering the *Memoirs of Felix Neff,* is Miss Eliza Pratt; and the small elderly lady in dowdy clothing, who is also working diligently, is Mrs. Pettifer, a superior-minded widow, much valued in Milby, being such a very respectable person to have in the house in case of illness, and of quite too good a family to receive any money-payment—you could always send her garden-stuff that would make her ample amends. Miss Pratt has enough to do in commenting on the heap of volumes before her, feeling it a responsibility entailed on her by her great powers of mind to leave nothing without the advantage of her opinion. Whatever was good must be sprinkled with the chrism of her approval; whatever was evil must be blighted by her condemnation.

"Upon my word," she said, in a deliberate high voice, as if she were dictating to an amanuensis, "it is a most admirable selection of works for popular reading, this that our excellent Mr. Tryan has made. I do not know whether, if the task had been confided to me, I could have made a selection, combining in a higher degree religious instruction and edification, with a due admixture of the purer species of amusement. This story of *Father Clement* is a library in itself on the errors of Romanism. I have ever considered fiction a suitable form for conveying moral and religious instruction, as I have shown in my little work *De Courcy,* which, as a very clever writer in the *Crompton Argus* said at the time of its appearance, is the light vehicle of a weighty moral."

"One 'ud think," said Mrs. Linnet, who also had her spectacles on, but chiefly for the purpose of seeing what the others were doing, "there didn't want much to drive people away from a religion as makes 'em walk barefoot over stone floors, like that girl in *Father Clement*—sending the blood up to the head frightful. Anybody might see that was an unnat'ral creed."

"Yes," said Miss Pratt, "but asceticism is not the root of the error, as Mr. Tryan was telling us the other evening—it is the denial of the great doctrine of justification by faith. Much as I had reflected on all subjects in the course of my life, I am indebted to Mr. Tryan for opening my eyes to the full importance of that cardinal doctrine of the Reformation. From a child I had a deep sense of religion, but in my early days the Gospel light was obscured in the English Church, notwithstanding the possession of our incomparable Liturgy, than which I know no human composition more faultless and sublime. As I tell Eliza, I was not blest as she is at the age of two-and-twenty, in knowing a clergyman who unites all that is great and admirable in intellect with the highest spiritual gifts. I am no contemptible judge of a man's acquirements, and I assure you I have tested Mr. Tryan's by questions which are a pretty severe touchstone. It is true, I sometimes carry him a little beyond the depth of the other listeners. Profound learning," continued Miss Pratt, shutting her spectacles, and tapping them on the book before her, "has not many to estimate it in Milby."

"Miss Pratt," said Rebecca, "will you please give me *Scott's Force of Truth*? There—that small book lying against the *Life of Legh Richmond.*"

"That's a book I'm very fond of—the *Life of Legh Richmond,*" said Mrs. Linnet. "He found out all about that woman at Tutbury as pretended to live without eating. Stuff and nonsense!"

Mrs. Linnet had become a reader of religious books since Mr. Tryan's advent, and as she was in the habit of confining her perusal to the purely secular portions, which bore a very small proportion to the whole, she could make rapid progress through a large number of volumes. On taking up the biography of a celebrated preacher, she immediately turned to the end to see what disease he died of; and if his legs swelled, as her own occasionally did, she felt a stronger interest in ascertaining any earlier facts in the history of the dropsical divine—whether he had ever fallen off a stage coach, whether he had married more than one wife, and, in general, any adventures or repartees recorded of him previous to the epoch of his conversion. She then glanced over the letters and diary, and wherever there was a predominance of Zion, the River of Life, and notes of exclamation, she turned over to the next page; but any passage in which she saw such promising nouns as "small-pox," "pony," or "boots and shoes," at once arrested her.

"It is half-past six now," said Miss Linnet, looking at her watch as the servant appeared with the tea-tray. "I suppose the delegates are come back by this time. If Mr. Tryan had not so kindly promised to call and let us know, I should hardly rest without walking to Milby myself to know what answer they have brought back. It is a great privilege for us, Mr. Tryan living at Mrs. Wagstaff's, for he is often able to take us on his way backwards and forwards into the town."

"I wonder if there's another man in the world who has been brought up as Mr. Tryan has, that would choose to live in those small close rooms on the common, among heaps of dirty cottages, for the sake of being near the poor people," said Mrs. Pettifer. "I'm afraid he hurts his health by it; he looks to me far from strong."

"Ah," said Miss Pratt, "I understand he is of a highly respectable family indeed, in Huntingdonshire. I heard him myself speak of his father's carriage—quite incidentally you know—and Eliza tells me what very fine cambric handkerchiefs he uses. My eyes are not good enough to see such things, but I know what breeding is as well as most people, and it is easy to see that Mr. Tryan is quite *comme il faw,* to use a French expression."

"I should like to tell him better nor use fine cambric i' this place, where there's such washing, it's a shame to be seen," said Mrs. Linnet; "he'll get 'em tore to pieces. Good lawn 'ud be far better. I saw what a color his linen looked at the sacrament last Sunday. Mary's making him a black silk case to hold his bands, but I told her she'd more need wash 'em for him."

"O mother!" said Rebecca, with solemn severity, "pray don't think of pocket-handkerchiefs and linen, when we are talking of such a man. And at this moment, too, when he is perhaps having to bear a heavy blow. We have more need to help him by prayer, as Aaron and Hur held up the hands of Moses. We don't know but wickedness may have triumphed, and Mr. Prendergast may have consented to forbid the lecture. There have been dispensations quite as mysterious, and Satan is evidently putting forth all his strength to resist the entrance of the Gospel into Milby Church."

"You niver spoke a truer word than that, my dear," said Mrs. Linnet, who accepted all religious phrases, but was extremely rationalistic in her interpretation; "for if iver Old Harry appeared in a human form, it's that Dempster. It was all through him as we got cheated out o' Pye's Croft, making out as the title wasn't good. Such lawyer's villainy! As if paying good money wasn't title enough to anything. If your father as is dead and gone had been worthy to know it! But he'll have a fall some day, Dempster will. Mark my words."

"Ah, out of his carriage, you mean," said Miss Pratt, who, in the movement occasioned by the clearing of the table, had lost the first part of Mrs. Linnet's speech. "It certainly is alarming to see him driving home from Rotherby, flogging his galloping horse like a madman. My brother has often said he expected every Thursday evening to be called in to set some of Dempster's bones; but I suppose he may drop that expectation now, for we are given to understand from good authority that he has forbidden his wife to call my brother in again either to herself or her mother. He swears no Tryanite doctor shall attend his family. I have reason to believe that Pilgrim was called in to Mrs. Dempster's mother the other day."

"Poor Mrs. Raynor! she's glad to do anything for the sake of peace and quietness," said Mrs. Pettifer; "but it's no trifle at her time of life to part with a doctor as knows her constitution."

"What trouble that poor woman has to bear in her old age!" said Mary Linnet, "to see her daughter leading such a life!—an only daughter, too, that she dotes on."

"Yes, indeed," said Miss Pratt. "We, of course, know more about it than most people, my brother having attended the family so many years. For my part, I never thought well of the marriage; and I endeavored to dissuade my brother when Mrs. Raynor asked him to give Janet away at the wedding. 'If you will take my advice, Richard,' I said, 'you will have nothing to do with that marriage.' And he has seen the justice of my opinion since. Mrs. Raynor herself was against the connection at first; but she always spoiled Janet, and I fear, too, she was won over by a foolish pride in having her daughter marry a professional man. I fear it was so. No one but myself, I think, foresaw the extent of the evil."

"Well," said Mrs. Pettifer, "Janet had nothing to look to but being a governess; and it was hard for Mrs. Raynor to have to work at millinering—a woman well brought up, and her husband a man who held his head as high as any man in Thurston. And it isn't everybody that sees everything fifteen years beforehand.

Robert Dempster was the cleverest man in Milby; and there weren't many young men fit to talk to Janet."

"It is a thousand pities," said Miss Pratt, choosing to ignore Mrs. Pettifer's slight sarcasm, "for I certainly did consider Janet Raynor the most promising young woman of my acquaintance;—a little too much lifted up, perhaps, by her superior education, and too much given to satire, but able to express herself very well indeed about any book I recommended to her perusal. There is no young woman in Milby now who can be compared with what Janet was when she was married, either in mind or person. I consider Miss Landor far, far below her. Indeed, I cannot say much for the mental superiority of the young ladies in our first families. They are superficial—very superficial."

"She made the handsomest bride that ever came out of Milby church, too," said Mrs. Pettifer. "Such a very fine figure! and it showed off her white poplin so well. And what a pretty smile Janet always had! Poor thing, she keeps that now for all her old friends. I never see her but she has something pretty to say to me—living in the same street, you know, I can't help seeing her often, though I've never been to the house since Dempster broke out on me in one of his drunken fits. She comes to me sometimes, poor thing, looking so strange, anybody passing her in the street may see plain enough what's the matter; but she's always got some little good-natured plan in her head for all that. Only last night when I met her, I saw five yards off she wasn't fit to be out; but she had a basin in her hand, full of something she was carrying to Sally Martin, the deformed girl that's in a consumption."

"But she is just as bitter against Mr. Tryan as her husband is, I understand," said Rebecca. "Her heart is very much set against the truth, for I understand she bought Mr. Tryan's sermons on purpose to ridicule them to Mrs. Crewe."

"Well, poor thing," said Mrs. Pettifer, "you know she stands up for everything her husband says and does. She never will admit to anybody that he's not a good husband."

"That is her pride," said Miss Pratt. "She married him in opposition to the advice of her best friends, and now she is not willing to admit that she was wrong. Why, even to my brother—and a medical attendant, you know, can hardly fail to be acquainted with family secrets—she has always pretended to have the highest respect for her husband's qualities. Poor Mrs. Raynor, however, is well aware that every one knows the real state of things. Latterly, she has not even avoided the subject with me. The very last time I called on her she said, 'Have you been to see my poor daughter?' and burst into tears."

"Pride or no pride," said Mrs. Pettifer, "I shall always stand up for Janet Dempster. She sat up with me night after night when I had that attack of rheumatic fever six years ago. There's great excuses for her. When a woman can't think of her husband coming home without trembling, it's enough to make her drink something to blunt her feelings—and no children either, to keep her from it. You and me might do the same, if we were in her place."

"Speak for yourself, Mrs. Pettifer," said Miss Pratt. "Under no circumstances can I imagine myself resorting to a practice so degrading. A woman should find support in her own strength of mind."

"I think," said Rebecca, who considered Miss Pratt still very blind in spiritual things, notwithstanding her assumption of enlightenment, "she will find poor support if she trusts only to her own strength. She must seek aid elsewhere than in herself."

Happily the removal of the tea-things just then created a little confusion, which aided Miss Pratt to repress her resentment at Rebecca's presumption in correcting her—a person like Rebecca Linnet! who six months ago was as flighty and vain a woman as Miss Pratt had ever known—so very unconscious of her unfortunate person!

The ladies had scarcely been seated at their work another hour, when the sun was sinking, and the clouds that flecked the sky to the very zenith were every moment taking on a brighter gold. The gate of the little garden opened, and Miss Linnet, seated at her small table near the window, saw Mr. Tryan enter.

"There is Mr. Tryan," she said, and her pale cheek was lighted up with a little blush that would have made her look more attractive to almost any one except Miss Eliza Pratt, whose fine gray eyes allowed few things to escape her silent observation. "Mary Linnet gets more and more in love with Mr. Tryan," thought Miss Eliza; "it is really pitiable to see such feelings in a woman of her age, with those old-maidish little ringlets. I dare say she flatters herself Mr. Tryan may fall in love with her, because he makes her useful among the poor." At the same time, Miss Eliza, as she bent her handsome head and large cannon curls with apparent calmness over her work, felt a considerable internal flutter when she heard the knock at the door. Rebecca had less self-command. She felt too much agitated to go on with her pasting, and clutched the leg of the table to counteract the trembling in her hands.

Poor women's hearts! Heaven forbid that I should laugh at you, and make cheap jests on your susceptibility towards the clerical sex, as if it had nothing deeper or more lovely in it than the mere vulgar angling for a husband. Even in these enlightened days, many a curate who, considered abstractedly, is nothing more than a sleek bimanous animal in a white neckcloth, with views more or less Anglican, and furtively addicted to the flute, is adored by a girl who has coarse brothers, or by a solitary woman who would like to be a helpmate in good works beyond her own means, simply because he seems to them the model of refinement and of public usefulness. What wonder, then, that in Milby society, such as I have told you it was a very long while ago, a zealous Evangelical clergyman, aged thirty-three, called forth all the little agitations that belong to the divine necessity of loving, implanted in the Miss Linnets, with their [thirty to forty years] and their unfashionable ringlets, no less than in Miss Eliza Pratt, with her youthful bloom and her ample cannon curls.

But Mr. Tryan has entered the room, and the strange light from the golden sky falling on his light brown hair, which is brushed high up round his head, makes it look almost like an auréole. His gray eyes, too, shine with unwonted brilliancy this evening. They were not remarkable eyes, but they accorded completely in their changing light with the changing expression of his person, which indicated the paradoxical character often observable in a large-limbed sanguine blond; at once mild and irritable, gentle and overbearing, indolent and resolute, self-conscious and dreamy. Except that the well-filled lips had something of the artificially compressed look which is often the sign of a struggle to keep the dragon undermost, and that the complexion was rather pallid, giving the idea of imperfect health, Mr. Tryan's face in repose was that of an ordinary whiskerless blond, and it seemed difficult to refer a certain air of distinction about him to anything in particular, unless it were his delicate hands and well-shapen feet.

It was a great anomaly to the Milby mind that a canting evangelical parson, who would take tea with tradespeople, and make friends of vulgar women like the Linnets, should have so much the air of a gentleman, and be so little like the splay-footed Mr. Stickney of Salem, to whom he approximated so closely in doctrine. And this want of correspondence between the physique and the creed had excited no less surprise in the larger town of Laxeter, where Mr. Tryan had formerly held a curacy; for of the two other Low Church clergymen in the neighborhood, one was a Welshman of globose figure and unctuous complexion, and the other a man of atrabiliar aspect, with lank black hair, and a redundance of limp cravat—in fact, the sort of thing you might expect in men who distributed the publications of the Religious Tract Society and introduced Dissenting hymns into the Church.

Mr. Tryan shook hands with Mrs. Linnet, bowed with rather a preoccupied air to the other ladies, and seated himself in the large horse-hair easy-chair which had been drawn forward for him, while the ladies ceased from their work, and fixed their eyes on him, awaiting the news he had to tell them.

"It seems," he began, in a low and silvery tone, "I need a lesson of patience; there has been something wrong in my thought or action about this evening lecture. I have been too much bent on doing good to Milby after my own plan—too reliant on my own wisdom."

Mr. Tryan paused. He was struggling against inward irritation.

"The delegates are come back, then?" "Has Mr. Prendergast given way?" "Has Dempster succeeded?"—were the eager questions of three ladies at once.

"Yes; the town is in an uproar. As we were sitting in Mr. Landor's drawing-room we heard a loud cheering, and presently Mr. Thrupp, the clerk at the bank, who had been waiting at the Red Lion to hear the result, came to let us know. He said Dempster had been making a speech to the mob out of the window. They were distributing drink to the people, and hoisting placards in great letters,—'Down with the Tryanites!' 'Down with cant!' They had a hideous caricature of me being tripped-up and pitched head foremost out of the pulpit. Good old Mr. Landor would insist on sending me round in the carriage; he thought I should not be safe from the mob; but I got down at the Crossways. The row was evidently preconcerted by Dempster before he set out. He made sure of succeeding."

Mr. Tryan's utterance had been getting rather louder and more rapid in the course of this speech, and he now added, in the energetic chest-voice, which, both in and out of the pulpit, alternated continually with his more silvery notes,—

"But his triumph will be a short one. If he thinks he can intimidate me by obloquy or threats, he has mistaken the man he has to deal with. Mr. Dempster and his colleagues will find themselves checkmated after all. Mr. Prendergast has been false to his own conscience in this business. He knows as well as I do that he is throwing away the souls of the people by leaving things as they are in the parish. But I shall appeal to the Bishop—I am confident of his sympathy."

"The Bishop will be coming shortly, I suppose," said Miss Pratt, "to hold a confirmation?"

"Yes; but I shall write to him at once, and lay the case before him. Indeed, I must hurry away now, for I have many matters to attend to. You, ladies, have been kindly helping me with your labors, I see," continued Mr. Tryan, politely, glancing at the canvas-covered books as he rose from his seat. Then, turning to Mary Linnet: "Our library is really getting on, I think. You and your sister have quite a heavy task of distribution now."

Poor Rebecca felt it very hard to bear that Mr. Tryan did not turn towards her too. If he knew how much she entered into his feelings about the lecture, and the interest she took in the library. Well! perhaps it was her lot to be overlooked—and it might be a token of mercy. Even a good man might not always know the heart that was most with him. But the next moment poor Mary had a pang, when Mr. Tryan turned to Miss Eliza Pratt, and the preoccupied expression of his face melted into that beaming timidity with which a man almost always addresses a pretty woman.

"I have to thank you, too, Miss Eliza, for seconding me so well in your visits to Joseph Mercer. The old man tells me how precious he finds your reading to him, now he is no longer able to go to church."

Miss Eliza only answered by a blush, which made her look all the handsomer, but her aunt said,

"Yes, Mr. Tryan, I have ever inculcated on my dear Eliza the importance of spending her leisure in being useful to her fellow-creatures. Your example and instruction have been quite in the spirit of the system which I have always pursued, though we are indebted to you for a clearer view of the motives that should actuate us in our pursuit of good works. Not that I can accuse myself of having ever had a self-righteous spirit, but my humility was rather instinctive than based on a firm ground of doctrinal knowledge, such as you so admirably impart to us."

Mrs. Linnet's usual entreaty that Mr. Tryan would "have something—some wine-and-water and a biscuit," was just here a welcome relief from the necessity of answering Miss Pratt's oration.

"Not anything, my dear Mrs. Linnet, thank you. You forget what [an abstainer] I am. By the by, when I went this morning to see a poor girl in Butcher's Lane, whom I had heard of as being in a consumption, I found Mrs. Dempster there. I had often met her in the street, but did not know it was Mrs. Dempster. It seems she goes among the poor a good deal. She is really an interesting-looking woman. I was quite surprised, for I have heard the worst account of her habits—that she is almost as bad as her husband. She went out hastily as soon as I entered. But," (apologetically) "I am keeping you all standing, and I must really hurry away. Mrs. Pettifer, I have not had the pleasure of calling on you for some time; I shall take an early opportunity of going your way. Good evening, good evening."

Chapter IV

Mr. Tryan was right in saying that the "row" in Milby had been preconcerted by Dempster. The placards and the caricature were prepared before the departure of the delegates; and it had been settled that Mat Paine, Dempster's clerk, should ride out on Thursday morning to meet them at Whitlow, the last place where they would change horses, that he might gallop back and prepare an ovation for the triumvirate in case of their success. Dempster had determined to dine at Whitlow: so that Mat Paine was in Milby again two hours before the entrance of the delegates, and had time to send a whisper up the back streets that there was promise of a "spree" in the Bridge Way, as well as to assemble two knots of picked men—one to feed the flame of orthodox zeal with gin-and-water, at the Green Man, near High Street; the other to solidify their church principles with heady beer at the Bear and Ragged Staff, in the Bridge Way.

The Bridge Way was an irregular straggling street, where the town fringed off raggedly into the Whitlow road: rows of new red-brick houses, in which ribbon-looms were rattling behind long lines of window, alternating with old, half-thatched, half-tiled cottages—one of those dismal wide streets where dirt and misery have no long shadows thrown on them to soften their ugliness. Here, about half-past five o'clock, Silly Caleb, an idiot well known in Dog Lane, but more of a stranger in the Bridge Way, was seen slouching along with a string of boys hooting at his heels; presently another group, for the most part out at elbows, came briskly in the same direction, looking round them with an air of expectation; and at no long interval, Deb Traunter, in a pink flounced gown and floating ribbons, was observed talking with great affability to two men in seal-skin caps and fustian, who formed her cortège. The Bridge Way began to have a presentiment of something in the wind. Phib Cook left her evening wash-tub and appeared at her door in soap-suds, a bonnet-poke, and general dampness; three narrow-chested ribbon-weavers, in rusty black streaked with shreds of many-colored silk, sauntered out with their hands in their pockets; and Molly Beale, a brawny old virago, descrying wiry Dame Ricketts peeping out from her entry, seized the opportunity of renewing the morning's skirmish. In short, the Bridge Way was in that state of excitement which is understood to announce a "demonstration" on the part of the British public; and the afflux of remote townsmen increasing, there was soon so large a crowd that it was time for Bill Powers, a plethoric Goliath, who presided over the knot of beer-drinkers at the Bear and Ragged Staff, to issue forth with his companions, and, like the enunciator of the ancient myth, make the assemblage distinctly conscious of the common sentiment that had drawn them together. The expectation of the delegates' chaise, added to the fight between Molly Beale and Dame Ricketts, and the ill-advised appearance of a lean bull-terrier, were a sufficient safety-valve to the popular excitement during the remaining quarter of an hour; at the end of which, the chaise was seen approaching along the Whitlow road, with oak boughs ornamenting the horses' heads, and, to quote the account of this interesting scene which was sent to the *Rotherby Guardian,* "loud cheers immediately testified to the sympathy of the honest fellows collected there, with the public-spirited exertions of their fellow-townsmen." Bill Powers, whose bloodshot eyes, bent hat, and protuberant altitude, marked him out as the natural leader of the assemblage, undertook to interpret the common sentiment by stopping the chaise, advancing to the door with raised hat, and begging to know of Mr. Dempster, whether the Rector had forbidden the "canting lecture."

"Yes, yes," said Mr. Dempster. "Keep up a jolly good hurray."

No public duty could have been more easy and agreeable to Mr. Powers and his associates, and the chorus swelled all the way to the High Street, where, by a mysterious coincidence often observable in these spontaneous "demonstrations," large placards on long poles were observed to shoot upward from among the crowd, principally in the direction of Tucker's Lane, where the Green Man was situated. One bore, "Down with the Tryanites!" another, "No Cant!" another, "Long live our venerable Curate!" and one in still larger letters, "Sound Church Principles and no Hypocrisy!" But a still more remarkable impromptu was a huge caricature of Mr. Tryan in gown and band, with an enormous aureole of yellow hair and upturned eyes, standing on the pulpit stairs and trying to pull down old Mr. Crewe. Groans, yells, and hisses—hisses, yells, and groans—only stemmed by the appearance of another caricature representing Mr. Tryan being pitched head-foremost from the pulpit stairs by a hand which the artist, either from subtlety of intention or want of space, had left unindicated. In the midst of the tremendous cheering that saluted this piece of symbolical art, the chaise had reached the door of the Red Lion, and loud cries of "Dempster for ever!" with a feebler cheer now and then for Tomlinson and Budd, were presently responded to by the appearance of the public-spirited attorney at the large upper window, where also were visible a little in the background the small sleek head of Mr. Budd, and the blinking countenance of Mr. Tomlinson.

Mr. Dempster held his hat in his hand, and poked his head forward with a butting motion by way of bow. A storm of cheers subsided at last into dropping sounds of "Silence!" "Hear him!" "Go it, Dempster!" and the lawyer's rasping voice became distinctly audible.

"Fellow Townsmen! It gives us the sincerest pleasure—I speak for my respected colleagues as well as myself—to witness these strong proofs of your attachment to the principles of our excellent Church, and your zeal for the honor of our venerable pastor. But it is no more than I expected of you. I know you well. I've known you for the last twenty years to be as honest and respectable a set of rate-payers as any in this county. Your hearts are sound to the core! No man had better try to thrust his cant and hypocrisy down *your* throats. You're used to wash them with liquor of a better flavor. This is the proudest moment in my own life, and I think I may say in that of my colleagues, in which I have to tell you that our exertions in the cause of sound religion and manly morality have been crowned with success. Yes, my fellow Townsmen! I have the gratification of announcing to you thus formally what you have already learned indirectly. The pulpit from which our venerable pastor has fed us with sound doctrine for half a century is not to be invaded by a fanatical, sectarian, double-faced, Jesuitical interloper! We are not to have our young people demoralized and corrupted by the temptations to vice, notoriously connected with Sunday evening lectures! We are not to have a preacher obtruding himself upon us, who decries good works, and sneaks into our homes perverting the faith of our wives and daughters! We are not to be poisoned with doctrines which damp every innocent enjoyment, and pick a poor man's pocket of the sixpence with which he might buy himself a cheerful glass after a hard day's work, under pretense of paying for bibles to send to the Chicktaws!

"But I'm not going to waste your valuable time with unnecessary words. I am a man of deeds." ("Aye, damn you, that you are, and you charge well for 'em too," said a voice from the crowd, probably that of a gentleman who was immediately afterwards observed with his hat crushed over his head.) "I shall always be at the service of my fellow-townsmen, and whoever dares to hector over you, or interfere with your innocent pleasures, shall have an account to settle with Robert Dempster.

"Now, my boys! you can't do better than disperse and carry the good news to all your fellow-townsmen, whose hearts are as sound as your own. Let some of you go one way and some another, that every man, woman, and child in Milby may know what you know yourselves. But before we part, let us have three cheers for True Religion, and down with Cant!"

When the last cheer was dying, Mr. Dempster closed the window, and the judiciously instructed placards and caricatures moved off in divers directions, followed by larger or smaller divisions of the crowd. The greatest attraction apparently lay in the direction of Dog Lane, the outlet towards Paddiford Common, whither the caricatures were moving; and you foresee, of course, that those works of symbolical art were consumed with a liberal expenditure of dry gorse-bushes and vague shouting.

After these great public exertions, it was natural that Mr. Dempster and his colleagues should feel more in need than usual of a little social relaxation; and a party of their friends was already beginning to assemble in the large parlor of the Red Lion, convened partly by their own curiosity, and partly by the invaluable Mat Paine. The most capacious punch-bowl was put in requisition; and that born gentleman, Mr. Lowme, seated opposite Mr. Dempster as "Vice," undertook to brew the punch, defying the criticisms of the envious men out of office, who, with the readiness of irresponsibility, ignorantly suggested more lemons. The social festivities were continued till long past midnight, when several friends of sound religion were conveyed home with some difficulty, one of them showing a dogged determination to seat himself in the gutter.

Mr. Dempster had done as much justice to the punch as any of the party; and his friend Boots, though aware that the lawyer could "carry his liquor like Old Nick," with whose social demeanor Boots seemed to be particularly well acquainted, nevertheless thought it might be as well to see so good a customer in safety to his own door, and walked quietly behind his elbow out of the innyard. Dempster, however, soon became aware of him, stopped short, and, turning slowly round upon him, recognized the well-known drab waistcoat sleeves, conspicuous enough in the starlight.

"You twopenny scoundrel! What do you mean by dogging a professional man's footsteps in this way? I'll break every bone in your skin if you attempt to track me, like a beastly cur sniffing at one's pocket. Do you think a gentleman will make his way home any the better for having the scent of your blacking-bottle thrust up his nostrils?"

Boots slunk back, in more amusement than ill-humor, thinking the lawyer's "rum talk" was doubtless part and parcel of his professional ability; and Mr. Dempster pursued his slow way alone.

His house lay in Orchard Street, which opened on the prettiest outskirt of the town—the church, the parsonage, and a long stretch of green fields. It was an old-fashioned house, with an overhanging upper story; outside, it had a face of rough stucco, and casement windows with green frames and shutters; inside, it was full of long passages, and rooms with low ceilings. There was a large heavy knocker on the green door, and though Mr. Dempster carried a latch-key, he sometimes chose to use the knocker. He chose to do so now. The thunder resounded through Orchard Street, and, after a single minute, there was a second clap louder than the first. Another minute, and still the door was not opened; whereupon Mr. Dempster, muttering, took out his latch-key, and, with less difficulty than might have been expected, thrust it into the door. When he opened the door the passage was dark.

"Janet!" in the loudest rasping tone, was the next sound that rang through the house.

"Janet!" again—before a slow step was heard on the stairs, and a distant light began to flicker on the wall of the passage.

"Curse you! you creeping idiot! Come faster, can't you?"

Yet another few seconds, and the figure of a tall woman, holding aslant a heavy-plated drawing-room candlestick, appeared at the turning of the passage that led to the broader entrance.

See, she has on a light dress which sits loosely about her figure, but does not disguise its liberal, graceful outline. A heavy mass of straight jet-black hair has escaped from its fastening, and hangs over her shoulders. Her grandly-cut features, pale with the natural paleness of a brunette, have premature lines about them telling that the years have been lengthened by sorrow, and the delicately-curved nostril, which seems made to quiver with the proud consciousness of power and beauty, must have quivered to the heart-piercing griefs which have given that worn look to the corners of the mouth. Her wide open black eyes have a strangely fixed, sightless gaze, as she pauses at the turning, and stands silent before her husband.

"I'll teach you to keep me waiting in the dark, you pale staring fool!" advancing with his slow drunken step. "What, you've been drinking again, have you? I'll beat you into your senses."

He laid his hand with a firm grip on her shoulder, turned her round, and pushed her slowly before him along the passage and through the dining-room door which stood open on their left hand.

There was a portrait of Janet's mother, a gray-haired, dark-eyed old woman, in a neatly-fluted cap, hanging over the mantelpiece. Surely the aged eyes take on a look of anguish as they see Janet—not trembling, no! it would be better if she trembled—standing stupidly unmoved in her great beauty, while the heavy arm is lifted to strike her. The blow falls—another—and another. Surely the mother hears that cry—"O Robert! pity! pity!"

Poor gray-haired woman! Was it for this you suffered a mother's pangs in your lone widowhood five-and-thirty years ago? Was it for this you kept the little worn morocco shoes Janet had first run in, and kissed them day by day when she was away from you, a tall girl at school? Was it for this you looked proudly at her when she came back to you in her rich pale beauty, like a tall white arum that has just unfolded its grand pure curves to the sun?

The mother lies sleepless and praying in her lonely house, weeping the hard tears of age, because she dreads this may be a cruel night for her child.

She too has a picture over her mantelpiece, drawn in chalk by Janet long years ago. She looked at it before she went to bed. It is a head bowed beneath a cross and wearing a crown of thorns.

Chapter V

It was half-past nine o'clock in the morning. The midsummer sun was already warm on the roofs and weathercocks of Milby. The church-bells were ringing, and many families were conscious of Sunday sensations, chiefly referable to the fact that the daughters had come down to breakfast in their best frocks, and with their hair particularly well dressed. For it was not Sunday, but Wednesday; and though the Bishop was going to hold a Confirmation, and to decide whether or not there should be a Sunday evening lecture in Milby, the sunbeams had the usual working-day look to the haymakers already long out in the fields, and to laggard weavers just "setting up" their week's "piece." The notion of its being Sunday was the strongest in young ladies like Miss Phipps, who was going to accompany her younger sister to the confirmation, and to wear a "sweetly pretty" transparent bonnet with marabout feathers on the interesting occasion, thus throwing into relief the suitable simplicity of her sister's attire, who was, of course, to appear in a new white frock; or in the pupils at Miss Townley's, who were absolved from all lessons, and were going to church to see the Bishop, and to hear the Honorable and Reverend Mr. Prendergast, the rector, read prayers—a high intellectual treat, as Miss Townley assured them. It seemed only natural that a rector, who was honorable, should read better than old Mr. Crewe, who was only a curate, and not honorable; and when little Clara Robins wondered why some clergymen were rectors and others not, Ellen Marriott assured her with great confidence that it was only the clever men who were made rectors. Ellen Marriott was going to be confirmed. She was a short, fair, plump girl, with blue eyes and sandy hair, which was this morning arranged in taller cannon curls than usual, for the reception of the Episcopal benediction, and some of the young ladies thought her the prettiest girl in the school; but others gave the preference to her rival, Maria Gardner, who was much taller, and had a lovely "crop" of dark-brown ringlets, and who, being also about to take upon herself the vows made in her name at her baptism, had oiled and twisted her ringlets with especial care. As she seated herself at the breakfast-table before Miss Townley's entrance to dispense the weak coffee, her crop excited so strong a sensation that Ellen Marriott was at length impelled to look at it, and to say with suppressed but bitter sarcasm, "Is that Miss Gardner's head?" "Yes," said Maria, amiable and stuttering, and no match for Ellen in retort; "Th—th—this is my head." "Then I don't admire it at all!" was the crushing rejoinder of Ellen, followed by a murmur of approval among her friends. Young ladies, I suppose, exhaust their sac of venom in this way at school. That is the reason why they have such a harmless tooth for each other in after life.

The only other candidate for confirmation at Miss Townley's was Mary Dunn, a draper's daughter in Milby, and a distant relation of the Miss Linnets. Her pale lanky hair could never be coaxed into permanent curl, and this morning the heat had brought it down to its natural condition of lankiness earlier than usual. But that was not what made her sit melancholy and apart at the lower end of the form. Her parents were admirers of Mr. Tryan, and had been persuaded, by the Miss Linnets' influence, to insist that their daughter should be prepared for confirmation by him, over and above the preparation given to Miss Townley's pupils by Mr. Crewe. Poor Mary Dunn! I am afraid she thought it too heavy a price to pay for these spiritual advantages, to be excluded from every game at ball, to be obliged to walk with none but little girls—in fact, to be the object of an aversion that nothing short of an incessant supply of plumcakes would have neutralized. And Mrs. Dunn was of opinion that plumcake was unwholesome. The anti-Tryanite spirit, you perceive, was very strong at Miss Townley's, imported probably by day scholars, as well as encouraged by the fact that that clever woman was herself strongly opposed to innovation, and remarked every Sunday that Mr. Crewe had preached an "excellent discourse." Poor Mary Dunn dreaded the moment when school-hours would be over, for then she was sure to be the butt of those very explicit remarks which, in young ladies' as well as young gentlemen's seminaries, constitute the most subtle and delicate form of the innuendo. "I'd never be a Tryanite, would you?" "O here comes the lady that knows so much more about religion than we do!" "Some people think themselves so very pious!"

It is really surprising that young ladies should not be thought competent to the same curriculum as young gentlemen. I observe that their powers of sarcasm are quite equal; and if there had been a genteel academy for young gentlemen at Milby, I am inclined to think that, notwithstanding Euclid and the classics, the party spirit there would not have exhibited itself in more pungent irony, or more incisive satire, than was heard in Miss Townley's seminary. But there was no such academy, the existence of the grammar-school under Mr. Crewe's superintendence probably discouraging speculations of that kind; and the genteel youths of Milby were chiefly come home for the midsummer holidays from distant schools. Several of us had just assumed coat-tails, and the assumption of new responsibilities apparently following as a matter of course, we were among the candidates for confirmation. I wish I could say that the solemnity of our feelings was on a level with the solemnity of the occasion; but unimaginative boys find it difficult to recognize apostolical institutions in their developed form, and I fear our chief emotion concerning the ceremony was a sense of sheepishness, and our chief opinion, the speculative and heretical position, that it ought to be confined to the girls. It was a pity, you will say; but it is the way with us men in other crises, that come a long while after confirmation. The golden moments in the stream of life rush past us, and we see nothing but sand; the angels come to visit us, and we only know them when they are gone. . . .

And who is this bright-looking woman walking with hasty step along Orchard Street so early, with a large nosegay in her hand? Can it be Janet Dempster, on whom we looked with such deep pity, one sad midnight, hardly a fortnight ago? Yes; no other woman in Milby has those searching black eyes, that tall graceful unconstrained figure, set off by her simple muslin dress and black lace shawl, that massy black hair now so neatly braided in glossy contrast with the white satin ribbons of her modest cap and bonnet. No other woman has that sweet speaking smile, with which she nods to Jonathan Lamb, the old parish clerk. And, ah!—now she comes nearer—there are those sad lines about the mouth and eyes on which that sweet smile plays like sunbeams on the storm-beaten beauty of the full and ripened corn.

She is turning out of Orchard Street, and making her way as fast as she can to her mother's house, a pleasant cottage facing a roadside meadow from which the hay is being carried. Mrs. Raynor has had her breakfast, and is seated in her arm-chair reading, when Janet opens the door, saying, in her most playful voice,—

"Please mother, I'm come to show myself to you before I go to the Parsonage. Have I put on my pretty cap and bonnet to satisfy you?"

Mrs. Raynor looked over her spectacles, and met her daughter's glance with eyes as dark and loving as her own. She was a much smaller woman than Janet, both in figure and feature, the chief resemblance lying in the eyes and the clear brunette complexion. The mother's hair had long been gray, and was gathered under the neatest of caps, made by her own clever fingers, as all Janet's caps and bonnets were too. They were well-practiced fingers, for Mrs. Raynor had supported herself in her widowhood by keeping a millinery establishment, and in this way had earned money enough to give her daughter what was then thought a first-rate education, as well as to save a sum which, eked out by her son-in-law, sufficed to support her in her solitary old age. Always the same clean, neat old lady, dressed in black silk, was Mrs. Raynor: a patient, brave woman, who bowed with resignation under the burden of remembered sorrow, and bore with meek fortitude the new load that the new days brought with them.

"Your bonnet wants pulling a trifle forwarder, my child," she said, smiling, and taking off her spectacles, while Janet at once knelt down before her, and waited to be "set to rights," as she would have done when she was a child. "You're going straight to Mrs. Crewe's, I suppose? Are those flowers to garnish the dishes?"

"No, indeed, mother. This is a nosegay for the middle of the table. I've sent up the dinner-service and the ham we had cooked at our house yesterday, and Betty is coming directly with the garnish and the plate. We shall get our good Mrs. Crewe through her troubles famously. Dear tiny woman! You should have seen her lift up her hands yesterday, and pray heaven to take her before ever she should have another collation to get ready for the Bishop. She said, 'It's bad enough to have the Archdeacon, though he doesn't want half so many jelly-glasses. I wouldn't mind, Janet, if it was to feed all the old hungry cripples in Milby; but so much trouble and expense for people who eat too much every day of their lives!' We had such a cleaning and furbishing-up of the sitting-room yesterday! Nothing will ever do away with the smell of Mr. Crewe's pipes, you know; but we have thrown it into the background, with yellow soap and dry lavender. And now I must run away. You will come to church, mother?"

"Yes, my dear, I wouldn't lose such a pretty sight. It does my old eyes good to see so many fresh young faces. Is your husband going?"

"Yes, Robert will be there. I've made him as neat as a new pin this morning, and he says the Bishop will think him too buckish by half. I took him into Mammy Dempster's room to show himself. We hear Tryan is making sure of the Bishop's support; but we shall see. I would give my crooked guinea, and all the luck it will ever bring me, to have him beaten, for I can't endure the sight of the man coming to harass dear old Mr. and Mrs. Crewe in their last days. Preaching the Gospel indeed! That is the best Gospel that makes everybody happy and comfortable, isn't it, mother?"

"Ah, child, I'm afraid there's no Gospel will do that here below."

"Well, I can do something to comfort Mrs. Crewe, at least; so give me a kiss, and good-bye till church-time."

The mother leaned back in her chair when Janet was gone, and sank into a painful reverie. When our life is a continuous trial, the moments of respite seem only to substitute the heaviness of dread for the heaviness of actual suffering: the curtain of cloud seems parted an instant only that we may measure all its horror as it hangs low, black, and imminent, in contrast with the transient brightness; the water-drops that visit the parched lips in the desert, bear with them only the keen imagination of thirst. Janet looked glad and tender now—but what scene of misery was coming next? She was too like the cistus flowers in the little garden before the window, that, with the shades of evening, might lie with the delicate white and glossy dark of their petals trampled in the roadside dust. When the sun had sunk, and the twilight was deepening, Janet might be sitting there, heated, maddened, sobbing out her griefs with selfish passion, and wildly wishing herself dead.

Mrs. Raynor had been reading about the lost sheep, and the joy there is in heaven over the sinner that repenteth. Surely the eternal love she believed in through all the sadness of her lot, would not leave her child to wander farther and farther into the wilderness till there was no turning—the child so lovely, so pitiful to others, so good—till she was goaded into sin by woman's bitterest sorrows! Mrs. Raynor had her faith and her spiritual comforts, though she was not in the least evangelical, and knew nothing of doctrinal zeal. I fear most of Mr. Tryan's hearers would have considered her destitute of saving knowledge, and I am quite sure she had no well-defined views on justification. Nevertheless, she read her Bible a great deal, and thought she found divine lessons there—how to bear the cross meekly, and be merciful. Let us hope that there is a saving ignorance, and that Mrs. Raynor was justified without knowing exactly how.

She tried to have hope and trust, though it was hard to believe that the future would be anything else than the harvest of the seed that was being sown before her eyes. But always there is seed being sown silently and unseen, and everywhere there come sweet flowers without our foresight or labor. We reap what we sow, but Nature has love over and above that justice, and gives us shadow and blossom and fruit that spring from no planting of ours.

Chapter VI

. . . At length, the last stage in the long ceremony was over, the large assembly streamed warm and weary into the open afternoon sunshine, and the Bishop retired to the Parsonage, where, after honoring Mrs. Crewe's collation, he was to give audience to the delegates and Mr. Tryan on the great question of the evening lecture.

Between five and six o'clock the Parsonage was once more as quiet as usual under the shadow of its tall elms, and the only traces of the Bishop's recent presence there were the wheel-marks on the gravel, and the long table with its garnished dishes awry, its damask sprinkled with crumbs, and its decanters without their stoppers. . . .

Before that time, the Bishop's carriage had been seen driving through the High Street on its way to Lord Trufford's, where he was to dine. The question of the lecture was decided, then?

The nature of the decision may be gathered from the following conversation which took place in the bar of the Red Lion that evening.

"So you're done, eh, Dempster?" was Mr. Pilgrim's observation, uttered with some gusto. He was not glad Mr. Tryan had gained his point, but he was not sorry Dempster was disappointed.

"Done, sir? Not at all. It is what I anticipated. I knew we had nothing else to expect in these days, when the Church is infested by a set of men who are only fit to give out hymns from an empty cask, to tunes set by a journeyman cobbler. But I was not the less to exert myself in the cause of sound Churchmanship for the good of the town. Any coward can fight a battle when he's sure of winning; but give me the man who has pluck to fight when he's sure of losing. That's my way, sir; and there are many victories worse than a defeat, as Mr. Tryan shall learn to his cost."

"He must be a poor shuperannyated sort of a bishop, that's my opinion," said Mr. Tomlinson, "to go along with a sneaking Methodist like Tryan. And, for my part, I think we should be as well wi'out bishops, if they're no wiser than that. Where's the use o' havin' thousands a-year an' livin' in a pallis, if they don't stick to the Church?"

"No. There you're going out of your depth, Tomlinson," said Mr. Dempster. "No one shall hear me say a word against Episcopacy—it is a safeguard of the Church; we must have ranks and dignities there as well as everywhere else. No, sir! Episcopacy is a good thing; but it may happen that a bishop is not a good thing. Just as brandy is a good thing, though this particular bottle is British, and tastes like sugared rainwater caught down the chimney. Here, Ratcliffe, let me have something to drink, a little less like a decoction of sugar and soot."

"*I* said nothing again' Episcopacy," returned Mr. Tomlinson. "I only said I thought we should do as well wi'out bishops; an' I'll say it again for the matter o' that. Bishops never brought ony grist to my mill."

"Do you know when the lectures are to begin?" said Mr. Pilgrim.

"They are to *begin* on Sunday next," said Mr. Dempster in a significant tone; "but I think it will not take a long-sighted prophet to foresee the end of them. It strikes me Mr. Tryan will be looking out for another curacy shortly."

"He'll not get many Milby people to go and hear his lectures after a while, I'll bet a guinea," observed Mr. Budd. "I know I'll not keep a single workman on my ground who either goes to the lecture himself or lets anybody belonging to him go."

"Nor me nayther," said Mr. Tomlinson. "No Tryanite shall touch a sack or drive a wagon o' mine, that you may depend on. An' I know more besides me as are o' the same mind."

"Tryan has a good many friends in the town, though, and friends that are likely to stand by him too," said Mr. Pilgrim. "I should say it would be as well to let him and his lectures alone. If he goes on preaching as he does, with such a constitution as his, he'll get a relaxed throat by-and-by, and you'll be rid of him without any trouble."

"We'll not allow him to do himself that injury," said Mr. Dempster. "Since his health is not good, we'll persuade him to try change of air. Depend upon it, he'll find the climate of Milby too hot for him."

Chapter VII

Mr. Dempster did not stay long at the Red Lion that evening. He was summoned home to meet Mr. Armstrong, a wealthy client, and as he was kept in consultation till a late hour, it happened that this was one of the nights on which Mr. Dempster went to bed tolerably sober. Thus the day, which had been one of Janet's happiest, because it had been spent by her in helping her dear old friend Mrs. Crewe, ended for her with unusual quietude; and as a bright sunset promises a fair morning, so a calm lying down is a good augury for a calm waking. Mr. Dempster, on the Thursday morning, was in one of his best humors, and though perhaps some of the good humor might result from the prospect of a lucrative and exciting bit of business in Mr. Armstrong's probable lawsuit, the greater part of it was doubtless due to those stirrings of the more kindly, healthy sap of human feeling, by which goodness tries to get the upper hand in us whenever it seems to have the slightest chance—on Sunday mornings, perhaps, when we are set free from the grinding hurry of the week, and take the little three-year-old on our knee at breakfast to share our egg and muffin; in moments of trouble, when death visits our roof or illness makes us dependent on the tending hand of a slighted wife; in quiet talks with an aged mother, of the days when we stood at her knee with our first picture-book, or wrote her loving letters from school. In the man whose childhood has known caresses there is always a fiber of memory that can be touched to gentle issues, and Mr. Dempster, whom you have hitherto seen only as the orator of the Red Lion, and the drunken tyrant of a dreary midnight home, was the first-born darling son of a fair little mother. That mother was living still, and her own large black easy-chair, where she sat knitting through the live-long day, was now set ready for her at the breakfast-table, by her son's side, a sleek tortoise-shell cat acting as provisional incumbent.

"Good morning, Mamsey! why, you're looking as fresh as a daisy this morning. You're getting young again," said Mr. Dempster, looking up from his newspaper when the little old lady entered. A very little old lady she was, with a pale, scarcely wrinkled face, hair of that peculiar white which tells that the locks have once been blond, a natty pure white cap on her head, and a white shawl pinned over her shoulders. You saw at a glance that she had been a mignonne blonde, strangely unlike her tall, ugly, dingy-complexioned son; unlike her daughter-in-law, too, whose large-featured brunette beauty seemed always thrown into higher relief by the white presence of little Mamsey. The unlikeness between Janet and her mother-in-law went deeper than outline and complexion, and indeed there was little sympathy between them, for old Mrs. Dempster had not yet learned to believe that her son, Robert, would have gone wrong if he had married the right woman—a meek woman like herself, who would have borne him children, and been a deft, orderly housekeeper. In spite of Janet's tenderness and attention to her, she had had little love for her daughter-in-law from the first, and had witnessed the sad growth of home-misery through long years, always with a disposition to lay the blame on the wife rather than on the husband, and to reproach Mrs. Raynor for encouraging her daughter's faults by a too exclusive sympathy. But old Mrs. Dempster had that rare gift of silence and passivity which often supplies the absence of mental strength; and, whatever were her thoughts, she said no word to aggravate the domestic discord. Patient and mute she sat at her knitting through many a scene of quarrel and anguish; resolutely she appeared unconscious of the sounds that reached her ears, and the facts she divined after she had retired to her bed; mutely she witnessed poor Janet's faults, only registering them as a balance of excuse on the side of her son. The hard, astute, domineering attorney was still that little old woman's pet, as he had been when she watched with triumphant pride his first tumbling effort to march alone across the nursery floor. "See what a good son he is to me!" she often thought. "Never gave me a harsh word. And so he might have been a good husband."

O it is piteous—that sorrow of aged women! In early youth, perhaps, they said to themselves, "I shall be happy when I have a husband to love me best of all"; then, when the husband was too careless, "My child will comfort me"; then, through the mother's watching and toil, "My child will repay me all when it grows up." And at last, after the long journey of years has been wearily traveled through, the mother's heart is weighed down by a heavier burden, and no hope remains but the grave.

But this morning old Mrs. Dempster sat down in her easy-chair without any painful, suppressed remembrance of the preceding night.

"I declare mammy looks younger than Mrs. Crewe, who is only sixty-five," said Janet. "Mrs. Crewe will come to see you to-day, mammy, and tell you all about her troubles with the Bishop and the collation. She'll bring her knitting, and you'll have a regular gossip together."

"The gossip will be all on one side, then, for Mrs. Crewe gets so very deaf, I can't make her hear a word. And if I motion to her, she always understands me wrong."

"O, she will have so much to tell you to-day, you will not want to speak yourself. You, who have patience to knit those wonderful counterpanes, mammy, must not be impatient with dear Mrs. Crewe. Good old lady! I can't bear her to think she's ever tiresome to people, and you know she's very ready to fancy herself in the way. I think she would like to shrink up to the size of a mouse, that she might run about and do people good without their noticing her."

"It isn't patience I want, God knows; it's lungs to speak loud enough. But you'll be at home yourself, I suppose, this morning; and you can talk to her for me."

"No, mammy; I promised poor Mrs. Lowme to go and sit with her. She's confined to her room, and both the Miss Lowmes are out; so I'm going to read the newspaper to her and amuse her."

"Couldn't you go another morning? As Mr. Armstrong and that other gentleman are coming to dinner, I should think it would be better to stay at home. Can you trust Betty to see to everything? She's new to the place."

"O I couldn't disappoint Mrs. Lowme; I promised her. Betty will do very well, no fear."

Old Mrs. Dempster was silent after this, and began to sip her tea. The breakfast went on without further conversation for some time, Mr. Dempster being absorbed in the papers. At length, when he was running over the advertisements, his eye seemed to be caught by something that suggested a new thought to him. He presently thumped the table with an air of exultation, and said, turning to Janet,—

"I've a capital idea, Gypsy!" (that was his name for his dark-eyed wife when he was in an extraordinarily good humor), "and you shall help me. It's just what you're up to."

"What is it?" said Janet, her face beaming at the sound of the pet name, now heard so seldom. "Anything to do with conveyancing?"

"It's a bit of fun worth a dozen fees—a plan for raising a laugh against Tryan and his gang of hypocrites."

"What is it? Nothing that wants a needle and thread, I hope, else I must go and tease mother."

"No, nothing sharper than your wit—except mine. I'll tell you what it is. We'll get up a programme of the Sunday evening lecture, like a play-bill, you know—'Grand Performance of the celebrated Mountebank,' and so on. We'll bring in the Tryanites—old Landor and the rest—in appropriate characters. Proctor shall print it, and we'll circulate it in the town. It will be a capital hit."

"Bravo!" said Janet, clapping her hands. She would just then have pretended to like almost anything, in her pleasure at being appealed to by her husband, and she really did like to laugh at the Tryanites. "We'll set about it directly, and sketch it out before you go to the office. I've got Tryan's sermons up-stairs, but I don't think there's anything in them we can use. I've only just looked into them; they're not at all what I expected—dull, stupid things—nothing of the roaring fire-and-brimstone sort that I expected."

"Roaring? No; Tryan's as soft as a sucking dove—one of your honey-mouthed hypocrites. Plenty of devil and malice in him, though, I could see that, while he was talking to the Bishop; but as smooth as a snake outside. He's beginning a single-handed fight with me, I can see—persuading my clients away from me. We shall see who will be the first to cry ['I have sinned']. Milby will do better without Mr. Tryan than without Robert Dempster, I fancy! and Milby shall never be flooded with cant as long as I can raise a breakwater against it. But now, get the breakfast things cleared away, and let us set about the play-bill. Come, mamsey, come and have a walk with me round the garden, and let us see how the cucumbers are getting on. I've never taken you round the garden for an age. Come, you don't want a bonnet. It's like walking in a greenhouse this morning."

"But she will want a parasol," said Janet. "There's one on the stand against the garden-door, Robert."

The little old lady took her son's arm with placid pleasure. She could barely reach it so as to rest upon it, but he inclined a little towards her, and accommodated his heavy long-limbed steps to her feeble pace. The cat chose to sun herself too, and walked close beside them, with tail erect, rubbing her sleek sides against their legs, too well fed to be excited by the twittering birds. The garden was of the grassy, shady kind, often seen attached to old houses in provincial towns; the apple-trees had had time to spread their branches very wide, the shrubs and hardy perennial plants had grown into a luxuriance that required constant trimming to prevent them from intruding on the space for walking. But the farther end, which united with green fields, was open and sunny.

It was rather sad, and yet pretty, to see that little group passing out of the shadow into the sunshine, and out of the sunshine into the shadow again: sad, because this tenderness of the son for the mother was hardly more than a nucleus of healthy life in an organ hardening by disease, because the man who was linked in this way with an innocent past, had become callous in worldliness, fevered by sensuality, enslaved by chance impulses; pretty, because it showed how hard it is to kill the deep-down fibrous roots of human love and goodness—how the man from whom we make it our pride to shrink, has yet a close brotherhood with us through some of our most sacred feelings.

As they were returning to the house, Janet met them, and said, "Now, Robert, the writing things are ready. I shall be clerk, and Mat Paine can copy it out after."

Mammy once more deposited in her arm-chair, with her knitting in her hand, and the cat purring at her elbow, Janet seated herself at the table, while Mr. Dempster placed himself near her, took out his snuff-box, and plentifully suffusing himself with the inspiring powder, began to dictate.

What he dictated, we shall see by-and-by.

Chapter VIII

The next day, Friday, at five o'clock by the sundial, the large bow-window of Mrs. Jerome's parlor was open; and that lady herself was seated within its ample semicircle, having a table before her on which her best tea-tray, her best china, and her best urn-rug had already been standing in readiness for half an hour. Mrs. Jerome's best tea-service was of delicate white fluted china, with gold sprigs upon it—as pretty a tea-service as you need wish to see, and quite good enough for chimney ornaments; indeed, as the cups were without handles, most visitors who had the distinction of taking tea out of them, wished that such charming china had already been promoted to that honorary position. Mrs. Jerome was like her china, handsome and old-fashioned. She was a buxom lady of sixty, in an elaborate lace cap fastened by a frill under her chin, a dark, well-curled front concealing her forehead, a snowy neckerchief exhibiting its ample folds as far as her waist, and a stiff gray silk gown. She had a clean damask napkin pinned before her to guard her dress during the process of tea-making; her favorite geraniums in the bow-window were looking as healthy as she could desire; her own handsome portrait, painted when she was twenty years younger, was smiling down on her with agreeable flattery; and altogether she seemed to be in as peaceful and pleasant a position as a buxom, well-dressed elderly lady need desire. But, as in so many other cases, appearances were deceptive. Her mind was greatly perturbed and her temper ruffled by the fact that it was more than a quarter past five even by the losing timepiece, that it was half-past by her large gold watch, which she held in her hand as if she were counting the pulse of the afternoon, and that, by the kitchen clock, which she felt sure was not an hour too fast, it had already struck six. The lapse of time was rendered the more unendurable to Mrs. Jerome by her wonder that Mr. Jerome could stay out in the garden with Lizzie in that thoughtless way, taking it so easily that tea-time was long past, and that, after all the trouble of getting down the best tea-things, Mr. Tryan would not come.

This honor had been shown to Mr. Tryan, not at all because Mrs. Jerome had any high appreciation of his doctrine or of his exemplary activity as a pastor, but simply because he was a "Church clergyman," and as such was regarded by her with the same sort of exceptional respect that a white woman who had married a native of the Society Islands might be supposed to feel towards a white-skinned visitor from the land of her youth. For Mrs. Jerome had been reared a Churchwoman, and having attained the age of thirty before she was married, had felt the greatest repugnance in the first instance to renouncing the religious forms in which she had been brought up. "You know," she said in confidence to her Church acquaintances, "I wouldn't give no ear at all to Mr. Jerome at fust; but after all, I begun to think as there was a maeny things wuss nor goin' to chapel, an' you'd better do that nor not pay your way. Mr. Jerome had a very pleasant manner wi' him, an' there was niver another as kep a gig, an' 'ud make a settlement on me like him, chapel or no chapel. It seemed very odd to me for a lung while, the preachin' wi'out book, an' the stannin' up to one lung prayer, istid o' changin' yur postur. But la! there's nothin' as you mayn't get used to i' time; you can al'ys sit down, you know, afore the prayer's done. The ministers say welly the same things as the Church parsons, by what I could iver mek out, an' we're out o' chapel i' the mornin' a deal sooner nor they're out o' church. An' as for pews, ourn's a deal comfortabler nor aeny i' Milby church."

Mrs. Jerome, you perceive, had not a keen susceptibility to shades of doctrine, and it is probable that, after listening to Dissenting eloquence for thirty years, she might safely have re-entered the Establishment without performing any spiritual quarantine. Her mind, apparently, was of that non-porous flinty character which is not in the least danger from surrounding damp. But on the question of getting start of the sun in the day's business, and clearing her conscience of the necessary sum of meals and the consequent "washing up" as soon as possible, so that the family might be well in bed at nine, Mrs. Jerome *was* susceptible; and the present lingering pace of things, united with Mr. Jerome's unaccountable obliviousness, was not to be borne any longer. So she rang the bell for Sally.

"Goodness me, Sally! go into the garden an' see after your master. Tell him it's goin' on for six, an' Mr. Tryan 'ull niver think o' comin' now, an' it's time we got tea over. An' he's lettin' Lizzie stain her frock, I expect, among them strawberry beds. Mek her come in this minute."

No wonder Mr. Jerome was tempted to linger in the garden, for though the house was pretty and well deserved its name—"the White House," the tall damask roses that clustered over the porch being thrown into relief by rough stucco of the most brilliant white, yet the garden and orchards were Mr. Jerome's glory, as well they might be; and there was nothing in which he had a more innocent pride—peace to a good man's memory! all his pride was innocent—than in conducting a hitherto uninitiated visitor over his grounds, and making him in some degree aware of the incomparable advantages possessed by the inhabitants of the White House in the matter of red-streaked apples, russets, northern greens (excellent for baking), swan-egg pears, and early vegetables, to say nothing of flowering "srubs," pink hawthorns, lavender bushes more than ever Mrs. Jerome could use, and, in short, a superabundance of everything that a person retired from business could desire to possess himself or to share with his friends. The garden was one of those old-fashioned paradises which hardly exist any longer except as memories of our childhood: no finical separation between flower and kitchen garden there; no monotony of enjoyment for one sense to the exclusion of another; but a charming paradisiacal mingling of all that was pleasant to the eyes and good for food. The rich flower-border running along every walk, with its endless succession of spring flowers, anemones, auriculas, wall-flowers, sweet-williams, campanulas, snapdragons, and tiger-lilies, had its taller beauties. . . . Then what a high wall at one end . . . what alcoves and garden-seats in all directions; and along one side, what a hedge, tall, and firm, and unbroken, like a green wall!

It was near this hedge that Mr. Jerome was standing when Sally found him. He had set down the basket of strawberries on the gravel, and had lifted up little Lizzie in his arms to look at a bird's nest. Lizzie peeped, and then looked at her grandpa with round blue eyes, and then peeped again.

"D'ye see it, Lizzie?" he whispered.

"Yes," she whispered in return, putting her lips very near grandpa's face. At this moment Sally appeared.

"Eh, eh, Sally, what's the matter? Is Mr. Tryan come?"

"No, sir, an' Missis says she's sure he won't come now, an' she wants you to come in an' hev tea. Dear heart, Miss Lizzie, you've stained your pinafore, an' I shouldn't wonder if it's gone through to your frock. There'll be fine work! Come alonk wi' me, do."

"Nay, nay, nay, we've done no harm, we've done no harm, hev we Lizzie? The wash-tub 'll mek all right again."

Sally, regarding the wash-tub from a different point of view, looked sourly serious, and hurried away with Lizzie, who trotted submissively along, her little head in eclipse under a large nankin bonnet, while Mr. Jerome followed leisurely with his full broad shoulders in rather a stooping posture, and his large good-natured features and white locks shaded by a broad-brimmed hat.

"Mr. Jerome, I wonder at you," said Mrs. Jerome, in a tone of indignant remonstrance, evidently sustained by a deep sense of injury, as her husband opened the parlor door. "When will you leave off invitin' people to meals an' not lettin' 'em know the time? I'll answer for't, you niver said a word to Mr. Tryan as we should tek tea at five o'clock. It's just like you!"

"Nay, nay, Susan," answered the husband in a soothing tone, "there's nothin' amiss. I told Mr. Tryan as we took tea at five punctial; mayhap summat's a detainin' on him. He's a deal to do an' to think on, remember."

"Why, it's struck six i' the kitchen a'ready. It's nonsense to look for him comin' now. So you may's well ring for th' urn. Now Sally's got th' heater i' th' fire, we may's well hev th' urn in, though he doesn't come. I niver see the like o' you, Mr. Jerome, for axin' people an' givin' me the trouble o' gettin' things down an' hevin' crumpets made, an' after all they don't come. I shall hev to wash every one o' these tea-things myself, for there's no trustin' Sally—she'd break a fortin i' crockery i' no time!"

"But why will you give yourself sich trouble, Susan? Our everyday tea-things would ha' done as well for Mr. Tryan, an' they're a deal convenenter to hold."

"Yes, that's just your way, Mr. Jerome, you're al'ys a-findin' faut wi' my chany, because I bought it myself afore I was married. But let me tell you, I knowed how to choose chany if I didn't know how to choose a husband. An' where's Lizzie? You've niver left her i' the garden by herself, wi her white frock on an' clean stockins?"

"Be easy, my dear Susan, be easy; Lizzie's come in wi' Sally. She's hevin' her pinafore took off, I'll be bound. Ah! There's Mr. Tryan a-comin' through the gate."

Mrs. Jerome began hastily to adjust her damask napkin and the expression of her countenance for the reception of the clergyman, and Mr. Jerome went out to meet his guest, whom he greeted outside the door.

"Mr. Tryan, how do you do, Mr. Tryan? Welcome to the White House! I'm glad to see you, sir, I'm glad to see you."

If you had heard the tone of mingled goodwill, veneration, and condolence in which this greeting was uttered, even without seeing the face that completely harmonized with it, you would have no difficulty in inferring the ground-notes of Mr. Jerome's character. To a fine ear that tone said as plainly as possible—"Whatever recommends itself to me, Thomas Jerome, as piety and goodness, shall have my love and honor. Ah, friends, this pleasant world is a sad one, too, isn't it? Let us help one another, let us help one another." And it was entirely owing to this basis of character, not at all from any clear and precise doctrinal discrimination, that Mr. Jerome had very early in life become a Dissenter. In his boyish days he had been thrown where Dissent seemed to have the balance of piety, purity, and good works on its side, and to become a Dissenter seemed to him identical with choosing God instead of mammon. . . . Mr. Jerome's dissent being of this simple, non-polemical kind, it is easy to understand that the report he heard of Mr. Tryan as a good man and a powerful preacher, who was stirring the hearts of the people, had been enough to attract him to the Paddiford Church, and that having felt himself more edified there than he had of late been under Mr. Stickney's discourses at Salem, he had driven thither repeatedly in the Sunday afternoons, and had sought an opportunity of making Mr. Tryan's acquaintance. The evening lecture was a subject of warm interest with him, and the opposition Mr. Tryan met with gave that interest a strong tinge of partisanship; for there was a store of irascibility in Mr. Jerome's nature which must find a vent somewhere, and in so kindly and upright a man could only find it in indignation against those whom he held to be enemies of truth and goodness. Mr. Tryan had not hitherto been to the White House, but yesterday, meeting Mr. Jerome in the street, he had at once accepted the invitation to tea, saying there was something he wished to talk about. He appeared worn and fatigued now, and after shaking hands with Mrs. Jerome, threw himself into a chair and looked out on the pretty garden with an air of relief.

"What a nice place you have here, Mr. Jerome! I've not seen anything so quiet and pretty since I came to Milby. On Paddiford Common, where I live, you know, the bushes are all sprinkled with soot, and there's never any quiet except in the dead of night."

"Dear heart! dear heart! That's very bad—and for you, too, as hev to study. Wouldn't it be better for you to be somewhere more out i' the country like?"

"O no! I should lose so much time in going to and fro, and besides I like to be *among* the people. I've no face to go and preach resignation to those poor things in their smoky air and comfortless homes, when I come straight from every luxury myself. There are many things quite lawful for other men, which a clergyman must forgo if he would do any good in a manufacturing population like this."

Here the preparations for tea were crowned by the simultaneous appearance of Lizzie and the crumpet. It is a pretty surprise, when one visits an elderly couple, to see a little figure enter in a white frock with a blond head as smooth as satin, round blue eyes, and a cheek like an apple blossom. A toddling little girl is a center of common feeling which makes the most dissimilar people understand each other; and Mr. Tryan looked at Lizzie with that quiet pleasure which is always genuine.

"Here we are, here we are!" said proud grandpapa. "You didn't think we'd got such a little gell as this, did you, Mr. Tryan? Why, it seems but th' other day since her mother was just such another. This is our little Lizzie, this is. Come an' shake hands wi' Mr. Tryan, Lizzie; come."

Lizzie advanced without hesitation, and put out one hand, while she fingered her coral necklace with the other, and looked up into Mr. Tryan's face with a reconnoitering gaze. He stroked the satin head, and said in his gentlest voice, "How do you do, Lizzie? will you give me a kiss?" She put up her little bud of a mouth, and then retreating a little and glancing down at her frock, said,

"Dit id my noo fock. I put it on 'tod you wad toming. Tally taid you wouldn't 'ook at it."

"Hush, hush, Lizzie, little gells must be seen and not heard," said Mrs. Jerome; while grandpapa, winking significantly, and looking radiant with delight at Lizzie's extraordinary promise of cleverness, set her up on her high cane-chair by the side of grandma, who lost no time in shielding the beauties of the new frock with a napkin.

"Well now, Mr. Tryan," said Mr. Jerome, in a very serious tone when tea had been distributed, "let me hear how you're a-goin' on about the lectur. When I was i' the town yisterday, I heared as there was pessecutin' schemes a-bein' laid again' you. I fear me those raskills 'ull mek things very onpleasant to you."

"I've no doubt they will attempt it; indeed, I quite expect there will be a regular mob got up on Sunday evening, as there was when the delegates returned, on purpose to annoy me and the congregation on our way to church."

"Ah, they're capible o' anything, such men as Dempster an' Budd; an' Tomlinson backs 'em wi' money, though he can't wi' brains. Howiver, Dempster's lost one client by's wicked doins, an' I'm deceived if he won't lose more nor one. I little thought, Mr. Tryan, when I put my affairs into his hands twenty 'ear ago this Michaelmas, as he was to turn out a pessecutor o' religion. I niver lighted on a cliverer, promisiner young man nor he was then. They talked of his bein' fond of a extry glass now an' then, but niver nothin' like what he's come to since. An' it's headpiece you must look for in a lawyer, Mr. Tryan, it's headpiece. His wife, too, was al'ys an uncommon favorite o' mine—poor thing! I hear sad stories about her now. But she's druv to it, she's druv to it, Mr. Tryan. A tender-hearted woman to the poor, she is, as iver lived; an' as pretty-spoken a woman as you need wish to talk to. Yes! I'd al'ys a likin' for Dempster an' his wife, spite o' iverything. But as soon as iver I heared o' that dilegate business, I says, says I, that man shall hev no more to do wi' my affairs. It may put me t' inconvenience, but I'll encourage no man as pessecutes religion."

"He is evidently the brain and hand of the persecution," said Mr. Tryan. "There may be a strong feeling against me in a large number of the inhabitants—it must be so, from the great ignorance of spiritual things in this place. But I fancy there would have been no formal opposition to the lecture, if Dempster had not planned it. I am not myself the least alarmed at anything he can do; he will find I am not to be cowed or driven away by insult or personal danger. God has sent me to this place, and, by His blessing, I'll not shrink from anything I may have to encounter in doing His work among the people. But I feel it right to call on all those who know the value of the Gospel, to stand by me publicly. I think—and Mr. Landor agrees with me—that it will be well for my friends to proceed with me in a body to the church on Sunday evening. Dempster, you know, has pretended that almost all the respectable inhabitants are opposed to the lecture. Now, I wish that falsehood to be visibly contradicted. What do you think of the plan? I have to-day been to see several of my friends, who will make a point of being there to accompany me, and will communicate with others on the subject."

"I'll mek one, Mr. Tryan, I'll mek one. You shall not be wantin' in any support as I can give. Before you come to it, sir, Milby was a dead an' dark place; you are the fust man i' the Church to my knowledge as has brought the word o' God home to the people; an' I'll stan' by you, sir, I'll stan' by you. I'm a Dissenter, Mr. Tryan, I've been a Dissenter iver sin' I was fifteen 'ear old; but show me good i' the Church, an' I'm a Churchman too. When I was a boy I lived at Tilston; you mayn't know the place; the best part o' the land there belonged to Squire Sandeman; he'd a club-foot, hed Squire Sandeman—lost a deal o' money by canal shares. Well, sir, as I was sayin', I lived at Tilston, an' the rector there was a terrible drinkin', fox-huntin' man; you niver see such a parish i' your time for wickedness; Milby's nothin' to it. Well, sir, my father was a workin' man, an' couldn't afford to gi' me ony eddication, so I went to a night-school as was kep by a Dissenter, one Jacob Wright; an' it was from that man, sir, as I got my little schoolin' an' my knowledge o' religion. I went to chapel wi' Jacob—he was a good man was Jacob—an' to chapel I've been iver since. But I'm no enemy o' the Church, sir, when the Church brings light to the ignorant and the sinful; an' that's what you're a-doin', Mr. Tryan. Yes, sir, I'll stan' by you. I'll go to church wi' you o' Sunday evenin'."

"You'd fur better stay at home, Mr. Jerome, if I may give *my* opinion," interposed Mrs. Jerome. "It's not as I hevn't ivery respect for you, Mr. Tryan, but Mr. Jerome 'ull do you no good by his interferin'. Dissenters are not at all looked on i' Milby, an' he's as nervous as iver he can be; he'll come back as ill as ill, an' niver let me hev a wink o' sleep all night."

Mrs. Jerome had been frightened at the mention of a mob, and her retrospective regard for the religious communion of her youth by no means inspired her with the temper of a martyr. Her husband looked at her with an expression of tender and grieved remonstrance, which might have been that of the patient patriarch [Job] on the memorable occasion when he rebuked *his* wife.

"Susan, Susan, let me beg on you not to oppose me, an' put stumblin'-blocks i' the way o' doin' what's right. I can't give up my conscience, let me give up what else I may."

"Perhaps," said Mr. Tryan, feeling slightly uncomfortable, "since you are not very strong, my dear sir, it will be well, as Mrs. Jerome suggests, that you should not run the risk of any excitement."

"Say no more, Mr. Tryan. I'll stan' by you, sir. It's my duty. It's the cause o' God, sir; it's the cause o' God."

Mr. Tryan obeyed his impulse of admiration and gratitude, and put out his hand to the white-haired old man, saying, "Thank you, Mr. Jerome, thank you."

Mr. Jerome grasped the proffered hand in silence, and then threw himself back in his chair, casting a regretful look at his wife, which seemed to say, "Why don't you feel with me, Susan?"

The sympathy of this simple-minded old man was more precious to Mr. Tryan than any mere onlooker could have imagined. To persons possessing a great deal of that facile psychology which prejudges individuals by means of formulas, and casts them, without further trouble, into duly lettered pigeon-holes, the Evangelical curate might seem to be doing simply what all other men like to do—carrying out objects which were identified not only with his theory, which is but a kind of secondary egoism, but also with the primary egoism of his feelings. Opposition may become sweet to a man when he has christened it persecution: a self-obtrusive, over-hasty reformer complacently disclaiming all merit, while his friends call him a martyr, has not in reality a career the most arduous to the fleshly mind. But Mr. Tryan was not cast in the mold of the gratuitous martyr. With a power of persistence which had been often blamed as obstinacy, he had an acute sensibility to the very hatred or ridicule he did not flinch from provoking. Every form of disapproval jarred him painfully; and, though he fronted his opponents manfully, and often with considerable warmth of temper, he had no pugnacious pleasure in the contest. It was one of the weaknesses of his nature to be too keenly alive to every harsh wind of opinion; to wince under the frowns of the foolish; to be irritated by the injustice of those who could not possibly have the elements indispensable for judging him rightly; and with all this acute sensibility to blame, this dependence on sympathy, he had for years been constrained into a position of antagonism. No wonder, then, that good old Mr. Jerome's cordial words were balm to him. He had often been thankful to an old woman for saying "God bless you"; to a little child for smiling at him; to a dog for submitting to be patted by him.

Tea being over by this time, Mr. Tryan proposed a walk in the garden as a means of dissipating all recollection of the recent conjugal dissidence. Little Lizzie's appeal, "Me go, gandpa!" could not be rejected, so she was duly bonneted and pinafored, and then they turned out into the evening sunshine. Not Mrs. Jerome, however; she had a deeply-meditated plan of retiring *ad interim* to the kitchen and washing up the best tea-things, as a mode of getting forward with the sadly-retarded business of the day.

"This way, Mr. Tryan, this way," said the old gentleman; "I must take you to my pastur fust, an' show you our cow—the best milker i' the county. An' see here at these back-buildins, how convenent the dairy is; I planned it ivery bit myself. An' here I've got my little carpenter's shop an' my blacksmith's shop; I do no end o' jobs here myself. I niver could bear to be idle, Mr. Tryan; I must al'ys be at somethin' or other. It was time for me to ley by business and mek room for younger folks. I'd got money enough, wi' only one daughter to leave it to, an' I says to myself, says I, it's time to leave off moitherin' myself wi' this world so much, an' give more time to thinkin' of another. But there's a many hours atween getting up an' lyin' down, an' thoughts are no cumber; you can move about wi' a good many on 'em in your head. See here's the pastur."

A very pretty pasture it was, where the large-spotted short-horned cow quietly chewed the cud as she lay and looked sleepily at her admirers—a daintily-trimmed hedge all round, dotted here and there with a mountain-ash or a cherry-tree.

"I've a good bit more land besides this, worth your while to look at, but mayhap it's further nor you'd like to walk now. Bless you! I've welly an' acre o' potato-ground yonters; I've a good big family to supply, you know." (Here Mr. Jerome winked and smiled significantly.) "An' that puts me i' mind, Mr. Tryan, o' summat I wanted to say to you. Clergymen like you, I know, see a deal more poverty an' that, than other folks, an' hev a many claims on 'em more nor they can well meet; an' if you'll mek use o' my purse any time, or let me know where I can be o' any help, I'll tek it very kind on you."

"Thank you, Mr. Jerome, I will do so, I promise you. I saw a sad case yesterday; a collier—a fine broad-chested fellow about thirty—was killed by the falling of a wall in the Paddiford colliery. I was in one of the cottages near when they brought him home on a door, and the shriek of the wife has been ringing in my ears ever since. There are three little children. Happily the woman has her loom, so she will be able to keep out of the workhouse; but she looks very delicate."

"Give me her name, Mr. Tryan," said Mr. Jerome, drawing out his pocket-book. "I'll call an' see her, I'll call an' see her."

Deep was the fountain of pity in the good old man's heart! He often ate his dinner stintingly, oppressed by the thought that there were men, women, and children, with no dinner to sit down to, and would relieve his mind by going out in the afternoon to look for some need that he could supply, some honest struggle in which he could lend a helping hand. That any living being should want, was his chief sorrow; that any rational being should waste, was the next. Sally, indeed, having been scolded by master for a too lavish use of sticks in lighting the kitchen fire, and various instances of recklessness with regard to candle ends, considered him "as mean as aenythink"; but he had as kindly a warmth as the morning sunlight, and, like the sunlight, his goodness shone on all that came in his way, from the saucy rosy-cheeked lad whom he delighted to make happy with a Christmas box, to the pallid sufferers up dim entries, languishing under the tardy death of want and misery.

It was very pleasant to Mr. Tryan to listen to the simple chat of the old man—to walk in the shade of the incomparable orchard, and hear the story of the crops yielded by the red-streaked apple-tree, and the quite embarrassing plentifulness of the summer-pears—to drink in the sweet evening breath of the garden, as they sat in the alcove—and so, for a short interval, to feel the strain of his pastoral task relaxed.

Perhaps he felt the return to that task through the dusty roads all the more painfully, perhaps something in that quiet shady home had reminded him of the time before he had taken on him the yoke of self-denial. The strongest heart will faint sometimes under the feeling that enemies are bitter, and that friends only know half its sorrows. The most resolute soul will now and then cast back a yearning look in treading the rough mountain-path, away from the greensward and laughing voices of the valley. However it was, in the nine o'clock twilight that evening, when Mr. Tryan had entered his small study and turned the key in the door, he threw himself into the chair before his writing-table, and, heedless of the papers there, leaned his face low on his hand, and moaned heavily.

It is apt to be so in this life, I think. While we are coldly discussing a man's career, sneering at his mistakes, blaming his rashness, and labeling his opinions—"he is Evangelical and narrow," or "Latitudinarian and Pantheistic," or "Anglican and supercilious"—that man, in his solitude, is perhaps shedding hot tears because his sacrifice is a hard one, because strength and patience are failing him to speak the difficult word, and do the difficult deed.

Chapter IX

Mr. Tryan showed no such symptoms of weakness on the critical Sunday. He unhesitatingly rejected the suggestion that he should be taken to church in Mr. Landor's carriage—a proposition which that gentleman made as an amendment on the original plan, when the rumors of meditated insult became alarming. Mr. Tryan declared he would have no precautions taken, but would simply trust in God and his good cause. Some of his more timid friends thought this conduct rather defiant than wise, and reflecting that a mob has great talents for impromptu, and that legal redress is imperfect satisfaction for having one's head broken with a brickbat, were beginning to question their consciences very closely as to whether it was not a duty they owed to their families to stay at home on Sunday evening. These timorous persons, however, were in a small minority, and the generality of Mr. Tryan's friends and hearers rather exulted in an opportunity of braving insult for the sake of a preacher to whom they were attached on personal as well as doctrinal grounds. Miss Pratt spoke of Cranmer, Ridley, and Latimer, and observed that the present crisis afforded an occasion for emulating their heroism even in these degenerate times; while less highly instructed persons, whose memories were not well stored with precedents, simply expressed their determination, as Mr. Jerome had done, to "stan' by" the preacher and his cause, believing it to be the "cause of God."

On Sunday evening, then, at a quarter past six, Mr. Tryan, setting out from Mr. Landor's with a party of his friends who had assembled there, was soon joined by two other groups from Mr. Pratt's and Mr. Dunn's; and stray persons on their way to church naturally falling into rank behind this leading file, by the time they reached the entrance of Orchard Street, Mr. Tryan's friends formed a considerable procession, walking three or four abreast. It was in Orchard Street, and towards the church gates, that the chief crowd was collected; and at Mr. Dempster's drawing-room window, on the upper floor, a more select assembly of Anti-Tryanites were gathered, to witness the entertaining spectacle of the Tryanites walking to church amidst the jeers and hootings of the crowd.

To prompt the popular wit with appropriate sobriquets, numerous copies of Mr. Dempster's play-bill were posted on the walls, in suitably large and emphatic type. As it is possible that the most industrious collector of mural literature may not have been fortunate enough to possess himself of this production, which ought by all means to be preserved amongst the materials of our provincial religious history, I subjoin a faithful copy.

GRAND ENTERTAINMENT!!!

To be given at Milby on Sunday evening next, by the

FAMOUS COMEDIAN, TRY-IT-ON!

And his first-rate company, including not only an

UNPARALLELED CAST FOR COMEDY!

But a Large Collection of *reclaimed and converted Animals;*

Among the rest

A Bear, who used to *dance!*

A Parrot, once given to *swearing! !*
A Polygamous Pig! ! !
and
A Monkey who used to *catch fleas on a Sunday! ! ! !*
Together with a
Pair of *regenerated* LINNETS!
With an entirely new song, and *plumage.*
MR. TRY-IT-ON

Will first pass through the streets, in procession, with his unrivalled Company, warranted to have their *eyes turned up higher,* and the *corners of their mouths turned down lower,* than any other company of Mountebanks in this circuit!

AFTER WHICH
The Theatre will be opened, and the entertainment will
commence at HALF-PAST SIX,
When will be presented
A piece, never before performed on any stage, entitled,
THE WOLF IN SHEEP'S CLOTHING;
or
THE METHODIST IN A MASK

Mr. Boanerges Soft Sawder, ... Mr. TRY-IT-ON.
Old Ten-per-cent Godly, ... Mr. GANDER.
Dr. Feedemup, ... Mr. TONIC.
Mr. Lime-Twig Lady-winner, ... Mr. TRY-IT-ON.
Miss Piety Bait-the-hook, ... Miss TONIC.
Angelica, ... Miss SERAPHINA TONIC.

After which
A miscellaneous Musical Interlude, commencing with
The *Lamentations of Jerom-iah!*
In nasal recitative.
To be followed by
The favorite Cackling Quartette,
by
Two Hen-birds who are *no chickens!*
The well-known *counter*-tenor, Mr. Done, and a *Gander,*
lineally descended from the *Goose* that laid golden eggs!
To conclude with a
GRAND CHORUS by the
Entire Orchestra of converted Animals! !
But owing to the unavoidable absence (from illness) of
the *Bull-dog, who has left off fighting,* Mr. Tonic has kindly

undertaken, at a moment's notice, to supply the *"bark!"*
The whole to conclude with a
Screaming Farce of
THE PULPIT SNATCHER

Mr. Saintly Smooth-face, ... Mr. Try-it-on!
Mr. Worming Sneaker, ... Mr. Try-it-on! !
Mr. All-grace No-works, ... Mr. Try-it-on! ! !
Mr. Elect-and-Chosen Apewell, ... Mr. Try-it-on! ! ! !
Mr. Malevolent Prayerful, ... Mr. Try-it-on! ! ! ! !
Mr. Foist-himself Everywhere, ... Mr. Try-it-on! ! ! ! ! !
Mr. Flout-the-aged Upstart, ... Mr. Try-it-on! ! ! ! ! ! !

Admission Free. A *Collection* will be made at the Doors.
Vivat Rex!

This satire, though it presents the keenest edge of Milby wit, does not strike you as lacerating, I imagine. But hatred is like fire—it makes even light rubbish deadly. And Mr. Dempster's sarcasms were not merely visible on the walls; they were reflected in the derisive glances, and audible in the jeering voices of the crowd. Through this pelting shower of nicknames and bad puns, with an *ad libitum* accompaniment of groans, howls, hisses, and hee-haws, but of no heavier missiles, Mr. Tryan walked pale and composed, giving his arm to old Mr. Landor, whose step was feeble. On the other side of him was Mr. Jerome, who still walked firmly, though his shoulders were slightly bowed.

Outwardly Mr. Tryan was composed, but inwardly he was suffering acutely from these tones of hatred and scorn. However strong his consciousness of right, he found it no stronger armor against such weapons as derisive glances and virulent words, than against stones and clubs: his conscience was in repose, but his sensibility was bruised.

Once more only did the Evangelical curate pass up Orchard Street followed by a train of friends; once more only was there a crowd assembled to witness his entrance through the church gates. But that second time no voice was heard above a whisper, and the whispers were words of sorrow and blessing. That second time, Janet Dempster was not looking on in scorn and merriment; her eyes were worn with grief and watching, and she was following her beloved friend and pastor to the grave.

Chapter X

History, we know, is apt to repeat herself, and to foist very old incidents upon us with only a slight change of costume. From the time of Xerxes downwards, we have seen generals playing the braggadocio at the outset of their campaigns, and conquering the enemy with the greatest ease in after-dinner speeches. But events are apt to be in disgusting discrepancy with the anticipations of the most ingenious tacticians; the difficulties of the expedition are ridiculously at variance with able calculations; the enemy has the impudence not to fall into confusion as had been reasonably expected of him; the mind of the gallant general begins to be distracted by news of intrigues against him at home, and, notwithstanding the handsome compliments he paid to Providence as his undoubted patron before setting out, there seems every probability that the *Te Deums* will be all on the other side.

So it fell out with Mr. Dempster in his memorable campaign against the Tryanites. After all the premature triumph of the return from Elmstoke, the battle of the Evening Lecture had been lost; the enemy was in possession of the field; and the utmost hope remaining was, that by a harassing guerilla warfare he might be driven to evacuate the country.

For some time this sort of warfare was kept up with considerable spirit. The shafts of Milby ridicule were made more formidable by being poisoned with calumny; and very ugly stories, narrated with circumstantial minuteness, were soon in circulation concerning Mr. Tryan and his hearers, from which stories it was plainly deducible that Evangelicalism led by a necessary consequence to hypocritical indulgence in vice. Some old friendships were broken asunder, and there were near relations who felt that religious differences, unmitigated by any prospect of a legacy, were a sufficient ground for exhibiting their family antipathy. Mr. Budd harangued his workmen, and threatened them with dismissal if they or their families were known to attend the evening lecture; and Mr. Tomlinson, on discovering that his foreman was a rank Tryanite, blustered to a great extent, and would have cashiered that valuable functionary on the spot, if such a retributive procedure had not been inconvenient.

On the whole, however, at the end of a few months, the balance of substantial loss was on the side of the Anti-Tryanites. Mr. Pratt, indeed, had lost a patient or two besides Mr. Dempster's family; but as it was evident that Evangelicalism had not dried up the stream of his anecdote, or in the least altered his view of any lady's constitution, it is probable that a change accompanied by so few outward and visible signs, was rather the pretext than the ground of his dismissal in those additional cases. Mr. Dunn was threatened with the loss of several good customers, Mrs. Phipps and Mrs. Lowme having set the example of ordering him to send in his bill; and the draper began to look forward to his next stock-taking with an anxiety which was but slightly mitigated by the parallel his wife suggested between his own case and that of Shadrach, Meshech, and Abednego, who were thrust into a burning fiery furnace. For, as he observed to her the next morning, with that perspicacity which belongs to the period of shaving, whereas their deliverance consisted in the fact that their linen and woollen goods were not consumed, his own deliverance lay in precisely the opposite result. But convenience, that admirable branch system from the main line of self-interest, makes us all fellow-helpers in spite of adverse resolutions. It is probable that no speculative or theological hatred would be ultimately strong enough to resist the persuasive power of convenience. . . . In this persuasive power of convenience lay Mr. Dunn's ultimate security from martyrdom. His drapery was the best in Milby; the comfortable use and wont of procuring satisfactory articles at a moment's notice proved too strong for Anti-Tryanite zeal; and the draper could soon look forward to his next stock-taking without the support of a Scriptural parallel.

On the other hand, Mr. Dempster had lost his excellent client, Mr. Jerome—a loss which galled him out of proportion to the mere monetary deficit it represented. The attorney loved money, but he loved power still better. He had always been proud of having early won the confidence of a conventicle-goer, and of being able to "turn the prop of Salem round his thumb." Like most other men, too, he had a certain kindness towards those who had employed him when he was only starting in life; and just as we do not like to part with an old weather-glass from our study, or a two-feet ruler that we have carried in our pocket ever since we began business, so Mr. Dempster did not like having to erase his old client's name from the accustomed drawer in the bureau. Our habitual life is like a wall hung with pictures, which has been shone on by the suns of many years: take one of the pictures away, and it leaves a definite blank space, to which our eyes can never turn without a sensation of discomfort. Nay, the involuntary loss of any familiar object almost always brings a chill as from an evil omen; it seems to be the first finger-shadow of advancing death. . . .

Meanwhile, the evening lecture drew larger and larger congregations; not, perhaps, attracting many from that select aristocratic circle in which the Lowmes and Pittmans were predominant, but winning the larger proportion of Mr. Crewe's morning and afternoon hearers, and thinning Mr. Stickney's evening audiences at Salem. Evangelicalism was making its way in Milby, and gradually diffusing its subtle odor into chambers that were bolted and barred against it. The movement, like all other religious "revivals," had a mixed effect. . . .

. . . Whatever might be the weaknesses of the ladies who pruned the luxuriance of their lace and ribbons, cut out garments for the poor, distributed tracts, quoted Scripture, and defined the true Gospel, they had learned this—that there was a divine work to be done in life, a rule of goodness higher than the opinion of their neighbors; and if the notion of a heaven in reserve for themselves was a little too prominent, yet the theory of fitness for that heaven consisted in purity of heart, in Christ-like compassion, in the subduing of selfish desires. . . .

. . . Miss Rebecca Linnet, in quiet attire, with a somewhat excessive solemnity of countenance, teaching at the Sunday School, visiting the poor, and striving after a standard of purity and goodness, had surely more moral loveliness than in those flaunting peony-days, when she had no other model than the costumes of the heroines in the circulating library. Miss Eliza Pratt, listening in rapt attention to Mr. Tryan's evening lecture, no doubt found evangelical channels for vanity and egoism; but she was clearly in moral advance of Miss Phipps giggling under her feathers at old Mr. Crewe's peculiarities of enunciation. And even elderly fathers and mothers, with minds, like Mrs. Linnet's, too tough to imbibe much doctrine, were the better for having their hearts inclined towards the new preacher as a messenger from God. They became ashamed, perhaps, of their evil tempers, ashamed of their worldliness, ashamed of their trivial, futile past. The first condition of human goodness is something to love; the second, something to reverence. And this latter precious gift was brought to Milby by Mr. Tryan and Evangelicalism.

Yes, the movement was good, though it had that mixture of folly and evil which often makes what is good an offense to feeble and fastidious minds, who want human actions and characters riddled through the sieve of their own ideas, before they can accord their sympathy or admiration. Such minds, I dare say, would have found Mr. Tryan's character very much in need of that riddling process. . . .

Yet surely, surely the only true knowledge of our fellow-man is that which enables us to feel with him—which gives us a fine ear for the heart-pulses that are beating under the mere clothes of circumstance and opinion. Our subtlest analysis of schools and sects must miss the essential truth, unless it be lit up by the love that sees in all forms of human thought and work, the life and death struggles of separate human beings.

Chapter XI

Mr. Tryan's most unfriendly observers were obliged to admit that he gave himself no rest. Three sermons on Sunday, a night-school for young men on Tuesday, a cottage-lecture on Thursday, addresses to school-teachers, and catechizing of school-children, with pastoral visits, multiplying as his influence extended beyond his own district of Paddiford Common, would have been enough to tax severely the powers of a much stronger man. Mr. Pratt remonstrated with him on his imprudence, but could not prevail on him so far to economize time and strength as to keep a horse. On some ground or other, which his friends found difficult to explain to themselves, Mr. Tryan seemed bent on wearing himself out. His enemies were at no loss to account for such a course. The Evangelical curate's selfishness was clearly of too bad a kind to exhibit itself after the ordinary manner of a sound, respectable selfishness. "He wants to get the reputation of a saint," said one; "He's eaten up with spiritual pride," said another; "He's got his eye on some fine living, and wants to creep up the bishop's sleeve," said a third. . . .

As for Mr. Jerome, he drew the elements of his moral vision from the depths of his veneration and pity. If he himself felt so much for these poor things to whom life was so dim and meager, what must the clergyman feel who had undertaken before God to be their shepherd?

"Ah!" he whispered, interruptedly, "it's too big a load for his conscience, poor man! He wants to mek himself their brother, like; can't abide to preach to the fastin' on a full stomach. Ah! he's better nor we are, that's it—he's a deal better nor we are." . . .

Mr. Jerome's was not the only mind that was seriously disturbed by the idea that the curate was over-working himself. These were tender women's hearts in which anxiety about the state of his affections was beginning to be merged in anxiety about the state of his health. Miss Eliza Pratt had at one time passed through much sleepless cogitation on the possibility of Mr. Tryan's being attached to some lady at a distance—at Laxeter, perhaps, where he had formerly held a curacy; and her fine eyes kept close watch lest any symptom of engaged affections on his part should escape her. . . . Before Christmas, however, her cogitations began to take another turn. She heard her father say very confidently that "Tryan was consumptive, and if he didn't take more care of himself; his life would not be worth a year's purchase"; and shame at having speculated on suppositions that were likely to prove so false, sent poor Miss Eliza's feelings with all the stronger impetus into the one channel of sorrowful alarm at the prospect of losing the pastor who had opened to her a new life of piety and self-subjection. It is a sad weakness in us, after all, that the thought of a man's death hallows him anew to us; as if life were not sacred too—as if it were comparatively a light thing to fail in love and reverence to the brother who has to climb the whole toilsome steep with us, and all our tears and tenderness were due to the one who is spared that hard journey.

The Miss Linnets, too, were beginning to take a new view of the future, entirely uncolored by jealousy of Miss Eliza Pratt.

"Did you notice," said Mary, one afternoon when Mrs. Pettifer was taking tea with them—"did you notice that short dry cough of Mr. Tryan's yesterday? I think he looks worse and worse every week, and I only wish I knew his sister; I would write to her about him. I'm sure something should be done to make him give up part of his work, and he will listen to no one here."

"Ah," said Mrs. Pettifer, "it's a thousand pities his father and sister can't come and live with him, if he isn't to marry. But I wish with all my heart he could have taken to some nice woman as would have made a comfortable home for him. I used to think he might take to Eliza Pratt; she's a good girl, and very pretty; but I see no likelihood of it now."

"No, indeed," said Rebecca, with some emphasis; "Mr. Tryan's heart is not for any woman to win; it is all given to his work; and I could never wish to see him with a young inexperienced wife who would be a drag on him instead of a helpmate."

"He'd need have somebody, young or old," observed Mrs. Linnet, "to see as he wears a flannel wescoat, an' changes his stockins when he comes in. It's my opinion he's got that cough wi' sittin' i' wet shoes an' stockins; an' that Mrs. Wagstaff's a poor addle-headed thing; she doesn't half tek care on him."

"O, mother!" said Rebecca, "she's a very pious woman. And I'm sure she thinks it too great a privilege to have Mr. Tryan with her, not to do the best she can to make him comfortable. She can't help her rooms being shabby."

"I've nothing to say again' her piety, my dear; but I know very well I shouldn't like her to cook my victual. When a man comes in hungry an' tired, piety won't feed him; . . . I don't see as anybody 'ull go to heaven the sooner for not digestin' their dinner—providin' they don't die sooner, as mayhap Mr. Tryan will, poor dear man!"

"It will be a heavy day for us all when that comes to pass," said Mrs. Pettifer. "We shall never get anybody to fill up *that* gap. There's the new clergyman that's just come to Shepperton—Mr. Parry; I saw him the other day at Mrs. Bond's. He may be a very good man, and a fine preacher; they say he is; but I thought to myself, what a difference between him and Mr. Tryan! He's a sharp-sort-of-looking man, and hasn't that feeling way with him that Mr. Tryan has. What is so wonderful to me in Mr. Tryan is the way he puts himself on a level with one, and talks to one like a brother. I'm never afraid of telling him anything. He never seems to look down on anybody. He knows how to lift up those that are cast down, if ever man did."

"Yes," said Mary. "And when I see all the faces turned up to him in Paddiford church, I often think how hard it would be for any clergyman who had to come after him; he has made the people love him so."

Chapter XII

In her occasional visits to her near neighbor Mrs. Pettifer, too old a friend to be shunned because she was a Tryanite, Janet was obliged sometimes to hear allusions to Mr. Tryan, and even to listen to his praises, which she usually met with playful incredulity.

"Ah, well," she answered one day, "I like dear old Mr. Crewe and his pipes a great deal better than your Mr. Tryan and his Gospel. When I was a little toddle, Mr. and Mrs. Crewe used to let me play about in their garden, and have a swing between the great elm-trees, because mother had no garden. I like people who are kind; kindness is my religion; and that's the reason I like you, dear Mrs. Pettifer, though you *are* a Tryanite."

"But that's Mr. Tryan's religion too—at least partly. There's nobody can give himself up more to doing good amongst the poor; and he thinks of their bodies too, as well as their souls."

"O yes, yes; but then he talks about faith and grace, and all that, making people believe they are better than others, and that God loves them more than He does the rest of the world. I know he has put a great deal of that into Sally Martin's head, and it has done her no good at all. She was as nice, honest, patient a girl as need be before; and now she fancies she has new light and new wisdom. I don't like those notions."

"You mistake him, indeed you do, my dear Mrs. Dempster; I wish you'd go and hear him preach."

"Hear him preach! Why, you wicked woman, you would persuade me to disobey my husband, would you? O, shocking! I shall run away from you. Good-bye."

A few days after this conversation, however, Janet went to Sally Martin's about three o'clock in the afternoon. The pudding that had been sent in for herself and "Mammy," struck her as just the sort of delicate morsel the poor consumptive girl would be likely to fancy, and in her usual impulsive way she had started up from the dinner-table at once, put on her bonnet, and set off with a covered plateful to the neighboring street. When she entered the house there was no one to be seen; but in the little side-room where Sally lay, Janet heard a voice. It was one she had not heard before, but she immediately guessed it to be Mr. Tryan's. Her first impulse was to set down her plate and go away, but Mrs. Martin might not be in, and then there would be no one to give Sally that delicious bit of pudding. So she stood still, and was obliged to hear what Mr. Tryan was saying. He was interrupted by one of the invalid's violent fits of coughing.

"It is very hard to bear, is it not?" he said, when she was still again. "Yet God seems to support you under it wonderfully. Pray for me, Sally, that I may have strength too when the hour of great suffering comes. It is one of my worst weaknesses to shrink from bodily pain, and I think the time is perhaps not far off when I shall have to bear what you are bearing. But now I have tired you. We have talked enough. Good-bye."

Janet was surprised, and forgot her wish not to encounter Mr. Tryan; the tone and the words were so unlike what she had expected to hear. There was none of the self-satisfied unction of the teacher, quoting, or exhorting, or expounding, for the benefit of the hearer, but a simple appeal for help, a confession of weakness. Mr. Tryan had his deeply-felt troubles, then? Mr. Tryan, too, like herself, knew what it was to tremble at a foreseen trial—to shudder at an impending burden, heavier than he felt able to bear?

The most brilliant deed of virtue could not have inclined Janet's goodwill towards Mr. Tryan so much as this fellowship in suffering, and the softening thought was in her eyes when he appeared in the doorway, pale, weary, and depressed. The sight of Janet standing there with the entire absence of self-consciousness which belongs to a new and vivid impression, made him start and pause a little. Their eyes met, and they looked at each other gravely for a few moments. Then they bowed, and Mr. Tryan passed out.

There is a power in the direct glance of a sincere and loving human soul, which will do more to dissipate prejudice and kindle charity than the most elaborate arguments. The fullest exposition of Mr. Tryan's doctrine might not have sufficed to convince Janet that he had not an odious self-complacency in believing himself a peculiar child of God; but one direct, pathetic look of his had dissociated him with that conception for ever.

This happened late in the autumn, not long before Sally Martin died. Janet mentioned her new impression to no one, for she was afraid of arriving at a still more complete contradiction of her former ideas. We have all of us considerable regard for our past self, and are not fond of casting reflections on that respected individual by a total negation of his opinions. Janet could no longer think of Mr. Tryan without sympathy, but she still shrank from the idea of becoming his hearer and admirer. That was a reversal of the past which was as little accordant with her inclination as her circumstances.

And indeed this interview with Mr. Tryan was soon thrust into the background of poor Janet's memory by the daily thickening miseries of her life.

Chapter XIII

The loss of Mr. Jerome as a client proved only the beginning of annoyances to Dempster. That old gentleman had in him the vigorous remnant of an energy and perseverance which had created his own fortune; and being, as I have hinted, given to chewing the cud of a righteous indignation with considerable relish, he was determined to carry on his retributive war against the persecuting attorney. Having some influence with Mr. Pryme, who was one of the most substantial rate-payers in the neighboring parish of Dingley, and who had himself a complex and long-standing private account with Dempster, Mr. Jerome stirred up this gentleman to an investigation of some suspicious points in the attorney's conduct of the parish affairs. The natural consequence was a personal quarrel between Dempster and Mr. Pryme; the client demanded his account, and then followed the old story of an exorbitant lawyer's bill, with the unpleasant anti-climax of taxing.

These disagreeables, extending over many months, ran along side by side with the pressing business of Mr. Armstrong's lawsuit, which was threatening to take a turn rather depreciatory of Dempster's professional prevision; and it is not surprising that, being thus kept in a constant state of irritated excitement about his own affairs, he had little time for the further exhibition of his public spirit, or for rallying the forlorn hope of sound churchmanship against cant and hypocrisy. Not a few persons who had a grudge against him, began to remark, with satisfaction, that "Dempster's luck was forsaking him"; particularly Mrs. Linnet, who thought she saw distinctly the gradual ripening of a providential scheme, whereby a just retribution would be wrought on the man who had deprived her of Pye's Croft. On the other hand, Dempster's well-satisfied clients, who were of opinion that the punishment of his wickedness might conveniently be deferred to another world, noticed with some concern that he was drinking more than ever, and that both his temper and his driving were becoming more furious. Unhappily those additional glasses of brandy, that exasperation of loud-tongued abuse, had other effects than any that entered into the contemplation of anxious clients: they were the little superadded symbols that were perpetually raising the sum of home misery.

Poor Janet! how heavily the months rolled on for her, laden with fresh sorrows as the summer passed into autumn, the autumn into winter, and the winter into spring again. Every feverish morning, with its blank listlessness and despair, seemed more hateful than the last; every coming night more impossible to brave without arming herself in leaden stupor. The morning light brought no gladness to her: it seemed only to throw its glare on what had happened in the dim candle-light—on the cruel man seated immovable in drunken obstinacy by the dead fire and dying lights in the dining-room, rating her in harsh tones, reiterating old reproaches—or on a hideous blank of something unremembered, something that must have made that dark bruise on her shoulder, which aches as she dresses herself.

Do you wonder how it was that things had come to this pass—what offense Janet had committed in the early years of marriage to rouse the brutal hatred of this man? The seeds of things are very small: the hours that lie between sunrise and the gloom of midnight are traveled through by tiniest markings of the clock: and Janet, looking back along the fifteen years of her married life, hardly knew how or where this total misery began; hardly knew when the sweet wedded love and hope that had set for ever had ceased to make a twilight of memory and relenting, before the oncoming of the utter dark.

Old Mrs. Dempster thought she saw the true beginning of it all in Janet's want of housekeeping skill and exactness. "Janet," she said to herself, "was always running about doing things for other people, and neglecting her own house. That provokes a man: what use is it for a woman to be loving, and making a fuss with her husband, if she doesn't take care and keep his home just as he likes it; if she isn't at hand when he wants anything done; if she doesn't attend to all his wishes, let them be as small as they may? That was what I did when I was a wife, though I didn't make half so much fuss about loving my husband. Then, Janet had no children." . . . Ah! there Mammy Dempster had touched a true spring, not perhaps of her son's cruelty, but of half Janet's misery. If she had had babes to rock to sleep—little ones to kneel in their night-dress and say their prayers at her knees—sweet boys and girls to put their young arms round her neck and kiss away her tears, her poor hungry heart would have been fed with strong love, and might never have needed that fiery poison to still its cravings. Mighty is the force of motherhood! says the great tragic poet to us across the ages. . . . It transforms all things by its vital heat: it turns timidity into fierce courage, and dreadless defiance into tremulous submission; it turns thoughtlessness into foresight, and yet stills all anxiety into calm content; it makes selfishness become self-denial, and gives even to hard vanity the glance of admiring love. Yes; if Janet had been a mother, she might have been saved from much sin, and therefore from much of her sorrow.

But do not believe that it was anything either present or wanting in poor Janet that formed the motive of her husband's cruelty. Cruelty, like every other vice, requires no motive outside itself—it only requires opportunity. You do not suppose Dempster had any motive for drinking beyond the craving for drink; the presence of brandy was the only necessary condition. And an unloving, tyrannous, brutal man needs no motive to prompt his cruelty; he needs only the perpetual presence of a woman he can call his own. A whole park full of tame or timid-eyed animals to torment at his will would not serve him so well to glut his lust of torture; they could not *feel* as one woman does; they could not throw out the keen retort which whets the edge of hatred.

Janet's bitterness would overflow in ready words; she was not to be made meek by cruelty; she would repent of nothing in the face of injustice, though she was subdued in a moment by a word or a look that recalled the old days of fondness; and in times of comparative calm would often recover her sweet woman's habit of caressing playful affection. But such days were become rare, and poor Janet's soul was kept like a vexed sea, tossed by a new storm before the old waves have fallen. Proud, angry resistance and sullen endurance were now almost the only alternations she knew. She would bear it all proudly to the world, but proudly towards him too; her woman's weakness might shriek a cry for pity under a heavy blow, but voluntarily she would do nothing to mollify him, unless he first relented. What had she ever done to him but love him too well—but believe in him too foolishly? He had no pity on her tender flesh; he could strike the soft neck he had once asked to kiss. Yet she would not admit her wretchedness; she had married him blindly, and she would bear it out to the terrible end, whatever that might be. Better this misery than the blank that lay for her outside her married home.

But there was one person who heard all the plaints and all the outbursts of bitterness and despair which Janet was never tempted to pour into any other ear; and alas! in her worst moments, Janet would throw out wild reproaches against that patient listener. For the wrong that rouses our angry passions finds only a medium in us; it passes through us like a vibration, and we inflict what we have suffered.

Mrs. Raynor saw too clearly all through the winter that things were getting worse in Orchard Street. She had evidence enough of it in Janet's visits to her; and, though her own visits to her daughter were so timed that she saw little of Dempster personally, she noticed many indications not only that he was drinking to greater excess, but that he was beginning to lose that physical power of supporting excess which had long been the admiration of such fine spirits as Mr. Tomlinson. It seemed as if Dempster had some consciousness of this—some new distrust of himself; for, before winter was over, it was observed that he had renounced his habit of driving out alone, and was never seen in his gig without a servant by his side.

Nemesis is lame, but she is of colossal stature, like the gods; and sometimes, while her sword is not yet unsheathed, she stretches out her huge left arm and grasps her victim. The mighty hand is invisible, but the victim totters under the dire clutch.

The various symptoms that things were getting worse with the Dempsters afforded Milby gossip something new to say on an old subject. Mrs. Dempster, every one remarked, looked more miserable than ever, though she kept up the old pretense of being happy and satisfied. She was scarcely ever seen, as she used to be, going about on her good-natured errands; and even old Mrs. Crewe, who had always been willfully blind to anything wrong in her favorite Janet, was obliged to admit that she had not seemed like herself lately. "The poor thing's out of health," said the kind little old lady, in answer to all gossip about Janet; "her headaches always were bad, and I know what headaches are; why, they make one quite delirious sometimes." Mrs. Phipps, for her part, declared she would never accept an invitation to Dempster's again; it was getting so very disagreeable to go there, Mrs. Dempster was often "so strange." To be sure, there were dreadful stories about the way Dempster used his wife; but in Mrs. Phipps's opinion, it was six of one and half-a-dozen of the other. Mrs. Dempster had never been like other women: she had always a flighty way with her, carrying parcels of snuff to old Mrs. Tooke, and going to drink tea with Mrs. Brinley, the carpenter's wife; and then never taking care of her clothes, always wearing the same things week-day or Sunday. A man has a poor look-out with a wife of that sort. Mr. Phipps, amiable and laconic, wondered how it was women were so fond of running each other down.

Mr. Pratt, having been called in previously to a patient of Mr. Pilgrim's in a case of compound fracture, observed in a friendly colloquy with his brother surgeon the next day,

"So Dempster has left off driving himself, I see; he won't end with a broken neck after all. You'll have a case of meningitis and delirium tremens instead."

"Ah," said Mr. Pilgrim, "he can hardly stand it much longer at the rate he's going on, one would think. He's been confoundedly cut up about that business of Armstrong's, I fancy. It may do him some harm, perhaps, but Dempster must have feathered his nest pretty well; he can afford to lose a little business."

"His business will outlast him, that's pretty clear," said Pratt; "he'll run down like a watch with a broken spring one of these days."

Another prognostic of evil to Dempster came at the beginning of March. For then "little Mamsey" died—died suddenly. The housemaid found her seated motionless in her arm-chair, her knitting fallen down, and the tortoise-shell cat reposing on it unreproved. The little white old woman had ended her wintry age of patient sorrow, believing to the last that "Robert might have been a good husband as he had been a good son."

When the earth was thrown on Mamsey's coffin, and the son, in crape scarf and hatband, turned away homeward, his good angel, lingering with outstretched wing on the edge of the grave, cast one despairing look after him, and took flight for ever.

Chapter XIV

The last week in March, three weeks after old Mrs. Dempster died—occurred the unpleasant winding-up of affairs between Dempster and Mr. Pryme, and under this additional source of irritation the attorney's diurnal drunkenness had taken on its most ill-tempered and brutal phase. On the Friday morning, before setting out for Rotherby, he told his wife that he had invited "four men" to dinner at half-past six that evening. The previous night had been a terrible one for Janet, and when her husband broke his grim morning silence to say these few words, she was looking so blank and listless that he added in a loud sharp key, "Do you hear what I say? or must I tell the cook?" She started, and said "Yes, I hear."

"Then mind and have a dinner provided, and don't go mooning about like Crazy Jane."

Half an hour afterwards Mrs. Raynor, quietly busy in her kitchen with her household labors—for she had only a little twelve-year-old girl as a servant—heard with trembling the rattling of the garden gate and the opening of the outer door. She knew the step, and in one short moment she lived beforehand through the coming scene. She hurried out of the kitchen, and there in the passage, as she had felt, stood Janet, her eyes worn as if by night-long watching, her dress careless, her step languid. No cheerful morning greeting to her mother—no kiss. She turned into the parlor, and, seating herself on the sofa opposite her mother's chair, looked vacantly at the walls and furniture until the corners of her mouth began to tremble, and her dark eyes filled with tears that fell unwiped down her cheeks. The mother sat silently opposite to her, afraid to speak. She felt sure there was nothing new the matter—sure that the torrent of words would come sooner or later.

"Mother! Why don't you speak to me!" Janet burst out at last; "you don't care about my suffering; you are blaming me because I feel—because I am miserable."

"My child, I am not blaming you—my heart is bleeding for you. Your head is bad this morning—you have had a bad night. Let me make you a cup of tea now. Perhaps you didn't like your breakfast."

"Yes, that is what you always think, mother. It is the old story, you think. You don't ask me what it is I have had to bear. You are tired of hearing me. You are cruel, like the rest; every one is cruel in this world. Nothing but blame—blame—blame; never any pity. God is cruel to have sent me into the world to bear all this misery."

"Janet, Janet, don't say so. It is not for us to judge; we must submit; we must be thankful for the gift of life."

"Thankful for life? Why should I be thankful? God has made me with a heart to feel and He has sent me nothing but misery. How could I help it? How could I know what would come? Why didn't you tell me, mother?—why did you let me marry? You knew what brutes men could be; and there's no help for me—no hope. I can't kill myself; I've tried; but I can't leave this world and go to another. There may be no pity for me there, as there is none here."

"Janet, my child, there *is* pity. Have I ever done anything but love you? And there is pity in God. Hasn't He put pity into your heart for many a poor sufferer? Where did it come from, if not from Him?"

Janet's nervous irritation now broke out into sobs instead of complainings; and her mother was thankful, for after that crisis there would very likely come relenting, and tenderness, and comparative calm. She went out to make some tea, and when she returned with the tray in her hands, Janet had dried her eyes and now turned them towards her mother with a faint attempt to smile; but the poor face, in its sad blurred beauty, looked all the more piteous.

"Mother will insist upon her tea," she said, "and I really think I can drink a cup. But I must go home directly, for there are people coming to dinner. Could you go with me and help me, mother?"

Mrs. Raynor was always ready to do that. She went to Orchard Street with Janet, and remained with her through the day—comforted, as evening approached, to see her become more cheerful and willing to attend to her toilette. At half-past five everything was in order; Janet was dressed; and when the mother had kissed her and said good-bye, she could not help pausing a moment in sorrowful admiration at the tall rich figure, looking all the grander for the plainness of the deep mourning dress, and the noble face with its massy folds of black hair, made matronly by a simple white cap. Janet had that enduring beauty which belongs to pure majestic outline and depth of tint. Sorrow and neglect leave their traces on such beauty, but it thrills us to the last, like a glorious Greek temple, which, for all the loss it has suffered from time and barbarous hands, has gained a solemn history, and fills our imagination the more because it is incomplete to the sense.

It was six o'clock before Dempster returned from Rotherby. He had evidently drunk a great deal, and was in an angry humor; but Janet, who had gathered some little courage and forbearance from the consciousness that she had done her best to-day, was determined to speak pleasantly to him.

"Robert," she said gently, as she saw him seat himself in the dining-room in his dusty snuffy clothes, and take some documents out of his pocket, "will you not wash and change your dress? It will refresh you."

"Leave me alone, will you?" said Dempster, in his most brutal tone.

"Do change your coat and waistcoat, they are so dusty. I've laid all your things out ready."

"O, you have, have you?" After a few minutes he rose very deliberately and walked up-stairs into his bedroom. Janet had often been scolded before for not laying out his clothes, and she thought now, not without some wonder, that this attention of hers had brought him to compliance.

Presently he called out, "Janet!" and she went up-stairs.

"Here! Take that!" he said, as soon as she reached the door, flinging at her the coat she had laid out. "Another time, leave me to do as I please, will you?"

The coat, flung with great force, only brushed her shoulder, and fell some distance within the drawing-room, the door of which stood open just opposite.

She hastily retreated as she saw the waistcoat coming, and one by one the clothes she had laid out were all flung into the drawing-room.

Janet's face flushed with anger, and for the first time in her life her resentment overcame the long-cherished pride that made her hide her griefs from the world. There are moments when by some strange impulse we contradict our past selves—fatal moments, when a fit of passion, like a lava stream, lays low the work of half our lives. Janet thought, "I will not pick up the clothes; they shall lie there until the visitors come, and he shall be ashamed of himself."

There was a knock at the door, and she made haste to seat herself in the drawing-room, lest the servant should enter and remove the clothes, which were lying half on the table and half on the ground. Mr. Lowme entered with a less familiar visitor, a client of Dempster's, and the next moment Dempster himself came in.

His eye fell at once on the clothes, and then turned for an instant with a devilish glance of concentrated hatred on Janet, who, still flushed and excited, affected unconsciousness. After shaking hands with his visitors he immediately rang the bell.

"Take those clothes away," he said to the servant, not looking at Janet again.

During dinner, she kept up her assumed air of indifference, and tried to seem in high spirits, laughing and talking more than usual. In reality, she felt as if she had defied a wild beast within the four walls of his den, and he was crouching backward in preparation for his deadly spring. Dempster affected to take no notice of her, talked obstreperously, and drank steadily.

About eleven the party dispersed, with the exception of Mr. Budd, who had joined them after dinner, and appeared disposed to stay drinking a little longer. Janet began to hope that he would stay long enough for Dempster to become heavy and stupid, and so to fall asleep down stairs, which was a rare but occasional ending of his nights. She told the servants to sit up no longer, and she herself undressed and went to bed, trying to cheat her imagination into the belief that the day was ended for her. But when she lay down, she became more intensely awake than ever. Everything she had taken this evening seemed only to stimulate her senses and her apprehensions to new vividness. Her heart beat violently, and she heard every sound in the house.

At last, when it was twelve, she heard Mr. Budd go out; she heard the door slam. Dempster had not moved. Was he asleep? Would he forget? The minute seemed long, while, with a quickening pulse, she was on the stretch to catch every sound.

"Janet!" The loud jarring voice seemed to strike her like a hurled weapon.

"Janet!" he called again, moving out of the dining-room to the foot of the stairs.

There was a pause of a minute.

"If you don't come, I'll kill you."

Another pause, and she heard him turn back into the dining-room. He was gone for a light—perhaps for a weapon. Perhaps he *would* kill her. Let him. Life was as hideous as death. For years she had been rushing on to some unknown but certain horror; and now she was close upon it. She was almost glad. She was in a state of flushed feverish defiance that neutralized her woman's terrors.

She heard his heavy step on the stairs; she saw the slowly advancing light. Then she saw the tall massive figure, and the heavy face, now fierce with drunken rage. He had nothing but the candle in his hand. He set it down on the table, and advanced close to the bed.

"So you think you'll defy me, do you? We'll see how long that will last. Get up, madam; out of bed this instant!"

In the close presence of the dreadful man—of this huge crushing force, armed with savage will—poor Janet's desperate defiance all forsook her, and her terrors came back. Trembling she got up, and stood helpless in her night-dress before her husband.

He seized her with his heavy grasp by the shoulder, and pushed her before him.

"I'll cool your hot spirit for you! I'll teach you to brave me!"

Slowly he pushed her along before him, down stairs and through the passage, where a small oil-lamp was still flickering. What was he going to do to her? She thought every moment he was going to dash her before him on the ground. But she gave no scream—she only trembled.

He pushed her on to the entrance, and held her firmly in his grasp, while he lifted the latch of the door. Then he opened the door a little way, thrust her out, and slammed it behind her.

For a short space, it seemed like a deliverance to Janet. The harsh north-east wind, that blew through her thin night-dress, and sent her long heavy black hair streaming, seemed like the breath of pity after the grasp of that threatening monster. But soon the sense of release from an overpowering terror gave way before the sense of the fate that had really come upon her.

This, then, was what she had been traveling towards through her long years of misery! Not yet death. O! if she had been brave enough for it, death would have been better. The servants slept at the back of the house; it was impossible to make them hear, so that they might let her in again quietly, without her husband's knowledge. And she would not have tried. He had thrust her out, and it should be for ever.

There would have been dead silence in Orchard Street but for the whistling of the wind and the swirling of the March dust on the pavement. Thick clouds covered the sky; every door was closed; every window was dark. No ray of light fell on the tall white figure that stood in lonely misery on the door-step; no eye rested on Janet as she sank down on the cold stone, and looked into the dismal night. She seemed to be looking into her own blank future.

Chapter XV

The stony street, the bitter north-east wind and darkness—and in the midst of them a tender woman thrust out from her husband's home in her thin night-dress, the harsh wind cutting her naked feet, and driving her long hair away from her half-clad bosom, where the poor heart is crushed with anguish and despair. . . .

When Janet sat down shivering on the door-stone, with the door shut upon her past life, and the future black and unshapen before her as the night, the scenes of her childhood, her youth and her painful womanhood, rushed back upon her consciousness, and made one picture with her present desolation. The petted child taking her newest toy to bed with her—the young girl, proud in strength and beauty, dreaming that life was an easy thing, and that it was pitiful weakness to be unhappy—the bride, passing with trembling joy from the outer court to the inner sanctuary of woman's life—the wife, beginning her initiation into sorrow, wounded, resenting, yet still hoping and forgiving—the poor bruised woman, seeking through weary years the one refuge of despair, oblivion:—Janet seemed to herself all these in the same moment that she was conscious of being seated on the cold stone under the shock of a new misery. All her early gladness, all her bright hopes and illusions, all her gifts of beauty and affection, served only to darken the riddle of her life; they were the betraying promises of a cruel destiny which had brought out those sweet blossoms only that the winds and storms might have a greater work of desolation, which had nursed her like a pet fawn into tenderness and fond expectation, only that she might feel a keener terror in the clutch of the panther. Her mother had sometimes said that troubles were sent to make us better and draw us nearer to God. What mockery that seemed to Janet! *Her* troubles had been sinking her lower from year to year, pressing upon her like heavy fever-laden vapors, and perverting the very plenitude of her nature into a deeper source of disease. Her wretchedness had been a perpetually tightening instrument of torture, which had gradually absorbed all the other sensibilities of her nature into the sense of pain and the maddened craving for relief. Oh, if some ray of hope, of pity, of consolation, would pierce through the horrible gloom, she might believe *then* in a Divine love—in a heavenly Father who cared for His children! But now she had no faith, no trust. There was nothing she could lean on in the wide world, for her mother was only a fellow-sufferer in her own lot. The poor patient woman could do little more than mourn with her daughter: she had humble resignation enough to sustain her own soul, but she could no more give comfort and fortitude to Janet, than the withered ivy-covered trunk can bear up its strong, full-boughed offspring crashing down under an Alpine storm. Janet felt she was alone: no human soul had measured her anguish, had understood her self-despair, had entered into her sorrows and her sins with that deep-sighted sympathy which is wiser than all blame, more potent than all reproof—such sympathy as had swelled her own heart for many a sufferer. And if there was any Divine Pity, she could not feel it; it kept aloof from her, it poured no balm into her wounds, it stretched out no hand to bear up her weak resolve, to fortify her fainting courage. . . .

The loud sound of the church clock striking one, startled her. She had not been there more than half an hour, then? And it seemed to her as if she had been there half the night. She was getting benumbed with cold. With that strong instinctive dread of pain and death which had made her recoil from suicide, she started up, and the disagreeable sensation of resting on her benumbed feet helped to recall her completely to the sense of the present. The wind was beginning to make rents in the clouds, and there came every now and then a dim light of stars that frightened her more than the darkness; it was like a cruel finger pointing her out in her wretchedness and humiliation; it made her shudder at the thought of the morning twilight. What could she do? Not go to her mother—not rouse her in the dead of night to tell her this. Her mother would think she was a specter; it would be enough to kill her with horror. And the way there was so long . . . if she should meet some one . . . yet she must seek some shelter, somewhere to hide herself. Five doors off there was Mrs. Pettifer's; that kind woman would take her in. It was of no use now to be proud and mind about the world's knowing: she had nothing to wish for, nothing to care about; only she could not help shuddering at the thought of braving the morning light, there, in the street—she was frightened at the thought of spending long hours in the cold. Life might mean anguish, might mean despair; but—oh, she must clutch it, though with bleeding fingers; her feet must cling to the firm earth that the sunlight would revisit, not slip into the untried abyss, where she might long even for familiar pains.

Janet trod slowly with her naked feet on the rough pavement, trembling at the fitful gleams of starlight, and supporting herself by the wall, as the gusts of wind drove right against her. The very wind was cruel: it tried to push her back from the door where she wanted to go and knock and ask for pity.

Mrs. Pettifer's house did not look into Orchard Street: it stood a little way up a wide passage which opened into the street through an archway. Janet turned up the archway, and saw a faint light coming from Mrs. Pettifer's bedroom window. The glimmer of a rushlight from a room where a friend was lying, was like a ray of mercy to Janet, after that long, long time of darkness and loneliness; it would not be so dreadful to awake Mrs. Pettifer as she had thought. Yet she lingered some minutes at the door before she gathered courage to knock; she felt as if the sound must betray her to others besides Mrs. Pettifer, though there was no other dwelling that opened into the passage—only warehouses and outbuildings. There was no gravel for her to throw up at the window, nothing but heavy pavement; there was no door-bell; she must knock. Her first rap was very timid—one feeble fall of the knocker; and then she stood still again for many minutes; but presently she rallied her courage and knocked several times together, not loudly, but rapidly, so that Mrs. Pettifer, if she only heard the sound, could not mistake it. And she *had* heard it, for by-and-by the casement of her window was opened, and Janet perceived that she was bending out to try and discern who it was at the door.

"It is I, Mrs. Pettifer; it is Janet Dempster. Take me in, for pity's sake."

"Merciful God! what has happened?"

"Robert has turned me out. I have been in the cold a long while."

Mrs. Pettifer said no more, but hurried away from the window, and was soon at the door with a light in her hand.

"Come in, my poor dear, come in," said the good woman in a tremulous voice, drawing Janet within the door. "Come into my warm bed, and may God in heaven save and comfort you."

The pitying eyes, the tender voice, the warm touch, caused a rush of new feeling in Janet. Her heart swelled, and she burst out suddenly, like a child, into loud passionate sobs. Mrs. Pettifer could not help crying with her, but she said, "Come up-stairs, my dear, come. Don't linger in the cold."

She drew the poor sobbing thing gently up-stairs, and persuaded her to get into the warm bed. But it was long before Janet could lie down. She sat leaning her head on her knees, convulsed by sobs, while the motherly woman covered her with clothes and held her arms round her to comfort her with warmth. At last the hysterical passion had exhausted itself, and she fell back on the pillow; but her throat was still agitated by piteous after-sobs, such as shake a little child even when it has found a refuge from its alarms on its mother's lap.

Now Janet was getting quieter, Mrs. Pettifer determined to go down and make a cup of tea, the first thing a kind old woman thinks of as a solace and restorative under all calamities. Happily there was no danger of awaking her servant, a heavy girl of sixteen, who was snoring blissfully in the attic, and might be kept ignorant of the way in which Mrs. Dempster had come in. So Mrs. Pettifer busied herself with rousing the kitchen fire, which was kept in under a huge "raker"—a possibility by which the coal of the midland counties atones for all its slowness and white ashes.

When she carried up the tea, Janet was lying quite still; the spasmodic agitation had ceased, and she seemed lost in thought; her eyes were fixed vacantly on the rushlight shade, and all the lines of sorrow were deepened in her face.

"Now, my dear," said Mrs. Pettifer, "let me persuade you to drink a cup of tea; you'll find it warm you and soothe you very much. Why, dear heart, your feet are like ice still. Now, do drink this tea, and I'll wrap 'em up in flannel, and then they'll get warm."

Janet turned her dark eyes on her old friend and stretched out her arms. She was too much oppressed to say anything; her suffering lay like a heavy weight on her power of speech; but she wanted to kiss the good kind woman. Mrs. Pettifer, setting down the cup, bent towards the sad beautiful face, and Janet kissed her with earnest sacramental kisses—such kisses as seal a new and closer bond between the helper and the helped.

She drank the tea obediently. "It *does* warm me," she said. "But now you will get into bed. I shall lie still now."

Mrs. Pettifer felt it was the best thing she could do to lie down quietly, and say no more. She hoped Janet might go to sleep. As for herself, with that tendency to wakefulness common to advanced years, she found it impossible to compose herself to sleep again after this agitating surprise. She lay listening to the clock, wondering what had led to this new outrage of Dempster's, praying for the poor thing at her side, and pitying the mother who would have to hear it all to-morrow.

Chapter XVI

Janet lay still, as she had promised; but the tea, which had warmed her and given her a sense of greater bodily ease, had only heightened the previous excitement of her brain. Her ideas had a new vividness, which made her feel as if she had only seen life through a dim haze before; her thoughts, instead of springing from the action of her own mind, were external existences, that thrust themselves imperiously upon her like haunting visions. The future took shape after shape of misery before her, always ending in her being dragged back again to her old life of terror, and stupor, and fevered despair. Her husband had so long overshadowed her life that her imagination could not keep hold of a condition in which that great dread was absent; and even his absence—what was it? only a dreary vacant flat, where there was nothing to strive after, nothing to long for. . . .

She had scarcely been asleep an hour when her movements became more violent, her mutterings more frequent and agitated, till at last she started up with a smothered cry, and looked wildly round her, shaking with terror.

"Don't be frightened, dear Mrs. Dempster," said Mrs. Pettifer, who was up and dressing, "you are with me, your old friend, Mrs. Pettifer. Nothing will harm you."

Janet sank back again on her pillow, still trembling. After lying silent a little while, she said, "It was a horrible dream. Dear Mrs. Pettifer, don't let any one know I am here. Keep it a secret. If he finds out, he will come and drag me back again."

"No, my dear, depend on me. I've just thought, I shall send the servant home on a holiday—I've promised her a good while. I'll send her away as soon as she's had her breakfast, and she'll have no occasion to know you're here. There's no holding servants' tongues, if you let 'em know anything. What they don't know, they won't tell; you may trust 'em so far. But shouldn't you like me to go and fetch your mother?"

"No, not yet, not yet. I can't bear to see her yet."

"Well, it shall be just as you like. Now try and get to sleep again. I shall leave you for an hour or two, and send off Phoebe, and then bring you some breakfast. I'll lock the door behind me, so as the girl mayn't come in by chance."

The daylight changes the aspect of misery to us, as of everything else. In the night it presses on our imagination—the forms it takes are false, fitful, exaggerated; in broad day it sickens our sense with the dreary persistence of definite measurable reality. The man who looks with ghastly horror on all his property aflame in the dead of night, has not half the sense of destitution he will have in the morning, when he walks over the ruins lying blackened in the pitiless sunshine. That moment of intensest depression was come to Janet, when the daylight which showed her the walls, and chairs, and tables, and all the commonplace reality that surrounded her, seemed to lay bare the future too, and bring out into oppressive distinctness all the details of a weary life to be lived from day to day, with no hope to strengthen her against that evil habit, which she loathed in retrospect and yet was powerless to resist. Her husband would never consent to her living away from him: she was become necessary to his tyranny; he would never willingly loosen his grasp on her. She had a vague notion of some protection the law might give her, if she could prove her life in danger from him; but she shrank utterly, as she had always done, from any active, public resistance or vengeance: she felt too crushed, too faulty, too liable to reproach, to have the courage, even if she had had the wish, to put herself openly in the position of a wronged woman seeking redress. She had no strength to sustain her in a course of self-defense and independence: there was a darker shadow over her life than the dread of her husband—it was the shadow of self-despair. The easiest thing would be to go away and hide herself from him. But then there was her mother: Robert had all her little property in his hands, and that little was scarcely enough to keep her in comfort without his aid. If Janet went away alone, he would be sure to persecute her mother; and if she *did* go away—what then? She must work to maintain herself; she must exert herself, weary and hopeless as she was, to begin life afresh. How hard that seemed to her! Janet's nature did not belie her grand face and form: there was energy, there was strength in it; but it was the strength of the vine, which must have its broad leaves and rich clusters borne up by a firm stay. And now she had nothing to rest on—no faith, no love. If her mother had been very feeble, aged, or sickly, Janet's deep pity and tenderness might have made a daughter's duties an interest and a solace; but Mrs. Raynor had never needed tendance; she had always been giving help to her daughter; she had always been a sort of humble ministering spirit; and it was one of Janet's pangs of memory, that instead of being her mother's comfort, she had been her mother's trial. Everywhere the same sadness! Her life was a sun-dried, barren tract, where there was no shadow, and where all the waters were bitter.

No! She suddenly thought—and the thought was like an electric shock—there was one spot in her memory which seemed to promise her an untried spring, where the waters might be sweet. That short interview with Mr. Tryan had come back upon her—his voice, his words, his look, which told her that he knew sorrow. His words had implied that he thought his death was near, yet he had a faith which enabled him to labor—enabled him to give comfort to others. That look of his came back on her with a vividness greater than it had had for her in reality: surely he knew more of the secrets of sorrow than other men; perhaps he had some message of comfort, different from the feeble words she had been used to hear from others. She was tired, she was sick of that barren exhortation—Do right, and keep a clear conscience, and God will reward you, and your troubles will be easier to bear. She wanted *strength* to do right—she wanted something to rely on besides her own resolutions; for was not the path behind her all strewn with *broken* resolutions? How could she trust in new ones? She had often heard Mr. Tryan laughed at for being fond of great sinners. She began to see a new meaning in those words; he would perhaps understand her helplessness, her wants. If she could pour out her heart to him! if she could for the first time in her life unlock all the chambers of her soul!

The impulse to confession almost always requires the presence of a fresh ear and a fresh heart; and in our moments of spiritual need, the man to whom we have no tie but our common nature, seems nearer to us than mother, brother, or friend. Our daily familiar life is but a hiding of ourselves from each other behind a screen of trivial words and deeds, and those who sit with us at the same hearth, are often the farthest off from the deep human soul within us, full of unspoken evil and unacted good.

When Mrs. Pettifer came back to her, turning the key and opening the door very gently, Janet, instead of being asleep, as her good friend had hoped, was intensely occupied with her new thought. She longed to ask Mrs. Pettifer if she could see Mr. Tryan; but she was arrested by doubts and timidity. He might not feel for her—he might be shocked at her confession—he might talk to her of doctrines she could not understand or believe. She could not make up her mind yet; but she was too restless under this mental struggle to remain in bed.

"Mrs. Pettifer," she said, "I can't lie here any longer; I must get up. Will you lend me some clothes?"

Wrapt in such drapery as Mrs. Pettifer could find for her tall figure, Janet went down into the little parlor, and tried to take some of the breakfast her friend had prepared for her. But her effort was not a successful one; her cup of tea and bit of toast were only half finished. The leaden weight of discouragement pressed upon her more and more heavily. The wind had fallen, and a drizzling rain had come on; there was no prospect from Mrs. Pettifer's parlor but a blank wall; and as Janet looked out at the window, the rain and the smoke-blackened bricks seemed to blend themselves in sickening identity with her desolation of spirit and the headachy weariness of her body.

Mrs. Pettifer got through her household work as soon as she could, and sat down with her sewing, hoping that Janet would perhaps be able to talk a little of what had passed, and find some relief by unbosoming herself in that way. But Janet could not speak to her; she was importuned with the longing to see Mr. Tryan, and yet hesitating to express it.

Two hours passed in this way. The rain went on drizzling, and Janet sat still, leaning her aching head on her hand, and looking alternately at the fire and out of the window. She felt this could not last—this motionless, vacant misery. She must determine on something, she must take some step; and yet everything was so difficult.

It was one o'clock, and Mrs. Pettifer rose from her seat, saying, "I must go and see about dinner."

The movement and the sound startled Janet from her reverie. It seemed as if an opportunity were escaping her, and she said hastily, "Is Mr. Tryan in the town to-day, do you think?"

"No, I should think not, being Saturday, you know," said Mrs. Pettifer, her face lighting up with pleasure; "but he *would* come, if he was sent for. I can send Jesson's boy with a note to him any time. Should you like to see him?"

"Yes, I think I should."

"Then I'll send for him this instant."

Chapter XVII

When Dempster awoke in the morning, he was at no loss to account to himself for the fact that Janet was not by his side. His hours of drunkenness were not cut off from his other hours by any blank wall of oblivion; he remembered what Janet had done to offend him the evening before, he remembered what he had done to her at midnight, just as he would have remembered if he had been consulted about a right of road.

The remembrance gave him a definite ground for the extra ill-humor which had attended his waking every morning this week, but he would not admit to himself that it cost him any anxiety. "Pooh," he said inwardly, "she would go straight to her mother's. She's as timid as a hare; and she'll never let anybody know about it. She'll be back again before night."

But it would be as well for the servants not to know anything of the affair; so he collected the clothes she had taken off the night before, and threw them into a fire-proof closet of which he always kept the key in his pocket. When he went down stairs he said to the housemaid, "Mrs. Dempster is gone to her mother's; bring in the breakfast."

The servants, accustomed to hear domestic broils, and to see their mistress put on her bonnet hastily and go to her mother's, thought it only something a little worse than usual that she should have gone thither in consequence of a violent quarrel, either at midnight, or in the early morning before they were up. The housemaid told the cook what she supposed had happened; the cook shook her head and said, "Eh, dear, dear!" but they both expected to see their mistress back again in an hour or two.

Dempster, on his return home the evening before, had ordered his man, who lived away from the house, to bring up his horse and gig from the stables at ten. After breakfast he said to the housemaid, "No one need sit up for me to-night; I shall not be at home till to-morrow evening"; and then he walked to the office to give some orders, expecting, as he returned, to see the man waiting with his gig. But though the church clock had struck ten, no gig was there. In Dempster's mood this was more than enough to exasperate him. He went in to take his accustomed glass of brandy before setting out, promising himself the satisfaction of presently thundering at Dawes for being a few minutes behind his time. An outbreak of temper towards his man was not common with him; for Dempster, like most tyrannous people, had that dastardly kind of self-restraint which enabled him to control his temper where it suited his own convenience to do so; and feeling the value of Dawes, a steady punctual fellow, he not only gave him high wages, but usually treated him with exceptional civility. This morning, however, ill-humor got the better of prudence, and Dempster was determined to rate him soundly; a resolution for which Dawes gave him much better ground than he expected. Five minutes, ten minutes, a quarter of an hour, had passed, and Dempster was setting off to the stables in a back street to see what was the cause of the delay, when Dawes appeared with the gig.

"What the devil do you keep me here for?" thundered Dempster, "kicking my heels like a beggarly tailor waiting for a carrier's cart? I ordered you to be here at ten. We might have driven to Whitlow by this time."

"Why, one o' the traces was welly i' two, an' I had to tek it to Brady's to be mended, an' he didn't get it done i' time."

"Then why didn't you take it to him last night? Because of your damned laziness, I suppose. Do you think I give you wages for you to choose your own hours, and come dawdling up a quarter of an hour after my time?"

"Come, give me good words, will yer?" said Dawes, sulkily, "I'm not lazy, nor no man shall call me lazy. I know well anuff what you gi' me wages for; it's for doin' what yer won't find many men as 'ull do."

"What, you impudent scoundrel," said Dempster, getting into the gig, "you think you're necessary to me, do you? As if a beastly bucket-carrying idiot like you wasn't to be got any day. Look out for a new master, then, who'll pay you for not doing as you're bid."

Dawes's blood was now fairly up. "I'll look out for a master as has got a better charicter nor a lyin', bletherin' drunkard, an' I shouldn't hev to go fur."

Dempster, furious, snatched the whip from the socket, and gave Dawes a cut, which he meant to fall across his shoulders, saying, "Take that, sir, and go to hell with you!"

Dawes was in the act of turning with the reins in his hand when the lash fell, and the cut went across his face. With white lips, he said, "I'll hev the law on yer for that, lawyer as yer are," and threw the reins on the horse's back.

Dempster leaned forward, seized the reins, and drove off.

"Why, there's your friend Dempster driving out without his man again," said Mr. Luke Byles, who was chatting with Mr. Budd in the Bridge Way. "What a fool he is to drive that two-wheeled thing! he'll get pitched on his head one of these days."

"Not he," said Mr. Budd, nodding to Dempster as he passed; "he's got nine lives, Dempster has."

Chapter XVIII

It was dusk, and the candles were lighted before Mr. Tryan knocked at Mrs. Pettifer's door. Her messenger had brought back word, that he was not at home, and all afternoon Janet had been agitated by the fear that he would not come; but as soon as that anxiety was removed by the knock at the door, she felt a sudden rush of doubt and timidity: she trembled and turned cold.

Mrs. Pettifer went to open the door, and told Mr. Tryan, in as few words as possible, what had happened in the night. As he laid down his hat and prepared to enter the parlor, she said, "I won't go in with you, for I think perhaps she would rather see you go in alone."

Janet, wrapped up in a large white shawl which threw her dark face into startling relief, was seated with her eyes turned anxiously towards the door when Mr. Tryan entered. He had not seen her since their interview at Sally Martin's long months ago; and he felt a strong movement of compassion at the sight of the pain-stricken face which seemed to bear written on it the signs of all Janet's intervening misery. Her heart gave a great leap, as her eyes met his once more. No! she had not deceived herself: there was all the sincerity, all the sadness, all the deep pity in them her memory had told her of; more than it had told her, for in proportion as his face had become thinner and more worn, his eyes appeared to have gathered intensity.

He came forward, and, putting out his hand, said, "I am so glad you sent for me—I am so thankful you thought I could be any comfort to you." Janet took his hand in silence. She was unable to utter any words of mere politeness, or even of gratitude; her heart was too full of other words that had welled up the moment she met his pitying glance, and felt her doubts fall away.

They sat down opposite each other, and she said in a low voice, while slow difficult tears gathered in her aching eyes:—

"I want to tell you how unhappy I am—how weak and wicked. I feel no strength to live or die. I thought you could tell me something that would help me." She paused.

"Perhaps I can," Mr. Tryan said, "for in speaking to me you are speaking to a fellow-sinner who has needed just the comfort and help you are needing."

"And you did find it?"

"Yes; and I trust you will find it."

"O, I should like to be good and to do right," Janet burst forth, "but indeed, indeed, my lot has been a very hard one. I loved my husband very dearly when we were married, and I meant to make him happy—I wanted nothing else. But he began to be angry with me for little things and . . . I don't want to accuse him . . . but he drank and got more and more unkind to me, and then very cruel, and he beat me. And that cut me to the heart. It made me almost mad sometimes to think all our love had come to that. . . . I couldn't bear up against it. I had never been used to drink anything but water. I hated wine and spirits because Robert drank them so; but one day when I was very wretched, and the wine was standing on the table, I suddenly. . . . I can hardly remember how I came to do it. . . . I poured some wine into a large glass and drank it. It blunted my feelings, and made me more indifferent. After that, the temptation was always coming, and it got stronger and stronger. I was ashamed, and I hated what I did; but almost while the thought was passing through my mind that I would never do it again, I did it. It seemed as if there was a demon in me always making me rush to do what I longed not to do. And I thought all the more that God was cruel; for if He had not sent me that dreadful trial, so much worse than other women have to bear, I should not have done wrong in that way. I suppose it is wicked to think so. . . . I feel as if there must be goodness and right above us, but I can't see it, I can't trust in it. And I have gone on in that way for years and years. At one time it used to be better now and then, but everything has got worse lately: I felt sure it must soon end somehow. And last night he turned me out of doors. . . . I don't know what to do. I will never go back to that life again if I can help it; and yet everything else seems so miserable. I feel sure that demon will be always urging me to satisfy the craving that comes upon me, and the days will go on as they have done through all those miserable years. I shall always be doing wrong, and hating myself after—sinking lower and lower, and knowing that I am sinking. O can you tell me any way of getting strength? Have you ever known any one like me that got peace of mind and power to do right? Can you give me any comfort—any hope?"

While Janet was speaking, she had forgotten everything but her misery and her yearning for comfort. Her voice had risen from the low tone of timid distress to an intense pitch of imploring anguish. She clasped her hands tightly, and looked at Mr. Tryan with eager questioning eyes, with parted, trembling lips, with the deep horizontal lines of overmastering pain on her brow. In this artificial life of ours, it is not often we see a human face with all a heart's agony in it, uncontrolled by self-consciousness; when we do see it, it startles us as if we had suddenly waked into the real world of which this everyday one is but a puppet-show copy. For some moments Mr. Tryan was too deeply moved to speak.

"Yes, dear Mrs. Dempster," he said at last, "there *is* comfort, there *is* hope for you. Believe me there is, for I speak from my own deep and hard experience." He paused, as if he had not made up his mind to utter the words that were urging themselves to his lips. Presently he continued, "Ten years ago, I felt as wretched as you do. I think my wretchedness was even worse than yours, for I had a heavier sin on my conscience. I had suffered no wrong from others as you have, and I had injured another irreparably in body and soul. The image of the wrong I had done pursued me everywhere, and I seemed on the brink of madness. I hated my life, for I thought, just as you do, that I should go on falling into temptation and doing more harm in the world; and I dreaded death, for with that sense of guilt on my soul, I felt that whatever state I entered on must be one of misery. But a dear friend to whom I opened my mind showed me it was just such as I—the helpless who feel themselves helpless—that God specially invites to come to Him, and offers all the riches of His salvation: not forgiveness only; forgiveness would be worth little if it left us under the powers of our evil passions; but strength—that strength which enables us to conquer sin."

"But," said Janet, "I can feel no trust in God. He seems always to have left me to myself. I have sometimes prayed to Him to help me, and yet everything has been just the same as before. If you felt like me, how did you come to have hope and trust?"

"Do not believe that God has left you to yourself. How can you tell but that the hardest trials you have known have been only the road by which He was leading you to that complete sense of your own sin and helplessness, without which you would never have renounced all other hopes, and trusted in His love alone? I know, dear Mrs. Dempster, I know it is hard to bear. I would not speak lightly of your sorrows. I feel that the mystery of our life is great, and at one time it seemed as dark to me as it does to you." Mr. Tryan hesitated again. He saw that the first thing Janet needed was to be assured of sympathy. She must be made to feel that her anguish was not strange to him; that he entered into the only half-expressed secrets of her spiritual weakness, before any other message of consolation could find its way to her heart. The tale of the Divine Pity was never yet believed from lips that were not felt to be moved by human pity. And Janet's anguish was not strange to Mr. Tryan. He had never been in the presence of a sorrow and a self-despair that had sent so strong a thrill through all the recesses of his saddest experience; and it is because sympathy is but a living again through our own past in a new form, that confession often prompts a response of confession. Mr. Tryan felt this prompting, and his judgment too told him that in obeying it he would be taking the best means of administering comfort to Janet. Yet he hesitated; as we tremble to let in the daylight on a chamber of relics which we have never visited except in curtained silence. But the first impulse triumphed, and he went on. "I had lived all my life at a distance from God. My youth was spent in thoughtless self-indulgence, and all my hopes were of a vain worldly kind. I had no thought of entering the Church; I looked forward to a political career, for my father was private secretary to a man high in the Whig Ministry, and had been promised strong interest in my behalf. At college I lived in intimacy with the gayest men, even adopting follies and vices for which I had no taste, out of mere pliancy and the love of standing well with my companions. You see, I was more guilty even then than you have been, for I threw away all the rich blessings of untroubled youth and health; I had no excuse in my outward lot. But while I was at college that event in my life occurred, which in the end brought on the state of mind I have mentioned to you—the state of self-reproach and despair, which enables me to understand to the full what you are suffering; and I tell you the facts, because I want you to be assured that I am not uttering mere vague words when I say that I have been raised from as low a depth of sin and sorrow as that in which you feel yourself to be. At college I had an attachment to a lovely girl of seventeen: she was very much below my own station in life, and I never contemplated marrying her; but I induced her to leave her father's house. I did not mean to forsake her when I left college, and I quieted all scruples of conscience by promising myself that I would always take care of poor Lucy. But on my return from a vacation spent in traveling, I found that Lucy was gone—gone away with a gentleman, her neighbors said. I was a good deal distressed, but I tried to persuade myself that no harm would come to her. Soon afterwards I had an illness which left my health delicate, and made all dissipation distasteful to me. Life seemed very wearisome and empty, and I looked with envy on every one who had some great and absorbing object—even on my cousin who was preparing to go out as a missionary, and whom I had been used to think a dismal, tedious person, because he was constantly urging religious subjects upon me. We were living in London then; it was three years since I had lost sight of Lucy; and one summer evening about nine o'clock, as I was walking along Gower Street, I saw a knot of people on the causeway before me. As I came up to them, I heard one woman say, 'I tell you, she's dead.' This awakened my interest, and I pushed my way within the circle. The body of a woman, dressed in fine clothes, was lying against a door-step. Her head was bent on one side, and the long curls had fallen over her cheek. A tremor seized me when I saw the hair: it was light chestnut—the color of Lucy's. I knelt down and turned aside the hair; it was Lucy—dead—with paint on her cheeks. I found out afterwards that she had taken poison—that she was in the power of a wicked woman—that the very clothes on her back were not her own. It was then that my past life burst upon me in all its hideousness. I wished I had never been born. I couldn't look into the future. Lucy's dead painted face would follow me there, as it did when I looked back into the past—as it did when I sat down to table with my friends, when I lay down in my bed, and when I rose up. There was only one thing that could make life tolerable to me; that was, to spend all the rest of it in trying to save others from the ruin I had brought on one. But how was that possible for me? I had no comfort, no strength, no wisdom in my own soul; how could I give them to others? My mind was dark, rebellious, at war with itself and with God."

Mr. Tryan had been looking away from Janet. His face was towards the fire, and he was absorbed in the images his memory was recalling. But now he turned his eyes on her, and they met hers, fixed on him with the look of rapt expectation with which one clinging to a slippery summit of rock, while the waves are rising higher and higher, watches the boat that has put from shore to his rescue.

"You see, Mrs. Dempster, how deep my need was. I went on in this way for months. I was convinced that if I ever got help and comfort, it must be from religion. I went to hear celebrated preachers, and I read religious books. But I found nothing that fitted my own need. The faith which puts the sinner in possession of salvation seemed, as I understood it, to be quite out of my reach. I had no faith; I only felt utterly wretched, under the power of habits and dispositions which had wrought hideous evil. At last, as I told you, I found a friend to whom I opened all my feelings—to whom I confessed everything. He was a man who had gone through very deep experience, and could understand the different wants of different minds. He made it clear to me that the only preparation for coming to Christ and partaking of His salvation, was that very sense of guilt and helplessness which was weighing me down. He said, You are weary and heavy laden; well, it is you Christ invites to come to Him and find rest. He asks you to cling to Him, to lean on Him; He does not command you to walk alone without stumbling. He does not tell you, as your fellow-men do, that you must first merit His love; He neither condemns nor reproaches you for the past, He only bids you come to Him that you may have life: He bids you stretch out your hands, and take of the fullness of His love. You have only to rest on Him as a child rests on its mother's arms, and you will be upborne by His divine strength. That is what is meant by faith. Your evil habits, you feel, are too strong for you; you are unable to wrestle with them; you know beforehand you shall fall. But when once we feel our helplessness in that way, and go to Christ, desiring to be freed from the power as well as the punishment of sin, we are no longer left to our own strength. As long as we live in rebellion against God, desiring to have our own will, seeking happiness in the things of this world, it is as if we shut ourselves up in a crowded stifling room, where we breathe only poisoned air; but we have only to walk out under the infinite heavens, and we breathe the pure free air that gives us health, and strength, and gladness. It is just so with God's spirit: as soon as we submit ourselves to His will, as soon as we desire to be united to Him, and made pure and holy, it is as if the walls had fallen down that shut us out from God, and we are fed with His spirit, which gives us new strength."

"That is what I want," said Janet; "I have left off minding about pleasure. I think I could be contented in the midst of hardship, if I felt that God cared for me, and would give me strength to lead a pure life. But tell me, did you soon find peace and strength?"

"Not perfect peace for a long while, but hope and trust, which is strength. No sense of pardon for myself could do away with the pain I had in thinking what I had helped to bring on another. My friend used to urge upon me that my sin against God was greater than my sin against her; but—it may be from want of deeper spiritual feeling—that has remained to this hour the sin which causes me the bitterest pang. I could never rescue Lucy; but by God's blessing I might rescue other weak and falling souls; and that was why I entered the Church. I asked for nothing through the rest of my life but that I might be devoted to God's work, without swerving in search of pleasure either to the right hand or to the left. It has been often a hard struggle—but God has been with me—and perhaps it may not last much longer."

Mr. Tryan paused. For a moment he had forgotten Janet, and for a moment she had forgotten her own sorrows. When she recurred to herself, it was with a new feeling.

"Ah, what a difference between our lives! you have been choosing pain, and working, and denying yourself; and I have been thinking only of myself. I was only angry and discontented because I had pain to bear. You never had that wicked feeling that I have had so often, did you? that God was cruel to send me trials and temptations worse than others have."

"Yes, I had; I had very blasphemous thoughts, and I know that spirit of rebellion must have made the worst part of your lot. You did not feel how impossible it is for us to judge rightly of God's dealings, and you opposed yourself to His will. But what do we know? We cannot foretell the working of the smallest event in our own lot: how can we presume to judge of things that are so much too high for us? There is nothing that becomes us but entire submission, perfect resignation. As long as we set up our own will and our own wisdom against God's, we make that wall between us and His love which I have spoken of just now. But as soon as we lay ourselves entirely at His feet, we have enough light given us to guide our own steps; as the foot-soldier who hears nothing of the councils that determine the course of the great battle he is in, hears plainly enough the word of command which he must himself obey. I know, dear Mrs. Dempster, I know it is hard—the hardest thing of all, perhaps—to flesh and blood. But carry that difficulty to Christ along with all your other sins and weaknesses, and ask Him to pour into you a spirit of submission. He enters into your struggles; He has drunk the cup of our suffering to the dregs; He knows the hard wrestling it costs us to say, 'Not my will, but Thine be done.' "

"Pray with me," said Janet—"pray now that I may have light and strength."

Chapter XIX

Before leaving Janet, Mr. Tryan urged her strongly to send for her mother.

"Do not wound her," he said, "by shutting her out any longer from your troubles. It is right that you should be with her."

"Yes, I will send for her," said Janet. "But I would rather not go to my mother's yet, because my husband is sure to think I am there, and he might come and fetch me. I can't go back to him. . . . At least, not yet. Ought I to go back to him?"

"No, certainly not, at present. Something should be done to secure you from violence. Your mother, I think, should consult some confidential friend, some man of character and experience, who might mediate between you and your husband."

"Yes, I will send for my mother directly. But I will stay here, with Mrs. Pettifer, till something has been done. I want no one to know where I am, except you. You will come again, will you not? you will not leave me to myself?"

"You will not be left to yourself. God is with you. If I have been able to give you any comfort, it is because His power and love have been present with us. But I am very thankful that He has chosen to work through me. I shall see you again to-morrow—not before evening, for it will be Sunday, you know; but after the evening lecture I shall be at liberty. You will be in my prayers till then. In the mean time, dear Mrs. Dempster, open your heart as much as you can to your mother and Mrs. Pettifer. Cast away from you the pride that makes us shrink from acknowledging our weakness to our friends. Ask them to help you in guarding yourself from the least approach of the sin you most dread. Deprive yourself as far as possible of the very means and opportunity of committing it. Every effort of that kind made in humility and dependence is a prayer. Promise me you will do this."

"Yes, I promise you. I know I have always been too proud; I could never bear to speak to any one about myself. I have been proud towards my mother, even; it has always made me angry when she has seemed to take notice of my faults."

"Ah, dear Mrs. Dempster, you will never say again that life is blank, and that there is nothing to live for, will you? See what work there is to be done in life, both in our own souls and for others. Surely it matters little whether we have more or less of this world's comfort in these short years, when God is training us for the eternal enjoyment of His love. Keep that great end of life before you, and your troubles here will seem only the small hardships of a journey. Now I must go."

Mr. Tryan rose and held out his hand. Janet took it and said, "God has been very good to me in sending you to me. I will trust in Him. I will try to do everything you tell me."

Blessed influence of one true loving human soul on another! Not calculable by algebra, not deducible by logic, but mysterious, effectual, mighty as the hidden process by which the tiny seed is quickened, and bursts forth into tall stem and broad leaf, and glowing tasseled flower. Ideas are often poor ghosts; our sun-filled eyes cannot discern them; they pass athwart us in thin vapor, and cannot make themselves felt. But sometimes they are made flesh; they breathe upon us with warm breath, they touch us with soft responsive hands, they look at us with sad sincere eyes, and speak to us in appealing tones; they are clothed in a living human soul, with all its conflicts, its faith, and its love. Then their presence is a power, then they shake us like a passion, and we are drawn after them with gentle compulsion, as flame is drawn to flame.

Janet's dark grand face, still fatigued, had become quite calm, and looked up, as she sat, with a humble childlike expression at the thin blond face and slightly sunken gray eyes which now shone with hectic brightness. She might have been taken for an image of passionate strength beaten and worn with conflict; and he for an image of the self-renouncing faith which has soothed that conflict into rest. As he looked at the sweet submissive face, he remembered its look of despairing anguish, and his heart was very full as he turned away from her. "Let me only live to see this work confirmed, and then. . . ."

It was nearly ten o'clock when Mr. Tryan left, but Janet was bent on sending for her mother, so Mrs. Pettifer, as the readiest plan, put on her bonnet and went herself to fetch Mrs. Raynor. The mother had been too long used to expect that every fresh week would be more painful than the last, for Mrs. Pettifer's news to come upon her with the shock of a surprise. Quietly, without any show of distress, she made up a bundle of clothes, and, telling her little maid that she should not return home that night, accompanied Mrs. Pettifer back in silence.

When they entered the parlor, Janet, wearied out, had sunk to sleep in the large chair, which stood with its back to the door. The noise of the opening door disturbed her and she was looking round wonderingly when Mrs. Raynor came up to her chair, and said, "It's your mother, Janet."

"Mother, dear mother!' Janet cried, clasping her closely. "I have not been a good tender child to you, but I *will* be—I will not grieve you any more."

The calmness which had withstood a new sorrow was overcome by a new joy, and the mother burst into tears.

Chapter XX

On Sunday morning the rain had ceased, and Janet, looking out of the bedroom window, saw, above the house-tops, a shining mass of white cloud rolling under the far-away blue sky. It was going to be a lovely April day. The fresh sky, left clear and calm after the long vexation of wind and rain, mingled its mild influence with Janet's new thoughts and prospects. She felt a buoyant courage that surprised herself after the cold crushing weight of despondency which had oppressed her the day before: she could think even of her husband's rage without the old overpowering dread. For a delicious hope—the hope of purification and inward peace—had entered into Janet's soul, and made it springtime there as well as in the outer world.

While her mother was brushing and coiling up her thick black hair—a favorite task, because it seemed to renew the days of her daughter's girlhood—Janet told how she came to send for Mr. Tryan, how she had remembered their meeting at Sally Martin's in the autumn, and had felt an irresistible desire to see him, and tell him her sins and her troubles.

"I see God's goodness now, mother, in ordering it so that we should meet in that way, to overcome my prejudice against him, and make me feel that he was good, and then bringing it back to my mind in the depth of my trouble. You know what foolish things I used to say about him, knowing nothing of him all the while. And yet he was the man who was to give me comfort and help when everything else failed me. It is wonderful how I feel able to speak to him as I never have done to any one before; and how every word he says to me enters my heart, and has a new meaning for me. I think it must be because he has felt life more deeply than others, and has a deeper faith. I believe everything he says at once. His words come to me like rain on the parched ground. It has always seemed to me before as if I could see behind people's words, as one sees behind a screen; but in Mr. Tryan it is his very soul that speaks."

"Well, my dear child, I love and bless him for your sake, if he has given you any comfort. I never believed the harm people said of him, though I had no desire to go and hear him, for I am contented with old-fashioned ways. I had more good teaching than I can practice in reading my Bible at home, and hearing Mr. Crewe at church. But your wants are different, my dear, and we are not all led by the same road. That was certainly good advice of Mr. Tryan's you told me of last night—that we should consult some one that may interfere for you with your husband; and I've been turning it over in my mind while I've been lying awake in the night. I think nobody will do so well as Mr. Benjamin Landor, for we must have a man that knows the law, and that Robert is rather afraid of. And perhaps he could bring about an agreement for you to live apart. Your husband's bound to maintain you, you know; and, if you liked, we could move away from Milby and live somewhere else."

"O, mother, we must do nothing yet; I must think about it a little longer. I have a different feeling this morning from what I had yesterday. Something seems to tell me that I must go back to Robert some time—after a little while. I loved him once better than all the world, and I have never had any children to love. There were things in me that were wrong, and I should like to make up for them if I can."

"Well, my dear, I won't persuade you. Think of it a little longer. But something must be done soon."

"How I wish I had my bonnet, and shawl, and black gown here!" said Janet, after a few minutes' silence. "I should like to go to Paddiford church and hear Mr. Tryan. There would be no fear of my meeting Robert, for he never goes out on a Sunday morning."

"I'm afraid it would not do for me to go to the house and fetch your clothes," said Mrs. Raynor.

"O no, no! I must stay quietly here while you two go to church. I will be Mrs. Pettifer's maid, and get the dinner ready for her by the time she comes back. Dear good woman! She was so tender to me when she took me in, in the night, mother, and all the next day, when I couldn't speak a word to her to thank her."

Chapter XXI

The servants at Dempster's felt some surprise when the morning, noon, and evening of Saturday had passed, and still their mistress did not reappear.

"It's very odd," said Kitty, the housemaid, as she trimmed her next week's cap, while Betty, the middle-aged cook, looked on with folded arms. "Do you think as Mrs. Raynor was ill, and sent for the missis afore we was up?"

"O," said Betty, "if it had been that, she'd ha' been back'ards an' for'ards three or four times afore now; leastways, she'd ha' sent little Ann to let us know."

"There's summat up more nor usal between her an' the master, that you may depend on," said Kitty. "I know those clothes as was lying i' the drawing-room yisterday, when the company was come, meant summat. I shouldn't wonder if that was what they've had a fresh row about. She's p'raps gone away, an's made up her mind not to come back again."

"An' i' the right on't, too," said Betty. "I'd ha' overrun him long afore now, if it had been me. I wouldn't stan' bein' mauled as she is by no husband, not if he was the biggest lord i' the land. It's poor work bein' a wife at that price: I'd sooner be a cook wi'out perkises, an' hev roast, an' boil, an' fry, an' bake all to mind at once. She may well do as she does. I know I'm glad enough of a drop o' summat myself when I'm plagued. I feel very low, like, to-night; I think I shall put my beer i' the saucepan an' warm it."

"What a one you are for warmin' your beer, Betty! I couldn't abide it—nasty bitter stuff!"

"It's fine talkin'; if you was a cook you'd know what belongs to bein' a cook. It's none so nice to hev a sinkin' at your stomach, I can tell you. You wouldn't think so much o' fine ribbins i' your cap then."

"Well, well, Betty, don't be grumpy. Liza Thomson, as is at Phipps's, said to me last Sunday, 'I wonder you'll stay at Dempster's,' she says, 'such goins on as there is.' But I says, 'There's things to put up wi' in ivery place, an' you may change, an' change, an' not better yourself when all's said an' done.' Lors! why, Liza told me herself as Mrs. Phipps was as skinny as skinny i' the kitchen, for all they keep so much company; and as for follyers, she's as cross as a turkey-cock if she finds 'em out. There's nothin' o' that sort i' the missis. How pretty she come an' spoke to Job last Sunday! There isn't a good-natur'der woman i' the world, that's my belief—an' hansome too. I al'ys think there's nobody looks half so well as the missis when she's got her 'air done nice. Lors! I wish I'd got long 'air like her—my 'air's a-comin' off dreadful."

"There'll be fine work to-morrow, I expect," said Betty, "when the master comes home, an' Dawes a-swearin' as he'll niver do a stroke o' work for him again. It'll be good fun if he sets the justice on him for cuttin' him wi' the whip; the master 'll p'raps get his comb cut for once in his life!"

"Why, he was in a temper like a fi-end this morning," said Kitty. "I dare say it was along o' what had happened wi' the missis. We shall hev a pretty house wi' him if she doesn't come back—he'll want to be leatherin' *us,* I shouldn't wonder. He must hev somethin' t' ill-use when he's in a passion."

"I'd tek care he didn't leather me—no, not if he was my husban' ten times o'er; I'd pour hot drippin' on him sooner. But the missis hesn't a sperrit like me. He'll mek her come back, you'll see; he'll come round her somehow. There's no likelihood of her coming back to-night, though; so I should think we might fasten the doors and go to bed when we like."

On Sunday morning, however, Kitty's mind became disturbed by more definite and alarming conjectures about her mistress. While Betty, encouraged by the prospect of unwonted leisure, was sitting down to continue a letter which had long lain unfinished between the leaves of her Bible, Kitty came running into the kitchen and said,

"Lor! Betty, I'm all of a tremble; you might knock me down wi' a feather. I've just looked into the missis's wardrobe, an' there's both her bonnets. She must ha' gone wi'out her bonnet. An' then I remember as her night-clothes wasn't on the bed yisterday mornin'; I thought she'd put 'em away to be washed; but she hedn't, for I've been lookin'. It's my belief he's murdered her, and shut her up i' that closet as he keeps locked al'ys. He's capible on't."

"Lors-ha'-massy, why you'd better run to Mrs. Raynor's an' see if she's there after all. It was p'raps all a lie."

Mrs. Raynor had returned home to give directions to her little maiden, when Kitty, with the elaborate manifestation of alarm which servants delight in, rushed in without knocking, and holding her hands on her heart as if the consequences to that organ were likely to be very serious, said,—

"If you please 'm, is the missis here?"

"No, Kitty; why are you come to ask?"

"Because 'm, she's niver been at home since yisterday mornin', since afore we was up; an' we thought somethin' must ha' happened to her."

"No, don't be frightened, Kitty. Your mistress is quite safe; I know where she is. Is your master at home?"

"No 'm; he went out yisterday mornin', an' said he shouldn't be back afore to-night."

"Well, Kitty, there's nothing the matter with your mistress. You needn't say anything to any one about her being away from home. I shall call presently and fetch her gown and bonnet. She wants them to put on."

Kitty, perceiving there was a mystery she was not to inquire into, returned to Orchard Street, really glad to know that her mistress was safe, but disappointed nevertheless at being told that she was not to be frightened. She was soon followed by Mrs. Raynor in quest of the gown and bonnet. The good mother, on learning that Dempster was not at home, had at once thought that she could gratify Janet's wish to go to Paddiford church.

"See, my dear," she said, as she entered Mrs. Pettifer's parlor; "I've brought you your black clothes. Robert's not at home, and is not coming till this evening. I couldn't find your best black gown, but this will do. I wouldn't bring anything else, you know; but there can't be any objection to my fetching clothes to cover you. You can go to Paddiford church now, if you like; and I will go with you."

"That's a dear mother! Then we'll all three go together. Come and help me to get ready. Good little Mrs. Crewe! It will vex her sadly that I should go to hear Mr. Tryan. But I must kiss her, and make it up with her."

Many eyes were turned on Janet with a look of surprise as she walked up the aisle of Paddiford church. She felt a little tremor at the notice she knew she was exciting, but it was a strong satisfaction to her that she had been able at once to take a step that would let her neighbors know her change of feeling towards Mr. Tryan: she had left herself now no room for proud reluctance or weak hesitation. The walk through the sweet spring air had stimulated all her fresh hopes, all her yearning desires after purity, strength, and peace. She thought she should find a new meaning in the prayers this morning; her full heart, like an overflowing river, wanted those ready-made channels to pour itself into; and then she should hear Mr. Tryan again, and his words would fall on her like precious balm, as they had done last night. There was a liquid brightness in her eyes as they rested on the mere walls, the pews, the weavers and colliers in their Sunday clothes. The commonest things seemed to touch the spring of love within her, just as, when we are suddenly released from an acute absorbing bodily pain, our heart and senses leap out in new freedom; we think even the noise of streets harmonious, and are ready to hug the tradesman who is wrapping up our change. A door had been opened in Janet's cold dark prison of self-despair, and the golden light of morning was pouring in its slanting beams through the blessed opening. There was sunlight in the world; there was a divine love caring for her; it had given her an earnest of good things; it had been preparing comfort for her in the very moment when she had thought herself most forsaken.

Mr. Tryan might well rejoice when his eye rested on her as he entered his desk; but he rejoiced with trembling. He could not look at the sweet hopeful face without remembering its yesterday's look of agony; and there was the possibility that that look might return.

Janet's appearance at church was greeted not only by wondering eyes, but by kind hearts, and after the service several of Mr. Tryan's hearers with whom she had been on cold terms of late, contrived to come up to her and take her by the hand.

"Mother," said Miss Linnet, "do let us go and speak to Mrs. Dempster. I'm sure there's a great change in her mind towards Mr. Tryan. I noticed how eagerly she listened to the sermon, and she's come with Mrs. Pettifer, you see. We ought to go and give her a welcome among us."

"Why, my dear, we've never spoke friendly these five year. You know she's been as haughty as anything since I quarreled with her husband. However, let bygones be bygones: I've no grudge again' the poor thing, more particular as she must ha' flew in her husband's face to come an' hear Mr. Tryan. Yis, let us go an' speak to her."

The friendly words and looks touched Janet a little too keenly, and Mrs. Pettifer wisely hurried her home by the least-frequented road. When they reached home, a violent fit of weeping, followed by continuous lassitude, showed that the emotions of the morning had overstrained her nerves. She was suffering, too, from the absence of the long-accustomed stimulant which she had promised Mr. Tryan not to touch again. The poor thing was conscious of this, and dreaded her own weakness, as the victim of intermittent insanity dreads the oncoming of the old illusion.

"Mother," she whispered, when Mrs. Raynor urged her to lie down and rest all the afternoon, that she might be the better prepared to see Mr. Tryan in the evening—"mother, don't let me have anything if I ask for it."

In the mother's mind there was the same anxiety, and in her it was mingled with another fear—the fear lest Janet, in her present excited state of mind, should take some premature step in relation to her husband, which might lead back to all the former troubles. The hint she had thrown out in the morning of her wish to return to him after a time, showed a new eagerness for difficult duties, that only made the long-saddened sober mother tremble.

But as evening approached, Janet's morning heroism all forsook her: her imagination, influenced by physical depression as well as by mental habits, was haunted by the vision of her husband's return home, and she began to shudder with the yesterday's dread. She heard him calling her, she saw him going to her mother's to look for her, she felt sure he would find her out, and burst in upon her.

"Pray, pray, don't leave me, don't go to church," she said to Mrs. Pettifer. "You and mother both stay with me till Mr. Tryan comes."

At twenty minutes past six the church bells were ringing for the evening service, and soon the congregation was streaming along Orchard Street in the mellow sunset. The street opened towards the west. The red half-sunken sun shed a solemn splendor on the everyday houses, and crimsoned the windows of Dempster's projecting upper story.

Suddenly a loud murmur arose and spread along the stream of church-goers, and one group after another paused and looked backward. At the far end of the street, men, accompanied by a miscellaneous group of onlookers, are slowly carrying something—a body stretched on a door. Slowly they pass along the middle of the street, lined all the way with awe-struck faces, till they turn aside and pause in the red sunlight before Dempster's door.

It is Dempster's body. No one knows whether he is alive or dead.

Chapter XXII

It was probably a hard saying to the Pharisees, that "there is more joy in heaven over one sinner that repenteth, than over ninety and nine just persons that need no repentance." And certain ingenious philosophers of our own day must surely take offense at a joy so entirely out of correspondence with arithmetical proportion. But a heart that has been taught by its own sore struggles to bleed for the woes of another—that has "learned pity through suffering"—is likely to find very imperfect satisfaction in the "balance of happiness," "doctrine of compensations," and other short and easy methods of obtaining thorough complacency in the presence of pain; and for such a heart that saying will not be altogether dark. The emotions, I have observed, are but slightly influenced by arithmetical considerations: the mother, when her sweet lisping little ones have all been taken from her one after another, and she is hanging over her last dead babe, finds small consolation in the fact that the tiny dimpled corpse is but one of a necessary average, and that a thousand other babes brought into the world at the same time are doing well, and are likely to live; and if you stood beside that mother—if you knew her pang and shared it—it is probable you would be equally unable to see a ground of complacency in statistics.

Doubtless a complacency resting on that basis is highly rational; but emotion, I fear, is obstinately irrational: it insists on caring for individuals; it absolutely refuses to adopt the quantitative view of human anguish, and to admit that thirteen happy lives are a set-off against twelve miserable lives, which leaves a clear balance on the side of satisfaction. This is the inherent imbecility of feeling, and one must be a great philosopher to have got quite clear of all that, and to have emerged into the serene air of pure intellect, in which it is evident that individuals really exist for no other purpose than that abstractions may be drawn from them—abstractions that may rise from heaps of ruined lives like the sweet savor of a sacrifice in the nostrils of philosophers, and of a philosophic Deity. And so it comes to pass that for the man who knows sympathy because he has known sorrow, that old, old saying about the joy of angels over the repentant sinner outweighing their joy over the ninety-nine just, has a meaning which does not jar with the language of his own heart. It only tells him, that for angels too there is a transcendent value in human pain, which refuses to be settled by equations; that the eyes of angels too are turned away from the serene happiness of the righteous to bend with yearning pity on the poor erring soul wandering in the desert where no water is; that for angels too the misery of one casts so tremendous a shadow as to eclipse the bliss of ninety-nine.

Mr. Tryan had gone through the initiation of suffering: it is no wonder, then, that Janet's restoration was the work that lay nearest his heart; and that, weary as he was in body when he entered the vestry after the evening service, he was impatient to fulfill the promise of seeing her. His experience enabled him to divine—what was the fact—that the hopefulness of the morning would be followed by a return of depression and discouragement, and his sense of the inward and outward difficulties in the way of her restoration was so keen, that he could only find relief from the foreboding it excited by lifting up his heart in prayer. There are unseen elements which often frustrate our wisest calculations—which raise up the sufferer from the edge of the grave, contradicting the prophecies of the clear-sighted physician, and fulfilling the blind clinging hopes of affection; such unseen elements Mr. Tryan called the Divine Will, and filled up the margin of ignorance which surrounds all our knowledge with the feelings of trust and resignation. Perhaps the profoundest philosophy could hardly fill it up better.

His mind was occupied in this way as he was absently taking off his gown, when Mr. Landor startled him by entering the vestry and asking abruptly,

"Have you heard the news about Dempster?"

"No," said Mr. Tryan, anxiously; "what is it?"

"He has been thrown out of his gig in the Bridge Way, and he was taken up for dead. They were carrying him home as we were coming to church, and I stayed behind to see what I could do. I went in to speak to Mrs. Dempster, and prepare her a little, but she was not at home. Dempster is not dead, however; he was stunned with the fall. Pilgrim came in a few minutes, and he says the right leg is broken in two places. It's likely to be a terrible case, with his state of body. It seems he was more drunk than usual, and they say he came along the Bridge Way flogging his horse like a madman, till at last it gave a sudden wheel, and he was pitched out. The servants said they didn't know where Mrs. Dempster was: she had been away from home since yesterday morning; but Mrs. Raynor knew."

"I know where she is," said Mr. Tryan; "but I think it will be better for her not to be told of this just yet."

"Ah, that was what Pilgrim said, and so I didn't go round to Mrs. Raynor's. He said it would be all the better if Mrs. Dempster could be kept out of the house for the present. Do you know if anything new has happened between Dempster and his wife lately? I was surprised to hear of her being at Paddiford church this morning."

"Yes, something has happened; but I believe she is anxious that the particulars of his behavior towards her should not be known. She is at Mrs. Pettifer's—there is no reason for concealing that, since what has happened to her husband; and yesterday, when she was in very deep trouble, she sent for me. I was very thankful she did so: I believe a great change of feeling has begun in her. But she is at present in that excitable state of mind—she has been shaken by so many painful emotions during the last two days, that I think it would be better, for this evening at least, to guard her from a new shock, if possible. But I am going now to call upon her, and I shall see how she is."

"Mr. Tryan," said Mr. Jerome, who had entered during the dialogue and had been standing by listening with a distressed face, "I shall tek it as a favor if you'll let me know if iver there's anything I can do for Mrs. Dempster. Eh, dear, what a world this is! I think I see 'em fifteen 'ear ago—as happy a young couple as iver was; and now, what it's all come to! I was in a hurry, like, to punish Dempster for pessecutin', but there was a stronger hand at work nor mine."

"Yes, Mr. Jerome; but don't let us rejoice in punishment, even when the hand of God alone inflicts it. The best of us are but poor wretches just saved from shipwreck: can we feel anything but awe and pity when we see a fellow-passenger swallowed by the waves?"

"Right, right, Mr. Tryan. I'm over hot an' hasty, that I am. But I beg on you to tell Mrs. Dempster—I mean, in course, when you've an opportunity—tell her she's a friend at the White House as she may send for any hour o' the day."

"Yes; I shall have an opportunity, I dare say, and I will remember your wish. I think," continued Mr. Tryan, turning to Mr. Landor, "I had better see Mr. Pilgrim on my way, and learn what is exactly the state of things by this time. What do you think?"

"By all means: if Mrs. Dempster is to know, there's no one can break the news to her so well as you. I'll walk with you to Dempster's door. I dare say Pilgrim is there still. Come, Mr. Jerome, you've got to go our way too, to fetch your horse."

Mr. Pilgrim was in the passage giving some directions to his assistant, when, to his surprise, he saw Mr. Tryan enter. They shook hands; for Mr. Pilgrim, never having joined the party of the Anti-Tryanites, had no ground for resisting the growing conviction, that the Evangelical curate was really a good fellow, though he was a fool for not taking better care of himself.

"Why, I didn't expect to see you in your old enemy's quarters," he said to Mr. Tryan. "However, it will be a good while before poor Dempster shows any fight again."

"I came on Mrs. Dempster's account," said Mr. Tryan. "She is staying at Mrs. Pettifer's; she has had a great shock from some severe domestic trouble lately, and I think it will be wise to defer telling her of this dreadful event for a short time."

"Why, what has been up, eh?" said Mr. Pilgrim, whose curiosity was at once awakened. "She used to be no friend of yours. Has there been some split between them? It's a new thing for her to turn round on him."

"O, merely an exaggeration of scenes that must often have happened before. But the question now is, whether you think there is any immediate danger of her husband's death; for in that case I think, from what I have observed of her feelings, she would be pained afterwards to have been kept in ignorance."

"Well, there's no telling in these cases, you know. I don't apprehend speedy death, and it is not absolutely impossible that we may bring him round again. At present he's in a state of apoplectic stupor; but if that subsides, delirium is almost sure to supervene, and we shall have some painful scenes. It's one of those complicated cases in which the delirium is likely to be of the worst kind—meningitis and delirium tremens together—and we may have a good deal of trouble with him. If Mrs. Dempster were told, I should say it would be desirable to persuade her to remain out of the house at present. She could do no good, you know. I've got nurses."

"Thank you," said Mr. Tryan. "That is what I wanted to know. Good-bye."

When Mrs. Pettifer opened the door for Mr. Tryan, he told her in few words what had happened, and begged her to take an opportunity of letting Mrs. Raynor know, that they might, if possible, concur in preventing a premature or sudden disclosure of the event to Janet.

"Poor thing!" said Mrs. Pettifer. "She's not fit to hear any bad news; she's very low this evening—worn out with feeling; and she's not had anything to keep her up, as she's been used to. She seems frightened at the thought of being tempted to take it."

"Thank God for it; that fear is her greatest security."

When Mr. Tryan entered the parlor this time, Janet was again awaiting him eagerly, and her pale sad face was lighted up with a smile as she rose to meet him. But the next moment she said, with a look of anxiety,

"How very ill and tired you look! You have been working so hard all day, and yet you are come to talk to me. O, you are wearing yourself out. I must go and ask Mrs. Pettifer to come and make you have some supper. But this is my mother; you have not seen her before, I think."

While Mr. Tryan was speaking to Mrs. Raynor, Janet hurried out, and he, seeing that this good-natured thoughtfulness on his behalf would help to counteract her depression, was not inclined to oppose her wish, but accepted the supper Mrs. Pettifer offered him, quietly talking the while about a clothing club he was going to establish in Paddiford, and the want of provident habits among the poor.

Presently, however, Mrs. Raynor said she must go home for an hour, to see how her little maiden was going on, and Mrs. Pettifer left the room with her to take the opportunity of telling her what had happened to Dempster. When Janet was left alone with Mr. Tryan, she said,

"I feel so uncertain what to do about my husband. I am so weak—my feelings change so from hour to hour. This morning, when I felt so hopeful and happy, I thought I should like to go back to him, and try to make up for what has been wrong in me. I thought, now God would help me, and I should have you to teach and advise me, and I could bear the troubles that would come. But since then—all this afternoon and evening—I have had the same feelings I used to have, the same dread of his anger and cruelty, and it seems to me as if I should never be able to bear it without falling into the same sins, and doing just what I did before. Yet, if it were settled that I should live apart from him, I know it would always be a load on my mind that I had shut myself out from going back to him. It seems a dreadful thing in life, when any one has been so near to one as a husband for fifteen years, to part and be nothing to each other any more. Surely that is a very strong tie, and I feel as if my duty can never lie quite away from it. It is very difficult to know what to do: what ought I to do?"

"I think it will be well not to take any decisive step yet. Wait until your mind is calmer. You might remain with your mother for a little while; I think you have no real ground for fearing any annoyance from your husband at present; he has put himself too much in the wrong; he will very likely leave you unmolested for some time. Dismiss this difficult question from your mind just now, if you can. Every new day may bring you new grounds for decision, and what is most needful for your health of mind is repose from that haunting anxiety about the future which has been preying on you. Cast yourself on God, and trust that He will direct you; He will make your duty clear to you, if you wait submissively on Him."

"Yes; I will wait a little, as you tell me. I will go to my mother's tomorrow, and pray to be guided rightly. You will pray for me, too."

Chapter XXIII

The next morning Janet was so much calmer, and at breakfast spoke so decidedly of going to her mother's, that Mrs. Pettifer and Mrs. Raynor agreed it would be wise to let her know by degrees what had befallen her husband, since as soon as she went out there would be danger of her meeting some one who would betray the fact. But Mrs. Raynor thought it would be well first to call at Dempster's, and ascertain how he was: so she said to Janet,

"My dear, I'll go home first, and see to things, and get your room ready. You needn't come yet, you know. I shall be back again in an hour or so, and we can go together."

"O no," said Mrs. Pettifer. "Stay with me till evening. I shall be lost without you. You needn't go till quite evening."

Janet had dipped into the *Life of Henry Martyn,* which Mrs. Pettifer had from the Paddiford Lending Library, and her interest was so arrested by that pathetic missionary story, that she readily acquiesced in both propositions, and Mrs. Raynor set out.

She had been gone more than an hour, and it was nearly twelve o'clock, when Janet put down her book; and after sitting meditatively for some minutes with her eyes unconsciously fixed on the opposite wall, she rose, went to her bedroom, and, hastily putting on her bonnet and shawl, came down to Mrs. Pettifer, who was busy in the kitchen.

"Mrs. Pettifer," she said, "tell mother, when she comes back, I'm gone to see what is become of those poor Lakins in Butcher Lane. I know they're half starving, and I've neglected them so, lately. And then, I think, I'll go on to Mrs. Crewe. I want to see the dear little woman, and tell her myself about my going to hear Mr. Tryan. She won't feel it half so much if I tell her myself."

"Won't you wait till your mother comes, or put it off till to-morrow?" said Mrs. Pettifer, alarmed. "You'll hardly be back in time for dinner, if you get talking to Mrs. Crewe. And you'll have to pass by your husband's, you know; and yesterday, you were so afraid of seeing him."

"O, Robert will be shut up at the office now, if he's not gone out of the town. I must go—I feel I must be doing something for some one—not be a mere useless log any longer. I've been reading about that wonderful Henry Martyn; he's just like Mr. Tryan—wearing himself out for other people, and I sit thinking of nothing but myself. I *must* go. Good-bye; I shall be back soon."

She ran off before Mrs. Pettifer could utter another word of dissuasion, leaving the good woman in considerable anxiety lest this new impulse of Janet's should frustrate all precautions to save her from a sudden shock.

Janet, having paid her visit in Butcher Lane, turned again into Orchard Street on her way to Mrs. Crewe's, and was thinking, rather sadly, that her mother's economical housekeeping would leave no abundant surplus to be sent to the hungry Lakins, when she saw Mr. Pilgrim in advance of her on the other side of the street. He was walking at a rapid pace, and when he reached Dempster's door he turned and entered without knocking.

Janet was startled. Mr. Pilgrim would never enter in that way unless there were some one very ill in the house. It was her husband; she felt certain of it at once. Something had happened to him. Without a moment's pause, she ran across the street, opened the door and entered. There was no one in the passage. The dining-room door was wide open—no one was there. Mr. Pilgrim, then, was already upstairs. She rushed up at once to Dempster's room—her own room. The door was open, and she paused in pale horror at the sight before her, which seemed to stand out only with the more appalling distinctness because the noonday light was darkened to twilight in the chamber.

Two strong nurses were using their utmost force to hold Dempster in bed, while the medical assistant was applying a sponge to his head, and Mr. Pilgrim was busy adjusting some apparatus in the background. Dempster's face was purple and swollen, his eyes dilated, and fixed with a look of dire terror on something he seemed to see approaching him from the iron closet. He trembled violently, and struggled as if to jump out of bed.

"Let me go, let me go," he said in a loud, hoarse whisper; "she's coming. . . . she's cold. . . . she's dead. . . . she'll strangle me with her black hair. Ah!" he shrieked aloud, "her hair is all serpents. . . . they're black serpents. . . . they hiss. . . . they hiss. . . . let me go. . . . let me go. . . . she wants to drag me with her cold arms. . . . her arms are serpents. . . . they are great white serpents. . . . they'll twine round me. . . . she wants to drag me into the cold water. . . . her bosom is cold. . . . it is black. . . . it is all serpents. . . ."

"No, Robert," Janet cried, in tones of yearning pity, rushing to the side of the bed, and stretching out her arms towards him, "no, here is Janet. She is not dead—she forgives you."

Dempster's maddened senses seemed to receive some new impression from her appearance. The terror gave way to rage.

"Ha! you sneaking hypocrite!" he burst out in a grating voice, "you threaten me. . . . you mean to have your revenge on me, do you? Do your worst! I've got the law on my side. . . . I know the law. . . . I'll hunt you down like a hare. . . . prove it. . . . prove that I was tampered with. . . . prove that I took the money. . . . prove it. . . . you can prove nothing. . . . you damned psalm-singing maggots! I'll make a fire under you, and smoke off the whole pack of you. . . . I'll sweep you up. . . . I'll grind you to powder. . . . small powder. . . . (here his voice dropped to a low tone of shuddering disgust). . . . powder on the bedclothes. . . . running about. . . . black lice. . . . they are coming in swarms. . . . Janet! come and take them away. . . . curse you! why don't you come? Janet!"

Poor Janet was kneeling by the bed with her face buried in her hands. She almost wished her worst moment back again rather than this. It seemed as if her husband was already imprisoned in misery, and she could not reach him—his ear deaf for ever to the sounds of love and forgiveness. His sins had made a hard crust round his soul; her pitying voice could not pierce it.

"Not there, isn't she?" he went on in a defiant tone. "Why do you ask me where she is? I'll have every drop of yellow blood out of your veins if you come questioning me. Your blood is yellow. . . . in your purse. . . . running out of your purse. . . . What! you're changing it into toads, are you? They're crawling. . . . they're flying. . . . they're flying about my head. . . . the toads are flying about. Ostler! ostler! bring out my gig. . . . bring it out, you lazy beast. . . . ha! you'll follow me, will you?. . . . you'll fly about my head. . . . you've got fiery tongues. . . . Ostler! curse you! why don't you come? Janet! come and take the toads away. . . . Janet!"

This last time he uttered her name with such a shriek of terror, that Janet involuntarily started up from her knees, and stood as if petrified by the horrible vibration. Dempster stared wildly in silence for some moments; then he spoke again in a hoarse whisper:—

"Dead. . . . is she dead? *She* did it, then. She buried herself in the iron chest. . . . she left her clothes out, though. . . . she isn't dead. . . . why do you pretend she's dead?. . . . she's coming. . . . she's coming out of the iron closet. . . . there are the black serpents. . . . stop her. . . . let me go. . . . stop her. . . . she wants to drag me away into the cold black water. . . . her bosom is black. . . . it is all serpents. . . . they are getting longer. . . . the great white serpents are getting longer. . . ."

Here Mr. Pilgrim came forward with the apparatus to bind him, but Dempster's struggles became more and more violent. "Ostler! ostler!" he shouted, "bring out the gig. . . . give me the whip!"—and bursting loose from the strong hands that held him, he began to flog the bed-clothes furiously with his right arm.

"Get along, you lame brute!—sc—sc—sc! that's it! there you go! They think they've outwitted me, do they? The sneaking idiots! I'll be up with them by-and-by. I'll make them say the Lord's Prayer backwards. . . . I'll pepper them so that the devil shall eat them raw. . . . sc—sc—sc—we shall see who'll be the winner yet . . . . get along, you damned limping beast. . . . I'll lay your back open. . . . I'll. . . ."

He raised himself with a stronger effort than ever to flog the bed-clothes, and fell back in convulsions. Janet gave a scream, and sank on her knees again. She thought he was dead.

As soon as Mr. Pilgrim was able to give her a moment's attention, he came to her, and, taking her by the arm, attempted to draw her gently out of the room.

"Now, my dear Mrs. Dempster, let me persuade you not to remain in the room at present. We shall soon relieve these symptoms, I hope; it is nothing but the delirium that ordinarily attends such cases."

"O, what is the matter? what brought it on?"

"He fell out of the gig; the right leg is broken. It is a terrible accident, and I don't disguise that there is considerable danger attending it, owing to the state of the brain. But Mr. Dempster has a strong constitution, you know: in a few days these symptoms may be allayed, and he may do well. Let me beg of you to keep out of the room at present: you can do no good until Mr. Dempster is better, and able to know you. But you ought not to be alone; let me advise you to have Mrs. Raynor with you."

"Yes, I will send for mother. But you must not object to my being in the room. I shall be very quiet now, only just at first the shock was so great; I knew nothing about it. I can help the nurses a great deal; I can put the cold things to his head. He may be sensible for a moment, and know me. Pray do not say any more against it: my heart is set on being with him."

Mr. Pilgrim gave way, and Janet, having sent for her mother and put off her bonnet and shawl, returned to take her place by the side of her husband's bed.

Chapter XXIV

Day after day, with only short intervals of rest, Janet kept her place in that sad chamber. No wonder the sick-room and the lazaretto have so often been a refuge from the tossings of intellectual doubt—a place of repose for the worn and wounded spirit. Here is a duty about which all creeds and all philosophies are at one: here, at least, the conscience will not be dogged by doubt, the benign impulse will not be checked by adverse theory; here you may begin to act without settling one preliminary question. To moisten the sufferer's parched lips through the long night-watches, to bear up the drooping head, to lift the helpless limbs, to divine the want that can find no utterance beyond the feeble motion of the hand or beseeching glance of the eye—these are offices that demand no self-questionings, no casuistry, no assent to propositions, no weighing of consequences. Within the four walls where the stir and glare of the world are shut out, and every voice is subdued—where a human being lies prostrate, thrown on the tender mercies of his fellow, the moral relation of man to man is reduced to its utmost clearness and simplicity: bigotry cannot confuse it, theory cannot pervert it, passion, awed into quiescence, can neither pollute nor perturb it. As we bend over the sick-bed, all the forces of our nature rush towards the channels of pity, of patience, and of love, and sweep down the miserable choking drift of our quarrels, our debates, our would-be wisdom, and our clamorous selfish desires. This blessing of serene freedom from the importunities of opinion lies in all simple direct acts of mercy, and is one source of that sweet calm which is often felt by the watcher in the sick-room, even when the duties there are of a hard and terrible kind.

Something of that benign result was felt by Janet during her tendance in her husband's chamber. When the first heart-piercing hours were over—when her horror at his delirium was no longer fresh, she began to be conscious of her relief from the burden of decision as to her future course. The question that agitated her, about returning to her husband, had been solved in a moment; and this illness, after all, might be the herald of another blessing, just as that dreadful midnight when she stood an outcast in cold and darkness, had been followed by the dawn of a new hope. Robert would get better; this illness might alter him; he would be a long time feeble, needing help, walking with a crutch, perhaps. She would wait on him with such tenderness, such all-forgiving love, that the old harshness and cruelty must melt away for ever under the heart-sunshine she would pour around him. Her bosom heaved at the thought, and delicious tears fell. Janet's was a nature in which hatred and revenge could find no place; the long bitter years drew half their bitterness from her ever-living remembrance of the too short years of love that went before; and the thought that her husband would ever put her hand to his lips again, and recall the days when they sat on the grass together, and he laid scarlet poppies on her black hair, and called her his gypsy queen, seemed to send a tide of loving oblivion over all the harsh and stony space they had traversed since. The Divine Love that had already shone upon her would be with her; she would lift up her soul continually for help; Mr. Tryan, she knew, would pray for her. If she felt herself failing, she would confess it to him at once; if her feet began to slip, there was that stay for her to cling to. O she could never be drawn back into that cold damp vault of sin and despair again; she had felt the morning sun, she had tasted the sweet pure air of trust and penitence and submission.

These were the thoughts passing through Janet's mind as she hovered about her husband's bed, and these were the hopes she poured out to Mr. Tryan when he called to see her. It was so evident that they were strengthening her in her new struggle—they shed such a glow of calm enthusiasm over her face as she spoke of them, that Mr. Tryan could not bear to throw on them the chill of premonitory doubts, though a previous conversation he had had with Mr. Pilgrim had convinced him that there was not the faintest probability of Dempster's recovery. Poor Janet did not know the significance of the changing symptoms, and when, after the lapse of a week, the delirium began to lose some of its violence, and to be interrupted by longer and longer intervals of stupor, she tried to think that these might be steps on the way to recovery, and she shrank from questioning Mr. Pilgrim, lest he should confirm the fears that began to get predominance in her mind. But before many days were past, he thought it right not to allow her to blind herself any longer. One day—it was just about noon, when bad news always seems most sickening—he led her from her husband's chamber into the opposite drawing-room, where Mrs. Raynor was sitting, and said to her, in that low tone of sympathetic feeling which sometimes gave a sudden air of gentleness to this rough man,—

"My dear Mrs. Dempster, it is right in these cases, you know, to be prepared for the worst. I think I shall be saving you pain by preventing you from entertaining any false hopes, and Mr. Dempster's state is now such that I fear we must consider recovery impossible. The affection of the brain might not have been hopeless, but, you see, there is a terrible complication; and I am grieved to say, the broken limb is mortifying."

Janet listened with a sinking heart. That future of love and forgiveness would never come, then: he was going out of her sight for ever, where her pity could never reach him. She turned cold, and trembled.

"But do you think he will die," she said, "without ever coming to himself? without ever knowing me?"

"One cannot say that with certainty. It is not impossible that the cerebral oppression may subside, and that he may become conscious. If there is anything you would wish to be said or done in that case, it would be well to be prepared. I should think," Mr. Pilgrim continued, turning to Mrs. Raynor, "Mr. Dempster's affairs are likely to be in order—his will is. . . ."

"O, I wouldn't have him troubled about those things," interrupted Janet; "he has no relations but quite distant ones—no one but me. I wouldn't take up the time with that. I only want to. . . ."

She was unable to finish; she felt her sobs rising, and left the room. "O God!" she said inwardly, "is not Thy love greater than mine? Have mercy on him! have mercy on him!"

This happened on Wednesday, ten days after the fatal accident. By the following Sunday, Dempster was in a state of rapidly increasing prostration; and when Mr. Pilgrim, who, in turn with his assistant, had slept in the house from the beginning, came in, about half-past ten, as usual, he scarcely believed that the feebly struggling life would last out till morning. For the last few days he had been administering stimulants to relieve the exhaustion which had succeeded the alternations of delirium and stupor. This slight office was all that now remained to be done for the patient; so at eleven o'clock Mr. Pilgrim went to bed, having given directions to the nurse, and desired her to call him if any change took place, or if Mrs. Dempster desired his presence.

Janet could not be persuaded to leave the room. She was yearning and watching for a moment in which her husband's eyes would rest consciously upon her, and he would know that she had forgiven him.

How changed he was since that terrible Monday, nearly a fortnight ago! He lay motionless, but for the irregular breathing that stirred his broad chest and thick muscular neck. His features were no longer purple and swollen; they were pale, sunken, and haggard. A cold perspiration stood in beads on the protuberant forehead, and on the wasted hands stretched motionless on the bed-clothes It was better to see the hands so, than convulsively picking the air, as they had been a week ago.

Janet sat on the edge of the bed through the long hours of candle-light, watching the unconscious half-closed eyes, wiping the perspiration from the brow and cheeks, and keeping her left hand on the cold unanswering right hand that lay beside her on the bed-clothes. She was almost as pale as her dying husband, and there were dark lines under her eyes, for this was the third night since she had taken off her clothes; but the eager straining gaze of her dark eyes, and the acute sensibility that lay in every line about her mouth, made a strange contrast with the blank unconsciousness and emaciated animalism of the face she was watching.

There was profound stillness in the house. She heard no sound but her husband's breathing and the ticking of the watch on the mantelpiece. The candle, placed high up, shed a soft light down on the one object she cared to see. There was a smell of brandy in the room; it was given to her husband from time to time; but this smell, which at first had produced in her a faint shuddering sensation, was now become indifferent to her; she did not even perceive it; she was too unconscious of herself to feel either temptations or accusations. She only felt that the husband of her youth was dying; far, far out of her reach, as if she were standing helpless on the shore, while he was sinking in the black storm-waves; she only yearned for one moment in which she might satisfy the deep forgiving pity of her soul by one look of love, one word of tenderness.

Her sensations and thoughts were so persistent that she could not measure the hours, and it was a surprise to her when the nurse put out the candle, and let in the faint morning light. Mrs. Raynor, anxious about Janet, was already up, and now brought in some fresh coffee for her; and Mr. Pilgrim, having awaked, had hurried on his clothes, and was come in to see how Dempster was.

This change from candle-light to morning, this recommencement of the same round of things that had happened yesterday, was a discouragement rather than a relief to Janet. She was more conscious of her chill weariness; the new light thrown on her husband's face seemed to reveal the still work that death had been doing through the night; she felt her last lingering hope that he would ever know her again forsake her.

But now Mr. Pilgrim, having felt the pulse, was putting some brandy in a tea-spoon between Dempster's lips; the brandy went down, and his breathing became freer. Janet noticed the change, and her heart beat faster as she leaned forward to watch him. Suddenly a slight movement, like the passing away of a shadow, was visible in his face, and he opened his eyes full on Janet.

It was almost like meeting him again on the resurrection morning, after the night of the grave.

"Robert, do you know me?"

He kept his eyes fixed on her, and there was a faintly perceptible motion of the lips, as if he wanted to speak.

But the moment of speech was for ever gone—the moment for asking pardon of her, if he wanted to ask it. Could he read the full forgiveness that was written in her eyes? She never knew; for, as she was bending to kiss him, the thick veil of death fell between them, and her lips touched a corpse.

Chapter XXV

The faces looked very hard and unmoved that surrounded Dempster's grave, while old Mr. Crewe read the burial-service in his low, broken voice. The pall-bearers were such men as Mr. Pittman, Mr. Lowme, and Mr. Budd—men whom Dempster had called his friends while he was in life; and worldly faces never look so worldly as at a funeral. They have the same effect of grating incongruity as the sound of a coarse voice breaking the solemn silence of night.

The one face that had sorrow in it was covered by a thick crape-veil, and the sorrow was suppressed and silent. No one knew how deep it was; for the thought in most of her neighbors' minds was, that Mrs. Dempster could hardly have had better fortune than to lose a bad husband who had left her the compensation of a good income. They found it difficult to conceive that her husband's death could be felt by her otherwise than as a deliverance. The person who was most thoroughly convinced that Janet's grief was deep and real, was Mr. Pilgrim, who in general was not at all weakly given to a belief in disinterested feeling.

"That woman has a tender heart," he was frequently heard to observe in his morning rounds about this time. "I used to think there was a great deal of palaver in her, but you may depend upon it there's no pretense about her. If he'd been the kindest husband in the world she couldn't have felt more. There's a great deal of good in Mrs. Dempster—a great deal of good."

"*I* always said so," was Mrs. Lowme's reply, when he made the observation to her; "she was always so very full of pretty attentions to me when I was ill. But they tell me now she's turned Tryanite; if that's it we shan't agree again. It's very inconsistent in her, I think, turning round in that way, after being the foremost to laugh at the Tryanite cant, and especially in a woman of her habits; she should cure herself of *them* before she pretends to be over-religious."

"Well, I think she means to cure herself, do you know," said Mr. Pilgrim, whose goodwill towards Janet was just now quite above that temperate point at which he could indulge his feminine patients with a little judicious detraction. "I feel sure she has not taken any stimulants all through her husband's illness; and, she has been constantly in the way of them. I can see she sometimes suffers a good deal of depression for want of them—it shows all the more resolution in her. Those cures are rare; but I've known them happen sometimes with people of strong will.

Mrs. Lowme took an opportunity of retailing Mr. Pilgrim's conversation to Mrs. Phipps, who, as a victim of Pratt and plethora, could rarely enjoy that pleasure at first-hand. Mrs. Phipps was a woman of decided opinions, though of wheezy utterance.

"For my part," she remarked, "I'm glad to hear there's any likelihood of improvement in Mrs. Dempster, but I think the way things have turned out seems to show that she was more to blame than people thought she was; else, why should she feel so much about her husband? And Dempster, I understand, has left his wife pretty nearly all his property to do as she likes with; *that* isn't behaving like such a very bad husband. I don't believe Mrs. Dempster can have had so much provocation as they pretended. I've known husbands who've laid plans for tormenting their wives when they're underground—tying up their money and hindering them from marrying again. Not that *I* should ever wish to marry again; I think one husband in one's life is enough in all conscience";—here she threw a fierce glance at the amiable Mr. Phipps, who was innocently delighting himself with the *facetiae* in the *Rotherby Guardian,* and thinking the editor must be a droll fellow—"but it's aggravating to be tied up in that way. Why, they say Mrs. Dempster will have as good as six-hundred a year at least. A fine thing for her, that was a poor girl without a farthing to her fortune. It's well if she doesn't make ducks and drakes of it somehow."

Mrs. Phipps's view of Janet, however, was far from being the prevalent one in Milby. Even neighbors who had no strong personal interest in her, could hardly see the noble-looking woman in her widow's dress, with a sad sweet gravity in her face, and not be touched with fresh admiration for her—and not feel, at least vaguely, that she had entered on a new life in which it was a sort of desecration to allude to the painful past. And the old friends who had a real regard for her, but whose cordiality had been repelled or chilled of late years, now came round her with hearty demonstrations of affection. Mr. Jerome felt that his happiness had a substantial addition now he could once more call on that "nice little woman Mrs. Dempster," and think of her with rejoicing instead of sorrow. The Pratts lost no time in returning to the footing of old-established friendship with Janet and her mother; and Miss Pratt felt it incumbent on her, on all suitable occasions, to deliver a very emphatic approval of the remarkable strength of mind she understood Mrs. Dempster to be exhibiting. The Miss Linnets were eager to meet Mr. Tryan's wishes by greeting Janet as one who was likely to be a sister in religious feeling and good works; and Mrs. Linnet was so agreeably surprised by the fact that Dempster had left his wife the money "in that handsome way, to do what she liked with it," that she even included Dempster himself, and his villainous discovery of the flaw in her title to Pye's Croft, in her magnanimous oblivion of past offenses. She and Mrs. Jerome agreed over a friendly cup of tea that there were "a maeny husbands as was very fine spoken an' all that, an' yit all the while kep' a will locked up from you, as tied you up as tight as aenything. I assure *you,*" Mrs. Jerome continued, dropping her voice in a confidential manner, "I know no more to this day about Mr. Jerome's will, nor the child as is unborn. I've no fears about a income—I'm well awear' Mr. Jerome 'ud niver leave me stret for that; but I should like t' hev a thousand or two at my own disposial; it meks a widder a deal more looked on."

Perhaps this ground of respect to widows might not be entirely without its influence on the Milby mind, and might do something towards conciliating those more aristocratic acquaintances of Janet's, who would otherwise have been inclined to take the severest view of her apostasy towards Evangelicalism. Errors look so very ugly in persons of small means—one feels they are taking quite a liberty in going astray; whereas people of fortune may naturally indulge in a few delinquencies. "They've got the money for it," as the girl said of her mistress who had made herself ill with pickled salmon. However it may have been, there was not an acquaintance of Janet's, in Milby, that did not offer her civilities in the early days of her widowhood. Even the severe Mrs. Phipps was not an exception; for heaven knows what would become of our sociality if we never visited people we speak ill of: we should live, like Egyptian hermits, in crowded solitude.

Perhaps the attentions most grateful to Janet were those of her old friend Mrs. Crewe, whose attachment to her favorite proved quite too strong for any resentment she might be supposed to feel on the score of Mr. Tryan. The little deaf old lady couldn't do without her accustomed visitor, whom she had seen grow up from child to woman, always so willing to chat with her and tell her all the news, though she *was* deaf; while other people thought it tiresome to shout in her ear, and irritated her by recommending ear-trumpets of various construction.

All this friendliness was very precious to Janet. She was conscious of the aid it gave her in the self-conquest which was the blessing she prayed for with every fresh morning. The chief strength of her nature lay in her affection, which colored all the rest of her mind: it gave a personal sisterly tenderness to her acts of benevolence; it made her cling with tenacity to every object that had once stirred her kindly emotions. Alas! it was unsatisfied, wounded affection that had made her trouble greater than she could bear. And now there was no check to the full flow of that plenteous current in her nature—no gnawing secret anguish—no overhanging terror—no inward shame. Friendly faces beamed on her; she felt that friendly hearts were approving her, and wishing her well, and that mild sunshine of goodwill fell beneficently on her new hopes and efforts, as the clear shining after rain falls on the tender leaf-buds of spring, and wins them from promise to fulfillment.

And she needed these secondary helps, for her wrestling with her past self was not always easy. The strong emotions from which the life of a human being receives a new bias, win their victory as the sea wins his: though their advance may be sure, they will often, after a mightier wave than usual, seem to roll back so far as to lose all the ground they had made. Janet showed the strong bent of her will by taking every outward precaution against the occurrence of a temptation. Her mother was now her constant companion, having shut up her little dwelling and come to reside in Orchard Street; and Janet gave all dangerous keys into her keeping, entreating her to lock them away in some secret place. Whenever the too well-known depression and craving threatened her, she would seek a refuge in what had always been her purest enjoyment—in visiting one of her poor neighbors, in carrying some food or comfort to a sick-bed, in cheering with her smile some of the familiar dwellings up the dingy back-lanes. But the great source of courage, the great help to perseverance, was the sense that she had a friend and teacher in Mr. Tryan: she could confess her difficulties to him; she knew he prayed for her; she had always before her the prospect of soon seeing him, and hearing words of admonition and comfort, that came to her charged with a divine power such as she had never found in human words before.

So the time passed, till it was far on in May, nearly a month after her husband's death, when, as she and her mother were seated peacefully at breakfast in the dining-room, looking through the open window at the old-fashioned garden, where the grass-plot was now whitened with apple-blossoms, a letter was brought in for Mrs. Raynor.

"Why, there's the Thurston post-mark on it," she said. "It must be about your Aunt Anna. Ah, so it is, poor thing; she's been taken worse this last day or two, and has asked them to send for me. That dropsy is carrying her off at last, I dare say. Poor thing! it will be a happy release. I must go, my dear—she's your father's last sister—though I'm sorry to leave you. However, perhaps I shall not have to stay more than a night or two."

Janet looked distressed as she said, "Yes, you must go, mother. But I don't know what I shall do without you. I think I shall run in to Mrs. Pettifer, and ask her to come and stay with me while you're away. I'm sure she will."

At twelve o'clock, Janet, having seen her mother in the coach that was to carry her to Thurston, called, on her way back, at Mrs. Pettifer's, but found, to her great disappointment, that her old friend was gone out for the day. So she wrote on a leaf of her pocket-book an urgent request that Mrs. Pettifer would come and stay with her while her mother was away; and, desiring the servant-girl to give it to her mistress as soon as she came home, walked on to the Vicarage to sit with Mrs. Crewe, thinking to relieve in this way the feeling of desolateness and undefined fear that was taking possession of her on being left alone for the first time since that great crisis in her life. And Mrs. Crewe, too, was not at home!

Janet, with a sense of discouragement for which she rebuked herself as childish, walked sadly home again; and when she entered the vacant dining-room, she could not help bursting into tears. It is such vague undefinable states of susceptibility as this—states of excitement or depression, half mental, half physical—that determine many a tragedy in women's lives. Janet could scarcely eat anything at her solitary dinner; she tried to fix her attention on a book in vain; she walked about the garden, and felt the very sunshine melancholy.

Between four and five o'clock, old Mr. Pittman called, and joined her in the garden, where she had been sitting for some time under one of the great apple-trees, thinking how Robert, in his best moods, used to take little Mamsey to look at the cucumbers, or to see the Alderney cow with its calf in the paddock. The tears and sobs had come again at these thoughts; and when Mr. Pittman approached her, she was feeling languid and exhausted. But the old gentleman's sight and sensibility were obtuse, and, to Janet's satisfaction, he showed no consciousness that she was in grief.

"I have a task to impose upon you, Mrs. Dempster," he said, with a certain toothless pomposity habitual to him: "I want you to look over those letters again in Dempster's bureau, and see if you can find one from Poole about the mortgage on those houses at Dingley. It will be worth twenty pounds, if you can find it; and I don't know where it can be, if it isn't among those letters in the bureau. I've looked everywhere at the office for it. I'm going home now, but I'll call again to-morrow, if you'll be good enough to look in the mean time."

Janet said she would look directly, and turned with Mr. Pittman into the house. But the search would take her some time, so he bade her good-bye, and she went at once to a bureau which stood in a small back room, where Dempster used sometimes to write letters and receive people who came on business out of office hours. She had looked through the contents of the bureau more than once; but to-day, on removing the last bundle of letters from one of the compartments, she saw what she had never seen before, a small nick in the wood, made in the shape of a thumb-nail, evidently intended as a means of pushing aside the movable back of the compartment. In her examination hitherto she had not found such a letter as Mr. Pittman had described—perhaps there might be more letters behind this slide. She pushed it back at once, and saw—no letters, but a small spirit decanter, half full of pale brandy, Dempster's habitual drink.

An impetuous desire shook Janet through all her members; it seemed to master her with the inevitable force of strong fumes that flood our senses before we are aware. Her hand was on the decanter; pale and excited she was lifting it out of its niche, when, with a start and a shudder, she dashed it to the ground, and the room was filled with the odor of the spirit. Without staying to shut up the bureau, she rushed out of the room, snatched up her bonnet and mantle which lay in the dining-room, and hurried out of the house.

Where should she go? In what place would this demon that had reentered her be scared back again? She walks rapidly along the street in the direction of the church. She is soon at the gate of the churchyard; she passes through it, and makes her way across the graves to a spot she knows—a spot where the turf was stirred not long ago, where a tomb is to be erected soon. It is very near the church wall, on the side which now lies in deep shadow, quite shut out from the rays of the westering sun by a projecting buttress.

Janet sat down on the ground. It was a somber spot. A thick hedge, surmounted by elm trees, was in front of her; a projecting buttress on each side. But she wanted to shut out even these objects. Her thick crape veil was down; but she closed her eyes behind it, and pressed her hands upon them. She wanted to summon up the vision of the past; she wanted to lash the demon out of her soul with the stinging memories of the bygone misery; she wanted to renew the old horror and the old anguish, that she might throw herself with the more desperate clinging energy at the foot of the cross, where the Divine Sufferer would impart divine strength. She tried to recall those first bitter moments of shame, which were like the shuddering discovery of the leper that the dire taint is upon him; the deeper and deeper lapse; the on-coming of settled despair; the awful moments by the bedside of her self-maddened husband. And then she tried to live through, with a remembrance made more vivid by that contrast, the blessed hours of hope, and joy, and peace that had come to her of late, since her whole soul had been bent towards the attainment of purity and holiness.

But now, when the paroxysm of temptation was past, dread and despondency began to thrust themselves, like cold heavy mists, between her and the heaven to which she wanted to look for light and guidance. The temptation would come again—that rush of desire might overmaster her the next time—she would slip back again into that deep slimy pit from which she had been once rescued, and there might be no deliverance for her more. Her prayers did not help her, for fear predominated over trust; she had no confidence that the aid she sought would be given; the idea of her future fall had grasped her mind too strongly. Alone, in this way, she was powerless. If she could see Mr. Tryan, if she could confess all to him, she might gather hope again. She *must* see him; she must go to him.

Janet rose from the ground, and walked away with a quick resolved step. She had been seated there a long while, and the sun had already sunk. It was late for her to walk to Paddiford and go to Mr. Tryan's, where she had never called before; but there was no other way of seeing him that evening, and she could not hesitate about it. She walked towards a footpath through the fields, which would take her to Paddiford without obliging her to go through the town. The way was rather long, but she preferred it, because it left less probability of her meeting acquaintances, and she shrank from having to speak to any one.

The evening red had nearly faded by the time Janet knocked at Mrs. Wagstaff's door. The good woman looked surprised to see her at that hour; but Janet's mourning weeds and the painful agitation of her face quickly brought the second thought, that some urgent trouble had sent her there.

"Mr. Tryan's just come in," she said. "If you'll step into the parlor, I'll go up and tell him you're here. He seemed very tired and poorly."

At another time Janet would have felt distress at the idea that she was disturbing Mr. Tryan when he required rest; but now her need was too great for that: she could feel nothing but a sense of coming relief, when she heard his step on the stair and saw him enter the room.

He went towards her with a look of anxiety, and said, "I fear something is the matter. I fear you are in trouble."

Then poor Janet poured forth her sad tale of temptation and despondency; and even while she was confessing she felt half her burden removed. The act of confiding in human sympathy, the consciousness that a fellow-being was listening to her with patient pity, prepared her soul for that stronger leap by which faith grasps the idea of the divine sympathy. When Mr. Tryan spoke words of consolation and encouragement, she could now believe the message of mercy; the water-floods that had threatened to overwhelm her rolled back again, and life once more spread its heaven-covered space before her. She had been unable to pray alone; but now his prayer bore her own soul along with it, as the broad tongue of flame carries upward in its vigorous leap the little flickering fire that could hardly keep alight by itself.

But Mr. Tryan was anxious that Janet should not linger out at this late hour. When he saw that she was calmed, he said, "I will walk home with you now; we can talk on the way." But Janet's mind was now sufficiently at liberty for her to notice the signs of feverish weariness in his appearance, and she would not hear of causing him any further fatigue.

"No, no," she said earnestly, "you will pain me very much—indeed you will, by going out again to-night on my account. There is no real reason why I should not go alone." And when he persisted, fearing that for her to be seen out so late alone might excite remark, she said imploringly, with a half sob in her voice, "What should I—what would others like me do, if you went from us? Why will you not think more of that, and take care of yourself?"

He had often had that appeal made to him before, but tonight—from Janet's lips—it seemed to have a new force for him, and he gave way. At first, indeed, he only did so on condition that she would let Mrs. Wagstaff go with her; but Janet had determined to walk home alone. She preferred solitude; she wished not to have her present feelings distracted by any conversation.

So she went out into the dewy starlight; and as Mr. Tryan turned away from her, he felt a stronger wish than ever that his fragile life might last out for him to see Janet's restoration thoroughly established—to see her no longer fleeing, struggling, clinging up the steep sides of a precipice whence she might be any moment hurled back into the depths of despair, but walking firmly on the level ground of habit. He inwardly resolved that nothing but a peremptory duty should ever take him from Milby—that he would not cease to watch over her until life forsook him.

Janet walked on quickly till she turned into the fields; then she slackened her pace a little, enjoying the sense of solitude which a few hours before had been intolerable to her. The Divine Presence did not now seem far off, where she had not wings to reach it; prayer itself seemed superfluous in those moments of calm trust. The temptation which had so lately made her shudder before the possibilities of the future, was now a source of confidence; for had she not been delivered from it? Had not rescue come in the extremity of danger? Yes, Infinite Love was caring for her. She felt like a little child whose hand is firmly grasped by its father, as its frail limbs make their way over the rough ground; if it should stumble, the father will not let it go.

That walk in the dewy starlight remained for ever in Janet's memory as one of those baptismal epochs, when the soul, dipped in the sacred waters of joy and peace, rises from them with new energies, with more unalterable longings.

When she reached home she found Mrs. Pettifer there, anxious for her return. After thanking her for coming, Janet only said, "I have been to Mr. Tryan's; I wanted to speak to him"; and then remembering how she had left the bureau and papers, she went into the back-room, where, apparently, no one had been since she quitted it; for there lay the fragments of glass, and the room was still full of the hateful odor. How feeble and miserable the temptation seemed to her at this moment! She rang for Kitty to come and pick up the fragments and rub the floor, while she herself replaced the papers and locked up the bureau.

The next morning, when seated at breakfast with Mrs. Pettifer, Janet said,

"What a dreary, unhealthy-looking place that is where Mr. Tryan lives! I'm sure it must be very bad for him to live there. Do you know, all this morning, since I've been awake, I've been turning over a little plan in my mind. I think it a charming one—all the more, because you are concerned in it.

"Why, what can that be?"

"You know that house on the Redhill road they call Holly Mount; it is shut up now. That is Robert's house; at least, it is mine now, and it stands on one of the healthiest spots about here. Now, I've been settling in my own mind, that if a dear good woman of my acquaintance, who knows how to make a home as comfortable and cozy as a bird's nest, were to take up her abode there, and have Mr. Tryan as a lodger, she would be doing one of the most useful deeds in all her useful life."

"You've such a way of wrapping up things in pretty words. You must speak plainer."

"In plain words, then, I should like to settle you at Holly Mount. You would not have to pay any more rent than where you are, and it would be twenty times pleasanter for you than living up that passage where you see nothing but a brick wall. And then, as it is not far from Paddiford, I think Mr. Tryan might be persuaded to lodge with you, instead of in that musty house, among dead cabbages and smoky cottages. I know you would like to have him live with you, and you would be such a mother to him."

"To be sure I should like it; it would be the finest thing in the world for me. But there'll be furniture wanted. My little bit of furniture won't fill that house."

"O, I can put some in out of this house; it is too full; and we can buy the rest. They tell me I'm to have more money than I shall know what to do with."

"I'm almost afraid," said Mrs. Pettifer, doubtfully, "Mr. Tryan will hardly be persuaded. He's been talked to so much about leaving that place; and he always said he must stay there—he must be among the people, and there was no other place for him in Paddiford. It cuts me to the heart to see him getting thinner and thinner, and I've noticed him quite short o' breath sometimes. Mrs. Linnet will have it, Mrs. Wagstaff half poisons him with bad cooking. I don't know about that, but he can't have many comforts. I expect he'll break down all of a sudden some day, and never be able to preach any more."

"Well, I shall try my skill with him by-and-by. I shall be very cunning, and say nothing to him till all is ready. You and I and mother, when she comes home, will set to work directly and get the house in order, and then we'll get you snugly settled in it. I shall see Mr. Pittman to-day, and I will tell him what I mean to do. I shall say I wish to have you for a tenant. Everybody knows I'm very fond of that naughty person, Mrs. Pettifer; so it will seem the most natural thing in the world. And then I shall by-and-by point out to Mr. Tryan that he will be doing you a service as well as himself by taking up his abode with you. I think I can prevail upon him; for last night, when he was quite bent on coming out into the night air, I persuaded him to give it up."

"Well, I only hope you may, my dear. I don't desire anything better than to do something towards prolonging Mr. Tryan's life, for I've sad fears about him."

"Don't speak of them—I can't bear to think of them. We will only think about getting the house ready. We shall be as busy as bees. How we shall want mother's clever fingers! I know the room up-stairs that will just do for Mr. Tryan's study. There shall be no seats in it except a very easy chair and a very easy sofa, so that he shall be obliged to rest himself when he comes home."

Chapter XXVI

That was the last terrible crisis of temptation Janet had to pass through. The goodwill of her neighbors, the helpful sympathy of the friends who shared her religious feelings, the occupations suggested to her by Mr. Tryan, concurred, with her strong spontaneous impulses towards works of love and mercy, to fill up her days with quiet social intercourse and charitable exertion. Besides, her constitution, naturally healthy and strong, was every week tending, with the gathering force of habit, to recover its equipoise and set her free from those physical solicitations which the smallest habitual vice always leaves behind it. The prisoner feels where the iron has galled him, long after his fetters have been loosed.

There were always neighborly visits to be paid and received; and as the months wore on, increasing familiarity with Janet's present self began to efface, even from minds as rigid as Mrs. Phipps's, the unpleasant impressions that had been left by recent years. Janet was recovering the popularity which her beauty and sweetness of nature had won for her when she was a girl; and popularity, as every one knows, is the most complex and self-multiplying of echoes. Even anti-Tryanite prejudice could not resist the fact that Janet Dempster was a changed woman—changed as the dusty, bruised, and sun-withered plant is changed when the soft rains of heaven have fallen on it—and that this change was due to Mr. Tryan's influence. The last lingering sneers against the Evangelical curate began to die out; and though much of the feeling that had prompted them remained behind, there was an intimidating consciousness that the expression of such feeling would not be effective—jokes of that sort had ceased to tickle the Milby mind. Even Mr. Budd and Mr. Tomlinson, when they saw Mr. Tryan passing pale and worn along the street, had a secret sense that this man was somehow not that very natural and comprehensible thing, a humbug; that, in fact, it was impossible to explain him from the stomach and pocket point of view. Twist and stretch their theory as they might, it would not fit Mr. Tryan; and so, with that remarkable resemblance as to mental processes which may frequently be observed to exist between plain men and philosophers, they concluded that the less they said about him the better.

Among all Janet's neighborly pleasures, there was nothing she liked better than to take an early tea at the White House, and to stroll with Mr. Jerome round the old-fashioned garden and orchard. There was endless matter for talk between her and the good old man, for Janet had that genuine delight in human fellowship which gives an interest to all personal details that come warm from truthful lips; and, besides, they had a common interest in good-natured plans for helping their poorer neighbors. One great object of Mr. Jerome's charities was, as he often said, "to keep industrious men an' women off the parish. I'd rether give ten shillin' an' help a man to stan' on his own legs, nor pay half-a-crown to buy him a parish crutch; it's the ruination on him if he once goes to the parish. I've see'd many a time, if you help a man wi' a present in a neeborly way, it sweetens his blood—he thinks it kind on you; but the parish shillins turn it sour—he niver thinks 'em enough." In illustration of this opinion Mr. Jerome had a large store of details about such persons as Jim Hardy, the coal-carrier, "as lost his hoss," and Sally Butts, "as hed to sell her mangle, though she was as decent a woman as need to be"; to the hearing of which details Janet seriously inclined, and you would hardly desire to see a prettier picture than the kind-faced white-haired old man telling these fragments of his simple experience as he walked, with shoulders slightly bent, among the moss-roses and espalier apple-trees, while Janet in her widow's cap, her dark eyes bright with interest, went listening by his side, and little Lizzie, with her nankin bonnet hanging down her back, toddled on before them. Mrs. Jerome usually declined these lingering strolls, and often observed, "I niver see the like to Mr. Jerome when he's got Mrs. Dempster to talk to; it sinnifies nothin' to him whether we've tea at four or at five o'clock; he'd goo on till six, if you'd let him alone—he's like off his head." . . .

The sight of little Lizzie often stirred in Janet's mind a sense of the childlessness which had made a fatal blank in her life. She had fleeting thoughts that perhaps among her husband's distant relatives there might be some children whom she could help to bring up, some little girl whom she might adopt; and she promised herself one day or other to hunt out a second cousin of his—a married woman of whom he had lost sight for many years.

But at present her hands and heart were too full for her to carry out that scheme. To her great disappointment, her project of settling Mrs. Pettifer at Holly Mount had been delayed by the discovery that some repairs were necessary in order to make the house habitable, and it was not till September had set in that she had the satisfaction of seeing her old friend comfortably installed, and the rooms destined for Mr. Tryan looking pretty and cozy to her heart's content. She had taken several of his chief friends into her confidence, and they were warmly wishing success to her plan for inducing him to quit poor Mrs. Wagstaff's dingy house and dubious cookery. That he should consent to some such change was becoming more and more a matter of anxiety to his hearers; for though no more decided symptoms were yet observable in him than increasing emaciation, a dry hacking cough, and an occasional shortness of breath, it was felt that the fulfillment of Mr. Pratt's prediction could not long be deferred, and that this obstinate persistence in labor and self-disregard must soon be peremptorily cut short by a total failure of strength. Any hopes that the influence of Mr. Tryan's father and sister would prevail on him to change his mode of life—that they would perhaps come to live with him, or that his sister at least might come to see him, and that the arguments which had failed from other lips might be more persuasive from hers—were now quite dissipated. His father had lately had an attack of paralysis, and could not spare his only daughter's tendance. On Mr. Tryan's return from a visit to his father, Miss Linnet was very anxious to know whether his sister had not urged him to try change of air. From his answers she gathered that Miss Tryan wished him to give up his curacy and travel, or at least go to the south Devonshire coast.

"And why will you not do so?" Miss Linnet said; "you might come back to us well and strong, and have many years of usefulness before you."

"No," he answered quietly, "I think people attach more importance to such measures than is warranted. I don't see any good end that is to be served by going to die at Nice, instead of dying amongst one's friends and one's work. I cannot leave Milby—at least I will not leave it voluntarily."

But though he remained immovable on this point, he had been compelled to give up his afternoon service on the Sunday, and to accept Mr. Parry's offer of aid in the evening service, as well as to curtail his weekday labors; and he had even written to Mr. Prendergast to request that he would appoint another curate to the Paddiford district, on the understanding that the new curate should receive the salary, but that Mr. Tryan should co-operate with him as long as he was able. The hopefulness which is an almost constant attendant on consumption, had not the effect of deceiving him as to the nature of his malady, or of making him look forward to ultimate recovery. He believed himself to be consumptive, and he had not yet felt any desire to escape the early death which he had for some time contemplated as probable. Even diseased hopes will take their direction from the strong habitual bias of the mind, and to Mr. Tryan death had for years seemed nothing else than the laying down of a burden, under which he sometimes felt himself fainting. He was only sanguine about his powers of work: he flattered himself that what he was unable to do one week he should be equal to the next, and he would not admit that in desisting from any part of his labor he was renouncing it permanently. He had lately delighted Mr. Jerome by accepting his long-proffered loan of the "little chacenut hoss"; and he found so much benefit from substituting constant riding exercise for walking, that he began to think he should soon be able to resume some of the work he had dropped.

That was a happy afternoon for Janet, when, after exerting herself busily for a week with her mother and Mrs. Pettifer, she saw Holly Mount looking orderly and comfortable from attic to cellar. It was an old red-brick house, with two gables in front, and two clipped holly-trees flanking the garden gate; a simple, homely-looking place, that quiet people might easily get fond of; and now it was scoured and polished and carpeted and furnished so as to look really snug within. When there was nothing more to be done, Janet delighted herself with contemplating Mr. Tryan's study, first sitting down in the easy-chair, and then lying for a moment on the sofa, that she might have a keener sense of the repose he would get from those well-stuffed articles of furniture, which she had gone to Rotherby on purpose to choose.

"Now, mother," she said, when she had finished her survey, "you have done your work as well as any fairy mother or god-mother that ever turned a pumpkin into a coach and horses. You stay and have tea cozily with Mrs. Pettifer while I go to Mrs. Linnet's. I want to tell Mary and Rebecca the good news, that I've got the exciseman to promise that he will take Mrs. Wagstaff's lodgings when Mr. Tryan leaves. They'll be so pleased to hear it, because they thought he would make her poverty an objection to his leaving her." . . .

. . . As she walked along the rough lane with a buoyant step, a half smile of innocent, kindly triumph played about her mouth. She was delighting beforehand in the anticipated success of her persuasive power, and for the time her painful anxiety about Mr. Tryan's health was thrown into abeyance. But she had not gone far along the lane before she heard the sound of a horse advancing at a walking pace behind her. Without looking back, she turned aside to make way for it between the ruts, and did not notice that for a moment it had stopped and had then come on with a slightly quickened pace. In less than a minute she heard a well-known voice say, "Mrs. Dempster"; and, turning, saw Mr. Tryan close to her, holding his horse by the bridle. It seemed very natural to her that he should be there. Her mind was so full of his presence at that moment, that the actual sight of him was only like a more vivid thought, and she behaved, as we are apt to do when feeling obliges us to be genuine, with a total forgetfulness of polite forms. She only looked at him with a slight deepening of the smile that was already on her face. He said gently, "Take my arm"; and they walked on a little way in silence.

It was he who broke it. "You are going to Paddiford, I suppose?" . . .

"Yes," she said, "I was going to Mrs. Linnet's. I knew Miss Linnet would like to hear that our friend Mrs. Pettifer is quite settled now in her new house. She is as fond of Mrs. Pettifer as I am—almost; I won't admit that any one loves her *quite* as well, for no one else has such good reason as I have. But now the dear woman wants a lodger, for you know she can't afford to live in so large a house by herself. But I knew when I persuaded her to go there that she would be sure to get one—she's such a comfortable creature to live with; and I didn't like her to spend all the rest of her days up that dull passage, being at every one's beck and call who wanted to make use of her."

"Yes," said Mr. Tryan, "I quite understand your feeling; I don't wonder at your strong regard for her."

"Well, but now I want her other friends to second me. There she is, with three rooms to let, ready furnished, everything in order; and I know some one, who thinks as well of her as I do, and who would be doing good all round—to every one that knows him, as well as to Mrs. Pettifer, if he would go to live with her. He would leave some uncomfortable lodgings which another person is already coveting and would take immediately; and he would go to breathe pure air at Holly Mount, and gladden Mrs. Pettifer's heart by letting her wait on him; and comfort all his friends, who are quite miserable about him."

Mr. Tryan saw it all in a moment—he saw that it had all been done for his sake. He could not be sorry; he could not say no; he could not resist the sense that life had a new sweetness for him, and that he should like it to be prolonged a little—only a little, for the sake of feeling a stronger security about Janet. When she had finished speaking, she looked at him with a doubtful, inquiring glance. He was not looking at her; his eyes were cast downward; but the expression of his face encouraged her, and she said, in a half-playful tone of entreaty,—

"You *will* go and live with her? I know you will. You will come back with me now and see the house."

He looked at her then, and smiled. There is an unspeakable blending of sadness and sweetness in the smile of a face sharpened and paled by slow consumption. That smile of Mr. Tryan's pierced poor Janet's heart: she felt in it at once the assurance of grateful affection and the prophecy of coming death. Her tears rose; they turned round without speaking, and went back again along the lane.

Chapter XXVII

In less than a week Mr. Tryan was settled at Holly Mount, and there was not one of his many attached hearers who did not sincerely rejoice at the event.

The autumn that year was bright and warm, and at the beginning of October Mr. Walsh, the new curate, came. The mild weather, the relaxation from excessive work, and perhaps another benignant influence, had for a few weeks a visibly favorable effect on Mr. Tryan. At least he began to feel new hopes, which sometimes took the guise of new strength. He thought of the cases in which consumptive patients remain nearly stationary for years, without suffering so as to make their life burdensome to themselves or to others; and he began to struggle with a longing that it might be so with him. He struggled with it, because he felt it to be an indication that earthly affection was beginning to have too strong a hold on him, and he prayed earnestly for more perfect submission, and for a more absorbing delight in the Divine Presence as the chief good. He was conscious that he did not wish for prolonged life solely that he might do God's work in reclaiming the wanderers and sustaining the feeble: he was conscious of a new yearning for those pure human joys which he had voluntarily and determinedly banished from his life—for a draught of that deep affection from which he had been cut off by a dark chasm of remorse. For now, that affection was within his reach; he saw it there, like a palm-shadowed well in the desert; he *could* not desire to die in sight of it.

And so the autumn rolled gently by in its "calm decay." Until November, Mr. Tryan continued to preach occasionally, to ride about visiting his flock, and to look in at his schools; but his growing satisfaction in Mr. Walsh as his successor saved him from too eager exertion and from worrying anxieties. Janet was with him a great deal now, for she saw that he liked her to read to him in the lengthening evenings, and it became the rule for her and her mother to have tea at Holly Mount, where, with Mrs. Pettifer and sometimes another friend or two, they brought Mr. Tryan the unaccustomed enjoyment of companionship by his own fireside.

Janet did not share his new hopes, for she was not only in the habit of hearing Mr. Pratt's opinion that Mr. Tryan could hardly stand out through the winter, but she also knew that it was shared by Dr. Madely of Rotherby, whom, at her request, he had consented to call in. It was not necessary or desirable to tell Mr. Tryan what was revealed by the stethoscope, but Janet knew the worst.

She felt no rebellion under this prospect of bereavement, but rather a quiet submissive sorrow. Gratitude that his influence and guidance had been given her, even if only for a little while—gratitude that she was permitted to be with him, to take a deeper and deeper impress from daily communion with him, to be something to him in these last months of his life, was so strong in her that it almost silenced regret. Janet had lived through the great tragedy of woman's life. Her keenest personal emotions had been poured forth in her early love—her wounded affection with its years of anguish—her agony of unavailing pity over that death-bed seven months ago. The thought of Mr. Tryan was associated for her with repose from that conflict of emotion, with trust in the unchangeable, with the influx of a power to subdue self. To have been assured of his sympathy, his teaching, his help, all through her life, would have been to her like a heaven already begun—a deliverance from fear and danger; but the time was not yet come for her to be conscious that the hold he had on her heart was any other than that of the heaven-sent friend who had come to her like the angel in the prison, and loosed her bonds, and led her by the hand till she could look back on the dreadful doors that had once closed her in.

Before November was over Mr. Tryan had ceased to go out. A new crisis had come on: the cough had changed its character, and the worst symptoms developed themselves so rapidly that Mr. Pratt began to think the end would arrive sooner than he had expected. Janet became a constant attendant on him now, and no one could feel that she was performing anything but a sacred office. She made Holly Mount her home, and, with her mother and Mrs. Pettifer to help her, she filled the painful days and nights with every soothing influence that care and tenderness could devise. There were many visitors to the sick-room, led thither by venerating affection; and there could hardly be one who did not retain in after years a vivid remembrance of the scene there—of the pale wasted form in the easy-chair (for he sat up to the last), of the gray eyes so full even yet of inquiring kindness, as the thin, almost transparent hand was held out to give the pressure of welcome; and of the sweet woman, too, whose dark watchful eyes detected every want, and who supplied the want with a ready hand.

There were others who would have had the heart and the skill to fill this place by Mr. Tryan's side, and who would have accepted it as an honor; but they could not help feeling that God had given it to Janet by a train of events which were too impressive not to shame all jealousies into silence.

That sad history, which most of us know too well, lasted more than three months. He was too feeble and suffering for the last few weeks to see any visitors, but he still sat up through the day. The strange hallucinations of the disease which had seemed to take a more decided hold on him just at the fatal crisis, and had made him think he was perhaps getting better at the very time when death had begun to hurry on with more rapid movement, had now given way, and left him calmly conscious of the reality. One afternoon, near the end of February, Janet was moving about gently in the room, in the fire-lit dusk, arranging some things that would be wanted in the night. There was no one else in the room, and his eyes followed her as she moved with the firm grace natural to her, white the bright fire every now and then lit up her face, and gave an unusual glow to her dark beauty. Even to follow her in this way with his eyes was an exertion that gave a painful tension to his face; while *she* looked like an image of life and strength.

"Janet," he said presently, in his faint voice—he always called her Janet now. In a moment she was close to him, bending over him. He opened his hand as he looked up at her, and she placed hers within it.

"Janet," he said again, "you will have a long while to life after I am gone."

A sudden pang of fear shot through her. She thought he felt himself dying, and she sank on her knees at his feet, holding his hand, while she looked up at him, almost breathless.

"But you will not feel the need of me as you have done . . . You have a sure trust in God . . . I shall not look for you in vain at the last."

"No . . . no . . . I shall be there. . . . God will not forsake me."

She could hardly utter the words, though she was not weeping. She was waiting with trembling eagerness for anything else he might have to say.

"Let us kiss each other before we part."

She lifted up her face to his, and the full life-breathing lips met the wasted dying ones in a sacred kiss of promise.

Chapter XVIII

It soon came—the blessed day of deliverance, the sad day of bereavement; and in the second week of March they carried him to the grave. He was buried as he had desired: there was no hearse, no mourning-coach; his coffin was borne by twelve of his humbler hearers, who relieved each other by turns. But he was followed by a long procession of mourning friends, women as well as men.

Slowly, amid deep silence, the dark stream passed along Orchard Street, where eighteen months before the Evangelical curate had been saluted with hooting and hisses. Mr. Jerome and Mr. Landor were the eldest pall-bearers; and behind the coffin, led by Mr. Tryan's cousin, walked Janet in quiet submissive sorrow. She could not feel that he was quite gone from her; the unseen world lay so very near her—it held all that had ever stirred the depths of anguish and joy within her.

It was a cloudy morning, and had been raining when they left Holly Mount; but as they walked, the sun broke out, and the clouds were rolling off in large masses when they entered the churchyard, and Mr. Walsh's voice was heard saying, "I am the Resurrection and the Life." The faces were not hard at this funeral; the burial-service was not a hollow form. Every heart there was filled with the memory of a man who, through a self-sacrificing life, and in a painful death, had been sustained by the faith which fills that form with breath and substance.

When Janet left the grave, she did not return to Holly Mount; she went to her home in Orchard Street, where her mother was waiting to receive her. She said quite calmly, "Let us walk round the garden, mother." And they walked round in silence, with their hands clasped together, looking at the golden crocuses bright in the spring sunshine. Janet felt a deep stillness within. She thirsted for no pleasure; she craved no worldly good. She saw the years to come stretch before her like an autumn afternoon, filled with resigned memory. Life to her could never more have any eagerness; it was a solemn service of gratitude and patient effort. She walked in the presence of unseen witnesses—of the Divine love that had rescued her, of the human love that waited for its eternal repose until it had seen her endure to the end.

Janet is living still. Her black hair is gray, and her step is no longer buoyant; but the sweetness of her smile remains, the love is not gone from her eyes; and strangers sometimes ask, Who is that noble-looking elderly woman, that walks about holding a little boy by the hand? The little boy is the son of Janet's adopted daughter, and Janet in her old age has children about her knees, and loving young arms round her neck.

There is a simple gravestone in Milby churchyard, telling that in this spot lie the remains of Edgar Tryan, for two years officiating curate at the Paddiford Chapel-of-Ease, in this parish. It is a meager memorial, and tells you simply that the man who lies there took upon him, faithfully or unfaithfully, the office of guide and instructor to his fellow-men.

But there is another memorial of Edgar Tryan, which bears a fuller record: it is Janet Dempster, rescued from self-despair, strengthened with divine hopes, and now looking back on years of purity and helpful labor. The man who has left such a memorial behind him, must have been one whose heart beat with true compassion, and whose lips were moved by fervent faith.

Domestic Violence in "The White Stocking"

A LAWRENCEAN CASE STUDY

No reading of D. H. Lawrence's "The White Stocking" can proceed very far without acknowledging Keith Cushman's useful precedent. In chapter 6 of *D. H. Lawrence at Work,* Cushman traces the story's development from its conception in 1907 through its magazine publication in *The Smart Set* in October 1914 to its final appearance in *The Prussian Officer and Other Stories* in December of that year. His most startling discovery, moreover, is one on which my own speculations depend: for it was not until that final version that Lawrence would include the episode of domestic violence that gives the story its remarkably modern resonance. As Cushman demonstrates, the original story was merely an amusing anecdote, and the more serious *Smart Set* revision had avoided violence through the heroine's timely change of heart and mind in the final paragraphs. Thus, when Elsie Whiston sees how upset her husband, Ted, has become over the Valentine's Day gifts and messages she has received from her former employer, she embraces him, stops her defiant flirtation, and quietly sends the gifts back the next day. In the final version, however, Whiston bloodies her mouth with a backslap of his hand, advances as if to destroy her, then backs off "in shame and nausea," before returning the offending gifts himself. His closing embrace of his wife combines his own guilty penitence, moreover, with her equally anguished repentance.[1]

Cushman calls the first ending "sentimental" and considers the second ending a great improvement. "[T]he addition of the blow makes the story more psychologically persuasive," he claims, "and greatly increases its effectiveness. The blow provides a needed catharsis." Later he embellishes these points by arguing that "violence is a transgression of the mores of modern life" and that husband and wife "are shocked back to social reality" by it.[2]

1. *D.H. Lawrence at Work: The Emergence of the* Prussian Officer *Stories,* 149–50, 162–65.
2. Ibid., 164, 165.

Such aesthetic considerations are not uncommon among critical discussions of domestic violence in our time. They suggest a certain edginess about dealing directly with moral implications. Cushman himself exhibits such edginess in his preceding remarks: "Too much has been written about the dishes Lawrence and Frieda sometimes threw at each other, but we do know that Lawrence believed that a strong passional impulse should not be resisted." As if to reinforce this odd authorial sanction for violence, Cushman then quotes George Orwell's flip deduction of the story's moral: "women behave better if they get a sock on the jaw occasionally"—"an interpretation," says Cushman, "that might not have upset Lawrence."[3] Nor Hemingway, one might add, nor Steinbeck, nor many a male writer of hard-boiled film and fiction in our time. The incorporation of domestic violence into modern literary fare is legion; it often proceeds without moral comment, or with the implicit sanction of harsh domestic realism or naturalism, a sort of tonic male version of how things really are.

My own comments are going to be less tonic, but no less realistic. They are also going to be much more insistent on the moral and social hazards of aesthetic treatments of this theme. I have used "A Lawrencean Case Study" as my subtitle, for instance, for two good reasons: first, because the story seems to me an almost classic narration of the terms and stages of domestic violence as defined today by professionals in that social service field; second, it not only prefigures the directions Lawrence himself would take in his later treatments of domestic violence, it also contains an implicit critique of those directions. I will combine these reasons in my remarks, as the occasion requires; but I want to point out now that the story itself anticipates the professional critique of domestic violence of the 1990s even as it makes its own prescient case against some of Lawrence's most cherished future convictions. As Lawrence himself wisely noted in his "The Study of Thomas Hardy," "every work of art . . . must contain the essential criticism on the morality to which it adheres."[4] The early story at hand not only contains that essential moral criticism; it helps us to understand how and where Lawrence himself lost sight of it in later fictions, and how and where he restored it.

I

I want to stress, in this light, the early appearance in this tale of the dominance-submission problem of Lawrence's later fictions. In his edginess about domestic violence, Cushman overlooks this theme almost entirely, but it is crucial to the

3. Ibid., 164.

4. "The Study of Thomas Hardy," *Selected Literary Criticism,* 185. See also *Phoenix: The Posthumous Papers of D. H. Lawrence,* 476.

story's dramatic tensions and unspoken assumptions and needs to be spelled out. From the opening sentence—" 'I'm getting up, Teddilinks,' said Mrs. Whiston, and she sprang out of bed briskly"—the story is about sex and power, or more precisely, about the liberating freedom Mrs. Whiston finds by leaving herself "utterly in [her husband's] power."[5] On this Valentine's Day she exercises this liberation, paradoxically enough, through her interest in the coming postman's delivery of expected Valentines from her former employer. She springs out of bed with a "careless abandon" that makes her husband's spirit glow; she seems a thoughtless "pretty little thing," an "untidy minx," "quick and handy" in her careless ways, intent on her secret rendezvous with the postman and with those confirming letters and packages that indicate that her former employer, Sam Adams, is following up for a second year a flirtation that began before her marriage to Teddilinks. And as her lighthearted name-play on tiddly-winks suggests, her liberation allows now for thoughtless romantic games with another power player, the bald bachelor roué who runs the local lace factory where he and she and her future husband once tiddled winks with each other at the Christmas ball.

This thoughtless but loving wife carries the heavy burden, then, of Lawrence's future concern with sexual politics. She is about to test the limits of her freedom in consequential ways that the early Lawrence wants to explore and understand. The problem he poses will recur in different ways in his mature fiction; but it surfaces from the very beginning—"The White Stocking" was among the first three stories that he and Jessie Chambers entered in a story contest in 1907; and by 1914—in sequence with the composition of *The Rainbow*—it receives its lasting imprint of domestic violence. Thus Elsie Whiston's paradoxical dependence on her husband's reassuring masculine power is carefully spelled out, in part 1, through the kind of washing scene that Lawrence would employ early and late to indicate male vitality:

> Presently he rose, and went to wash himself, rolling back his sleeves and pulling open his shirt at the breast. It was as if his fine, clear-cut temples and steady eyes were degraded by the lower, rather brutal part of his face. But she loved it. As she whisked about, clearing the table, she loved the way in which he stood washing himself. He was such a man. She liked to see his neck glistening with water as he swilled it. It amused her and pleased her and thrilled her. He was so sure, so permanent, he had her so utterly in his power. It gave her a delightful mischievous sense of liberty. Within his grasp, she could dart about excitingly. (327–28/171)

The physical description of Whiston's face recalls that of Lawrence himself, and the emphasis on the brutal lower jaw will have its fictional relevance to

5. "The White Stocking," 323, 328/167, 171. Further page references will be given in the text, with the first number referring to the edition listed in the bibliography and the second to the reprinting of the story below.

the author's marriage; but the frivolousness of this wife within her husband's power hardly recalls Frieda. These are ordinary Nottingham characters from whom Lawrence is able to gain some distance from his own marital troubles while speaking to the terms of every marriage. And the terms are those of male responsibility for female conduct. Thus in part 3 of the tale the theme of dominant responsibility is even more carefully articulated: "Inside of marriage she found her liberty. She was rid of the responsibility of herself. Her husband must look after that. She was free to get what she could out of her time" (338/181).

This is the rather biblical tenet to which Lawrence would return in *The Fox* and the American and Mexican stories and novels of his middle period, after striving so bravely for "star-equilibrium" in *Women in Love* and for balanced roles freely chosen in *The Captain's Doll.* It is also the tenet he would abandon by stressing mutual submission, in *Lady Chatterley's Lover,* to the spontaneities and responsibilities of tender passional love. Meanwhile he was able to see with startling clarity some limits of the tenet in this striking early tale.

II

Among those limits are the husband's secret dependency on his wife. Although Lawrence insists that Whiston has found himself in this marriage, that his wife's passionate abandon has given him "a permanent surety and sense of realness in himself," he is also a man who "would be miserable all day if he went without" his good-bye kiss from Elsie, and who feels "as if all his light and warmth were taken away" when she leaves the room (338, 328, 323/181, 172, 167). Cushman makes the nice point that Lawrence was equally dependent on Frieda in these early years of marital discovery, that he too had found himself in marriage yet felt hopeless without a woman at his back, upon whom he could draw for strength.[6] In this early story, then, he tests the limits of his own paradoxical dependency and self-discovery: in Elsie's defiant liberation tactics on this Valentine's morning, and in Whiston's violent reactions, he tests his own half-formed convictions about male responsibility and sheltering power, about female liberation and submission—and finds them sorely wanting!

Whiston's jealousy about Sam Adams's Valentine's Day attentions offers another biographical clue to these paradoxes. One thinks of Lawrence's rather platonic surface reactions to Frieda's defiant flirtations and infidelities, during their early relations, and of the comic alpine travel narrative that Lawrence would devote to that period in *Mr. Noon* (1920–1921), with its oddly calm acceptance of cuckoldry. Perhaps Lawrence's frequent fights with Frieda, his own angry

6. *D. H. Lawrence,* 150–51.

violence about apparently unrelated matters, speak more tellingly to those early triangulations than we have hitherto supposed. Certainly his recognition that Whiston, in his violence with Elsie, is paying back old scores has the ring of authorial self-knowledge behind it.

It rings also with the power side of sexual politics. Cushman's observation, that "Whiston's 'lust to see [Elsie] bleed, to break her and destroy her' and his desire for 'satisfaction' are obviously and violently sexual,"[7] is certainly well taken; and his tracing of the sensual emendations of the dance imagery in the middle section, as they prefigure similar rhythmic scenes of sexual import in *The Rainbow* (1915), is the triumphant heart of his valuable chapter on this story. But Cushman wrote before the development of an insightful discourse about domestic violence in the 1980s and 1990s. The more recent stress is on male power and control, on mastery and possession and the denial of female equality, and Lawrence's tale rings truer to that emphasis than Cushman is able to show us. The instructive difference between sexual and social potency in males, with its different basis in physical and sensual powers, is what matters here; and Elsie's confused attribution of Whiston's sensual powers in that washing scene—his male vitality—to his physical ability to hold her in his power ("He was such a man") helps to explain why it matters. One has only to recall Lady Chatterley's similar reaction to the gamekeeper's male vitality as she comes upon him washing his upper body in that later novel—her shock of recognition at the beauty of male sensual potency in a rather frail male physique—to grasp the crucial difference.[8]

The early game, then, is power and control, as our current professionals tell us. Men batter women, even as they rape them, for that very different and decidedly more deadly kind of satisfaction. And the story's structure and texture speak steadily to that deadly end.

III

Lawrence's use of the flashback in part 2 is a functional case in point. In part 1 he introduces the Valentine's Day flirtation between Elsie and Adams that has been going on for the past two years. When Whiston surprises Elsie in the front hall, where she has been winking at herself in the mirror, admiring her new earrings, she begins a sequence of delayed confessions by which she ultimately reveals that Adams is the sender of white handkerchiefs, white stockings, earrings, an amethyst brooch, and romantic verses. The confession is staggered over parts 1

7. Ibid., 164.

8. *Lady Chatterley's Lover,* 75–76. See also my early establishment of this stress on the body's vitality (not its physical strength) in *The Love Ethic of D. H. Lawrence,* 183–86.

and 3. By the end of part 1, Whiston has learned only that she has lied about the white stocking by calling it a sample, and that she has in fact met with Adams once for a drink of coffee and benedictine at a local pub. That is enough, however, to shake Whiston's sense of "permanent surety" and "realness in himself" that came with marriage. In fact, he leaves the house deeply hurt, burned by her flirtation, dangerously roused by her partial confession, and spends his day at work "yearning for surety, and kept tense by not getting it (329/172)."

Part 2, the flashback to the Christmas party for employees at Adams's house two years before, after which the Whistons quickly married, is accordingly our explanatory source for those old scores with Elsie that Whiston settles so violently in part 3. As Cushman shows, Lawrence has added two dance scenes to the original one and has emphasized in all three the seductive sensual power by which bachelor Adams appeals to Elsie, dazes her into unconscious connection, until she swims away "out of contact with the room," passing "into him" sensually, so that the "delicious" movements of his strong supporting body are her own.[9] In part 1 we have watched her swinging from her husband's neck, like a child who delights in the sheer physicality of masculine power. Now, in her passive submission to Adams's seductive movements, we see the blend of sexual and physical power that appeals to her. That Whiston also sees it, and is disturbed by her touch while she is roused by the other man, is the dynamic tension of part 2. Unable to dance himself, he is forced to play cards while his partner enjoys herself so thoroughly in the arms of their common boss that she resists going home; and when he warns her against being "too free" with the rakish Adams, she even admits to liking him. Then the tension breaks into the open when Adams comes to her for another dance, and she accidentally drops what she takes to be her pocket handkerchief, but which turns out as it falls to the floor to be a white stocking. Adams picks it up with a triumphant laugh:

> "That'll do for me," he whispered—seeming to take possession of her. And he stuffed the stocking in his trousers pocket, and quickly offered her his handkerchief.
>
> The dance began. She felt weak and faint, as if her will were turned to water. A heavy sense of loss came over her. She could not help herself any more. But it was peace. (336/179)

Plainly Elsie has become the unlucky pawn in an intimate power play. Throughout this scene her self-division between the attractions of these two men has been evident. Now she belongs to Adams. But Whiston intervenes and soon reclaims her. Incensed by the boss's appropriation of her stocking, and by her acquiescence in that seizure, he demands to know what it means, refuses to

9. Cushman, *D. H. Lawrence,* 159–60.

stay any longer, and explodes with rage outside when he faces her attachment to "That great hog, an' all." As the sequence ends he holds her safe in his arms while she pleads with him to be good to her, not to be cruel to her, and is restored at last by his "white-hot . . . love and belief in her." As part 3 begins we learn that they got married within a few weeks and that the episode of the white stocking, though touched upon once or twice, has never been resolved.

IV

The white stocking story had begun with an episode in the early life of Lawrence's mother. She had worked at a lace factory, had gone to the Christmas party for employees, and had been so embarrassed when the white handkerchief she pulled from her pocket turned out to be a white stocking that she never forgot the incident.[10] She told her children about it, and one of them at least understood the embarrassing sexual subtext so well that he made an artful story about it during his own early manhood. The sensual dancing and the problem of divided sexual attraction came from his own early experiences with fickle girlfriends at such parties and from his own troubled reactions to the infidelities and flirtations of his older wife; but the marvelous grasp of these matters comes from his characteristic identification with the woman's point of view. He was close to his mother, and (as we have seen) strongly dependent on his wife for the strength to create his new fictions; the revision of the story to include the new sensualized dancing scenes and the closing violence—this artful realization of the meaning of his early materials—comes from that strong identification with how the women in his life might think and feel. Troubled by his father's brutalities with his mother, and by his own repetition of those brutalities in his fights with Frieda, encouraged by the recent airing of cases of domestic violence during the lengthy public hearings of the Royal Commission on Divorce and Matrimonial Causes (1910–1912), he created this rare exposition of domestic violence and its causes in characters close to his own sense of himself, his own male and female aspects. There is nothing quite this intimate, quite this close to home, wife and mother, and to his own battering propensities, in his later fiction.[11] The story functions accordingly as a useful case study of the nature

10. Ibid., 149–50. See also John Worthen, *D. H. Lawrence: The Early Years, 1885–1912,* 189–90.

11. See Janice Harris's recent enlightening study, *Edwardian Stories of Divorce,* esp. chaps. 1 and 2 on "Stock Stories" and "Counterstories." See also my extensive account of Lawrence's treatment of domestic violence in "Hemingway and Lawrence as Abusive Husbands" and "Repossessing *The Captain's Doll.*" As I observe in the former (219–20), though Lawrence gave a powerful fictional account of his father's domestic violence in *Sons and Lovers,* he avoided direct autobiographical treatments of his own abusive behavior.

of domestic violence and of his early apprehension of the deadly struggle he would later place at the heart of modern marriage.

In part 3 Lawrence turns to the culmination of that deadly struggle in the Whiston household. As Cushman shows, he had worked in an intimation of impending violence in part 1.[12] Thus, when Elsie tells Whiston of her drink with Adams at a local pub,

> The blood came up into his neck and face, he stood motionless, dangerous.
>
> "It was cold, and it was such fun to go into the Royal," she said.
>
> "You'd go off with a nigger for a packet of chocolate," he said, in anger and contempt, and some bitterness. Queer how he drew away from her, cut her off from him.
>
> "Ted—how beastly!" she cried. "You know quite well—" She caught her lip, flushed, and the tears came to her eyes. (328/172)

That women and blacks share a subordinate status in our culture comes as no surprise in these days of raised consciousness about ethnic and gender differences. But it is worth citing Toni Morrison's recent observation of the disruptive presence of African darkness in white fictions as a sign of things "beastly" and black that threaten our white heterosexual partners.[13] Elsie has just fallen measurably in human and social status as the angry Whiston draws back in bitter contempt from his erstwhile prize possession. It is in this "dangerous" and demeaning manner that Whiston claims his dependent good-bye kiss and goes off to work as the sequence closes. Meanwhile Elsie is further trivialized as thoughtless by her return to the frivolous morning mood of delight in her new earrings, which Whiston has not noticed, but which she wears all day, hoping the tradesmen will notice them, as indeed they do:

> All the tradesmen left her door with a glow in them, feeling elated, and unconsciously favoring the delightful little creature, though there had been nothing to notice in her behavior.
>
> She was stimulated all the day. She did not think about her husband. He was the permanent basis from which she took these giddy little flights into nowhere. At night, like chickens and curses, she would come home to him, to roost. (328–29/172)

That ominous reference to curses indicates Lawrence's participation in Elsie's indictment in this story as a provocative, thoughtless minx, while she is at the same time being cherished as a woman who rests confident in her husband's power, his willingness to take responsibility for her behavior and her willingness to allow it. These contradictory meanings—or perhaps more accurately, these

12. *D. H. Lawrence,* 154.

13. *Playing in the Dark: Whiteness and the Literary Imagination,* 76, 91.

ambivalent leanings—are now exposed as Lawrence further develops Elsie's sportive play with her Valentine's Day fantasies of the past two years and her plans for future innocent deceptions of her now discouraged husband. Thus, when he returns home tired and depressed from his male insecurities, she is still caught up in imagined "liberations" and begins to mock and jeer and cut him off. Although these additional provocations make her uneasy, she can't help goading him on, as if testing the limits of her sportive freedom like a child asking for clarifying punishment.

Or perhaps like a woman who no longer wants to be treated like a child. That construction is my own, but it seems to me implicit in the story's ultimate exposure of its own ambivalences. "Elsie's Rebellion, or The White Stocking Revisited," might be a fair way of retitling this essay, in keeping with my reading of her supposedly thoughtless conduct and its contradictory meanings. If she is to learn to take more seriously her sportive ways, her harmless and supposedly innocent flirtations, she must herself be taken more seriously by her husband, her creator, and her self. In all fairness to Lawrence and his awareness of more serious infidelities, I think he does arrive at a similar weighting of the inadequacy of his own assumptions here. He is true to the psychodynamics of this situation—to where the tale is taking him—and so creates a tale we can trust while at the same time questioning the artist's mixed intentions.[14]

Meanwhile he provides us with a nice version of the standard complaint of male batterers: "she drove me to it." Thus Elsie does all she can to madden and infuriate her already jealous husband. When he asks why she doesn't put the stockings on the fire-back where they belong, she goes upstairs, pulls them onto her legs, and comes down to dance around her husband tauntingly, in defiant resentment of his commanding ways. His anger mounts dangerously.

> It was a war now. She bent forward, in a ballet-dancer's fashion, and put her tongue between her teeth.
>
> "I shan't backfire them stockings," she sang, repeating his words, "I shan't, I shan't, I shan't."
>
> And she danced round the room doing a high kick to the tune of her words. There was a real biting indifference in her behavior.
>
> "We'll see whether you will or not . . . trollops! You'd like Sam Adams to know you was wearing 'em, wouldn't you? . . ."
>
> "Yes, I'd like him to see how nicely they fit me, he might give me some more then."

---

14. I am referring, of course, to Lawrence's famous dictum in his introduction to *Studies in Classic American Literature:* "Never trust the artist. Trust the tale. The proper function of a critic is to save the tale from the artist who created it."

> And she looked down at her pretty legs. . . . It made his anger go deep, almost to hatred.
>
> "Yer nasty trolley," he cried. "Put your petticoats down, and stop being so foul-minded."
>
> "I'm not foul-minded," she said. "My legs are my own. And why shouldn't Sam Adams think they're nice?" . . . .
>
> "Them who has anything to do wi' him is too bad for me, I tell you."
>
> "Why, what are you frightened of him for?" she mocked.
>
> She was rousing all his uncontrollable anger. . . . Every one of her sentences stirred him up like a red-hot iron. Soon it would be too much. . . . . A curious little grin of hate came on his face. He had a long score against her.
>
> "What am I frightened of him for?" he repeated automatically. . . . . "Why for you, you stray-running little bitch."
>
> She flushed. The insult went deep into her, right home. (340–41/183)

Bad, nasty, trollops, trolley, foul-minded, stray-running little bitch—the abusive litany of sexually degrading terms betrays Whiston's fear of dispossession by another man. His long score against Elsie has its roots in those seductive dancing scenes two years back, in Adams's possession of her pawnlike body upon seizing the white stocking and making it his own. That unresolved incident still rankles Whiston, rouses what Lawrence calls his "uncontrollable anger"—which, as domestic violence professionals know, is the rage at the bottom of the Anger Iceberg Chart (see below, 358), where old scores are stored below our half-conscious feelings of resentment, loss, jealousy, inadequacy, insecurity, contempt, bitter hostility: old scores, that is, against the women in our lives, our sweethearts, wives, and mothers before them, as in those pre-oedipal infant rages that Margaret Storch explores through Melanie Klein,[15] or in those oedipal resentments that Lawrence and Freud explore between rivalrous sons and fathers. Long scores indeed, but scarcely uncontrollable. We work them up as we need them, we exploit them in our need for power and control, and then blame anger itself for our violent conduct, or blame our provocative partners, as the story now demonstrates.

Thus, when Elsie jeeringly suggests that she won't tell her husband about any future meetings with Adams, a strange thing happens:

> Her jeering scorn made him go white-hot, molten. He knew he was incoherent, scarcely responsible for what he might do. Slowly, unseeing, he rose and went out of doors, stifled, moved to kill her.
>
> He stood leaning against the garden fence, unable either to see or hear. Below him, far off, fumed the lights of the town. He stood still, unconscious with a black storm of rage, his face lifted to the night. (341/184)

---

15. See *Sons and Adversaries: Women in William Blake and D. H. Lawrence.*

Here Whiston does instinctively what domestic violence counselors advise their clients to do: butt out, cool off when rage rises, find time and space to talk yourself down, to regain full control of your hostile feelings. But "instinctively" is perhaps misleading since Whiston here *chooses* to go outside, exhibits the very control and responsibility he claims not to possess, and seeks to reinforce it. Actually he merely allows his rage to simmer. There is no talking down; when he returns to the house, Lawrence emphasizes that he is "still unconscious of what he was doing."

It is at this point in the magazine version of the story that Elsie goes outside to look for him, calls his name, and returns inside when he does not answer. He then feels sorry for her and comes inside to confront her. "Taking courage," she moves into his embrace, and they reach each other's deepest feelings by holding fast, overcoming fear and hostility, until she finally draws his head down to kiss him, murmuring "My love, my love." The next day she sends back both the stockings and the earrings, never telling her husband about the latter.[16]

This "sentimental ending," as Cushman calls it, is oddly true to Elsie's integrity as a responsible person, able to judge and act for herself, but not to the biblical wife, the fallen Eve whose punishment is to look to her husband for spiritual and moral guidance. The revised ending is indeed an "improvement" on this easy moral gain, not as an aesthetic catharsis as Cushman argues, but in its recognition of the realities of sexual politics in our time. The story is true, that is to say, to the actualities of domestic violence, to its repetitive and recurrent nature, and to those devastatingly false assumptions about biblical responsibilities, about male power and control and female submission and childish "liberation," that go with the territory. Thus, when Whiston returns inside, Elsie confronts him stubbornly with his commanding ways: "*You're* not going to tell me everything I shall do, and everything I shan't," she declares; and then for the first time, when he threatens to break her neck, she tells him defiantly about the jewels that Adams has sent her over the past two years without his knowledge:

> "He what?" said Whiston, in a suddenly normal voice. His eyes were fixed on her.
>
> "Sent me a pair of pearl ear-rings and an amethyst brooch," she repeated, mechanically, pale to the lips.
>
> And her big, black, childish eyes watched him, fascinated, held in [his] spell.
>
> He seemed to thrust his face and eyes forward at her, as he rose slowly and came to her. She watched transfixed in terror. Her throat made a small sound, as she tried to scream.

16. Cushman, *D. H. Lawrence,* 162–63.

> Then, quick as lightning, the back of his hand struck her with a crash across the mouth, and she was flung back blinded against the wall. The shock shook a queer sound out of her. And then she saw him still coming on, his eyes holding her, his fist drawn back, advancing slowly. (342/184–85)

As Whiston's "suddenly normal voice" attests, he is able now to focus his full attention on the apparent meaning of his wife's defiant confession. In that sense he is in full control of his long-simmering rage when he slaps her; it is a deliberate slap, a choice of punishments, an interpretive response to those surprise romantic properties, those telltale jewels and their apparent confirmation of lost power and control over his own romantic "property." His slow advance with fist drawn back indicates another deliberate action; but this time he is "slowly arrested" by the sight of his terrified wife:

> He hung before her, looking at her fixedly, as she stood crouched against the wall with open, bleeding mouth, and wide-staring eyes, and two hands clawing over her temples. And his lust to see her bleed, to break her and destroy her, rose from an old source against her. It carried him. He wanted satisfaction.
>
> But he had seen her standing there, a piteous, horrified thing, and he turned his face aside in shame and nausea. He went and sat heavily in his chair, and a curious ease, almost like sleep, came over his brain. (342/185)

Again Lawrence refers to the "old source against [Elsie]," the old scores to be settled, as the origin of violence and of the rage that carries Whiston toward it: but what Whiston demonstrates is a controlled use of that rage, a series of choices, and a decision now to desist out of "shame and nausea" over the observed consequences of his own chosen conduct. Indeed, a moment later, after discovering that his wife has merely kept the jewelry for its own sake and has had no carnal dealings with Adams, a weariness comes over him; he feels dreary and sick, and the sight of his wife's bloody handkerchief makes him "only more tired and sick of the responsibility of it, the violence, the shame."

The doubling here of the meaning of responsibility, the reference now to his own guilt and shame at striking her, along with the old biblical concern with responsibility for her conduct, is the story's striking reversal, its critique of its own moral system, here sharply undercut by Whiston's recognition of the double folly of his own assumptions. Still, those grimly doubled responsibilities continue as he now goes slowly about his unfinished biblical business: when his wife refuses to fetch the jewels, he goes upstairs to find them, wraps them up, and walks out in his slippers to post them back to Adams. The Valentine's Day Massacre, such as it has been, is over. When he returns to his wife and sees "her tear-stained, swollen face," a flash of anguish goes over his body: *he* embraces *her* now, in this revised version of the ending, and it is he who says "My love—my little love" as the story ends.

As Cushman wisely observes, "Lawrence's art here is more convincing than the couple's reconciliation."[17] The event has been much too traumatic for easy resolution. A terrifying breach in the marriage has just occurred. Indeed, we have just witnessed what professionals call "the honeymoon phase" of the cycle of violence: the remorseful pleasures of kissing and making up after the dramatic flare-up of ugly violence, with its damaging wounds and bruises, its anguished tears and hostile recriminations, its demeaning and bloody consequences for the wife, its exhilarating high for the power-hungry husband, his reactive guilt and shame as he reassures himself and his wife that it won't happen again, and her own mistaken concurrence in that guilt. It is this honeymoon phase, with its mutually anguished repentance, that Lawrence records as the story closes. For in a way nothing has really changed: the wife's littleness, her childishness, and the husband's controlling role remain intact. The cycle of violence will continue; it will repeat itself again and again, as in Lawrence's marriage to Frieda and in his own artistic reworkings of the theme. As with those battle-scarred antagonists Walter and Gertrude Morel, in *Sons and Lovers,* there will be many, many stages in the ebbing of the Whistons' love, but it will always be ebbing.[18]

V

What are we to make, then, of Lawrence's undercutting of his own assumptions in this tale? What did he learn from revising and strengthening this story? Well, for one thing, he seems to have reached that mature understanding of the powerful psychodynamics of marital conflict, with its death-or-life options, that marks the next phase of his development; for another, he seems to have revised upward his estimate of women's strength and worth and the seriousness of their own search for responsible freedom. In *The Rainbow* and *Women in Love,* where the new ethic of star-equilibrium emerges, his creation of strong questing women, his choice of creative life for questing characters of either sex, the personal resistance of such characters to the death-pulls of northern ice-destruction, is a decided cultural and moral advance over the merely personal predicament of the anguished and imbalanced Whistons. As late as *The Captain's Doll* (1921), moreover, he would balance the chauvinist premise that every woman wants to make a doll of the man she loves with the more strikingly accountable view that every man makes "a ghastly fool of *himself* with a woman at some time or other."[19]

---

17. Ibid., 165.

18. *Sons and Lovers,* 46: "There were many, many stages in the ebbing of her love for him, but it was always ebbing." See also Cycle of Violence, below, 359.

19. My emphasis. For a full discussion of this balanced opposition and the striking sense of male accountability it implies, see my "Repossessing *The Captain's Doll.*"

Meanwhile the deadly weight of World War I, the police persecution in Cornwall, the estrangement of old friends, the suppression of *The Rainbow* and the delay of *Women in Love* (1920) took their cultural and personal toll. By the time Lawrence began his own postwar quest for political power and purpose, he had given himself permission to revive the dominance-submission ethos, with its essentially abusive posture toward women and its reduction of their common claim to life-responsibility, its biblical insistence that women should freely yield that claim in marriage to their supposedly protective partners.[20] In such disastrous cosmic fantasies as *The Plumed Serpent* and "The Woman Who Rode Away," he would even try to reshape the world and its wives to conform to that ethos. At this point, however, two related personal changes of great moment occurred: he became impotent and ill himself from the inroads of tuberculosis, and his own good wife, Frieda, rode away from him to England and the arms of John Middleton Murry.

Of necessity, then, and with no little wisdom and courage, the phoenixlike Lawrence veered sharply away from the deadly willfulness of "the militant ideal," as he then called it, toward the mutual creaturely tenderness and sensual renewals and responsibilities of *Lady Chatterley's Lover* and *The Man Who Died,* and toward the final haunting humanity of his great poem, *The Ship of Death.* In these last wiser "poems," moreover, he also veered away from the emotional dependency of the physically strong young Teddilinks in "The White Stocking" toward the acknowledged vulnerability and frailness of his three older male personas, all of whom cultivate and strengthen their isolate selfhood without blaming women for their frailties.

In these last years, then, Lawrence had apparently learned something valuable about his own battered manhood. Whatever the case, his own deadly propensities, his own cycle of violence had finally been broken.

---

20. As early as *The White Peacock* Lawrence had granted the principle of life-responsibility (that is, personal responsibility for the quality and direction of one's life) to women as well as to men. The intrusions of the dominance theme led to doctrinal conflicts in his thinking and to the dubious resolution of asking women characters to yield their claims to free choice in marriage to their male partners—as in "The White Stocking" and in later derivative situations in *The Fox, The Plumed Serpent,* and "The Woman Who Rode Away." In *The Captain's Doll* he even tried the expedient of freely chosen submissive and dominant *roles* as defined by the marriage service, as distinct from unpossessable modes of *being* for both partners. In *Lady Chatterley,* however, he returned to vital modes of being for equal partners and showed in several ways how the dominance drive can work against that freely chosen goal. Indeed, the dominance drive here dwindles and transmogrifies, in my view, into the "sexual refinements" and expungings of shame through anal intercourse during the last of many stages of sexual conflict and change—a stage that some critics aggrandize into the novel's true and final goal.

The White Stocking

by D. H. Lawrence

I

"I'm getting up, Teddilinks," said Mrs. Whiston, and she sprang out of bed briskly.

"What the Hanover's got you?" asked Whiston.

"Nothing. Can't I get up?" she replied animatedly.

It was about seven o'clock, scarcely light yet in the cold bedroom. Whiston lay still and looked at his wife. She was a pretty little thing, with her fleecy, short black hair all tousled . . . He watched her as she dressed quickly, flicking her small, delightful limbs, throwing her clothes about her. Her slovenliness and untidiness did not trouble him. When she picked up the edge of her petticoat, ripped off a torn string of white lace, and flung it on the dressing-table, her careless abandon made his spirit glow. She stood before the mirror and roughly scrambled together her profuse little mane of hair. He watched the quickness and softness of her young shoulders, calmly, like a husband, and appreciatively.

"Rise up," she cried, turning to him with a quick wave of her arm—"and shine forth."

They had been married two years. But still, when she had gone out of the room, he felt as if all his light and warmth were taken away, he became aware of the raw, cold morning. So he rose himself, wondering casually what had roused her so early. Usually she lay in bed as late as she could.

Whiston fastened a belt round his loins and went downstairs in shirt and trousers. He heard her singing in her snatchy fashion. The stairs creaked under his weight. He passed down the narrow little passage, which she called a hall, of the seven and sixpenny house which was his first home.

He was a shapely young fellow of about twenty-eight, sleepy now and easy with well-being. He heard the water drumming into the kettle, and she began to whistle. He loved the quick way she dodged the supper cups under the tap to wash them for breakfast. She looked an untidy minx, but she was quick and handy enough.

"Teddilinks," she cried.

"What?"

"Light a fire, quick."

She wore an old, sack-like dressing-jacket of black silk pinned across her breast. But one of the sleeves, coming unfastened, showed some delightful pink upper-arm.

"Why don't you sew your sleeve up?" he said, suffering from the sight of the exposed soft flesh.

"Where?" she cried, peering round. "Nuisance," she said, seeing the gap, then with light fingers went on drying the cups.

The kitchen was of fair size, but gloomy. Whiston poked out the dead ashes.

Suddenly a thud was heard at the door down the passage.

"I'll go," cried Mrs. Whiston, and she was gone down the hall.

The postman was a ruddy-faced man who had been a soldier. He smiled broadly, handing her some packages.

"They've not forgot you," he said impudently.

"No—lucky for them," she said, with a toss of the head. But she was interested only in her envelopes this morning. The postman waited inquisitively, smiling in an ingratiating fashion. She slowly, abstractedly, as if she did not know anyone was there, closed the door in his face, continuing to look at the addresses on her letters.

She tore open the thin envelope. There was a long, hideous, cartoon valentine. She smiled briefly and dropped it on the floor. Struggling with the string of a packet, she opened a white cardboard box, and there lay a white silk handkerchief packed neatly under the paper lace of the box, and her initial, worked in heliotrope, fully displayed. She smiled pleasantly, and gently put the box aside. The third envelope contained another white packet—apparently a cotton handkerchief neatly folded. She shook it out. It was a long white stocking, but there was a little weight in the toe. Quickly, she thrust down her arm, wriggling her fingers into the toe of the stocking, and brought out a small box. She peeped inside the box, then hastily opened a door on her left hand, and went into the little, cold sitting-room. She had her lower lip caught earnestly between her teeth.

With a little flash of triumph, she lifted a pair of pearl ear-rings from the small box, and she went to the mirror. There, earnestly, she began to hook them through her ears, looking at herself sideways in the glass. Curiously concentrated and intent she seemed as she fingered the lobes of her ears, her head bent on one side.

Then the pearl ear-rings dangled under her rosy, small ears. She shook her head sharply, to see the swing of the drops. They went chill against her neck, in little, sharp touches. Then she stood still to look at herself, bridling her head in the dignified fashion. Then she simpered at herself. Catching her own eye, she could not help winking at herself and laughing.

She turned to look at the box. There was a scrap of paper with this posy:

> "Pearls may be fair, but thou art fairer.
> Wear these for me, and I'll love the wearer."

She made a grimace and a grin. But she was drawn to the mirror again, to look at her ear-rings.

Whiston had made the fire burn, so he came to look for her. When she heard him, she started round quickly, guiltily. She was watching him with intent blue eyes when he appeared.

He did not see much, in his morning-drowsy warmth. He gave her, as ever, a feeling of warmth and slowness. His eyes were very blue, very kind, his manner simple.

"What ha' you got?" he asked.

"Valentines," she said briskly, ostentatiously turning to show him the silk handkerchief. She thrust it under his nose. "Smell how good," she said.

"Who's that from?" he replied, without smelling.

"It's a valentine," she cried. "How do I know who it's from?"

"I'll bet you know," he said.

"Ted!—I don't!" she cried, beginning to shake her head, then stopping because of the ear-rings.

He stood still a moment, displeased.

"They've no right to send you valentines, now," he said.

"Ted!—Why not? You're not jealous, are you? I haven't the least idea who it's from. Look—there's my initial"—she pointed with an emphatic finger at the heliotrope embroidery—

> "E for Elsie,
> Nice little gelsie,"

she sang.

"Get out," he said. "You know who it's from."

"Truth, I don't," she cried.

He looked round, and saw the white stocking lying on a chair.

"Is this another?" he said.

"No, that's a sample," she said. "There's only a comic." And she fetched in the long cartoon.

He stretched it out and looked at it solemnly.

"Fools!" he said, and went out of the room.

She flew upstairs and took off the ear-rings. When she returned, he was crouched before the fire blowing the coals. The skin of his face was flushed, and slightly pitted, as if he had had small-pox. But his neck was white and smooth and goodly. She hung her arms round his neck as he crouched there, and clung to him. He balanced on his toes.

"This fire's a slow-coach," he said.

"And who else is a slow-coach?" she said.

"One of us two, I know," he said, and he rose carefully. She remained clinging round his neck, so that she was lifted off her feet.

"Ha!—swing me," she cried.

He lowered his head, and she hung in the air, swinging from his neck, laughing. Then she slipped off.

"The kettle is singing," she sang, flying for the teapot. He bent down again to blow the fire. The veins in his neck stood out, his shirt collar seemed too tight.

> "Doctor Wyer,
> Blow the fire,
> Puff! puff! puff!"

she sang, laughing.

He smiled at her.

She was so glad because of her pearl ear-rings.

Over the breakfast she grew serious. He did not notice. She became portentous in her gravity. Almost it penetrated through his steady good-humor to irritate him.

"Teddy!" she said at last.

"What?" he asked.

"I told you a lie," she said, humbly tragic.

His soul stirred uneasily.

"Oh aye?" he said casually.

She was not satisfied. He ought to be more moved.

"Yes," she said.

He cut a piece of bread.

"Was it a good one?" he asked.

She was piqued. Then she considered—was it a good one? Then she laughed.

"No," she said, "it wasn't up to much."

"Ah!" he said easily, but with a steady strength of fondness for her in his tone. "Get it out then."

It became a little more difficult.

"You know that white stocking," she said earnestly. "I told you a lie. It wasn't a sample. It was a valentine."

A little frown came on his brow.

"Then what did you invent it as a sample for?" he said. But he knew this weakness of hers. The touch of anger in his voice frightened her.

"I was afraid you'd be cross," she said pathetically.

"I'll bet you were vastly afraid," he said.

"I *was,* Teddy."

There was a pause. He was resolving one or two things in his mind.

"And who sent it?" he asked.

"I can guess," she said, "though there wasn't a word with it—except—"

She ran to the sitting-room and returned with a slip of paper.

> "Pearls may be fair, but thou art fairer.
> Wear these for me, and I'll love the wearer."

He read it twice, then a dull red flush came on his face.

"And *who* do you guess it is?" he asked, with a ringing of anger in his voice.

"I suspect it's Sam Adams," she said, with a little virtuous indignation.

Whiston was silent for a moment.

"Fool!" he said. "An' what's it got to do with pearls?—and how can he say 'wear these for me' when there's only one? He hasn't got the brain to invent a proper verse."

He screwed the slip of paper into a ball and flung it into the fire.

"I suppose he thinks it'll make a pair with the one last year," she said.

"Why, did he send one then?"

"Yes. I thought you'd be wild if you knew."

His jaw set rather sullenly.

Presently he rose, and went to wash himself, rolling back his sleeves and pulling open his shirt at the breast. It was as if his fine, clear-cut temples and steady eyes were degraded by the lower, rather brutal part of his face. But she loved it. As she whisked about, clearing the table, she loved the way in which he stood washing himself. He was such a man. She liked to see his neck glistening with water as he swilled it. It amused her and pleased her and thrilled her. He was so sure, so permanent, he had her so utterly in his power. It gave her a delightful, mischievous sense of liberty. Within his grasp, she could dart about excitingly.

He turned round to her, his face red from the cold water, his eyes fresh and very blue.

"You haven't been seeing anything of him, have you?" he asked roughly.

"Yes," she answered, after a moment, as if caught guiltily. "He got into the tram with me, and he asked me to drink a coffee and a Benedictine in the Royal."

"You've got it off fine and glib," he said sullenly. "And did you?"

"Yes," she replied, with the air of a traitor before the rack.

The blood came up into his neck and face, he stood motionless, dangerous.

"It was cold, and it was such fun to go into the Royal," she said.

"You'd go off with a nigger for a packet of chocolate," he said, in anger and contempt, and some bitterness. Queer how he drew away from her, cut her off from him.

"Ted—how beastly!" she cried. "You know quite well—" She caught her lip, flushed, and the tears came to her eyes.

He turned away, to put on his necktie. She went about her work, making a queer pathetic little mouth, down which occasionally dripped a tear.

He was ready to go. With his hat jammed down on his head, and his overcoat buttoned up to his chin, he came to kiss her. He would be miserable all the day if he went without. She allowed herself to be kissed. Her cheek was wet under his lips, and his heart burned. She hurt him so deeply. And she felt aggrieved, and did not quite forgive him.

In a moment she went upstairs to her ear-rings. Sweet they looked nestling in the little drawer—sweet! She examined them with voluptuous pleasure, she threaded them in her ears, she looked at herself, she posed and postured and smiled, and looked sad and tragic and winning and appealing, all in turn before the mirror. And she was happy, and very pretty.

She wore the ear-rings all morning, in the house. She was self-conscious, and quite brilliantly winsome, when the baker came, wondering if he would notice. All the tradesmen left her door with a glow in them, feeling elated, and unconsciously favoring the delightful little creature, though there had been nothing to notice in her behavior.

She was stimulated all the day. She did not think about her husband. He was the permanent basis from which she took these giddy little flights into nowhere. At night, like chickens and curses, she would come home to him, to roost.

Meanwhile Whiston, a traveler and confidential support of a small firm, hastened about his work, his heart all the while anxious for her, yearning for surety, and kept tense by not getting it.

II

She had been a warehouse girl in Adams's lace factory before she was married. Sam Adams was her employer. He was a bachelor of forty, growing stout, a man well dressed and florid, with a large brown moustache and thin hair. From the rest of his well-groomed, showy appearance, it was evident his baldness was a chagrin to him. He had a good presence, and some Irish blood in his veins.

His fondness for the girls, or the fondness of the girls for him, was notorious. And Elsie, quick, pretty, almost witty little thing—she *seemed* witty, although, when her sayings were repeated, they were entirely trivial—she had a great attraction for him. He would come into the warehouse dressed in a rather sporting reefer coat, of fawn color, and trousers of fine black-and-white check, a cap with a big peak and a scarlet carnation in his button-hole, to impress her. She was only half impressed. He was too loud for her good taste. Instinctively perceiving this, he sobered down to navy blue. Then a well-built man, florid, with large brown whiskers, smart navy blue suit, fashionable boots, and manly hat, he was the irreproachable. Elsie was impressed.

But meanwhile Whiston was courting her, and she made splendid little gestures, before her bedroom mirror, of the constant-and-true sort.

"True, true till death—"

That was her song. Whiston was made that way, so there was no need to take thought for him.

Every Christmas Sam Adams gave a party at his house, to which he invited his superior work-people—not factory hands and laborers, but those above. He was a generous man in his way, with a real warm feeling for giving pleasure.

Two years ago Elsie had attended this Christmas-party for the last time. Whiston had accompanied her. At that time he worked for Sam Adams.

She had been very proud of herself, in her close-fitting, full-skirted dress of blue silk. Whiston called for her. Then she tripped beside him, holding her large cashmere shawl across her breast. He strode with long strides, his trousers handsomely strapped under his boots, and her silk shoes bulging the pockets of his full-skirted overcoat.

They passed through the park gates, and her spirits rose. Above them the Castle Rock looked grandly in the night, the naked trees stood still and dark in the frost, along the boulevard.

They were rather late. Agitated with anticipation, in the cloakroom she gave up her shawl, donned her silk shoes, and looked at herself in the mirror. The loose bunches of curls on either side her face danced prettily, her mouth smiled.

She hung a moment in the door of the brilliantly lighted room. Many people were moving within the blaze of lamps, under the crystal chandeliers, the full skirts of the women balancing and floating, the side-whiskers and white cravats of the men bowing above. Then she entered the light.

In an instant Sam Adams was coming forward, lifting both his arms in boisterous welcome. There was a constant red laugh on his face.

"Come late, would you," he shouted, "like royalty."

He seized her hands and led her forward. He opened his mouth wide when he spoke, and the effect of the warm, dark opening behind the brown whiskers was disturbing. But she was floating into the throng on his arm. He was very gallant.

"Now then," he said, taking her card to write down the dances, "I've got carte blanche, haven't I?"

"Mr. Whiston doesn't dance," she said.

"I am a lucky man!" he said, scribbling his initials. "I was born with an *amourette* in my mouth."

He wrote on, quietly. She blushed and laughed, not knowing what it meant.

"Why, what is that?" she said.

"It's you, even littler than you are, dressed in little wings," he said.

"I should have to be pretty small to get in your mouth," she said. "You think you're too big, do you!" he said easily.

He handed her her card, with a bow.

"Now I'm set up, my darling, for this evening," he said.

Then, quick, always at his ease, he looked over the room. She waited in front of him. He was ready. Catching the eye of the band, he nodded. In a moment, the music began. He seemed to relax, giving himself up.

"Now then, Elsie," he said, with a curious caress in his voice that seemed to lap the outside of her body in a warm glow, delicious. She gave herself to it. She liked it.

He was an excellent dancer. He seemed to draw her close in to him by some male warmth of attraction, so that she became all soft and pliant to him, flowing to his form, whilst he united her with him and they lapsed along in one movement. She was just carried in a kind of strong, warm flood, her feet moved of themselves, and only the music threw her away from him, threw her back to him, to his clasp, in his strong form moving against her, rhythmically, deliciously.

When it was over, he was pleased and his eyes had a curious gleam which thrilled her and yet had nothing to do with her. Yet it held her. He did not speak to her. He only looked straight into her eyes with a curious, gleaming look that disturbed her fearfully and deliciously. But also there was in his look some of the automatic irony of the *roué*. It left her partly cold. She was not carried away.

She went, driven by an opposite, heavier impulse, to Whiston. He stood looking gloomy, trying to admit that she had a perfect right to enjoy herself apart from him. He received her with rather grudging kindliness.

"Aren't you going to play whist?" she asked.

"Aye," he said. "Directly."

"I do wish you could dance."

"Well, I can't," he said. "So you enjoy yourself."

"But I should enjoy it better if I could dance with you."

"Nay, you're all right," he said. "I'm not made that way."

"Then you ought to be!" she cried.

"Well, it's my fault, not yours. You enjoy yourself," he bade her. Which she proceeded to do, a little bit irked.

She went with anticipation to the arms of Sam Adams, when the time came to dance with him. It *was* so gratifying, irrespective of the man. And she felt a little grudge against Whiston, soon forgotten when her host was holding her near to him, in a delicious embrace. And she watched his eyes, to meet the gleam in them, which gratified her.

She was getting warmed right through, the glow was penetrating into her, driving away everything else. Only in her heart was a little tightness, like conscience.

When she got a chance, she escaped from the dancing-room to the card-room. There, in a cloud of smoke, she found Whiston playing cribbage. Radiant, roused, animated, she came up to him and greeted him. She was too strong, too vibrant a note in the quiet room. He lifted his head, and a frown knitted his gloomy forehead.

"Are you playing cribbage? Is it exciting? How are you getting on?" she chattered.

He looked at her. None of these questions needed answering, and he did not feel in touch with her. She turned to the cribbage-board.

"Are you white or red?" she asked.

"He's red," replied the partner.

"Then you're losing," she said, still to Whiston. And she lifted the red peg from the board. "One—two—three—four—five—six—seven—eight—Right up there you ought to jump—"

"Now put it back in its right place," said Whiston.

"Where was it?" she asked gaily, knowing her transgression. He took the little red peg away from her and stuck it in its hole.

The cards were shuffled.

"What a shame you're losing!" said Elsie.

"You'd better cut for him," said the partner.

She did so, hastily. The cards were dealt. She put her hand on his shoulder, looking at his cards.

"It's good," she cried, "isn't it?"

He did not answer, but threw down two cards. It moved him more strongly than was comfortable, to have her hand on his shoulder, her curls dangling and touching his ears, whilst she was roused to another man. It made the blood flame over him.

At that moment Sam Adams appeared, florid and boisterous, intoxicated more with himself, with the dancing, than with wine. In his eyes the curious, impersonal light gleamed.

"I thought I should find you here, Elsie," he cried boisterously, a disturbing, high note in his voice.

"What made you think so?" she replied, the mischief rousing in her.

The florid, well-built man narrowed his eyes to a smile.

"I should never look for you among the ladies," he said, with a kind of intimate, animal call to her. He laughed, bowed, and offered her his arm.

"Madam, the music waits."

She went almost helplessly, carried along with him, unwilling, yet delighted.

That dance was an intoxication to her. After the first few steps, she felt herself slipping away from herself. She almost knew she was going, she did not even want to go. Yet she must have chosen to go. She lay in the arm of the steady, close man with whom she was dancing, and she seemed to swim away out of contact with the room, into him. She had passed into another, denser element of him, an essential privacy. The room was all vague around her, like an atmosphere, like under sea, with a flow of ghostly, dumb movements. But she herself was held real against her partner, and it seemed she was connected with him, as if the movements of his body and limbs were her own movements, yet not her own movements—and oh, delicious! He also was given up, oblivious, concentrated, into the dance. His eye was unseeing. Only his large, voluptuous body gave off a subtle activity. His fingers seemed to search into her flesh. Every moment, and every moment, she felt she would give way utterly, and sink molten: the fusion point was coming when she would fuse down into perfect unconsciousness at his feet and knees. But he bore her round the room in the dance, and he seemed to sustain all her body with his limbs, his body, and his warmth seemed to come closer into her, nearer, till it would fuse right through her, and she would be as liquid to him, as an intoxication only.

It was exquisite. When it was over, she was dazed, and was scarcely breathing. She stood with him in the middle of the room as if she were alone in a remote place. He bent over her. She expected his lips on her bare shoulder, and waited. Yet they were not alone, they were not alone. It was cruel.

" 'Twas good, wasn't it, my darling?" he said to her, low and delighted. There was a strange impersonality about his low, exultant call that appealed to her irresistibly. Yet why was she aware of some part shut off in her? She pressed his arm, and he led her toward the door.

She was not aware of what she was doing, only a little grain of resistant trouble was in her. The man, possessed, yet with a superficial presence of mind, made way to the dining-room, as if to give her refreshment, cunningly working to his own escape with her. He was molten hot, filmed over with presence of mind, and bottomed with cold disbelief.

In the dining-room was Whiston, carrying coffee to the plain, neglected ladies. Elsie saw him, but felt as if he could not see her. She was beyond his reach and ken. A sort of fusion existed between her and the large man at her side. She ate her custard, but an incomplete fusion all the while sustained and contained her within the being of her employer.

But she was growing cooler. Whiston came up. She looked at him, and saw him with different eyes. She saw his slim, young man's figure real and enduring before her. That was he. But she was in the spell with the other man, fused with him, and she could not be taken away.

"Have you finished your cribbage?" she asked, with hasty evasion of him.

"Yes," he replied. "Aren't you getting tired of dancing?"

"Not a bit," she said.

"Not she," said Adams heartily. "No girl with any spirit gets tired of dancing. —Have something else, Elsie. Come—sherry. Have a glass of sherry with us, Whiston."

Whilst they sipped the wine, Adams watched Whiston almost cunningly, to find his advantage.

"We'd better be getting back—there's the music," he said. "See the women get something to eat, Whiston, will you, there's a good chap."

And he began to draw away. Elsie was drifting helplessly with him. But Whiston put himself beside them, and went along with them. In silence they passed through to the dancing-room. There Adams hesitated, and looked round the room. It was as if he could not see.

A man came hurrying forward, claiming Elsie, and Adams went to his other partner. Whiston stood watching during the dance. She was conscious of him standing there observant of her, like a ghost, or a judgment, or a guardian angel. She was also conscious, much more intimately and impersonally, of the body of the other man moving somewhere in the room. She still belonged to him, but a feeling of distraction possessed her, and helplessness. Adams danced on, adhering to Elsie, waiting his time, with the persistence of cynicism.

The dance was over. Adams was detained. Elsie found herself beside Whiston. There was something shapely about him as he sat, about his knees and his distinct figure, that she clung to. It was as if he had enduring form. She put her hand on his knee.

"Are you enjoying yourself?" he asked.

"*Ever* so," she replied, with a fervent, yet detached tone.

"It's going on for one o'clock," he said.

"Is it?" she answered. It meant nothing to her.

"Should we be going?" he said.

She was silent. For the first time for an hour or more an inkling of her normal consciousness returned. She resented it.

"What for?" she said.

"I thought you might have had enough," he said.

A slight soberness came over her, an irritation at being frustrated of her illusion.

"Why?" she said.

"We've been here since nine," he said.

That was no answer, no reason. It conveyed nothing to her. She sat detached from him. Across the room Sam Adams glanced at her. She sat there exposed for him.

"You don't want to be too free with Sam Adams," said Whiston cautiously, suffering. "You know what he is."

"How, free?" she asked.

"Why—you don't want to have too much to do with him."

She sat silent. He was forcing her into consciousness of her position. But he could not get hold of her feelings, to change them. She had a curious, perverse desire that he should not.

"I like him," she said.

"What do you find to like in him?" he said, with a hot heart.

"I don't know—but I like him," she said.

She was immutable. He sat feeling heavy and dulled with rage. He was not clear as to what he felt. He sat there unliving whilst she danced. And she, distracted, lost to herself between the opposing forces of the two men, drifted. Between the dances, Whiston kept near to her. She was scarcely conscious. She glanced repeatedly at her card, to see when she would dance again with Adams, half in desire, half in dread. Sometimes she met his steady, glaucous eye as she passed him in the dance. Sometimes she saw the steadiness of his flank as he danced. And it was always as if she rested on his arm, were borne along, upborne by him, away from herself. And always there was present the other's antagonism. She was divided.

The time came for her to dance with Adams. Oh, the delicious closing of contact with him, of his limbs touching her limbs, his arm supporting her. She seemed to resolve. Whiston had not made himself real to her. He was only a heavy place in her consciousness.

But she breathed heavily, beginning to suffer from the closeness of strain. She was nervous. Adams also was constrained. A tightness, a tension was coming over them all. And he was exasperated, feeling something counteracting physical magnetism, feeling a will stronger with her than his own, intervening in what was becoming a vital necessity to him.

Elsie was almost lost to her own control. As she went forward with him to take her place at the dance, she stooped for her pocket-handkerchief. The music sounded for quadrilles. Everybody was ready. Adams stood with his body near her, exerting his attraction over her. He was tense and fighting. She stooped for her pocket-handkerchief, and shook it as she rose. It shook out and fell from her hand. With agony, she saw she had taken a white stocking instead of a handkerchief. For a second it lay on the floor, a twist of white stocking. Then, in an instant, Adams picked it up, with a little, surprised laugh of triumph.

"That'll do for me," he whispered—seeming to take possession of her. And he stuffed the stocking in his trousers pocket, and quickly offered her his handkerchief.

The dance began. She felt weak and faint, as if her will were turned to water. A heavy sense of loss came over her. She could not help herself any more. But it was peace.

When the dance was over, Adams yielded her up. Whiston came to her.

"What was it as you dropped?" Whiston asked.

"I thought it was my handkerchief—I'd taken a stocking by mistake," she said, detached and muted.

"And he's got it?"

"Yes."

"What does he mean by that?"

She lifted her shoulders.

"Are you going to let him keep it?" he asked.

"I don't let him."

There was a long pause.

"Am I to go and have it out with him?" he asked, his face flushed, his blue eyes going hard with opposition.

"No," she said, pale.

"Why?"

"No —I don't want to say anything about it."

He sat exasperated and nonplussed.

"You'll let him keep it, then?" he asked.

She sat silent and made no form of answer.

"What do you mean by it?" he said, dark with fury. And he started up.

"No!" she cried. "Ted!" And she caught hold of him, sharply detaining him. It made him black with rage.

"Why?" he said.

Then something about her mouth was pitiful to him. He did not understand, but he felt she must have her reasons.

"Then I'm not stopping here," he said. "Are you coming with me?"

She rose mutely, and they went out of the room. Adams had not noticed.

In a few moments they were in the street.

"What the hell do you mean?" he said, in a black fury.

She went at his side, in silence, neutral.

"That great hog, an' all," he added.

Then they went a long time in silence through the frozen, deserted darkness of the town. She felt she could not go indoors. They were drawing near her house.

"I don't want to go home," she suddenly cried in distress and anguish. "I don't want to go home."

He looked at her.

"Why don't you?" he said.

"I don't want to go home," was all she could sob.

He heard somebody coming.

"Well, we can walk a bit further," he said.

She was silent again. They passed out of the town into the fields. He held her by the arm—they could not speak.

"What's a-matter?" he asked at length, puzzled.

She began to cry again.

At last he took her in his arms, to soothe her. She sobbed by herself, almost unaware of him.

"Tell me what's a-matter, Elsie," he said. "Tell me what's a-matter—my dear—tell me, then—"

He kissed her wet face, and caressed her. She made no response. He was puzzled and tender and miserable.

At length she became quiet. Then he kissed her, and she put her arms round him, and clung to him very tight, as if for fear and anguish. He held her in his arms, wondering.

"Ted!" she whispered, frantic. "Ted!"

"What, my love?" he answered, becoming also afraid.

"Be good to me," she cried. "Don't be cruel to me."

"No, my pet," he said, amazed and grieved. "Why?"

"Oh, be good to me," she sobbed.

And he held her very safe, and his heart was white-hot with love for her. His mind was amazed. He could only hold her against his chest that was white-hot with love and belief in her. So she was restored at last.

III

She refused to go to her work at Adams's any more. Her father had to submit and she sent in her notice—she was not well. Sam Adams was ironical. But he had a curious patience. He did not fight.

In a few weeks, she and Whiston were married. She loved him with passion and worship, a fierce little abandon of love that moved him to the depths of his being, and gave him a permanent surety and sense of realness in himself. He did not trouble about himself any more: he felt he was fulfilled and now he had only the many things in the world to busy himself about. Whatever troubled him, at the bottom was surety. He had found himself in this love.

They spoke once or twice of the white stocking.

"Ah!" Whiston exclaimed. "What does it matter?"

He was impatient and angry, and could not bear to consider the matter. So it was left unresolved.

She was quite happy at first, carried away by her adoration of her husband. Then gradually she got used to him. He always was the ground of her happiness, but she got used to him, as to the air she breathed. He never got used to her in the same way.

Inside of marriage she found her liberty. She was rid of the responsibility of herself. Her husband must look after that. She was free to get what she could out of her time.

So that, when, after some months, she met Sam Adams, she was not quite as unkind to him as she might have been. With a young wife's new and exciting knowledge of men, she perceived he was in love with her, she knew he had always kept an unsatisfied desire for her. And, sportive, she could not help playing a little with this, though she cared not one jot for the man himself.

When Valentine's day came, which was near the first anniversary of her wedding day, there arrived a white stocking with a little amethyst brooch. Luckily Whiston did not see it, so she said nothing of it to him. She had not the faintest intention of having anything to do with Sam Adams, but once a little brooch was in her possession, it was hers, and she did not trouble her head for a moment how she had come by it. She kept it.

Now she had the pearl ear-rings. They were a more valuable and a more conspicuous present. She would have to ask her mother to give them to her, to explain their presence. She made a little plan in her head. And she was extraordinarily pleased. As for Sam Adams, even if he saw her wearing them, he would not give her away. What fun, if he saw her wearing his ear-rings! She would pretend she had inherited them from her grandmother, her mother's mother. She laughed to herself as she went down town in the afternoon, the pretty drops dangling in front of her curls. But she saw no one of importance.

Whiston came home tired and depressed. All day the male in him had been uneasy, and this had fatigued him. She was curiously against him, inclined, as she sometimes was nowadays, to make mock of him and jeer at him and cut him off. He did not understand this, and it angered him deeply. She was uneasy before him.

She knew he was in a state of suppressed irritation. The veins stood out on the backs of his hands, his brow was drawn stiffly. Yet she could not help goading him.

"What did you do wi' that white stocking?" he asked, out of a gloomy silence, his voice strong and brutal.

"I put it in a drawer—why?" she replied flippantly.

"Why didn't you put it on the fire back?" he said harshly. "What are you hoarding it up for?"

"I'm not hoarding it up," she said. "I've got a pair."

He relapsed into gloomy silence. She, unable to move him, ran away upstairs, leaving him smoking by the fire. Again she tried on the ear-rings. Then another little inspiration came to her. She drew on the white stockings, both of them.

Presently she came down in them. Her husband still sat immoveable and glowering by the fire.

"Look!" she said. "They'll do beautifully."

And she picked up her skirts to her knees, and twisted round, looking at her pretty legs in the neat stockings.

He filled with unreasonable rage, and took the pipe from his mouth.

"Don't they look nice?" she said. "One from last year and one from this, they just do. Save you buying a pair."

And she looked over her shoulders at her pretty calves, and the dangling frills of her knickers.

"Put your skirts down and don't make a fool of yourself," he said.

"Why a fool of myself?" she asked.

And she began to dance slowly round the room, kicking up her feet half reckless, half jeering, in a ballet-dancer's fashion. Almost fearfully, yet in defiance, she kicked up her legs at him, singing as she did so. She resented him.

"You little fool, ha' done with it," he said. "And you'll backfire them stockings, I'm telling you." He was angry. His face flushed dark, he kept his head bent. She ceased to dance.

"I shan't," she said. "They'll come in very useful."

He lifted his head and watched her, with lighted, dangerous eyes.

"You'll put 'em on the fire back, I tell you," he said.

It was a war now. She bent forward, in a ballet-dancer's fashion, and put her tongue between her teeth.

"I shan't backfire them stockings," she sang, repeating his words, "I shan't, I shan't, I shan't."

And she danced round the room doing a high kick to the tune of her words. There was a real biting indifference in her behavior.

"We'll see whether you will or not," he said, "trollops! You'd like Sam Adams to know you was wearing 'em, wouldn't you? That's what would please you."

"Yes, I'd like him to see how nicely they fit me, he might give me some more then."

And she looked down at her pretty legs.

He knew somehow that she *would* like Sam Adams to see how pretty her legs looked in the white stockings. It made his anger go deep, almost to hatred.

"Yer nasty trolley," he cried. "Put yer petticoats down, and stop being so foul-minded."

"I'm not foul-minded," she said. "My legs are my own. And why shouldn't Sam Adams think they're nice?"

There was a pause. He watched her with eyes glittering to a point.

"Have you been havin' owt to do with him?" he asked.

"I've just spoken to him when I've seen him," she said. "He's not as bad as you would make out."

"Isn't he?" he cried, a certain wakefulness in his voice. "Them who has anything to do wi' him is too bad for me, I tell you."

"Why, what are you frightened of him for?" she mocked.

She was rousing all his uncontrollable anger. He sat glowering. Every one of her sentences stirred him up like a red-hot iron. Soon it would be too much. And she was afraid herself; but she was neither conquered nor convinced.

A curious little grin of hate came on his face. He had a long score against her.

"What am I frightened of him for?" he repeated automatically. "What am I frightened of him for? Why, for you, you stray-running little bitch."

She flushed. The insult went deep into her, right home.

"Well, if you're so dull—" she said, lowering her eyelids, and speaking coldly, haughtily.

"If I'm so dull I'll break your neck the first word you speak to him," he said, tense.

"Pf!" she sneered. "Do you think I'm frightened of you?" She spoke coldly, detached.

She was frightened, for all that, white round the mouth.

His heart was getting hotter.

"You *will* be frightened of me, the next time you have anything to do with him," he said.

"Do you think *you'd* ever be told—ha!"

Her jeering scorn made him go white-hot, molten. He knew he was incoherent, scarcely responsible for what he might do. Slowly, unseeing, he rose and went out of doors, stifled, moved to kill her.

He stood leaning against the garden fence, unable either to see or hear. Below him, far off, fumed the lights of the town. He stood still, unconscious with a black storm of rage, his face lifted to the night.

Presently, still unconscious of what he was doing, he went indoors again. She stood, a small stubborn figure with tight-pressed lips and big, sullen, childish eyes, watching him, white with fear. He went heavily across the floor and dropped into his chair.

There was a silence.

"*You're* not going to tell me everything I shall do, and everything I shan't," she broke out at last.

He lifted his head.

"I tell you *this,*" he said, low and intense. "Have anything to do with Sam Adams, and I'll break your neck."

She laughed, shrill and false.

"How I hate your word 'break your neck,' " she said, with a grimace of the mouth. "It sounds so common and beastly. Can't you say something else—"

There was a dead silence.

"And besides," she said, with a queer chirrup of mocking laughter, "what do you know about anything? He sent me an amethyst brooch and a pair of pearl ear-rings."

"He what?" said Whiston, in a suddenly normal voice. His eyes were fixed on her.

"Sent me a pair of pearl ear-rings, and an amethyst brooch," she repeated, mechanically, pale to the lips.

And her big, black, childish eyes watched him, fascinated, held in her [his] spell.

He seemed to thrust his face and his eyes forward at her, as he rose slowly and came to her. She watched transfixed in terror. Her throat made a small sound, as she tried to scream.

Then, quick as lightning, the back of his hand struck her with a crash across the mouth, and she was flung back blinded against the wall. The shock shook a queer sound out of her. And then she saw him still coming on, his eyes holding her, his fist drawn back, advancing slowly. At any instant the blow might crash into her.

Mad with terror, she raised her hands with a queer clawing movement to cover her eyes and her temples, opening her mouth in a dumb shriek. There was no sound. But the sight of her slowly arrested him. He hung before her, looking at her fixedly, as she stood crouched against the wall with open, bleeding mouth, and wide-staring eyes, and two hands clawing over her temples. And his lust to see her bleed, to break her and destroy her, rose from an old source against her. It carried him. He wanted satisfaction.

But he had seen her standing there, a piteous, horrified thing, and he turned his face aside in shame and nausea. He went and sat heavily in his chair, and a curious ease, almost like sleep, came over his brain.

She walked away from the wall toward the fire, dizzy, white to the lips, mechanically wiping her small, bleeding mouth. He sat motionless. Then, gradually, her breath began to hiss, she shook, and was sobbing silently, in grief for herself. Without looking, he saw. It made his mad desire to destroy her come back.

At length he lifted his head. His eyes were glowing again, fixed on her.

"And what did he give them you for?" he asked, in a steady, unyielding voice.

Her crying dried up in a second. She also was tense.

"They came as valentines," she replied, still not subjugated, even if beaten.

"When, to-day?"

"The pearl ear-rings to-day—the amethyst brooch last year."

"You've had it a year?"

"Yes."

She felt that now nothing would prevent him if he rose to kill her. She could not prevent him any more. She was yielded up to him. They both trembled in the balance, unconscious.

"What have you had to do with him?" he asked, in a barren voice.

"I've not had anything to do with him," she quavered.

"You just kept 'em because they were jewelry?" he said.

A weariness came over him. What was the worth of speaking any more of it? He did not care any more. He was dreary and sick.

She began to cry again, but he took no notice. She kept wiping her mouth on her handkerchief. He could see it, the blood-mark. It made him only more sick and tired of the responsibility of it, the violence, the shame.

When she began to move about again, he raised his head once more from his dead, motionless position.

"Where are the things?" he said.

"They are upstairs," she quavered. She knew the passion had gone down in him.

"Bring them down," he said.

"I won't," she wept, with rage. "You're not going to bully me and hit me like that on the mouth."

And she sobbed again. He looked at her in contempt and compassion and in rising anger.

"Where are they?" he said.

"They're in the little drawer under the looking-glass," she sobbed.

He went slowly upstairs, struck a match, and found the trinkets. He brought them downstairs in his hand.

"These?" he said, looking at them as they lay in his palm.

She looked at them without answering. She was not interested in them any more.

He looked at the little jewels. They were pretty.

"It's none of their fault," he said to himself.

And he searched round slowly, persistently, for a box. He tied the things up and addressed them to Sam Adams. Then he went out in his slippers to post the little package.

When he came back she was still sitting crying.

"You'd better go to bed," he said.

She paid no attention. He sat by the fire. She still cried.

"I'm sleeping down here," he said. "Go you to bed."

In a few moments she lifted her tear-stained, swollen face and looked at him with eyes all forlorn and pathetic. A great flash of anguish went over his body. He went over, slowly, and very gently took her in his hands. She let herself be taken. Then as she lay against his shoulder, she sobbed aloud:

"I never meant—"

"My love—my little love—" he cried, in anguish of spirit, holding her in his arms.

Power Games in Joyce's "Counterparts"

That male batterers are made and not born is one of the more obvious axioms among counselors in the field of domestic violence. Although there are genetic and psychological theories about propensities for violent or criminal behavior, their usefulness to rehabilitation workers in this field is negligible. They purport to separate batterers from nonviolent and law-abiding citizens—in other words, from the rest of us—when in fact the evidence is all too clear that batterers are normal and quite ordinary people. They are not crazies or criminals by birth or predisposition. They exist among all classes, races, and ethnic groups; they are supported in their behavior by social sanctions and precedents; they become violent because in one way or another they have been taught to be violent. They have learned that, in the sanctity of the home, it is all right for men to seek power and control over their wives and children through violence. The problem faced by counselors in the field, therefore, is how to make batterers unlearn that socially sanctioned lesson.

At Brother to Brother, the social service agency in Rhode Island where I worked for a time as a co-counselor for the group reeducation of male batterers, the seventh week in our program was devoted in this light to "Issues of Oppression, Control, & Power." The week before that was devoted to "Gender Role Stereotypes," and the weeks before that to defining abuse as a choice men made, for which they were responsible—a choice designed to force their partners to do or think something against their will, a choice often abetted by drinking or taking drugs but not defined by them, and one likely to have a lasting and traumatic effect upon their partners. Our progression through these stages was itself designed, of course, to change our clients' attitudes and beliefs about domestic violence. With lessons six and seven we moved beyond the immediacies of such attitudes into the arena of their social and political formation.

The aim of lesson seven, for instance, was to look at "issues of oppression and how they contribute to men being abusive in their relationships." For this purpose each lead counselor pinned blank newsprint on the wall and asked the clients to suggest items for two conflicting lists: "those who have power and those who don't have power in our society." The chief categories were gender (men/women), race (whites/people of color), economic status (wealthy/unwealthy), and sexual identity (heterosexual/gay and lesbian). Other relevant categories were religion (Christians/Jews, Muslims), education (college/lower schools), health or physical ability (able-bodied/disabled), age (youth and maturity/old age, infancy), and ethnicity (Anglo-Saxon/others). The idea behind these lists was to bring out the prevalence of hierarchical groupings in our society and to suggest the kinds of subordination, oppression, or prejudicial treatment they might foster. (See Power Ladder, below, 357.)

The clients were then asked how we know the "have-nots" on these lists are oppressed. Relevant answers included their underrepresentation in positions of power in federal and state governments, business, the judiciary, police and fire departments, and so forth; their difficulties with hiring, housing, finance, medical care, legal justice; and their minimal presence in histories and the mass media. The same question was then specifically pursued with the categories of gender, race, and sexual identity and the kinds of daily abuses that the "have-nots" in these categories (women, people of color, gays and lesbians) might suffer. Then the clients were asked to identify their own contributions "to power staying where it is in our society" and to their power relations with their partners. The closing statement of the agency's perspective reads as follows:

> Oppression is about power and control. As long as you feel that you can oppress anyone based on who they are then you will be at risk of oppressing your partner. By accepting the perspective that oppression is a legitimate way of being, you give up the ideal that all people should have equal opportunity to develop their full potential.[1]

The obvious assumption here is that we are all conditioned to accept oppression as a social norm, and therefore at risk of oppressing those beneath us not only on the social ladders discussed here but also in our homes, where women and children have less power and status than men. They exist, as it were, at the bottom of the domestic ladder.

I

In 1914, in a *Dubliners* tale called "Counterparts," James Joyce anticipated and dramatized these charged assumptions in two telling ways. First, he developed a grim view of power relations in a Dublin law office and in nearby public houses; second he focused on the peregrinations between these sites of a pub-hopping office clerk who exhibits several kinds of male egoism under stress. Thus the

1. Anonymous, "Part One: Ending Men's Violence," seventh week.

tale opens with a dramatic encounter between its chief "counterparts": the office boss, Mr. Alleyne, who uses his superior position to berate and humiliate the protagonist for not doing his job properly; and the protagonist himself, the lowly office clerk Farrington, whose accumulated resentments, fueled by steady drinking, will lead him to berate, humiliate, and physically abuse his innocent son Tom that night, though by then he cannot even distinguish Tom from his brother Charlie.

Note, in the opening lines, how Joyce stresses the angry thrust and counterthrust of power and resentment:

> The bell rang furiously and, when Miss Parker went to the tube, a furious voice called out in a piercing North of Ireland accent:
>
> "Send Farrington here!"
>
> Miss Parker returned to her machine, saying to a man who was writing at a desk:
>
> "Mr. Alleyne wants you upstairs."
>
> The man muttered "*Blast* him!" under his breath and pushed back his chair to stand up. When he stood up he was tall and of great bulk. He had a hanging face, dark wine-colored, with fair eyebrows and moustache: his eyes bulged forward slightly and the whites of them were dirty. He lifted up the counter and, passing by the clients, went out of the office with a heavy step.[2]

We begin, then, with the "furious voice" and "piercing accent" of empowered authority—the doubly imperative voice of "Send Farrington here!" Its geographical origin—Northern Ireland—suggests at once the thriving Protestant commercialism of that region, with its closer ties to England, intruding now into the more sluggish commerce of dirty, sleepy, penny-pinching, and decidedly Catholic Dublin. Thus Farrington, the offending Dublin clerk, is reduced to a wishful, resentful, smothered epithet—*Blast* him!—in response to his northern master's piercing voice. Later he will lose a barroom test of strength to a younger man, an English acrobat, while trying on still other grounds to uphold "the national honor." We are meant to see him, then, at the bottom of several status ladders—commercial, religious, national, regional, athletic—one of the many spiritually paralyzed Dublin citizens in Joyce's turn-of-the-century tales.

We learn still more troubling things about him, moreover, from Joyce's unsparing description. His great height, bulk, and heavy step suggest a displaced physique more suited to the region's agricultural past than to its urban commercial present, and in fact he is being called to book for his inefficient work as a copy clerk. His hanging face and forward-bulging eyes suggest further his

2. "Counterparts," 106/201. Further page references will be given in the text, with the first number referring to the edition listed in the bibliography and the second to the reprinting of the story below.

unsuitableness for squinting deskwork, though his alcoholism may account as much for the hanging face and the forward-bulging as for the dirty whiteness of his eyes. Certainly it accounts for his "dark wine-colored" complexion and contributes much to his heavy step. An unathletic alcoholic himself, slightly built, astigmatic, yet engaged more suitably in squinting work, Joyce mixes sympathy for this misplaced creature with a clear critical eye for shared shortcomings and envied strengths.

Thus it is Joyce himself who now describes Mr. Alleyne as "a little man wearing gold-rimmed glasses on a clean-shaven face," whose head looks "so pink and hairless" as it shoots up over a pile of papers that "it seemed like a large egg reposing on the papers" (106–7/201). This of course is what the vexed and puffing Farrington sees as he enters Alleyne's office, after laboring heavily up the stairs: but it is Joyce, not Farrington, who carefully reports this seeming vision, as if to explain and support the clerk's vengeful responses to it. Thus, after Alleyne dresses him down on two counts, and turns again to his pile of papers, "a spasm of rage" grips Farrington's throat; he stares fixedly "at the polished skull which directed the affairs of Crosbie & Alleyne, gauging its fragility" (107/202). Plainly he wants to crush that fragile egglike skull and has the physical strength to do so. Indeed, as we are told after a second tirade, "the man could hardly restrain his fist from descending upon the head of the manikin before him" (112/204).

Elsewhere Joyce deplores physical brutality as a solution for human problems, and by the end of this tale he will deplore it more directly. Yet it is Joyce himself, before the first tirade, who dishes that egghead up for crushing, and who presents it thereby as a kind of severed instance of bodiless commercial intellect. After the second tirade, moreover, it is Joyce again who intentionally yokes "the man" with "the manikin" whose head he wants to crush. It is the shrill voice, then, of almost bodiless commercialism that abruptly greets this big, hulking man as the story opens. Consider, in that physically oppositional light, the dressing down that follows:

> "Farrington? What is the meaning of this? Why have I always to complain of you? May I ask you why you haven't made a copy of that contract between Bodley and Kirwan? I told you it must be ready by four o'clock."
>
> "But Mr. Shelley said, sir—"
>
> "*Mr. Shelley said, sir.* . . . Kindly attend to what I say and not to what *Mr. Shelley says, sir.* You have always some excuse or another for shirking work. Let me tell you that if the contract is not copied before this evening I'll lay the matter before Mr. Crosbie. . . . Do you hear me now?"
>
> "Yes, sir."
>
> "Do you hear me now? . . . Ay and another little matter! I might as well be talking to the wall as talking to you. Understand once for all that you get a half an

hour for your lunch and not an hour and a half. How many courses do you want, I'd like to know. . . . Do you mind me now?

"Yes, sir." (107/201–2)

Alleyne's mimicry of Farrington's voice is a payoff for the first incident between them, shortly after hiring, when "Mr. Alleyne had overheard him mimicking his North of Ireland accent to amuse Higgins and Miss Parker." As Farrington later muses, "that had been the beginning of it"—they had "never pulled together . . . since that day" (114/205). Plainly Alleyne has a sharp mind for storing and retrieving grudges. As his soon-repeated threat to "lay the matter" of Farrington's lapse before his partner Mr. Crosbie now reveals, Joyce himself has a sharp memory for literary precedents for such office power tactics: he seems to derive this one, for instance, from a famous Dickensian law firm, Spenlow and Jorkin in *David Copperfield,* where the visible partner, Spenlow, refers all unpleasant decisions to his invisible partner, Jorkin. Indeed, Joyce's brief portrait of Alleyne—an egghead mannikin with a "dwarf's passion" for abuse—is plainly more Dickensian than Flaubertian in its comic artistry. An office bully, then, in good Dickensian standing, Alleyne clearly relishes his commercial power: he lectures his clerk as if he were a disobedient schoolboy or a witless servant, with all the bloodless contempt of a long line of comically disembodied intellects. A different sort of egghead himself, concerned here and elsewhere with his own lack of human sympathies, Joyce understood the risk of cold indifference to less gifted fellow creatures. He faults this bodiless Northern Irish boss for the typically devitalizing sins of commercial intellect and, with an odd verbal twist, arranges for his brief comeuppance.

Farrington has slipped out of the office, between tirades, for a penny's worth of porter. As he returns upstairs "a moist pungent odor of perfumes" salutes his nose, letting him know that a favored client, Miss Delacour, is now with Mr. Alleyne (109/203). When a call for the Delacour correspondence comes, he hopes that Alleyne will not discover still another lapse—his failure to copy the last two letters. Meanwhile we learn that "Miss Delacour was a middle-aged woman of Jewish appearance" and that Alleyne "was said to be sweet on her or on her money" (110/203). This mixed erotic/avaricious hint gives unexpected zest to the second tirade, when Alleyne appears with Miss Delacour outside the clerk's counter and berates him with bitter, provocative violence for the missing letters. Farrington's sudden "felicitous moment" soon follows:

"I know nothing about any other two letters," he said stupidly.

"*You—know—nothing.* Of course you know nothing," said Mr. Alleyne. "Tell me," he added, glancing first for approval to the lady beside him, "do you take me for a fool? Do you think me an utter fool?"

> The man glanced from the lady's face to the little egg-shaped head and back again; and, almost before he was aware of it, his tongue had found a felicitous moment:
>
> "I don't think, sir," he said, "that that's a fair question to put to me." (112/204)

Everyone, including Farrington and the surrounding clerks, is astounded. Miss Delacour begins to smile. Mr. Alleyne flushes and his mouth twitches "with a dwarf's passion." He shakes his fist at Farrington "till it seemed to vibrate like the knob of some electric machine":

> "You impertinent ruffian! You impertinent ruffian! I'll make short work of you! Wait till you see! You'll apologize to me for your impertinence or you'll quit the office instanter! You'll quit this, I'm telling you, or you'll apologise to me!" (113/204)

Alleyne's demand is not unlike that of little Stephen Dedalus's Aunt Dante, in the opening pages of Joyce's *A Portrait of the Artist as a Young Man*—a threat to pull out the boy's eyes if he doesn't apologize, a fate the terrified boy then tries to avoid by hiding under the table. Farrington's adult reaction is not much braver. He apologizes abjectly, feels like "a proper fool" himself, realizes his quick tongue has cost him his job, that Alleyne will hound him out of the office now as he had once hounded another man "to make room for his own nephew" (113/205).

Meanwhile he has decidedly won a kind of pyrrhic victory that he can trade on in the pubs. For a moment, with the reactive brilliance of an Irish underdog, he has made a sudden breakthrough of subversive defiance and has mastered his Northern master. Joyce is careful to show, moreover, that he owes his brief triumph to the presence of Miss Delacour, to whom Alleyne has turned for approval before voicing his unusual question, "do you take me for a fool? Do you think me an utter fool?" His previous questions—"Do you hear me now?" "Do you mind me now?"—have been demands for attention; but his present question, designed to impress Miss Delacour with his power to toy with and humiliate a witless hulking clerk, has exposed to direct attack his most cherished attribute, his disembodied commercial intellect. Farrington has finally smashed that egghead with a word, if not a blow. His own responsive glance "from the lady's face to the little egg-shaped head and back again" has released a "felicitous" retort, also designed to please and amuse the Jewish lady, a power game at which he has always been more effective than Alleyne—witness his previous mimicry with Higgins and Miss Parker and his later barroom expectations.

But as we have seen, his victory is short-lived and all too self-destructive. He will now continue his own downward progress toward becoming Alleyne's counterpart. Joyce has been careful to show, in this regard, the cumulative contributions of alcoholism to Farrington's descent. He is decidedly a patron rather than a victim of this national addiction: it is his chosen mode of self-destruction, his chosen mode of escape from urban and domestic responsibilities. Late in the story, for instance, Joyce informs us that Farrington's wife "was a little sharp-faced woman who bullied her husband when he was sober and was bullied by him when he was drunk" (120/208). This odd glimpse of marital dynamics confirms what we already know about Farrington's office behavior: whether at home or at work, he drinks to fortify his vengeful courage, his flagging self-esteem. He uses alcohol to revive illusions of manly power and the energies to pursue them. He uses it to restore lost forms of power and control.

This is what happens after that first humiliating tirade, when he gauges the fragility of "the polished skull" before him and a "spasm of rage" grips his throat for a moment, "leaving after it a sharp sensation of thirst." In an almost physiological sense, he needs alcohol to compensate for the frustration of unspent rage. Thus, as Joyce immediately adds: "The man recognized the sensation and felt he must have a good night's drinking" (107/202). He is unable to concentrate on his work, even in the face of Alleyne's warnings, and slips off, as we have seen, to "the dark snug of O'Neill's shop" for a comforting drink. As the Delacour incident begins, "the porter he had gulped down so hastily" further confuses and retards his work: "The dark damp night was coming and he longed to spend it in the bars, drinking with his friends amid the glare of gas and the clatter of glasses" (110/203). When he tries to return to his first uncompleted task, his head is still unclear and his mind wanders back to the bar-dream. "It was a night for hot punches," he concludes, and struggles on with the copy until the clock strikes five. Then, like so many modern batterers, he begins to "talk up" the rage within him:

> Blast it! He couldn't finish it in time. He longed to execrate aloud, to bring his fist down on something violently. . . . He felt strong enough to clear out the whole office single-handed. His body ached to do something, to rush out and revel in violence. All the indignities of his life enraged him. . . . He knew where he would meet the boys: Leonard and O'Halloran and Nosey Flynn. The barometer of his emotional nature was set for a spell of riot. (111–12/204)

It is then that the second tirade occurs, and Farrington has his momentary triumph, followed by abject reckoning. But there is no change in his emotional barometer: he feels "savage and thirsty and revengeful, annoyed with himself and with everyone else"; his great body aches for "the comfort of the public-house"; "they could all go to hell," he concludes, "he was going to have a good night of it" (113–14/205). Then, deciding to pawn his watch, he holds out for six shillings instead of five, wins that minor victory, and emerges joyfully with his spoils. Passing through crowded streets, he looks now at the spectacle "with proud satisfaction," "stare[s] masterfully at the office-girls," and rehearses a selective version of his "felicitous moment" to tell "to the boys" (115/205).

II

In the pubs he becomes a kind of office hero, a boss killer, an Irish warrior using wit instead of force to master all tyrants. And storytelling itself becomes a form of compensatory bonding among bibulous brothers, each willing to stand a round for a tale that flatters crushed egos and eases hurt pride. They are all penny-pinchers, moreover, short of cash, but willing to parlay their pennies in return for ego-massaging retorts, tales of urban commercial valor, triumphs of the Dublin Irish tongue over assorted paternal oppressors. Thus Nosey Flynn stands Farrington "a half-one," when he hears the story, and calls it "as smart a thing as ever he heard." Farrington responds to this praise by standing another round. O'Halloran and Paddy Leonard do the same when they hear the story; and when O'Halloran gallantly admits that his own past retort to a chief clerk "was not as clever as Farrington's," that worthy hero stands his second round (115/206).

Then Higgins enters and an odd thing happens. This fellow clerk at Crosbie & Alleyne has witnessed the whole "felicitous moment," from witty retort to abject apology: yet he too, like Farrington, selects his material, makes everyone laugh by showing how the discomfited Alleyne had shaken his fist in Farrington's face while Farrington, now upgraded to "my nabs," had remained "as cool as you please." Thus the abject apology is erased, at least temporarily, by wholly triumphant retellings. In this mutually self-deceptive world the underdog always wins.

Still, it is a rivalrous cover-up world with its own hidden agendas. Since money is running short the group begins to break up. Higgins and Flynn move off by themselves while Farrington, Leonard, and O'Halloran turn back to the city as rain begins to fall. At the Scotch House, Leonard introduces them to a young English acrobat named Weathers, now performing at the Tivoli. When Farrington stands "a drink all round" this alien asks for "a small Irish and Apollinaris" instead of the cheaper hot toddies ordered by the others, and Farrington is secretly vexed at the extra drain on his funds. Weathers then promises to introduce them all to "some nice girls" at the Tivoli, and as the evening mellows three performers enter and another kind of barroom fantasy begins:

> Farrington's eyes wandered at every moment in the direction of one of the young women. There was something striking in her appearance. An immense scarf of

> peacock-blue muslin was wound round her hat and knotted in a great bow under her chin; and she wore bright yellow gloves, reaching to the elbow. Farrington gazed admiringly at the plump arm which she moved very often and with much grace; and when, after a little time, she answered his gaze he admired still more her large dark brown eyes. The oblique staring expression in them fascinated him. She glanced at him once or twice and, when the party was leaving the room, she brushed against his chair and said *"O, pardon!"* in a London accent. He watched her leave the room in the hope that she would look back at him, but he was disappointed. He cursed his want of money and cursed all the rounds he had stood, particularly all the whiskies and Apollinaris which he had stood to Weathers. If there was one thing he hated it was a sponge. He was so angry that he lost count of the conversation of his friends. (117–18/207)

The English sponger will soon drain more than his money. Indeed, that youthful athlete now boasts so much, while showing his biceps to the company, that Farrington's friends call on him to "uphold the national honor" through "a trial of strength." In the arm wrestle that follows young Weathers takes about thirty seconds to bring Farrington's hand down upon the table. As Joyce then pointedly notes, the older man's "dark wine-colored face flushed darker still with anger and humiliation at having been defeated by such a stripling." When Farrington says that he hasn't played fair and calls for "two best out of three," a longer and more valiant struggle occurs: the wine-colored Irish veins darken further, the pale English face further pales—but the results are finally the same. Age and drink have weakened Farrington's strength for such national/ethnic battles, and now an odd form of political betrayal almost moves him to compensatory violence:

> There was a murmur of applause from the spectators. The curate [bartender], who was standing beside the table, nodded his red head towards the victor and said with loutish familiarity:
>
> "Ah! That's the knack!"
>
> "What the hell do you know about it?" said Farrington fiercely, turning on the man. "What do you put in your gab for?"
>
> "Sh, sh!" said O'Halloran, observing the violent expression on Farrington's face. "Pony up, boys. We'll just have one little smahan more and then we'll be off." (119/207–8)

His comrades' applause, and the Irish bartender's "loutish" affirmation of the Englishman's knack for arm wrestling, moves our vengeful Dublin hero to his first near-knockdown of a naive and intrusive betrayer from a protected lower order.[3]

---

3. For the slang equation of *curates* with *bartenders,* see Robert Scholes and A. Walton Litz, eds., *Dubliners: Text, Criticism, and Notes,* 476, note 57.11: " 'curates'—bartenders in Dublin

III

Fittingly, Joyce's powerful summation of that thrice-defeated hero's feelings heads the last section:

> A very sullen-faced man stood at the corner of O'Connell Bridge waiting for the little Sandymount tram to take him home. He was full of smoldering anger and revengefulness. He felt humiliated and discontented; he did not even feel drunk; and he had only twopence in his pocket. He cursed everything. He had done for himself in the office, pawned his watch, spent all his money; and he had not even got drunk. He began to feel thirsty again and he longed to be back again in the hot reeking public-house. He had lost his reputation as a strong man, having been defeated twice by a mere boy. His heart swelled with fury and, when he thought of the woman in the big hat who had brushed against him and said *Pardon!* his fury nearly choked him. (119–20/208)

As the summary affirms, Farrington has been put down by a Northern Irish office boss, an English acrobat, and a bartender whose slang title—curate—has religious connotations. More oddly still, his real failures with these commercial, regional, national, youthful, healthful, athletic, and quasi-clerical figures do not enrage him quite so much as his erotic failure—more imagined than enacted—to "conquer" the London actress. That seems to be the worst aspect of his present lowly condition, one that bears significantly on what we now learn about his relations with his wife.

Joyce's sympathies are evenly divided about this briefly delineated couple. As we have already seen, the wife is "a little sharp-faced woman." She bullies Farrington when he is sober; he bullies her when he is drunk. As we now learn, they have five children, one of the usual signs of a Catholic marriage. In line with that sign, and in contrast with Farrington's anger at the quasi-clerical bartender, she is "out at the chapel" when he arrives home, so we understand where the real devotion to religion lies. From these few hints of her domestic sharpness and religious devotions, we may also suppose a grimly divisive marriage. But since she never appears herself in the story we have little else to go on.

Fortunately, some sixteen months after composing this story Joyce had written a helpful note about its ambience to his brother Stanislaus: "I am no friend of tyranny, as you know, but if many husbands are brutal the atmosphere

---

slang. The term properly refers to ecclesiastics who have charge of a body of laymen. Unlike the owner of a public house, the 'curate' would not be expected to mingle socially with the customers." Apparently this slightly removed or projected advantage, along with the ministering of spirits and its associations with the wine administered in the mass, accounts for the use of the mock- or quasi-religious title *curate* for bartenders. Joyce seems to be suggesting then that even this mildly spoofing publican version of the Catholic clergy sides with the English arm wrestler.

in which they live is brutal and few wives and homes can satisfy the desire for happiness."[4] Joyce's outlook here on the function of an Irish woman in the home is fairly traditional: she ought to satisfy the husband's desire for happiness. But, as we see, in the tale at hand she doesn't. Perhaps that explains why Farrington now "loathe[s] returning to his home." Although his fair-minded comrades have betrayed him by applauding his Anglo-Saxon conqueror at arm wrestling, and though he has himself failed to pick up the pretty London actress in the pub—though these compensatory pub-dreams have been shattered—he still feels thirsty and longs "to be back again in the hot reeking public-house." Significantly, he has even failed to get drunk there, which helps to place his alcoholism as the final compensation for missing domestic and public happiness.

Here the story takes a peculiar turn, one that suggests Joyce's need to dodge the implications of his own prejudices about women and their domestic and sexual roles. When Farrington enters the house he finds "the kitchen empty and the kitchen fire nearly out" and calls out for his wife, Ada. A little boy comes running down the stairs and reports her absence. If it weren't so late at night that absence would seem unremarkable. The last incident in the office had taken place after five o'clock. Farrington had then waited in the office until the cashier came out, moved next to the pawn shop in Fleet Street, headed afterward to Davy Byrne's pub, where the first four rounds of drinks took place, then walked back to the Scotch House, where the Englishman Weathers first appeared and another four rounds were imbibed, then took off to Mulligan's pub in Poolbeg Street, where Farrington saw the attractive actress and failed at arm wrestling; then, when his funds ran out, he had waited alone for a tram on Sandymount Bridge. At a conservative estimate he must have arrived home anywhere from 11:00 p.m. to midnight. It seems almost too convenient that his wife has gone out to an unusually late chapel service, for she would be the obvious—perhaps the intended—victim of Farrington's need for vengeance if she were present.

It is a nice point that he doesn't even feel drunk. He is primed for violence by his several defeats that day and night, and Joyce has wisely seen that alcohol only fuels, never determines, that priming and the choices that follow from it. As we know, he usually fears his wife when he is sober. But tonight he shows no such fear; he is out for vicarious revenge and she would just as obviously serve for it as the hapless son Tom who now comes down the stairs. Why did Joyce choose to keep her away at this odd hour? My own hunch is his Dickensian preference for dealing with children rather than women as victims of domestic abuse. Like Dickens himself, who often saw women as more powerful than men when it came to domestic disputes—witness Pickwick's imprisonment for

4. *Letters of James Joyce,* 192.

breach of promise, or Mr. Beadle's fear of his shrewish wife in *Oliver Twist*—Joyce often saw women as more emotionally powerful than men and, in *Ulysses* at least, in the person of Molly Bloom, took them as earth goddesses and potential stand-ins for the feminine principle that moved his art. Leopold Bloom's abject adoration of Molly's adulterous rump was both a comic and a serious metaphor, then, for the sexual and emotional power that Joyce also feared and worshiped. One thinks also, in this respect, of the fear of and attraction to powerful women evinced by other modern novelists—Steinbeck, Hemingway, Lawrence, even Isaac Bashevis Singer. But these novelists could imagine the domestic abuse of women and Joyce could not, or did not, or did so only peripherally—possibly out of his own strong distaste for violence of any kind, or his even stronger admiration for the feminine principle in life and art. In *Dubliners* itself there are weak women, such as Eveline or Maria in "Clay" or Mrs. Sinico in "A Painful Case," unable to break free of difficult circumstances; but more tellingly there are also tough ones—including the boardinghouse mother, Mrs. Mooney, who leaves home when her butcher husband goes after her with a cleaver; the bitter Mrs. Kearney in "A Mother," who insists on fair payment for her daughter's work; and the magnificent Gretta Conroy in "The Dead," for whose early love a young man dies—and there are no comparably strong male characters to match them. Joyce was also like Dickens, Lawrence, Hemingway or Steinbeck, one might add, in his youthful resentment of cold women who withheld sexual favors—though more happily he was also aware of his own youthful coldness.

In "A Painful Case," for instance, a story based nominally on his brother Stanislaus, he deals powerfully with male withdrawal as a form of relational abuse he must also have feared in himself. Similarly, in "The Dead" he deals indirectly with a rabid form of male egoism from which he might have suffered had he remained in Ireland. Interestingly, he also deals with and largely overcomes the problem of jealousy over his wife's early affairs with other men, using Gabriel Conroy's generous tears on discovering one such early affair, and his sudden sympathy then for his wife and for his aging maiden aunts, as an artistic outlet for his own troubled feelings about women. In these tales, certainly, he is accountable for his own stake in the patriarchal oppression of women for which all men are in some degree responsible, if only because they were raised to enjoy the top rung on the gender ladder. But in "A Little Cloud," another tale about a would-be artist who remains in Ireland, Joyce is again painfully subject to his own penchant for self-pity at the hands of stronger women, as when the protagonist, Little Chandler, sustains the hatred in his wife's eyes for his failure to comfort the sobbing child whom he has further frightened by shouting "Stop!" in its all-too-innocent face. Although his actions are angry and abusive, they are placed on a moral par with the hatred in his wife's eyes, even though that cold-eyed, thin-lipped, mean-spirited, penny-pinching woman appears only for the story's final moments. It is this kind of supposedly even-steven outlook, in "Counterparts" as in "A Little Cloud," that leads me to believe that Joyce was unable to face the test on domestic power relations that violence to an adult woman would entail—unable to accept the unmistakable evidence that men can always master women, and restore lost dominance and control, through dehumanizing violence.

IV

His choices among the violent events of his early life support this thesis. His father had lost many positions and suffered many disillusionments before receiving a barely sustaining pension. Then, according to biographer Richard Ellmann, further troubles led to domestic violence:

> At home, John Joyce's temper was frayed by the old economic stress. In the late summer or early fall [of 1894] a new son, Freddie, died a few weeks after birth. His wife was scarcely recovered when John Joyce, as Stanislaus remembers, attempted to strangle her. In a drunken fit he grabbed at her throat and roared, "Now, by God, is the time to finish it." The children ran screaming between them, but James jumped on his father's back and toppled both father and mother over. Mrs. Joyce snatched up the youngest children from the melee and ran to a neighbor's house. . . . A few days later, Stanislaus says, a police sergeant called and had a long conversation with his father and mother. From then on John Joyce contented himself with the threat of violence.[5]

This story was open to Joyce as a model for "Counterparts." He had based the character of Farrington partly on his father, who had once worked as a calligrapher for a solicitor on the Dublin quays named Aylward, and who considered himself quite a lady's man. But more obviously Farrington was based on Joyce's maternal uncle, William Murray, who worked as a billing clerk for the well-known firm of solicitors Collis and Ward, treated his children savagely when he was drunk, and whose child actually cried out, on one such occasion, "I'll say a *Hail, Mary* for you, pa, if you don't beat me."[6] That Joyce chose to work with this story of his uncle's child abuse, rather than that of his father's wife abuse, supports my hunch about his fear of testing the power implications of marital violence.

Whatever the case, Joyce chooses a hapless boy for Farrington's domestic victim. Given his own early paddlings by priestly schoolmasters, on the one

5. *James Joyce,* 41.

6. Ibid., 19. See also the last line of "Counterparts."

hand, and his awareness of Dickensian precedents for beating children on the other, he plainly felt much sympathy for the innocent victim. But when Farrington mistakes that victim for his brother, Charlie, we sense not only his own lack of intimacy with his children, and his own slight buzz of postdrunken befuddlement, but also the dilemma in a Catholic home of too many children to feed and care for. Given Chandler's failure in child care in "A Little Cloud," which precedes this story in *Dubliners,* that last criticism takes on added force as the husband's as well as the wife's dilemma. But it is the husband now who orders the child to light the lamp, mimics the boy's accent, bangs his fist on the table, shouts for his dinner, jumps up and twice threatens to teach the child not to let the fire go out, then beats him with a stick. It is the husband, then, who takes out his adult frustrations on the lowest creature on the domestic power ladder, just as Chandler does on the sobbing infant left in his care. But at least "tears of remorse" start to Chandler's eyes, in the final lines of "A Little Cloud," as his wife comforts the child she plainly prefers to her would-be artist husband. We can make no such claim for Farrington's closing sense of personal accountability. That issue is raised rather by the Dickensian child who now offers Farrington the bribe of Christian redemption in return for mere compassion, and so keeps alive the unanswered question of their common human worth.

Counterparts

by James Joyce

The bell rang furiously and, when Miss Parker went to the tube, a furious voice called out in a piercing North of Ireland accent:

"Send Farrington here!"

Miss Parker returned to her machine, saying to a man who was writing at a desk:

"Mr. Alleyne wants you upstairs."

The man muttered "*Blast* him!" under his breath and pushed back his chair to stand up. When he stood up he was tall and of great bulk. He had a hanging face, dark wine-colored, with fair eyebrows and moustache: his eyes bulged forward slightly and the whites of them were dirty. He lifted up the counter and, passing by the clients, went out of the office with a heavy step.

He went heavily upstairs until he came to the second landing, where a door bore a brass plate with the inscription *Mr. Alleyne.* Here he halted, puffing with labor and vexation, and knocked. The shrill voice cried:

"Come in!"

The man entered Mr. Alleyne's room. Simultaneously Mr. Alleyne, a little man wearing gold-rimmed glasses on a clean-shaven face, shot his head up over a pile of documents. The head itself was so pink and hairless it seemed like a large egg reposing on the papers. Mr. Alleyne did not lose a moment:

"Farrington? What is the meaning of this? Why have I always to complain of you? May I ask you why you haven't made a copy of that contract between Bodley and Kirwan? I told you it must be ready by four o'clock."

"But Mr. Shelley said, sir—"

"*Mr. Shelley said, sir.* . . . Kindly attend to what I say and not to what *Mr. Shelley says, sir.* You have always some excuse or another for shirking work. Let me tell you that if the contract is not copied before this evening I'll lay the matter before Mr. Crosbie. . . . Do you hear me now?"

"Yes, sir."

"Do you hear me now? . . . Ay and another little matter! I might as well be talking to the wall as talking to you. Understand once for all that you get a half an hour for your lunch and not an hour and a half. How many courses do you want, I'd like to know. . . . Do you mind me now?"

"Yes, sir."

Mr. Alleyne bent his head again upon his pile of papers. The man stared fixedly at the polished skull which directed the affairs of Crosbie & Alleyne, gauging its fragility. A spasm of rage gripped his throat for a few moments and then passed, leaving after it a sharp sensation of thirst. The man recognized the sensation and felt that he must have a good night's drinking. The middle of the month was passed and, if he could get the copy done in time, Mr. Alleyne might give him an order on the cashier. He stood still, gazing fixedly at the head upon the pile of papers. Suddenly Mr. Alleyne began to upset all the papers, searching for something. Then, as if he had been unaware of the man's presence till that moment, he shot up his head again, saying:

"Eh? Are you going to stand there all day? Upon my word, Farrington, you take things easy!"

"I was waiting to see . . ."

"Very good, you needn't wait to see. Go downstairs and do your work."

The man walked heavily towards the door and, as he went out of the room, he heard Mr. Alleyne cry after him that if the contract was not copied by evening Mr. Crosbie would hear of the matter.

He returned to his desk in the lower office and counted the sheets which remained to be copied. He took up his pen and dipped it in the ink but he continued to stare stupidly at the last words he had written: *In no case shall the said Bernard Bodley be* . . . The evening was falling and in a few minutes they would be lighting the gas: then he could write. He felt that he must slake the thirst in his throat. He stood up from his desk and, lifting the counter as before, passed out of the office. As he was passing out the chief clerk looked at him inquiringly.

"It's all right Mr. Shelley," said the man, pointing with his finger to indicate the objective of his journey.

The chief clerk glanced at the hat-rack, but, seeing the row complete, offered no remark. As soon as he was on the landing the man pulled a shepherd's plaid cap out of his pocket, put it on his head and ran quickly down the rickety stairs. From the street door he walked on furtively on the inner side of the path towards the corner and all at once dived into a doorway. He was now safe in the dark snug of O'Neill's shop, and, filling up the little window that looked into the bar with his inflamed face, the color of dark wine or dark meat, he called out:

"Here, Pat, give us a g.p., like a good fellow."

The curate brought him a glass of plain porter. The man drank it at a gulp and asked for a caraway seed. He put his penny on the counter and, leaving the curate to grope for it in the gloom, retreated out of the snug as furtively as he had entered it.

Darkness, accompanied by a thick fog, was gaining upon the dusk of February and the lamps in Eustace Street had been lit. The man went up by the houses until he reached the door of the office, wondering whether he could finish his copy in time. On the stairs a moist pungent odor of perfumes saluted his nose: evidently Miss Delacour had come while he was out in O'Neill's. He crammed his cap back again into his pocket and re-entered the office, assuming an air of absent mindedness.

"Mr. Alleyne has been calling for you," said the chief clerk severely. "Where were you?"

The man glanced at the two clients who were standing at the counter as if to intimate that their presence prevented him from answering. As the clients were both male the chief clerk allowed himself a laugh.

"I know that game," he said. "Five times in one day is a little bit. . . . Well, you better look sharp and get a copy of our correspondence in the Delacour case for Mr. Alleyne."

This address in the presence of the public, his run upstairs and the porter he had gulped down so hastily confused the man and, as he sat down at his desk to get what was required, he realized how hopeless was the task of finishing his copy of the contract before half past five. The dark damp night was coming and he longed to spend it in the bars, drinking with his friends amid the glare of gas and the clatter of glasses. He got out the Delacour correspondence and passed out of the office. He hoped Mr. Alleyne would not discover that the last two letters were missing.

The moist pungent perfume lay all the way up to Mr. Alleyne's room. Miss Delacour was a middle-aged woman of Jewish appearance. Mr. Alleyne was said to be sweet on her or on her money. She came to the office often and stayed a long time when she came. She was sitting beside his desk now in an aroma of perfumes, smoothing the handle of her umbrella and nodding the great black feather in her hat. Mr. Alleyne had swivelled his chair round to face her and thrown his right foot jauntily upon his left knee. The man put the correspondence on the desk and bowed respectfully but neither Mr. Alleyne nor Miss Delacour took any notice of his bow. Mr. Alleyne tapped a finger on the correspondence and then flicked it towards him as if to say: *"That's all right: you can go."*

The man returned to the lower office and sat down again at his desk. He stared intently at the incomplete phrase: *In no case shall the said Bernard Bodley be . . .* and thought how strange it was that the last three words began with the same letter. The chief clerk began to hurry Miss Parker, saying she would never have the letters typed in time for post. The man listened to the clicking of the machine for a few minutes and then set to work to finish his copy. But his head was not clear and his mind wandered away to the glare and rattle of the public-house. It was a night for hot punches. He struggled on with his copy, but when the clock struck five he had still fourteen pages to write. Blast it! He couldn't finish it in time. He longed to execrate aloud, to bring his fist down on something violently. He was so enraged that he wrote *Bernard Bernard* instead of *Bernard Bodley* and had to begin again on a clean sheet.

He felt strong enough to clear out the whole office single-handed. His body ached to do something, to rush out and revel in violence. All the indignities of his life enraged him. . . . Could he ask the cashier privately for an advance? No, the cashier was no good, no damn good: he wouldn't give an advance. . . . He knew where he would meet the boys: Leonard and O'Halloran and Nosey Flynn. The barometer of his emotional nature was set for a spell of riot.

His imagination had so abstracted him that his name was called twice before he answered. Mr. Alleyne and Miss Delacour were standing outside the counter and all the clerks had turned round in anticipation of something. The man got up from his desk. Mr. Alleyne began a tirade of abuse, saying that two letters were missing. The man answered that he knew nothing about them, that he had made a faithful copy. The tirade continued: it was so bitter and violent that the man could hardly restrain his fist from descending upon the head of the manikin before him:

"I know nothing about any other two letters," he said stupidly.

"*You—know—nothing*. Of course you know nothing," said Mr. Alleyne. "Tell me," he added, glancing first for approval to the lady beside him, "do you take me for a fool? Do you think me an utter fool?"

The man glanced from the lady's face to the little egg-shaped head and back again; and, almost before he was aware of it, his tongue had found a felicitous moment:

"I don't think, sir," he said, "that that's a fair question to put to me."

There was a pause in the very breathing of the clerks. Everyone was astounded (the author of the witticism no less than his neighbors) and Miss Delacour, who was a stout amiable person, began to smile broadly. Mr. Alleyne flushed to the hue of a wild rose and his mouth twitched with a dwarf's passion. He shook his fist in the man's face till it seemed to vibrate like the knob of some electric machine:

"You impertinent ruffian! You impertinent ruffian! I'll make short work of you! Wait till you see! You'll apologize to me for your impertinence or you'll quit the office instanter! You'll quit this, I'm telling you, or you'll apologize to me!"

He stood in a doorway opposite the office watching to see if the cashier would come out alone. All the clerks passed out and finally the cashier came out with the chief clerk. It was no use trying to say a word to him when he was with the chief clerk. The man felt that his position was bad enough. He had been obliged to offer an abject apology to Mr. Alleyne for his impertinence but he knew what a hornet's nest the office would be for him. He could remember the way in which Mr. Alleyne had hounded little Peake out of the office in order to make room for his own nephew. He felt savage and thirsty and revengeful, annoyed with himself and with everyone else. Mr. Alleyne would never give him an hour's rest; his life would be a hell to him. He had made a proper fool of himself this time. Could he not keep his tongue in his cheek? But they had never pulled together from the first, he and Mr. Alleyne, ever since the day Mr. Alleyne had overheard him mimicking his North of Ireland accent to amuse Higgins and Miss Parker: that had been the beginning of it. He might have tried Higgins for the money, but sure Higgins never had anything for himself. A man with two establishments to keep up, of course he couldn't. . . .

He felt his great body again aching for the comfort of the public-house. The fog had begun to chill him and he wondered could he touch Pat in O'Neill's. He could not touch him for more than a bob—and a bob was no use. Yet he must get money somewhere or other: he had spent his last penny for the g.p. and soon it would be too late for getting money anywhere. Suddenly, as he was fingering his watch-chain, he thought of Terry Kelly's pawn-office in Fleet Street. That was the dart! Why didn't he think of it sooner?

He went through the narrow alley of Temple Bar quickly, muttering to himself that they could all go to hell because he was going to have a good night of it. The clerk in Terry Kelly's said *A crown!* but the consignor held out for six shillings; and in the end the six shillings was allowed him literally. He came out of the pawn-office joyfully, making a little cylinder of the coins between his thumb and fingers. In Westmoreland Street the footpaths were crowded with young men and women returning from business and ragged urchins ran here and there yelling out the names of the evening editions. The man passed through the crowd, looking on the spectacle generally with proud satisfaction and staring masterfully at the office-girls. His head was full of the noises of tram-gongs and swishing trolleys and his nose already sniffed the curling fumes of punch. As he walked on he preconsidered the terms in which he would narrate the incident to the boys:

"So, I just looked at him—coolly, you know, and looked at her. Then I looked back at him again—taking my time, you know. 'I don't think that that's a fair question to put to me,' says I."

Nosey Flynn was sitting up in his usual corner of Davy Byrne's and, when he heard the story, he stood Farrington a half-one, saying it was as smart a thing as ever he heard. Farrington stood a drink in his turn. After a while O'Halloran and Paddy Leonard came in and the story was repeated to them. O'Halloran stood tailors of malt, hot, all round and told the story of the retort he had made to the chief clerk when he was in Callan's of Fownes's Street; but, as the retort was after the manner of the liberal shepherds in the eclogues, he had to admit that it was not as clever as Farrington's retort. At this Farrington told the boys to polish off that and have another.

Just as they were naming their poisons who should come in but Higgins! Of course he had to join in with the others. The men asked him to give his version of it, and he did so with great vivacity for the sight of five small hot whiskeys was very exhilarating. Everyone roared laughing when he showed the way in which Mr. Alleyne shook his fist in Farrington's face. Then he imitated Farrington, saying, *"And here was my nabs, as cool as you please,"* while Farrington looked at the company out of his heavy dirty eyes, smiling and at times drawing forth stray drops of liquor from his moustache with the aid of his lower lip.

When that round was over there was a pause. O'Halloran had money but neither of the other two seemed to have any; so the whole party left the shop somewhat regretfully. At the corner of Duke Street Higgins and Nosey Flynn beveled off to the left while the other three turned back towards the city. Rain was drizzling down on the cold streets and, when they reached the Ballast Office, Farrington suggested the Scotch House. The bar was full of men and loud with the noise of tongues and glasses. The three men pushed past the whining match-sellers at the door and formed a little party at the corner of the counter. They began to exchange stories. Leonard introduced them to a young fellow named Weathers who was performing at the Tivoli as an acrobat and knockabout *artiste.* Farrington stood a drink all round. Weathers said he would take a small Irish and Apollinaris. Farrington, who had definite notions of what was what, asked the boys would they have an Apollinaris too; but the boys told Tim to make theirs hot. The talk became theatrical. O'Halloran stood a round and then Farrington stood another round, Weathers protesting that the hospitality was too Irish. He promised to get them in behind the scenes and introduce them to some nice girls. O'Halloran said that he and Leonard would go, but that Farrington wouldn't go because he was a married man; and Farrington's heavy dirty eyes leered at the company in token that he understood he was being chaffed. Weathers made them all have just one little tincture at his expense and promised to meet them later on at Mulligan's in Poolbeg Street.

When the Scotch House closed they went round to Mulligan's. They went into the parlor at the back and O'Halloran ordered small hot specials all round. They were all beginning to feel mellow. Farrington was just standing another round when Weathers came back. Much to Farrington's relief he drank a glass of bitter this time. Funds were getting low but they had enough to keep them going.

Presently two young women with big hats and a young man in a check suit came in and sat at a table close by. Weathers saluted them and told the company that they were out of the Tivoli. Farrington's eyes wandered at every moment in the direction of one of the young women. There was something striking in her appearance. An immense scarf of peacock-blue muslin was wound round her hat and knotted in a great bow under her chin; and she wore bright yellow gloves, reaching to the elbow. Farrington gazed admiringly at the plump arm which she moved very often and with much grace; and when, after a little time, she answered his gaze he admired still more her large dark brown eyes. The oblique staring expression in them fascinated him. She glanced at him once or twice and, when the party was leaving the room, she brushed against his chair and said *"O, pardon!"* in a London accent. He watched her leave the room in the hope that she would look back at him, but he was disappointed. He cursed his want of money and cursed all the rounds he had stood, particularly all the whiskies and Apollinaris which he had stood to Weathers. If there was one thing that he hated it was a sponge. He was so angry that he lost count of the conversation of his friends.

When Paddy Leonard called him he found that they were talking about feats of strength. Weathers was showing his biceps muscle to the company and boasting so much that the other two had called on Farrington to uphold the national honor. Farrington pulled up his sleeve accordingly and showed his biceps muscle to the company. The two arms were examined and compared and finally it was agreed to have a trial of strength. The table was cleared and the two men rested their elbows on it, clasping hands. When Paddy Leonard said *"Go!"* each was to try to bring down the other's hand on to the table. Farrington looked very serious and determined.

The trial began. After about thirty seconds Weathers brought his opponent's hand slowly down on to the table. Farrington's dark wine-colored face flushed darker still with anger and humiliation at having been defeated by such a stripling.

"You're not to put the weight of your body behind it. Play fair," he said.

"Who's not playing fair?" said the other.

"Come on again. The two best out of three."

The trial began again. The veins stood out on Farrington's forehead, and the pallor of Weathers' complexion changed to peony. Their hands and arms trembled under the stress. After a long struggle Weathers again brought his opponent's hand slowly on to the table. There was a murmur of applause from the spectators. The curate, who was standing beside the table, nodded his red head towards the victor and said with stupid familiarity:

"Ah! that's the knack!"

"What the hell do you know about it?" said Farrington fiercely, turning on the man. "What do you put in your gab for?"

"Sh, sh!" said O'Halloran, observing the violent expression of Farrington's face. "Pony up, boys. We'll have just one little smahan more and then we'll be off."

A very sullen-faced man stood at the corner of O'Connell Bridge waiting for the little Sandymount tram to take him home. He was full of smoldering anger and revengefulness. He felt humiliated and discontented; he did not even feel drunk; and he had only twopence in his pocket. He cursed everything. He had done for himself in the office, pawned his watch, spent all his money; and he had not even got drunk. He began to feel thirsty again and he longed to be back again in the hot reeking public-house. He had lost his reputation as a strong man, having been defeated twice by a mere boy. His heart swelled with fury and, when he thought of the woman in the big hat who had brushed against him and said *Pardon!* his fury nearly choked him.

His tram let him down at Shelbourne Road and he steered his great body along in the shadow of the wall of the barracks. He loathed returning to his home. When he went in by the side-door he found the kitchen empty and the kitchen fire nearly out. He bawled upstairs:

"Ada! Ada!"

His wife was a little sharp-faced woman who bullied her husband when he was sober and was bullied by him when he was drunk. They had five children. A little boy came running down the stairs.

"Who is that?" said the man, peering through the darkness.

"Me, pa."

"Who are you? Charlie?"

"No, pa. Tom."

"Where's your mother?"

"She's out at the chapel."

"That's right. . . . Did she think of leaving any dinner for me?"

"Yes, pa. I—"

"Light the lamp. What do you mean by having the place in darkness? Are the other children in bed?"

The man sat down heavily on one of the chairs while the little boy lit the lamp. He began to mimic his son's flat accent, saying half to himself: *"At the chapel. At the chapel, if you please!"* When the lamp was lit he banged his fist on the table and shouted:

"What's for my dinner?"

"I'm going . . . to cook it, pa," said the little boy.

The man jumped up furiously and pointed to the fire.

"On that fire! You let the fire out! By God, I'll teach you to do that again!"

He took a step to the door and seized the walking-stick which was standing behind it.

"I'll teach you to let the fire out!" he said, rolling up his sleeve in order to give his arm free play.

The little boy cried *"O, pa!"* and ran whimpering round the table, but the man followed him and caught him by the coat. The little boy looked about him wildly but, seeing no way of escape, fell upon his knees.

"Now, you'll let the fire out the next time!" said the man, striking at him vigorously with the stick. "Take that, you little whelp!"

The boy uttered a squeal of pain as the stick cut his thigh. He clasped his hands together in the air and his voice shook with fright.

"O, pa!" he cried. "Don't beat me, pa! And I'll . . . I'll say a *Hail Mary* for you. . . . I'll say a *Hail Mary* for you, pa, if you don't beat me. I'll say a *Hail Mary. . . .*"

Abusive and Nonabusive Dying in Hemingway's Fiction

When I first became a counselor for Brother to Brother, I began to attend meetings for counselors and was even invited to sit in on the organization's coordinating council. At one of the weekly meetings of the latter council, the question was raised as to how to deal with a client who was dying of AIDS and therefore treated sympathetically by other clients, but who was also still quite abusive with his partner. Since most of these abusive clients already considered themselves victims of their female partners, and of the new laws in the state protecting their partners from domestic violence, it was necessary to separate somehow their sympathy for a victim of disease from their need to confront his and their own accountability for abusiveness. As the discussion continued I was oddly reminded of Hemingway's interest in dying well. I accordingly remarked to my fellow counselors that there was a difference between dying abusively and dying nonabusively and that attention could be focused for the therapy group upon that difference. And then I added, somewhat to my own surprise: "That's what's wrong with 'The Snows of Kilimanjaro'—the dying hero repeatedly abuses his safari wife verbally, but since he also defies death verbally, by trying to write stories in his mind, he is presented as dying well." Indeed, he is rewarded for it.

That last sentence came later, as I thought more about the story and about the intriguing notion that then came to me as to how Hemingway might have benefited from being a client in our therapy groups for male batterers. No doubt about it: he was an abusive husband, sometimes violently so, though more characteristically inclined toward vicious tongue-lashings and projected blame. Still later, when I was asked to write a new essay for a collection of my essays on D. H. Lawrence, I wrote at some length and with much enthusiasm an essay combining my literary and counseling interests called "Hemingway and Lawrence as Abusive Husbands." The pitch of the essay was the new way of seeing their work if we begin from the premise that both writers had physically abused female partners and were therefore liable for probation sentences as male batterers, but that both had also tried in their fictions to cope with their own propensities for domestic violence. As we all know, writers are often their best selves in their fictions, if not in their lives. Could we therefore save the works from the lives, and from our new and chiefly feminist concerns with how works by male writers can impinge damagingly upon our lives, by attending to the self-corrective concerns of such fictions?

We need not search far, of course, for the opposite concerns. Hemingway was not alone, among male writers of the 1920s and after, in seeing his male characters as victims of castrating bitches, spiritual vampires, and devouring mothers. Lawrence and Joyce were there before him; Faulkner and Fitzgerald, Wolfe and Nathanael West, would keep him good company. But Hemingway's pernicious stress on the fates of "men without women" was perhaps more central to the new definitions of manliness, its redirection as a strictly male concern, which began in England and America with the imperialist trends of the late nineteenth century. If he had served well as our "gauge of morale," as Edmund Wilson has argued,[1] he had also served, more dubiously, as our distinctly masculine gauge of male morale. It was characteristic of his fiction, for instance, that mothers controlled weak husbands with a firm and heavy hand; that they were spiritual and emotional bullies, capable of driving a man like Nick Adams's father, or Robert Jordan's father, to suicide, and of reducing even grown sons to infantile obedience. Such women were, in short, the truly abusive or battering partners and men were their hapless victims. In the same vein, bitch heroines like Brett Ashley in *The Sun Also Rises* or Margot Macomber in "The Short Happy Life of Francis Macomber" were their youthful counterparts, capable of destroying young bullfighters who loved them or of accidentally killing off rich husbands who threatened to leave them. Even the adoring heroines in his fiction, the fictional counterparts of his several adoring sisters, were sometimes threatening to their male partner's manhood and so better off dead, the only good woman being a dead woman, as Judith Fetterley so aptly argues of the death of Catherine Barkley in *A Farewell to Arms*.[2] Obviously, in the face of such victimizing options, it was better to seek the company of other men, or to identify with men who were able to live "without women," and so avoid the "softening feminine influence" of mothers, sisters, wives, and sweethearts.[3] Indeed, it was only in the company of other men, or through their standards, that manhood itself could be defined.

All this is familiar ground. Let me draw now upon my treatment, in my long comparative essay, of the more promising question of Hemingway's corrective

1. "Hemingway: Gauge of Morale," 92–114.
2. "*A Farewell to Arms:* Hemingway's Resentful Cryptogram," 46–71.
3. Ernest Hemingway, *Selected Letters, 1917–1961,* 245.

sense of himself and of his characters as male batterers. The most obvious case, if also the most paradoxical, is that of Harry, the self-styled married loner in "The Snows of Kilimanjaro."

I

"The Snows of Kilimanjaro" is about a writer who has traded his talent for money and comfort but who dies well by writing stories in his mind. On safari in Africa with his rich wife, he leaves a scratched leg untended, and when the leg turns gangrenous there is no quick way to get medical attention. The safari truck has broken down; the airplane they have radioed for has not yet arrived. For the writer, Harry, the situation seems Hardyesque: he is trapped by circumstances beyond his control and incommensurate with his initial failure to avoid them: he ignored the scratch, he failed to hire a good mechanic to fix the truck, he let his rich wife leave her own people to marry him.[4] The third lapse is a well-placed insult indicating his desire to blame much of his failed life and present predicament on his wife; but it is of a piece with the other minor failures to act well on his own behalf. Death catches up with you, even if life doesn't, and foils even your good intentions: he had meant to use this trip to train himself back into writing shape, like a boxer trying to lose weight for his next bout. Now that chance is gone.

The action of the story, then, is to fight death in his mind, to go down fighting by sketching out all the stories he had meant to write but hadn't. That is why the story focuses on and moves between five italicized passages of remembrance of untold tales; that is why it ends with an imagined flight in the rescue plane, which takes Harry toward what must be his private heavenly reward at the top of Mount Kilimanjaro. Actually the story has a second ending, designed to confirm the first: his wife wakes up in the night in their tent, sees that Harry's gangrenous leg has fallen out of bed, and cries for Harry's personal black "boy," Molo; the last thing we hear is the ironic beating of her heart when she realizes that Harry is dead and that she wants him back, even though she had just been dreaming that she was at her Long Island house on the night before her daughter's debut, and that her father was somehow there and "had been very rude" to her (77/241).

Harry's rudeness to his wife is the other part of the story, what happens in between the italicized remembrances. The story begins, for instance, with a ragging process. Harry deliberately pretends consideration for his wife's feelings; she is the target for his own bitterness about dying, and he wants to

4. "The Snows of Kilimanjaro," 55/225–26. Further page references will be given in the text, with the first number referring to the edition listed in the bibliography and the second to the reprinting of the story below.

hurt her as sharply as is passively possible. He is the insider even about dying, moreover, and begins by telling her that when the pain stops, death starts; he even muses aloud about those knowing harbingers, the vultures: is it the sight or the scent of death that brings them on? Then his jabs turn sardonic: "I'm awfully sorry about the odor, though. That must bother you." "I'm only talking. . . . It's much easier if I talk. But I don't want to bother you." "There is no sense in moving now except to make it easier for you" (52–53/223–24). These false courtesies have their desired effect and are followed by the wife's sharp cries: "Don't! Please don't." "I wish you wouldn't." "Please don't talk that way." But he prefers to talk, to quarrel, to tell her frankly that he doesn't love her, for instance, and never has (55/226), because it makes time pass. Before that, however, he goads her through his deliberate passivities into making the first open insult:

> "That's cowardly."
>
> "Can't you let a man die as comfortably as he can without calling him names? What's the use of slanging me?"
>
> "You're not going to die."
>
> "Don't be silly. I'm dying now. Ask those bastards." He looked over to where the huge, filthy birds sat, their naked heads sunk in the hunched feathers. A fourth planed down, to run quick-legged and then waddle slowly toward the others.
>
> "They're around every camp. You never notice them. You can't die if you don't give up."
>
> "Where did you read that? You're such a bloody fool."
>
> "You might think about some one else."
>
> "For Christ's sake," he said. "That's been my trade." (53/224)

Certainly Hemingway is practicing his own trade well, catching Harry's provoking and undercutting style, laying open his real concern with the betrayal of his own writing skills as the basis for these baiting tactics, following up Helen's shrewd observation—the birds are always there—with Harry's insult about her bookish expertise on dying compared implicitly with his insider's knowledge, then following her meek exposure of her own bruised feelings—"You might think about some one else"—with Harry's literary concern with people, his substitute now for caring about his wife's feelings, as if being nonabusive had nothing to do with dying well.

Ultimately we learn, in this male-oriented story, that being nonabusive has in fact little to do with dying well; but for a good while at least Hemingway is being his best self, judging Harry's selfishness sharply and effectively, and even letting the wife define it for us a short time later, after Harry delivers his famous epithet: "Love is a dunghill. . . . And I'm the cock that gets on it to crow." "If you have to go away," his wife responds, "is it absolutely necessary to kill off everything you leave behind? I mean do you have to take away everything? Do you have to kill your horse, and your wife and burn your saddle and your armour?" (57–58/227–28). That is certainly a shrewd perception, showing her insight not only into her husband's abusiveness but also into his literary pretensions, which Hemingway both acknowledges and exploits by letting Harry pun about them and further expose the sources of his abusiveness in his anger with himself:

> "Yes," he said. "Your damned money was my armour. My Swift and my Armour."
> "Don't."
> "All right, I'll stop that. I don't want to hurt you."
> "It's a little bit late now."
> "All right then. I'll go on hurting you. It's more amusing. The only thing I ever really liked to do with you I can't do now."
> "No, that's not true. You liked to do many things and everything you wanted to do I did."
> "Oh, for Christ sake stop bragging, will you?"
> He looked at her and saw her crying.
> "Listen," he said. "Do you think it is fun to do this? I don't know why I'm doing it. It's trying to kill to keep yourself alive, I imagine. I was all right when we started talking. I didn't mean to start this, and now I'm crazy as a coot and being as cruel to you as I can be. Don't pay any attention, darling, to what I say. I love you, really. You know I love you. I've never loved anyone else the way I love you."
> He slipped into the familiar lie he made his bread and butter by.
> "You're sweet to me."
> "You bitch," he said. "You rich bitch. That's poetry. I'm full of poetry now. Rot and poetry. Rotten poetry."
> "Stop it. Harry, Why do you have to turn into a devil now?"
> "I don't like to leave anything," the man said. "I don't like to leave things behind." (58/228)

The passage is extremely moving because it is also extremely insightful. Harry comes to terms for a moment with his own feelings, sees that he's out of control, taking out his bitterness with himself on his wife, killing her off to keep himself alive, punishing her for his own mistakes, then lapsing back into them, the literary warrior who has failed at his trade and is now barbarically trying to bury his wife with himself, or even before himself. Hemingway's mastery of these moods, his best artistic sense of his own bastardliness, is what makes the passage stick. He even catches and prepares here for the closing revelation that in pleasing him Harry's wife wants to please and appease a rude father, that Harry dislikes her "bragging" because he senses that she is using him, as he is certainly using her, to work out her own problems. The only problem for us is that her humanity and her own potential for heroism are secondary matters for both Harry and Hemingway, both of whom want to get on with the problem of dying well as a strictly male concern. As Harry will eventually tell us, he would like to die in better company, that is to say male company, and Hemingway provides it for him. For the moment, however, Hemingway at least stands away from Harry in some distaste, calling him "the man" who doesn't like to leave things like his wife behind.

Even more tellingly, he focuses now on Harry's self-examination as Harry acknowledges in his mind that it was not his wife's fault "that when he went to her he was already over"(59/228), that it was not her fault that he was dying just when he was ready to work again (60/229), and meanwhile that it was not she who had destroyed his talent; he had done that himself "by not using it, by betrayals of himself and what he believed in, by drinking so much that he blunted the edge of his perceptions, by laziness, by sloth, and by snobbery, by pride and by prejudice, by hook and by crook" (60/229). It is an impressive litany of confessed sins, a fine account of belated accountability; but it now takes an interestingly mythic turn as Harry claims he has traded on his talented pen so as to make a living by his talented penis.

Hemingway underwrites this shift from one kind of male egoism to another. Whatever his many talents, his own mixed sexual performance and androgynous propensities scarcely fit the unexamined myth of sexual prowess that he endorses here. And endorses is the word for it: there is much talk now of "the good destruction" in marriage that Harry and Helen have enjoyed (63/231); his admirations are of her "pleasant body" and her "great talent and appreciation for the bed" (61/230). It seems to me curious in this context that the androgynous Hemingway endows Harry with such orthodox sexual pizzazz. I find it also troubling in this light that the character he builds for Helen, of a woman who has lost a husband who "never bored her" and who has taken many lovers who did, and who after losing a child in a plane crash has become "acutely frightened of being alone" and has "wanted some one that she respected with her" (61/230), should get so little respect in return from Hemingway himself. Or rather that's almost all he gives her: summary respect. Harry's decision not to quarrel with her any more if he can help it, his modest attempts also to acknowledge to her and himself that she is after all "a damned nice woman" whose niceness he has exploited (62/230) but who "*was* very good to him" (64/232) seem similarly shallow.

His Shakespearean excuse, and Hemingway's, is that he has "never quarreled much with this woman, while with the women that he loved he had quarreled so much they had finally, always, with the corrosion of the quarreling, killed what they had together. He had loved too much, demanded too much, and he wore it all out" (64/232). One trouble with this passage is that we have every impression from previous pages that Harry and Helen have always quarreled destructively, that his present attempts to destroy her are familiar to them both, and that he is being alternately cruel and sweet to her now as he has always been alternately sweet and cruel. Another trouble is that Hemingway underwrites these all-too-personal sentiments; he sympathizes with a fellow sufferer who has loved not wisely but too well. Thus, like Ernest the wife slapper and tongue-lasher, Harry the verbal batterer has loved colorfully—that is to say, to Shakespearean excess. Poor suffering artist-hero, he just can't help it.

Yet in fact he can, at least with Helen. As the tale progresses Harry cuts down on the insults, probably because he is more into dying well through his remembered untold tales. At any rate he stops badgering Helen. After the fifth remembered passage, however, he thinks devastatingly that he would rather die "in better company" (73/239). Then, feeling death come by again, he works off a parting insult about "How little a woman knows" (74/239), how feeble her vaunted intuition is compared, no doubt, with his own insider's knowledge, just displayed. Then old Compton arrives in the rescue plane, an old Puss Moth in which there is just room for one passenger, namely the "old cock" Harry (75/240), who once crowed about dunghill love but who now writes well in his mind and so flies off with Compie toward his hard-earned reward. Male bonding is what matters, then, when it comes to dying. If Helen is given a final coda so that we know that in fact Harry has died and died well, we also know that he is in better company than she could ever offer. Compton, of course, is a British pilot borrowed from Kipling's imaginary world of imperial male comrades.[5]

II

In some ways *To Have and Have Not* is an attempt to do more justice to women like Helen, unwitting victims of abusive males like Harry. More obviously it is an attempt to write about the rich, whom Harry had dismissed as being too dull and repetitious to write about, and about poor but honestly dishonest pirates, present-day Harry Morgans who make their living running contraband between Florida and Cuba. Surprisingly, this novel is much more sympathetic to women than anything else Hemingway wrote. For the first time he empathizes with some range, goes inside a variety of women's minds, and attempts to show, or at least to identify with, how they think and feel. He doesn't do it well, but the attempt itself suggests his discomfort with the hardening and brutalizing of his outlook during the 1930s, as in *Death in the Afternoon, Green Hills of Africa,* and his two great African stories. Indeed, his years with Pauline seem to have

5. See my reflections on "The Kipling Impress" and "The Snows of Kilimanjaro" in *Hemingway's Quarrel with Androgyny,* 91–124, 240–45.

had this oddly polarizing effect: the emergence of his "tough guy" image and its attendant mythology, on the one hand, and of a deeper sympathy for the sufferings of women on the other. It seems probable that Pauline deserves some credit for both polarities. Hemingway blamed her, for instance, for the loss of Hadley, which critics now relate to the hardening process; but he also called her his best literary critic, his best adviser about his writing, and as *The Garden of Eden* shows, his best conversational model also for how a suffering woman thinks and feels. Certainly her Catholic presence looms large in the marital quarrels between Helen and Richard Gordon in *To Have and Have Not.*

Richard Gordon is a fashionably leftist writer nominally based on John Dos Passos, with whom Hemingway had recently quarreled. He is also an unwitting projection of Hemingway's worst husbandly traits, a kind of alter ego whipping boy. Thus, like Hemingway, he is openly unfaithful to his wife and slaps her cravenly when she decides to leave him. Meanwhile his wife is portrayed with great sympathy as the victim of her husband's abusive ways. In chapter 15, for instance, he leaves her in a bar with the public announcement that he is going to seek out and sleep with the rich and beautiful Helene Bradley because a writer "can't restrict his experience to conform to Bourgeois standards."[6] In chapter 21, however, when Gordon returns home, his face smeared with lipstick, his wife tells him the marriage is over. She then compares him to a conceited barnyard rooster, always crowing about his virility and his writing, and announces her intention to marry Professor Walsey, who has just proposed to her. When Gordon says she is still married to him, she says "Not really. Not in the church," and then makes her long and famous rejection of his kind of love:

> "Everything I believed in and everything I cared about I left for you because you were so wonderful and you loved me so much that love was all that mattered. Love was the greatest thing, wasn't it? Love was what we had that no one else had or could ever have? And you were a genius and I was your whole life. I was your partner and your little black flower. Slop. Love is just another dirty lie. Love is ergoapiol pills to make me come around because you were afraid to have a baby. Love is quinine and quinine and quinine until I'm deaf with it. Love is that dirty aborting horror you took me to. Love is my insides all messed up. It's half catheters and half whirling douches. I know about love. Love always hangs up behind the bathroom door. It smells like lysol. To hell with love. Love is you making me happy and then going off to sleep with your mouth open while I lie awake all night afraid to say my prayers even because I know I have no right to any more. Love is all the dirty little tricks you taught me that you probably got out of some book. All right. I'm through with you and I'm through with love. Your kind of picknose love. You writer." (185–86)

6. *To Have and Have Not,* 140. Further page references will be given in the text.

Because the victimized speaker's name is Helen, perhaps this can be called the wifely counterstatement to Harry the writer's dunghill definition of love in "The Snows of Kilimanjaro." Certainly this Helen extends her victim's wrath to Gordon's pen and penis:

> "If you were just a good writer I could stand for all the rest of it maybe. But I've seen you bitter, jealous, changing your politics to suit the fashion, sucking up to people's faces and talking about them behind their backs. I've seen you until I'm sick of you. Then that dirty rich bitch of a Bradley woman today. Oh, I'm sick of it. I've tried to take care of you and humor you and look after you and cook for you and keep quiet when you wanted and cheerful when you wanted and give you your little explosions and pretend it made me happy, and put up with your rages and jealousies and meannesses and now I'm through." (186–87)

A moment later she compares him to her father, who might have been unfaithful to her mother, but who "didn't do it out of curiosity, or from barnyard pride, or to tell his wife what a great man he was" (187). "He was a man," she adds, and then tells him she is going to get her religion back and he "won't be there to take it away" as he's taken everything else away. Taker Gordon now slaps his wife "hard and suddenly" for leaving him, and to pay her back for his own humiliation earlier in the day when Helene Bradley had slapped *him* for leaving her in the sexual lurch.

As in Joyce's "Counterparts," where a father humiliated at work takes it out at home by slapping his innocent son, so the puerile writer/lover Gordon takes out his worldly humiliations on his verbal, emotional, and sexual punching bag, his good wife Helen. He comes off poorly, if credibly, compared with the gentle if alcoholic Professor Walsey, who would rather take his licks than see another man suffer; and he seems oddly off-kilter as a fictional foil for latter-day pirate Harry Morgan, the novel's tough-guy hero. But then the real comparison is with Hemingway himself, or with the author's better self, as when Gordon imagines how Harry's wife, Marie, must feel about him:

> He was writing a novel about a strike in a textile factory. In today's chapter he was going to use the big woman with the tear-reddened eyes he had just seen on the way home. Her husband when he came home at night hated her, hated the way she had coarsened and grown heavy, was repelled by her bleached hair, her too big breasts, her lack of sympathy with his work as an organizer. He would compare her to the young, firm-breasted, full-lipped little Jewess that had spoken at the meeting that evening. It was good. It was, it could be easily, terrific, and it was true. He had seen, in a flash of perception, the whole inner life of that type of woman.
>
> Her early indifference to her husband's caresses. Her desire for children and security. Her lack of sympathy with her husband's aims. Her sad attempts to simulate

> an interest in the sexual act that had become actually repugnant to her. It would be a fine chapter. (176–77)

To undercut his alter ego, Hemingway now tells us that the woman is Marie Morgan, returning from the sheriff's office with news of Harry's involvement with Cuban revolutionaries who have just robbed a bank. He has already given us his own rich view of the marriage of Harry and Marie, perhaps the only happy marriage in his literary canon, including several glimpses of Marie's inner life in which she congratulates herself on how lucky she's been to have Harry for her man, admires him lovingly as he sleeps (114–15), or watches him leave the house like a graceful animal and begins to cry at the tough beauty of "his goddamn face" (128). He has already shown us, moreover, how much Harry loves and admires his big, still handsome wife and is excited by her bleached hair, and how zestful they are in bed.

But it is androgynous Marie who must give us pause as a big, mannish, bleached-blonde woman wearing a man's felt hat, for whom Hemingway feels and creates such strong empathy. Gordon to the contrary notwithstanding, she loves Harry more than she loves their three daughters; she supports him in his risky work; in bed or out, she delights in his manliness; she is Harry's match also in toughness and independent strength. Indeed, they are not only the only happy couple in Hemingway's canon, they are his only Lawrencean couple, and much of the book is given over to satiric contrast between their joyful lovemaking and marital balance and the dubious sexual fates (as Hemingway sees them) of the idle rich—impotence, divorce, infidelity, homosexuality, masturbation.

As if making up, moreover, for Helen's brief coda in "The Snows of Kilimanjaro," Hemingway gives Marie a long last word on this novel's actions. The focus is on her feelings about Harry's death, the love between them while he lived, and the sad life ahead for herself. Three chapters earlier Harry was given his own famous last word: "No matter how a man alone ain't got no bloody fucking chance" (225). His words go unheard, however, and there is no apotheosis, no uplifting plane ride over Mount Kilimanjaro. Marie's last words are similarly grim. She streams for five pages, Hemingway's longest time inside a woman's mind until Pilar's bloody tale of the Loyalist takeover of a Spanish town in *For Whom the Bell Tolls*. This warmup for his own apotheosis as a tough woman narrator is not as impressive, but it has its moments. Marie begins by complaining about "the goddamned nights" without Harry. If she cared about her three girls it might be different. She might get over "being dead inside" (257). She is afraid of forgetting Harry's face but recalls him now as "snotty and strong and quick, and like some kind of expensive animal." She condemns the Cubans who killed him, lashes out at the "niggers" among them, remembers a happier time when Harry smacked a "nigger" in Cuba who had "said something" to her, and how she laughed when Harry sailed the man's straw hat "about half a block and a taxi ran over it" (258). This brutalizing bit of racial prejudice recalls the more tender point of the trip, the first time she ever made her hair blonde in a beauty parlor on the Prado:

> They were working on it all afternoon and it was naturally so dark they didn't want to do it and I was afraid I'd look terrible, but I kept telling them to see if they couldn't make it a little lighter, and the man would go over it with that orange wood stick with cotton on the end, dipping it in that bowl that had the stuff in it sort of smoky like the way it steamed . . . ; parting the strands with one end of the stick and the comb and going over them and letting it dry and I was sitting there scared inside my chest of what I was having done and all I'd say was, just see if you can't make it a little lighter.
>
> And finally he said, that's just as light as I can make it safely, Madame, and then he shampooed it, and put a wave in, and I was afraid to look even for fear it would be terrible, and he waved it parted on one side and high behind my ears with little tight curls in back, and it still wet I couldn't tell how it looked except it looked all changed and I looked strange to myself. And he put a net over it wet and put me under the dryer and all the time I was scared about it. And then when I came out from under the dryer he took the net off and the pins out and combed it out and it was just like gold.
>
> And I came out of the place and saw myself in the mirror and it shone so in the sun and was so soft and silky when I . . . touched it, and I couldn't believe it was me and I was so excited I was choked with it.
>
> I walked down [to] where Harry was waiting and I was so excited feeling all funny inside, sort of faint like, and he stood up when he saw me coming and he couldn't take his eyes off me and his voice was thick and funny when he said, "Jesus, Marie, you're beautiful."
>
> And I said, "You like me blonde?"
>
> "Don't talk about it," he said. "Let's go to the hotel."
>
> And I said, "O.K., then. Let's go." I was twenty-six then. (258–59)

It is Marie, of course, who is apotheosized here. The novel ends with this evocation of the powerful bond between this pair, their sexual excitement over her transformation, her discovered beauty, which is still there for them when she is forty-five and he is forty-three, and which returns now at his death as a memory of appreciative love. Whatever this novel's crudities, Hemingway has brought it to a moving androgynous close not only as Marie's female impersonator but as the vulnerable woman also inside his blonde-haired hero who likes as well as identifies with big masculine artificial blondes in old felt hats. When on the next page Marie says, "I'm big now and ugly and old and he ain't here to tell me that I ain't," we can only say that Hemingway has for once put his hair fetishisms and female toughnesses to poignant and appreciative uses. If Marie now goes dead inside "like most people are most of the time" (261), if she tells us again that she's been lucky to have Harry (258), she has evoked something other here than the tribute to male *cojones* we might have expected from earlier pages. The tribute is to male tenderness, male nurture, male appreciation of a woman's sense of her own personal loveliness—a kind of tribute not usually found in Hemingway.

III

In chapter 16 of *To Have and Have Not* Harry is talking to his friend Albert, who has just been cut back to three days a week "on the relief," and who wants Harry to hire him on his boat. When Harry agrees Albert thanks him and they exchange views about domestic life:

> "I was afraid to go home to see my old woman. She gave me hell this noon like it was me had laid off the relief."
>
> "What's the matter with your old woman?" asked Harry cheerfully. "Why don't you smack her?"
>
> "You smack her." Albert said. "I'd like to hear what she'd say. She's some old woman to talk." (144)

Hemingway's almost Dickensian treatment of Albert's wife, as the powerful domestic shrew whom no man can control, except perhaps Harry, is an interestingly comic preparation for later use. Thus, when Harry's boat returns to the dock as the novel ends without Albert's body on it, Hemingway takes care of his wife for him in a macabre scene where she rushes wailingly to the pier in search of Albert and is inadvertently pushed off into the water by the jostling crowd. We last see her shaking her fist at the crowd, lisping out "Basards! Bishes!" and then "Alber. Wheersh Alber?" because she has lost her dental plate in the water and cannot speak articulately, like a sober novelist (252). Thus Hemingway disposes of a termagant wife while preparing to praise a loving one.

Plainly Harry reserves to himself the ancient right to smack his wife if she ever needs smacking; and just as plainly Marie knows better than to tempt him: she never gives him hell, at home or anywhere else. As wives go, there is nothing the matter with her. She knows her place; she keeps her part of the marital bargain. But then so does Harry. The instructive contrast is with Pilar and Pablo in Hemingway's next novel, *For Whom the Bell Tolls*. Pablo is the guerrilla leader who turns cowardly and is therefore supplanted as leader by his tough wife, Pilar. But when Pablo recovers his courage, Pilar is wise enough to let him lead the guerrilla band again. Meanwhile he continues to beat her, though he has forfeited that marital right through cowardice: we are meant to see such beatings as craven acts. Harry, of course, is never cowardly. Marie knows this and is therefore never shrewish; but it is a good thing, one conjectures, that he spends so much time away from home, as did Hemingway, systematically, throughout his long marriage to Pauline.

Hemingway's fantasy of the good tough mother, in *For Whom the Bell Tolls,* who not only knows when to take her cowardly husband's place and when to leave it, but who also provides an adoring younger sisterly woman for the novel's brotherly hero, allows for what must be the best of the good deaths in his fiction. Thus, as Robert Jordan lies on the pine forest floor in Spain, which reminds us of the pine forests of upper Michigan, and waits for the approaching fascist troops, he invokes his American grandfather the Indian fighter to help him avoid his cowardly father's suicidal ways. Having suffered a broken leg when his horse fell on him, he has remained behind to delay the fascist troops so that the rest of the fleeing guerrilla band can make their escape. He will sacrifice his life, in other words, for the lives of others, among them Pilar and the girl Maria she has provided for him, who will also extend his own life into the future by androgynous identification, as when he tells her on parting, "If thou goest then I go, too. . . . Whichever one there is, is both."[7] That Maria will be Jordan's apotheosis when he dies takes us a step further, certainly, than Marie Morgan's remembrance of her appreciative husband's love during her own more dramatically focused apotheosis. This familial and androgynous self-extension is as far as Hemingway could go, in the way of nonabusive deaths, and should be kept in mind when we contemplate his own abusive death: in the foyer of the Idaho home he shared with his fourth wife, Mary, his body blocking the entrance to the house so that no one could leave or enter without confronting it, his brains spattered all over the foyer for others to clean up. Happily for us, and for his artistry, he imagined so much better for himself in his fictions.

7. Ernest Hemingway, *For Whom the Bell Tolls,* 463.

The Snows of Kilimanjaro

by Ernest Hemingway

Kilimanjaro is a snow covered mountain 19,710 feet high, and is said to be the highest mountain in Africa. Its western summit is called the Masai "Ngàje Ngài," the House of God. Close to the western summit there is the dried and frozen carcass of a leopard. No one has explained what the leopard was seeking at that altitude.

"The marvelous thing is that it's painless," he said. "That's how you know when it starts."

"Is it really?"

"Absolutely. I'm awfully sorry about the odor though. That must bother you."

"Don't! Please don't."

"Look at them," he said. "Now is it sight or is it scent that brings them like that?"

The cot the man lay on was in the wide shade of a mimosa tree and as he looked out past the shade onto the glare of the plain there were three of the big birds squatted obscenely, while in the sky a dozen more sailed, making quick-moving shadows as they passed.

"They've been there since the day the truck broke down," he said. "Today's the first time any have lit on the ground. I watched the way they sailed very carefully at first in case I ever wanted to use them in a story. That's funny now."

"I wish you wouldn't," she said.

"I'm only talking," he said. "It's much easier if I talk. But I don't want to bother you."

"You know it doesn't bother me," she said. "It's that I've gotten so very nervous not being able to do anything. I think we might make it as easy as we can until the plane comes."

"Or until the plane doesn't come."

"Please tell me what I can do. There must be something I can do."

"You can take the leg off and that might stop it, though I doubt it. Or you can shoot me. You're a good shot now. I taught you to shoot didn't I?"

"Please don't talk that way. Couldn't I read to you?"

"Read what?"

"Anything in the book bag that we haven't read."

"I can't listen to it," he said. "Talking is the easiest. We quarrel and that makes the time pass."

"I don't quarrel. I never want to quarrel. Let's not quarrel any more. No matter how nervous we get. Maybe they will be back with another truck today. Maybe the plane will come."

"I don't want to move," the man said. "There is no sense in moving now except to make it easier for you."

"That's cowardly."

"Can't you let a man die as comfortably as he can without calling him names? What's the use of slanging me?"

"You're not going to die."

"Don't be silly. I'm dying now. Ask those bastards." He looked over to where the huge, filthy birds sat, their naked heads sunk in the hunched feathers. A fourth planed down, to run quick-legged and then waddle slowly toward the others.

"They are around every camp. You never notice them. You can't die if you don't give up."

"Where did you read that? You're such a bloody fool."

"You might think about some one else."

"For Christ's sake," he said, "That's been my trade."

He lay then and was quiet for a while and looked across the heat shimmer of the plain to the edge of the bush. There were a few Tommies that showed minute and white against the yellow and, far off, he saw a herd of zebra, white against the green of the bush. This was a pleasant camp under big trees against a hill, with good water, and close by, a nearly dry water hole where sand grouse flighted in the mornings.

"Wouldn't you like me to read?" she asked. She was sitting on a canvas chair beside his cot. "There's a breeze coming up."

"No thanks."

"Maybe the truck will come."

"I don't give a damn about the truck."

"I do."

"You give a damn about so many things that I don't."

"Not so many, Harry."

"What about a drink?"

"It's supposed to be bad for you. It said in Black's to avoid all alcohol. You shouldn't drink."

"Molo!" he shouted.

"Yes Bwana."

"Bring whiskey-soda."

"Yes Bwana."

"You shouldn't," she said. "That's what I mean by giving up. It says it's bad for you. I know it's bad for you."

"No," he said. "It's good for me."

So now it was all over, he thought. So now he would never have a chance to finish it. So this was the way it ended in a bickering over a drink. Since the gangrene started in his right leg he had no pain and with the pain the horror had gone and all he felt now was a great tiredness and anger that this was the end of it. For this, that now was coming, he had very little curiosity. For years it had obsessed him; but now it meant nothing in itself. It was strange how easy being tired enough made it.

Now he would never write the things that he had saved to write until he knew enough to write them well. Well, he would not have to fail at trying to write them either. Maybe you could never write them, and that was why you put them off and delayed the starting. Well he would never know, now.

"I wish we'd never come," the woman said. She was looking at him holding the glass and biting her lip. "You never would have gotten anything like this in Paris. You always said you loved Paris. We could have stayed in Paris or gone anywhere. I'd have gone anywhere. I said I'd go anywhere you wanted. If you wanted to shoot we could have gone shooting in Hungary and been comfortable."

"Your bloody money," he said.

"That's not fair," she said. "It was always yours as much as mine. I left everything and I went wherever you wanted to go and I've done what you wanted to do. But I wish we'd never come here."

"You said you loved it."

"I did when you were all right. But now I hate it. I don't see why that had to happen to your leg. What have we done to have that happen to us?"

"I suppose what I did was to forget to put iodine on it when I first scratched it. Then I didn't pay any attention to it because I never infect. Then, later, when it got bad, it was probably using that weak carbolic solution when the other antiseptics ran out that paralyzed the minute blood vessels and started the gangrene." He looked at her, "What else?"

"I don't mean that."

"If we would have hired a good mechanic instead of a half baked kikuyu driver, he would have checked the oil and never burned out that bearing in the truck."

"I don't mean that."

"If you hadn't left your own people, your goddamned Old Westbury, Saratoga, Palm Beach people to take me on—"

"Why, I loved you. That's not fair. I love you now. I'll always love you. Don't you love me?"

"No," said the man. "I don't think so. I never have."

"Harry, what are you saying? You're out of your head."

"No. I haven't any head to go out of."

"Don't drink that," she said. "Darling, please don't drink that. We have to do everything we can."

"You do it," he said. "I'm tired."

Now in his mind he saw a railway station at Karagatch and he was standing with his pack and that was the headlight of the Simplon-Orient cutting the dark now and he was leaving Thrace then after the retreat. That was one of the things he had saved to write, with, in the morning at breakfast, looking out the window and seeing snow on the mountains in Bulgaria and Nansen's Secretary asking the old man if it were snow and the old man looking at it and saying, No, that's not snow. It's too early for snow. And the Secretary repeating to the other girls, No, you see. It's not snow and them all saying, It's not snow we were mistaken. But it was the snow all right and he sent them on into it when he evolved exchange of populations. And it was snow they tramped along in until they died that winter.

It was snow too that fell all Christmas week that year up in the Gauertal, that year they lived in the woodcutter's house with the big square porcelain stove that filled half the room, and they slept on mattresses filled with beech leaves, the time the deserter came with his feet bloody in the snow. He said the police were right behind him and they gave him woolen socks and held the gendarmes talking until the tracks had drifted over.

In Schrunz, on Christmas day, the snow was so bright it hurt your eyes when you looked out from the weinstube and saw every one coming home from church. That was where they walked up the sleigh-smoothed urine-yellowed road along the river with the steep pine hills, skis heavy on the shoulder, and where they ran that great run down the glacier above the Madlener-haus, the snow as smooth to see as cake frosting and as light as powder and he remembered the noiseless rush the speed made as you dropped down like a bird.

They were snow-bound a week in the Madlener-haus that time in the blizzard playing cards in the smoke by the lantern light and the stakes were higher all the time as Herr Lent lost more. Finally he lost it all. Everything, the skischule money and all the season's profit and then his capital. He could see him with his long nose, picking up the cards and then opening, "Sans Voir." There was always gambling then. When there was no snow you gambled and when there was too much you gambled. He thought of all the time in his life he had spent gambling.

But he had never written a line of that, nor of that cold, bright Christmas day with the mountains showing across the plain that Barker had flown across the lines to bomb the Austrian officers' leave train, machine-gunning them as they scattered and ran. He remembered Barker afterwards coming into the mess and starting to tell about it. And how quiet it got and then somebody saying, "You bloody murderous bastard."

Those were the same Austrians they killed then that he skied with later. No not the same. Hans, that he skied with all that year, had been in the Kaiser-Jägers and when they went hunting hares together up the little valley above the saw-mill they had talked of the fighting on Pasubio and of the attack on Perticara and Asalone and he had never written a word of that. Nor of Monte Coronoa, nor the Sette Communi, nor of Arsiero.

How many winters had he lived in the Voralberg and the Arlberg? It was four and then he remembered the man who had the fox to sell when they had walked into Bludenz, that time to buy presents, and the cherry-pit taste of good kirsch, the fast-slipping rush of running powder-snow on crust, singing "Hi! Ho! said Rolly!" as you ran down the last stretch to the steep drop, taking it straight, then running the orchard in three turns and out across the ditch and onto the icy road behind the inn. Knocking your bindings loose, kicking the skis free and leaning them up against the wooden wall of the inn, the lamplight coming from the window, where inside, in the smoky, new-wine smelling warmth, they were playing the accordion.

"Where did we stay in Paris?" he asked the woman who was sitting by him in a canvas chair, now, in Africa.

"At the Crillon. You know that."

"Why do I know that?"

"That's where we always stayed."

"No. Not always."

"There and at the Pavillion Henri-Quatre in St. Germain. You said you loved it there."

"Love is a dunghill," said Harry. "And I'm the cock that gets on it to crow."

"If you have to go away," she said, "is it absolutely necessary to kill off everything you leave behind? I mean do you have to take away everything?

Do you have to kill your horse, and your wife and burn your saddle and your armour?"

"Yes," he said. "Your damned money was my armour. My Swift and my Armour."

"Don't."

"All right. I'll stop that. I don't want to hurt you."

"It's a little bit late now."

"All right then. I'll go on hurting you. It's more amusing. The only thing I ever really liked to do with you I can't do now."

"No, that's not true. You liked to do many things and everything you wanted to do I did."

"Oh, for Christ sake stop bragging, will you?"

He looked at her and saw her crying.

"Listen," he said. "Do you think that it is fun to do this? I don't know why I'm doing it. It's trying to kill to keep yourself alive, I imagine. I was all right when we started talking. I didn't mean to start this, and now I'm crazy as a coot and being as cruel to you as I can be. Don't pay any attention, darling, to what I say. I love you, really. You know I love you. I've never loved any one else the way I love you."

He slipped into the familiar lie he made his bread and butter by.

"You're sweet to me."

"You bitch," he said. "You rich bitch. That's poetry. I'm full of poetry now. Rot and poetry. Rotten poetry."

"Stop it. Harry, why do you have to turn into a devil now?"

"I don't like to leave anything," the man said. "I don't like to leave things behind."

It was evening now and he had been asleep. The sun was gone behind the hill and there was a shadow all across the plain and the small animals were feeding close to camp; quick dropping heads and switching tails, he watched them keeping well out away from the bush now. The birds no longer waited on the ground. They were all perched heavily in a tree. There were many more of them. His personal boy was sitting by the bed.

"Memsahib's gone to shoot," the boy said. "Does Bwana want?"

"Nothing."

She had gone to kill a piece of meat and, knowing how he liked to watch the game, she had gone well away so she would not disturb this little pocket of the plain that he could see. She was always thoughtful, he thought. On anything she knew about, or had read, or that she had ever heard.

It was not her fault that when he went to her he was already over. How could a woman know that you meant nothing that you said; that you spoke only from habit and to be comfortable? After he no longer meant what he said, his lies were more successful with women than when he had told them the truth.

It was not so much that he lied as that there was no truth to tell. He had had his life and it was over and then he went on living it again with different people and more money, with the best of the same places, and some new ones.

You kept from thinking and it was all marvelous. You were equipped with good insides so that you did not go to pieces that way, the way most of them had, and you made an attitude that you cared nothing for the work you used to do, now that you could no longer do it. But, in yourself, you said that you would write about these people; about the very rich; that you were really not of them but a spy in their country; that you would leave it and write of it and for once it would be written by some one who knew what he was writing of. But he would never do it, because each day of not writing, of comfort, of being that which he despised, dulled his ability and softened his will to work so that, finally, he did no work at all. The people he knew now were all much more comfortable when he did not work. Africa was where he had been happiest in the good time of his life, so he had come out here to start again. They had made this safari with the minimum of comfort. There was no hardship; but there was no luxury and he had thought that he could get back into training that way. That in some way he could work the fat off his soul the way a fighter went into the mountains to work and train in order to burn it out of his body.

She had liked it. She said she loved it. She loved anything that was exciting, that involved a change of scene, where there were new people and where things were pleasant. And he had felt the illusion of returning strength of will to work. Now if this was how it ended, and he knew it was, he must not turn like some snake biting itself because its back was broken. It wasn't this woman's fault. If it had not been she it would have been another. If he lived by a lie he should try to die by it. He heard a shot beyond the hill.

She shot very well this good, this rich bitch, this kindly caretaker and destroyer of his talent. Nonsense. He had destroyed his talent himself. Why should he blame this woman because she kept him well? He had destroyed his talent by not using it, by betrayals of himself and what he believed in, by drinking so much that he blunted the edge of his perceptions, by laziness, by sloth, and by snobbery, by pride and by prejudice, by hook and by crook. What was this? A catalogue of old books? What was his talent anyway? It was a talent all right but instead of using it, he had traded on it. It was never what he had done, but always what he could do. And he had chosen to make his living with something else instead of a pen or a pencil. It was strange, too, wasn't it, that when he fell in love with another woman, that woman should always have more money than the last one? But when he no longer was in love, when he was only lying, as to this woman, now, who had the most money of all, who had all the money there was, who had had a husband and children, who had taken lovers and been dissatisfied with them, and who loved him dearly as a writer, as a man, as a companion and as a proud possession; it was strange that when he did not love her at all and was lying, that he should be able to give her more for her money than when he had really loved.

We must all be cut out for what we do, he thought. However you make your living is where your talent lies. He had sold vitality, in one form or another, all his life and when your affections are not too involved you give much better value for the money. He had found that out but he would never write that, now, either. No, he would not write that, although it was well worth writing.

Now she came in sight, walking across the open toward the camp. She was wearing jodhpurs and carrying her rifle. The two boys had a Tommie slung and they were coming along behind her. She was still a good-looking woman, he thought, and she had a pleasant body. She had a great talent and appreciation for the bed, she was not pretty, but he liked her face, she read enormously, liked to ride and shoot and, certainly, she drank too much. Her husband had died when she was still a comparatively young woman and for a while she had devoted herself to her two just-grown children, who did not need her and were embarrassed at having her about, to her stable of horses, to books, and to bottles. She liked to read in the evening before dinner and she drank Scotch and soda while she read. By dinner she was fairly drunk and after a bottle of wine at dinner she was usually drunk enough to sleep.

That was before the lovers. After she had the lovers she did not drink so much because she did not have to be drunk to sleep. But the lovers bored her. She had been married to a man who had never bored her and these people bored her very much.

Then one of her two children was killed in a plane crash and after that was over she did not want the lovers, and drink being no anaesthetic she had to make another life. Suddenly, she had been acutely frightened of being alone. But she wanted some one that she respected with her.

It had begun very simply. She liked what he wrote and she had always envied the life he led. She thought he did exactly what he wanted to. The steps by which she had acquired him and the way in which she had finally fallen in love with him were all part of a regular progression in which she had built herself a new life and he had traded away what remained of his old life.

He had traded it for security, for comfort too, there was no denying that, and for what else? He did not know. She would have bought him anything he wanted. He knew that. She was a damned nice woman too. He would as soon be in bed with her as any one; rather with her, because she was richer, because she was very pleasant and appreciative and because she never made scenes.

And now this life that she had built again was coming to a term because he had not used iodine two weeks ago when a thorn had scratched his knee as they moved forward trying to photograph a herd of waterbuck standing, their heads up, peering while their nostrils searched the air, their ears spread wide to hear the first noise that would send them rushing into the bush. They had bolted, too, before he got the picture.

Here she came now.

He turned his head on the cot to look toward her. "Hello," he said.

"I shot a Tommy ram," she told him. "He'll make you good broth and I'll have them mash some potatoes with the Klim. How do you feel?"

"Much better."

"Isn't that lovely? You know I thought perhaps you would. You were sleeping when I left."

"I had a good sleep. Did you walk far?"

"No. Just around behind the hill. I made quite a good shot on the Tommy."

"You shoot marvelously, you know."

"I love it. I've loved Africa. Really. If *you're* all right it's the most fun that I've ever had. You don't know the fun it's been to shoot with you. I've loved the country."

"I love it too.

"Darling, you don't know how marvelous it is to see you feeling better. I couldn't stand it when you felt that way. You won't talk to me like that again, will you? Promise me?"

"No," he said. "I don't remember what I said."

"You don't have to destroy me. Do you? I'm only a middle-aged woman who loves you and wants to do what you want to do. I've been destroyed two or three times already. You wouldn't want to destroy me again, would you?"

"I'd like to destroy you a few times in bed," he said.

"Yes. That's the good destruction. That's the way we're made to be destroyed. The plane will be here tomorrow."

"How do you know?"

"I'm sure. It's bound to come. The boys have the wood all ready and the grass to make the smudge. I went down and looked at it again today. There's plenty of room to land and we have the smudges ready at both ends."

"What makes you think it will come tomorrow?"

"I'm sure it will. It's overdue now. Then, in town, they will fix up your leg and then we will have some good destruction. Not that dreadful talking kind."

"Should we have a drink? The sun is down."

"Do you think you should?"

"I'm having one."

"We'll have one together. *Molo, letti dui whiskey-soda!*" she called.

"You'd better put on your mosquito boots," he told her.

"I'll wait till I bathe . . ."

While it grew dark they drank and just before it was dark and there was no longer enough light to shoot, a hyena crossed the open on his way around the hill.

"That bastard crosses there every night," the man said. "Every night for two weeks."

"He's the one makes the noise at night. I don't mind it. They're a filthy animal though."

Drinking together, with no pain now except the discomfort of lying in the one position, the boys lighting a fire, its shadow jumping on the tents, he could feel the return of acquiescence in this life of pleasant surrender. She *was* very good to him. He had been cruel and unjust in the afternoon. She was a fine woman, marvelous really. And just then it occurred to him that he was going to die.

It came with a rush; not as a rush of water nor of wind; but of a sudden evil-smelling emptiness and the odd thing was that the hyena slipped lightly along the edge of it.

"What is it, Harry?" she asked him.

"Nothing," he said. "You had better move over to the other side. To windward."

"Did Molo change the dressing?"

"Yes. I'm just using the boric now."

"How do you feel?"

"A little wobbly."

"I'm going in to bathe," she said. "I'll be right out. I'll eat with you and then we'll put the cot in."

So, he said to himself, we did well to stop the quarreling. He had never quarreled much with this woman, while with the women that he loved he had quarreled so much they had finally, always, with the corrosion of the quarreling, killed what they had together. He had loved too much, demanded too much, and he wore it all out.

He thought about alone in Constantinople that time, having quarrelled in Paris before he had gone out. He had whored the whole time and then, when that was over, and he had failed to kill his loneliness, but only made it worse, he had written her, the first one, the one who left him, a letter telling her how he had never been able to kill it. . . . How when he thought he saw her outside the Regence *one time it made him go all faint and sick inside, and that he would follow a woman who looked like her in some way, along the Boulevard, afraid to see it was not she, afraid to lose the feeling it gave him. How every one he had slept with had only made him miss her more. How what she had done could never matter since he knew he could not cure himself of loving her. He wrote this letter at the Club, cold sober, and mailed it to New York asking her to write him at the office in Paris. That seemed safe. And that night missing her so much it made him feel hollow sick inside, he wandered up past Taxim's, picked a girl up and took her out to supper. He had gone to a place to dance with her afterward, she danced badly, and left her for a hot Armenian slut, that swung her belly against him so it almost scalded. He took her away from a British gunner subaltern after a row. The gunner asked him outside and they fought in the street on the cobbles in the dark. He'd hit him twice, hard, on the side of the jaw and when he didn't go down he knew he was in for a fight. The gunner hit him in the body, then beside his eye. He swung with his left again and landed and the gunner fell on him and grabbed his coat and tore the sleeve off and he clubbed him twice behind the ear and then smashed him with his right as he pushed him away. When the gunner went down his head hit first and he ran with the girl because they heard the M.P.s coming. They got into a taxi and drove out to Rimmily Hissa along the Bosphorus, and around, and back in the cool night and went to bed and she felt as over-ripe as she looked but smooth, rose-petal, syrupy, smooth-bellied, big-breasted and needed no pillow under her buttocks, and he left her before she was awake looking blousy enough in the first daylight and turned up at the Pera Palace with a black eye, carrying his coat because one sleeve was missing.*

That same night he left for Anatolia and he remembered, later on that trip, riding all day through fields of the poppies that they raised for opium and how strange it made you feel, finally, and all the distances seemed wrong, to where they had made the attack with the newly arrived Constantine officers, that did not know a god-damned thing, and the artillery had fired into the troops and the British observer had cried like a child.

That was the day he'd first seen dead men wearing white ballet skirts and upturned shoes with pompons on them. The Turks had come steadily and lumpily and he had seen the skirted men running and the officers shooting into them and running then themselves and he and the British observer had run too until his lungs ached and his mouth was full of the taste of pennies and they stopped behind some rocks and there were the Turks coming as lumpily as ever. Later he had seen the things that he could never think of and later still he had seen much worse. So when he got back to Paris that time he could not talk about it or stand to have it mentioned. And there in the café as he passed was that American poet with a pile of saucers in front of him and a stupid look on his potato face talking about the Dada movement with a Roumanian who said his name was

Tristan Tzara, who always wore a monocle and had a headache, and, back at the apartment with his wife that now he loved again, the quarrel all over, the madness all over, glad to be home, the office sent his mail up to the flat. So then the letter in answer to the one he'd written came in on a platter one morning and when he saw the handwriting he went cold all over and tried to slip the letter underneath another. But his wife said, "Who is that letter from, dear?" and that was the end of the beginning of that.

He remembered the good times with them all, and the quarrels. They always picked the finest places to have the quarrels. And why had they always quarreled when he was feeling best? He had never written any of that because, at first, he never wanted to hurt any one and then it seemed as though there was enough to write without it. But he had always thought that he would write it finally. There was so much to write. He had seen the world change; not just the events; although he had seen many of them and had watched the people, but he had seen the subtler change and he could remember how the people were at different times. He had been in it and he had watched it and it was his duty to write of it; but now he never would.

"How do you feel?" she said. She had come out from the tent now after her bath.

"All right."

"Could you eat now?" He saw Molo behind her with the folding table and the other boy with the dishes.

"I want to write," he said.

"You ought to take some broth to keep your strength up."

"I'm going to die tonight," he said. "I don't need my strength up."

"Don't be melodramatic, Harry, please," she said.

"Why don't you use your nose? I'm rotted half way up my thigh now. What the hell should I fool with broth for? Molo bring whiskey-soda."

"Please take the broth," she said gently.

"All right."

The broth was too hot. He had to hold it in the cup until it cooled enough to take it and then he just got it down without gagging.

"You're a fine woman," he said. "Don't pay any attention to me."

She looked at him with her well-known, well-loved face from *Spur* and *Town and Country,* only a little the worse for drink, only a little the worse for bed, but *Town and Country* never showed those good breasts and those useful thighs and those lightly small-of-back-caressing hands, and as he looked and saw her well-known pleasant smile, he felt death come again. This time there was no rush. It was a puff, as of a wind that makes a candle flicker and the flame go tall.

"They can bring my net out later and hang it from the tree and build the fire up. I'm not going in the tent tonight. It's not worth moving. It's a clear night. There won't be any rain."

So this was how you died, in whispers that you did not hear. Well, there would be no more quarreling. He could promise that. The one experience that he had never had he was not going to spoil now. He probably would. You spoiled everything. But perhaps he wouldn't.

"You can't take dictation, can you?"

"I never learned," she told him.

"That's all right."

There wasn't time, of course, although it seemed as though it telescoped so that you might put it all into one paragraph if you could get it right.

There was a log house, chinked white with mortar, on a hill above the lake. There was a bell on a pole by the door to call the people in to meals. Behind the house were fields and behind the fields was the timber. A line of lombardy poplars ran from the house to the dock. Other poplars ran along the point. A road went up to the hills along the edge of the timber and along that road he picked blackberries. Then that log house was burned down and all the guns that had been on deer foot racks above the open fire place were burned and afterwards their barrels, with the lead melted in the magazines, and the stocks burned away, lay out on the heap of ashes that were used to make lye for the big iron soap kettles, and you asked Grandfather if you could have them to play with, and he said, no. You see they were his guns still and he never bought any others. Nor did he hunt any more. The house was rebuilt in the same place out of lumber now and painted white and from its porch you saw the poplars and the lake beyond; but there were never any more guns. The barrels of the guns that had hung on the deer feet on the wall of the log house lay out there on the heap of ashes and no one ever touched them.

In the Black Forest, after the war, we rented a trout stream and there were two ways to walk to it. One was down the valley from Triberg and around the valley road in the shade of the trees that bordered the white road, and then up a side road that went up through the hills past many small farms, with the big Schwarzwald houses, until that road crossed the stream. That was where our fishing began.

The other way was to climb steeply up to the edge of the woods and then go across the top of the hills through the pine woods, and then out to the edge of a meadow and down across this meadow to the bridge. There were birches along the stream and it was not big, but narrow, clear and fast, with pools where it had cut under the roots of the birches. At the Hotel in Triberg the proprietor had a fine season. It was very pleasant and we were all great friends. The next year came the inflation and the money he had made the year before was not enough to buy supplies to open the hotel and he hanged himself.

You could dictate that, but you could not dictate the Place Contrescarpe where the flower sellers dyed their flowers in the street and the dye ran over the paving where the autobus started and the old men and the women, always drunk on wine and bad marc; and the children with their noses running in the cold; the smell of dirty sweat and poverty and drunkenness at the Café des Amateurs and the whores at the Bal Musette they lived above. The Concierge who entertained the trooper of the Garde Republicaine in her loge, his horse-hair-plumed helmet on a chair. The locataire across the hall whose husband was a bicycle racer and her joy that morning at the Cremerie when she had opened L'Auto and seen where he placed third in Paris-Tours, his first big race. She had blushed and laughed and then gone upstairs crying with the yellow sporting paper in her hand. The husband of the woman who ran the Bal Musette drove a taxi and when he, Harry, had to take an early plane the husband knocked upon the door to wake him and they each drank a glass of white wine at the zinc of the bar before they started. He knew his neighbors in that quarter then because they all were poor.

Around that Place there were two kinds; the drunkards and the sportifs. The drunkards killed their poverty that way; the sportifs took it out in exercise. They were the descendants of the Communards and it was no struggle for them to know their politics. They knew who had shot their fathers, their relatives, their brothers, and their friends when the Versailles troops came in and took the town after the Commune and executed any one they could catch with calloused hands, or who wore a cap, or carried any other sign he was a working man. And in that poverty, and in that quarter across the street from a Boucherie Chevaline and a wine co-operative he had written the start of all he was to do. There never was another part of Paris that he loved like that, the sprawling trees, the old white plastered houses painted brown below, the long green of the autobus in that round square, the purple flower dye upon the paving, the sudden drop down the hill of the rue Cardinal Lemoine to the River, and the other way the narrow crowded world of the rue Mouffetard. The street that ran up toward the Pantheon and the other that he always took with the bicycle, the only asphalted street in all that quarter, smooth under the tires; with the high narrow houses and the cheap tall hotel where Paul Verlaine had died. There were only two rooms in the apartments where they lived and he had a room on the top floor of that hotel that cost him sixty francs a month where he did his writing, and from it he could see the roofs and chimney pots and all the hills of Paris.

From the apartment you could only see the wood and coal man's place. He sold wine too, bad wine. The golden horse's head outside the Boucherie

Chevaline where the carcasses hung yellow gold and red in the open window, and the green painted co-operative where they bought their wine; good wine and cheap. The rest was plaster walls and the windows of the neighbors. The neighbors who, at night, when some one lay drunk in the street, moaning and groaning in that typical French ivresse *that you were propaganded to believe did not exist, would open their windows and then the murmur of talk.*

"Where is the policeman? When you don't want him the bugger is always there. He's sleeping with some concierge. Get the Agent." *Till some one threw a bucket of water from a window and the moaning stopped. "What's that? Water. Ah, that's intelligent." And the windows shutting. Marie, his femme de menage, protesting against the eight-hour day saying, "If a husband works until six he gets only a little drunk on the way home and does not waste too much. If he works only until five he is drunk every night and one has no money. It is the wife of the working man who suffers from this shortening of hours."*

"Wouldn't you like some more broth?" the woman asked him now.

"No, thank you very much. It is awfully good."

"Try just a little."

"I would like a whiskey-soda."

"It's not good for you."

"No. It's bad for me. Cole Porter wrote the words and the music. This knowledge that you're going mad for me."

"You know I like you to drink."

"Oh yes. Only it's bad for me."

When she goes, he thought. I'll have all I want. Not all I want but all there is. Ayee he was tired. Too tired. He was going to sleep a little while. He lay still and death was not there. It must have gone around another street. It went in pairs, on bicycles, and moved absolutely silently on the pavements.

No, he had never written about Paris. Not the Paris that he cared about. But what about the rest that he had never written?

What about the ranch and the silvered gray of the sage brush, the quick, clear water in the irrigation ditches, and the heavy green of the alfalfa. The trail went up into the hills and the cattle in the summer were shy as deer. The bawling and the steady noise and slow moving mass raising a dust as you brought them down in the fall. And behind the mountains, the clear sharpness of the peak in the evening light and, riding down along the trail in the moonlight, bright across the valley. Now he remembered coming down through the timber in the dark holding the horse's tail when you could not see and all the stories that he meant to write.

About the half-wit chore boy who was left at the ranch that time and told not to let any one get any hay, and that old bastard from the Forks who had beaten the boy when he had worked for him stopping to get some feed. The boy refusing and the old man saying he would beat him again. The boy got the rifle from the kitchen and shot him when he tried to come into the barn and when they came back to the ranch he'd been dead a week, frozen in the corral, and the dogs had eaten part of him. But what was left you packed on a sled wrapped in a blanket and roped on and you got the boy to help you haul it, and the two of you took it out over the road on skis, and sixty miles down to town to turn the boy over. He having no idea that he would be arrested. Thinking he had done his duty and that you were his friend and he would be rewarded. He'd helped to haul the old man in so everybody could know how bad the old man had been and how he'd tried to steal some feed that didn't belong to him, and when the sheriff put the handcuffs on the boy he couldn't believe it. Then he'd started to cry. That was one story he had saved to write. He knew at least twenty good stories from out there and he had never written one. Why?

"You tell them why," he said.

"Why what, dear?"

"Why nothing."

She didn't drink so much, now, since she had him. But if he lived he would never write about her, he knew that now. Nor about any of them. The rich were dull and they drank too much, or they played too much backgammon. They were dull and they were repetitious. He remembered poor Julian and his romantic awe of them and how he had started a story once that began, "The very rich are different from you and me." And how some one had said to Julian, Yes, they have more money. But that was not humorous to Julian. He thought they were a special glamorous race and when he found they weren't it wrecked him just as much as any other thing that wrecked him.

He had been contemptuous of those who wrecked. You did not have to like it because you understood it. He could beat anything, he thought, because no thing could hurt him if he did not care.

All right. Now he would not care for death. One thing he had always dreaded was the pain. He could stand pain as well as any man, until it went on too long, and wore him out, but here he had something that had hurt frightfully and just when he had felt it breaking him, the pain had stopped.

He remembered long ago when Williamson, the bombing officer, had been hit by a stick bomb some one in a German patrol had thrown as he was coming in through the wire that night and, screaming, had begged every one to kill him. He was a fat man, very brave, and a good officer, although addicted to fantastic shows. But that night he was caught in the wire, with a flare lighting him up and his bowels spilled out into the wire, so when they brought him in, alive, they had to cut him loose. Shoot me, Harry. For Christ sake shoot me. They had had an argument one time about our Lord never sending you anything you could not bear and some one's theory had been that meant that at a certain time the pain passed you out automatically. But he had always remembered Williamson, that night. Nothing passed out Williamson until he gave him all his morphine tablets that he had always saved to use himself and then they did not work right away.

Still this now, that he had, was very easy; and if it was no worse as it went on there was nothing to worry about. Except that he would rather be in better company.

He thought a little about the company that he would like to have.

No, he thought, when everything you do, you do too long, and do too late, you can't expect to find the people still there. The people all are gone. The party's over and you are with your hostess now.

I'm getting as bored with dying as with everything else, he thought.

"It's a bore," he said out loud.

"What is, my dear?"

"Anything you do too bloody long."

He looked at her face between him and the fire. She was leaning back in the chair and the firelight shone on her pleasantly lined face and he could see that she was sleepy. He heard the hyena make a noise just outside the range of the fire.

"I've been writing," he said. "But I got tired."

"Do you think you will be able to sleep?"

"Pretty sure. Why don't you turn in?"

"I like to sit here with you."

"Do you feel anything strange?" he asked her.

"No. Just a little sleepy."

"I do," he said.

He had just felt death come by again.

"You know the only thing I've never lost is curiosity," he said to her.

"You've never lost anything. You're the most complete man I've ever known."

"Christ," he said. "How little a woman knows. What is that? Your intuition?"

Because, just then, death had come and rested its head on the foot of the cot and he could smell its breath.

"Never believe any of that about a scythe and a skull," he told her. "It can be two bicycle policemen as easily, or be a bird. Or it can have a wide snout like a hyena."

It had moved up on him now, but it had no shape any more. It simply occupied space.

"Tell it to go away."

It did not go away but moved a little closer.

"You've got a hell of a breath," he told it. "You stinking bastard."

It moved up closer to him still and now he could not speak to it, and when it saw he could not speak it came a little closer, and now he tried to send it away without speaking, but it moved in on him so its weight was all upon his chest, and while it crouched there and he could not move, or speak, he heard the woman say, "Bwana is asleep now. Take the cot up very gently and carry it into the tent."

He could not speak to tell her to make it go away and it crouched now, heavier, so he could not breathe. And then, while they lifted the cot, suddenly it was all right and the weight went from his chest.

It was morning and had been morning for some time and he heard the plane. It showed very tiny and then made a wide circle and the boys ran out and lit the fires, using kerosene, and piled on grass so there were two big smudges at each end of the level place and the morning breeze blew them toward the camp and the plane circled twice more, low this time, and then glided down and leveled off and landed smoothly and, coming walking toward him, was old Compton in slacks, a tweed jacket and a brown felt hat.

"What's the matter, old cock?" Compton said.

"Bad leg," he told him. "Will you have some breakfast?"

"Thanks. I'll just have some tea. It's the Puss Moth you know. I won't be able to take the Memsahib. There's only room for one. Your lorry is on the way."

Helen had taken Compton aside and was speaking to him. Compton came back more cheery than ever.

"We'll get you right in," he said. "I'll be back for the Mem. Now I'm afraid I'll have to stop at Arusha to refuel. We'd better get going."

"What about the tea?"

"I don't really care about it you know."

The boys had picked up the cot and carried it around the green tents and down along the rock and out onto the plain and along past the smudges that were burning brightly now, the grass all consumed, and the wind fanning the fire, to the little plane. It was difficult getting him in, but once in he lay back in the leather seat, and the leg was stuck straight out to one side of the seat where Compton sat. Compton started the motor and got in. He waved to Helen and to the boys and, as the clatter moved into the old familiar roar, they swung around with Compie watching for wart-hog holes and roared, bumping, along the stretch between the fires and with the last bump rose and he saw them all standing below, waving, and the camp beside the hill, flattening now, and the plain spreading, clumps of trees, and the bush flattening, while the game trails ran now smoothly to the dry waterholes, and there was a new water that he had never known of. The zebra, small rounded backs now, and the wildebeest, big-headed dots seeming to climb as they moved in long fingers across the plain, now scattering as the shadow came toward them, they were tiny now, and the movement had no gallop, and the plain as far as you could see, gray-yellow now and ahead old Compie's tweed back and the brown felt hat. Then they were over the first hills and the wildebeest were trailing up them, and then they were over mountains with sudden depths of green-rising forest and the solid bamboo slopes, and then the heavy forest again, sculptured into peaks and hollows until they crossed, and hills sloped down and then another plain, hot now, and purple brown, bumpy with heat and Compie looking back to see how he was riding. Then there were other mountains dark ahead.

And then instead of going on to Arusha they turned left, he evidently figured that they had the gas, and looking down he saw a pink sifting cloud, moving over the ground, and in the air, like the first snow in a blizzard, that comes from nowhere, and he knew the locusts were coming up from the South. Then they began to climb and they were going to the East it seemed, and then it darkened and they were in a storm, the rain so thick it seemed like flying through a waterfall, and then they were out and Compie turned his head and grinned and pointed and there, ahead, all he could see, as wide as all the world, great, high, and unbelievably white in the sun, was the square top of Kilimanjaro. And then he knew that there was where he was going.

Just then the hyena stopped whimpering in the night and started to make a strange, human, almost crying sound. The woman heard it and stirred uneasily. She did not wake. In her dream she was at the house on Long Island and it was the night before her daughter's début. Somehow her father was there and he had been very rude. Then the noise the hyena made was so loud she woke and for a moment she did not know where she was and she was very afraid. Then she took the flashlight and shone it on the other cot that they had carried in after Harry had gone to sleep. She could see his bulk under the mosquito bar but somehow he had gotten his leg out and it hung down alongside the cot. The dressings had all come down and she could not look at it.

"Molo," she called, "Molo! Molo!"

Then she said, "Harry, Harry!" Then her voice rising, "Harry! Please, Oh Harry!"

There was no answer and she could not hear him breathing.

Outside the tent the hyena made the same strange noise that had awakened her. But she did not hear him for the beating of her heart.

Sweet Violence in Steinbeck's Eden

In 1974 I published an essay called "Of George and Lennie and Curley's Wife: Sweet Violence in Steinbeck's Eden," from which my present title is drawn. About ten years later, when I became a volunteer worker for a Rhode Island agency engaged in the rehabilitation of male batterers, I learned some of the more practical approaches to the puzzling nature of "sweet violence" that I had touched on in the essay. Appropriately enough, I had also touched upon "the perplexities of sexual rage," especially in Steinbeck's famous novella *Of Mice and Men,* but also in related fictions including "The Murder," "The Red Pony," *The Grapes of Wrath, Tortilla Flat,* and *East of Eden.* That concept had also figured as immediately in the agency's work as in these tales. Beyond that, I had demonstrated in the essay the blatant gender biases that furthered sexual rage, and the paradox of "responsibility" for supposedly "blameless violence" that framed it. In other words, I had unwittingly found confirmation in Steinbeck for those practical approaches I would later encounter in the social service field of domestic violence.

More interesting still, I had begun to deal with Steinbeck's marvelously predictive parable, in linking two migrant farmworkers with a straying ranch-house wife, for the conscious and unconscious aspects of domestic violence in male batterers—a parable, that is to say, for those cultivated rages—those sweet grapes of wrath—that fuel such violence. That rages can be cultivated, then, and that there are professional confirmations of that paradoxical process, will be my present justification for reviewing some relevant aspects of my original essay.

I

As I then demonstrated at some length, Steinbeck was attracted in many of his tales to the innocent pleasures of childhood and to the low threshold of rage in children whenever those pleasures are threatened or thwarted. He was aware also, among those innocent pleasures, of a penchant in children for "lordful violence" against lesser forms of life—melons, birds, dogs, vultures—of which adults might disapprove. He was further attracted to adult modes of "justifiable homicide," like Tom Joad's impulsive murder in self-defense of a jealous friend who knifed him at a dance, in *The Grapes of Wrath;* or like Jim Moore's vengeful killing, in "The Murder," of his foreign wife's lover when he finds them in bed together, a killing for which no western jury will convict him. Finally, he was keenly aware of the connecting links between these modes of violence in the painful passage from childhood innocence to adult carnal knowledge. Indeed, it is the puzzling nature of that often violent transition that is dramatized—one might even say allegorized—in *Of Mice and Men.*

It seems evident enough, for instance, that George Milton and Lennie Small bear allegorical names suggestive of their parent-child relations. It is further evident that George himself is inclined to be childish, rather than mature, in his dealings with Lennie, and that their friendship reflects the tensions created by his facile guidance. Thus, George the Miltonic god-player finds pleasure in playing tricks on Lennie, in complaining about the burden of his care, and in punishing him for his many failures to follow instructions and do what he is told. More positively, he cultivates a friendship dream with Lennie on which the novella's sentimental plot is based. But on closer inspection, that dream of the simple pleasures of an all-male friendship farm seems more like a boy's fantasized escape from threatening aspects of adulthood than the universal expression of man's "earth-longings," his need for land of his own, that Steinbeck tries to emphasize. In any event, these petty satisfactions and simple pleasures serve to characterize the mixed quality of the master-slave, parent-child relation between George and Lennie and its oddly adolescent cast.

Lennie's contribution to this mixture is evident, of course, in his enormous capacity for innocent childhood pleasures—stroking furry animals, dipping his whole head bearlike into the Salinas River, relishing the oft-told tale of the friendship farm in all its small details—and in his enormous capacity also for innocent childhood rages whenever his dreams or pleasures are thwarted, or whenever he feels threatened with discovery and punishment for his mistakes. Steinbeck's attraction to that capacity for innocent rage, that low threshold for its release in a grown man blessed with enormous physical strength, is another instance of his concern with "blameless murder" in adulthood, here portrayed in terms of its childhood origins. But his awareness of George's part in the release of Lennie's rages, and of George's manipulations in bringing about such releases for his own selfish ends, is one of the obvious sources of this popular novella's undeniable power, its forceful transcendence of its own sentimental assumptions.

As I try to show in my original essay, it is George's active sharing in the gender biases of the bunkhouse world that he and Lennie inhabit that determines the tragic events of the tale. It is George who dislikes the boss's son, Curley, and who resents his gloveful of vaseline for the hand that strokes his wife's genitals; it is George who sees Curley's wife as jailbait, bitch, rat-trap, and warns Lennie to avoid her seductive ways; finally, it is George who hates and distrusts the ranch boss for his authority and his favored dependents for their special privileges. Thus, as I originally argued, it is George who lordfully creates the troubles for which Lennie will himself be punished—though he only obeys his master's vengeful voice.

If we consider George and Lennie as in some sense aspects of one person, we can begin to understand how Steinbeck anticipates our present view of the conscious and unconscious aspects of domestic violence in male batterers. Such clients often depict themselves as being overwhelmed by anger, unable to control the powerful rages that sweep over them—they are the victims of their own uncontrollable rages. But as we try to demonstrate through the Anger Iceberg Chart used in educational therapy sessions, there are deep-seated feelings in all of us, old scores to settle, old hurts and resentments that can be brought to the surface only by conscious cultivation; they have to be "talked up," worked up—literally called up—before an emotional eruption can occur and the iceberg becomes—in a doubly mixed metaphor—a volcano of supposedly uncontrollable feelings. (See Anger Iceberg Chart, below, 358.)

This is what Steinbeck dramatizes when he has George deliberately instruct Lennie to crush Curley's hand, or when he shows George, even before that, vehemently sharing with Lennie his powerful resentment of the ranch boss, the boss's son Curley, and Curley's straying wife. As I note in the original essay, George pins such frightening taboos on these family figures that Lennie is bound to panic in their presence, to clutch with his tremendous strength—like a child caught with some forbidden object—and so punish people whom George openly dislikes. This is Steinbeck's marvelous parable, then, for the conscious cultivation of those unconscious rages to which we are all susceptible; this is how we call them up so they can seemingly seize and overwhelm us. Then we too can blame our emotions, after the fact, on the powerful giant within us who forces us to commit forbidden acts, just as George can initially blame Lennie, the personified bearer of his own cultivated rages. It may be true, as Steinbeck holds, that children and idiots really do have low thresholds for uncultivated and therefore wholly impulsive rages; but normal adults are neither children nor idiots. Our threshold for rage has been raised by familial and social prohibitions—we have to cultivate or call up those once more easily rousable rages of infancy and early childhood.

This is what George does, then, through Lennie: he manipulates his enormous strength for selfish ends, for which the supposedly impulsive Lennie can then be blamed. Indeed, even when George takes responsibility, at the end of the tale, for shooting Lennie, the analogy is with shooting a mad dog or an old one, an irresponsible animal that has to be put out of its misery or prevented from committing further destructive acts of violence. Only when we convert that analogy to our own ends can we say that George is getting rid thereby of his own propensities for violence, and in that sense taking responsibility for them, like an accountable male batterer who finally understands the moral implications of his own acts and attitudes. Steinbeck's story is of course richer than our professional approach allows: he is rightly troubled by the implied loss of animal energy and strength when Lennie is put to death. But our response to that loss must again be professional: we don't put male batterers to death unless they become murderers like "George-through-Lennie"; we, too, would like to convert such destructive energy and strength to responsibly creative ends.

II

"The Murder" was published in 1934, three years before *Of Mice and Men,* and was then selected for inclusion in *O. Henry Prize Stories.* In retrospect, that sign of public approval seems troubling. Although the tale is decidedly well wrought, it now appears more obviously sexist than *Of Mice and Men,* and less transcendent of its own biases. In my original essay I had only noted that it deals with another instance of "blameless murder." In keeping with my own partial blindness, I had forgotten to mention that it also deals with blameless wife-whipping, and deals with it in a socially biased way. Indeed, it is a splendidly sexist example of social attitudes in fiction that reflect and extend our sanctioned prejudices about domestic violence, and it deserves more attention on those demonstrable grounds.

There is, of course, much in this story that is simply peculiar to Steinbeck himself. Careful readers of the opening description of a back canyon in Monterey County, California, called the Canon del Castillo for its illusion of "a tremendous stone castle, buttressed and towered like those strongholds the Crusaders put up in the path of their conquests,"[1] will note the trace here of Steinbeck's boyhood zest for Arthurian legends, and may therefore legitimately suspect him of forecasting his rival-slaying wife-beating hero as a modern crusader who overcomes the grievous pagan iniquities ahead through bloody conquests. That our hero also chases away troops of boys who tramp through his abandoned house, in the next paragraph, adds unwitting support to such suspicions. But there is nothing suspicious about Steinbeck's blatant depiction of social attitudes at

1. "The Murder," 171/252. Further page references will be given in the text, with the first number referring to the edition listed in the bibliography and the second to the reprinting of the story below.

work in this part of California when he writes that the people in town now "turn and look at [the hero's] retreating back with awe and some admiration" whenever he and his "plump and still pretty wife" pass by (172/252). Indeed, they all too plainly admire a man who has killed his wife's lover, bullwhipped his unfaithful wife, and so won her abiding love.

The story offers local qualifications to that admiration. The wife is "a Jugo-Slav girl," a foreigner, and her father bluntly tells the hero that "he's" not like American girls, that "he" needs to be beaten if "he's" bad, and even if "he's" good, that it's an old and honored custom where they come from: "I beat *his* mama. Papa beat my mama." A Slav girl does "not like a man that don't beat hell out of *him*" (173/253). I have emphasized here the father's foreign inability to master English grammar—his substitutions of "he" for "she" and "him" for "her" in talking about his daughter, as if projecting his own gender views upon her. Whatever the case, his clumsiness with American speech chiefly helps to distance him and his daughter from American readers, and to reassure those readers that American girls need not be beaten when they marry, that the custom itself is a foreign import, not native to this Anglo-Saxon land.

It comes as no surprise, then, when Steinbeck tells us that his Anglo-Saxon hero, Jim Moore, "was not proud of [his wife's] foreign family, of her many brothers and sisters and cousins," and that he later faults the woman herself for being "a damn foreigner" (172, 175/253, 255). Nor does it surprise us that he nonetheless delights in her animal beauty, finds her eyes "as large and questioning as a doe's eyes," or pats her head and neck "under the same impulse that made him stroke a horse" (172, 173/253). Indeed, when the marriage quickly cools down and his girlfriends at a local bar ask him where his wife, Jelka, is, he even answers jokingly that she's "Home in the barn" (175/254). Thus he shares not only in his community's sense of superiority over foreigners but also in its double standards, its gender-shared beliefs that married women may be treated like domestic animals, and that men may betray them by frequent fraternizations with jolly prostitutes at the local bars, without being held morally responsible.

Readers will have to decide for themselves whether Steinbeck complicates his plot by letting us in on these male privileges, or whether he shares in the several prejudices that discount them as a possible explanation of the wife's later infidelity with her cousin. At any rate, it is Steinbeck who lets us know that Moore first goes to prostitutes in town when he fails to reach his foreign wife on the level of intimate sharing. They have been passionate lovers. She has served him faultlessly and apparently humbly as a self-styled subordinate. Indeed, she has carefully studied and met his every physical need. But she cannot or will not talk to him as an intimate companion. Apparently her "foreign ways" prevent it and therefore justify Moore's return to his old American ways, at least on Saturday nights, as a carefree bachelor.

Among those foreign ways are Jelka's conspicuous religious devotions, which reassure Moore as he makes his self-serving Saturday night visits to town. The lamp she puts in the window, on one such occasion, is our first hint of her covert affair with an overattentive and oft-mentioned cousin. Moore discovers the affair only by accident, when a friend alerts him that night to the presence of cattle thieves in the neighborhood, and he returns home unexpectedly to find the lovers asleep together in bed. The "crime of passion" that follows is nicely delineated, of course, as a deliberate and considered murder of the sleeping cousin. Thus Moore goes back outside, after discovering the lovers, as if to pull himself together, cries "a few dry, hard, smothered sobs," recalls "the way his mother used to hold a bucket to catch the throat blood when his father killed a pig," then returns inside and shoots the foreign pig asleep beside his now awakened wife (182–83/258–59). Whether Jelka avoids the blood that splashes on the pillow beside her, as Moore's mother had carefully kept her clothes from being spattered by the American pig's blood, we never know. Steinbeck only notes that her nose was running, presumably like a child's, and that she "whined softly, like a cold puppy," as if pleading for better treatment for herself. Moore turns away in panic, moves quickly outside, dips his whole head in the water trough—like an anguished Lennie Small—and then vomits on the ground. Inside the house his wife moves about, still whimpering "like a puppy" (183/259). He then decides to saddle a horse and report his crime in town.

If the murder has been a deliberate act, the whipping that follows is even more deliberate. Moore returns the next morning with a deputy sheriff and a coroner. These men go inside, at Moore's request, to look around and clean things up "a little." They return with the body wrapped in a comforter and reassure him that the technical murder charge against him will be dismissed. Then the sheriff asks him to "go kind of light" on his wife. "I won't hurt her," Moore replies (185/260). But after they leave he goes slowly into the house, finds his bullwhip, and returns to the barn, where his wife waits in the loft, still whimpering like a puppy:

> When Jim came out of the barn again, he carried Jelka over his shoulder. By the water-trough he set her tenderly on the ground. Her hair was littered with bits of hay. The back of her shirtwaist was streaked with blood. . . .
>
> "You hurt me," she said. "You hurt me bad."
>
> He nodded gravely. "Bad as I could without killing you." . . .
>
> Jelka's thickened lips tried to smile. "Did you have any breakfast at all?"

> "No," he said. "None at all."
>
> "Well, then, I'll fry you up some eggs." She struggled painfully to her feet.
>
> "Let me help you," he said. "I'll help you get your shirtwaist off. It's drying stuck to your back. It'll hurt."
>
> "No. I'll do it myself." Her voice had a peculiar resonance in it. Her dark eyes dwelt warmly on him for a moment, and then she turned and limped into the house. (185–86/260)

What we are witnessing here is the confirmation of her father's prediction that Slav girls don't "like a man that don't beat hell out of [them]." It is of course one of the standard rationalizations used for wife beating by male batterers: the women like it; they want you to beat them; they admire, respect, even love you for it. So the story shows, at least for foreign women—though as everybody knows, including Steinbeck, all women are foreign to all men: in their inscrutable "otherness," they all come from another country.

This seems to be Steinbeck's working subtext, in any case, for this otherwise exotic California canyon tale. Thus when Jelka asks, as the story ends, "Will you whip me any more—for this?" Jim firmly replies with the standing threat behind all abusive marriages of whatever venue: "No, not any more, for this." Then, as she sits down beside him, eyes smiling, he again pats her hair and neck as if stroking a well-trained horse.

III

Fortunately, we do have one clue to Steinbeck's intentions in writing "The Murder" that helps to confirm the above interpretation. In a letter to his friend George Albee dated February 25, 1934, he comments about his friend's response to that story: "I think you got out of the murder story about what I wanted you to. You got no character. I didn't want any there. You got color and a dream like movement. I was writing it more as a dream than anything else, so if you got this vague and curiously moving feeling out of it that is all I ask."[2]

To write a dreamlike story in this deliberately obscure way is, of course, to identify with the action, the local color, and the minimized characters, and to appropriate them for one's own dreamlike, if artistic, purposes. It amounts, I would argue, to giving oneself permission to dream this particular dream of "blameless" violence in public, without acknowledging one's own peculiar stake in its unraveling. In some sense, that may describe Steinbeck's intentions in many of his fictions, early and late.

---

2. *Steinbeck: A Life in Letters,* 91.

I began my original essay on *Of Mice and Men,* for instance, with an epigraph from Steinbeck's postwar novel *East of Eden,* which nicely indicates a similar attraction to secret motives and subsurface feelings:

> Nearly everyone has appetites and impulses, trigger emotions, islands of selfishness, lusts just beneath the surface. And most people either hold such things in check or indulge them secretly. Cathy knew not only these impulses in others but how to use them for her own gain. It is quite possible that she did not believe in any other tendencies in humans, for while she was preternaturally alert in some directions she was completely blind in others. Cathy learned when she was very young that sexuality with all its attendant yearnings and pains, jealousies and taboos, is the most disturbing impulse humans have.

This epigraph, I then explained, concerns a woman named Cathy Ames who deserts her husband and newborn twins to become the successful proprietor of a California whorehouse:

> In his diaries for the composition of the novel Steinbeck calls this woman a "monster" and says he will prove to his readers that such monsters actually exist. His choice of her as the archetypal mother of a California family, his peculiarly Miltonic view of her as an exploiter of men's lusts, and his awareness of the exploitability of such feelings—this complex of psychological tendencies in the later Steinbeck has much to do, I think, with the force behind his early social fiction.[3]

I then applied that "complex of psychological tendencies" to *Of Mice and Men* and turned, at one point, to a story from *Tortilla Flat* that helps to explain Steinbeck's ongoing need to demonize sexual exploiters like Cathy Ames and to justify subsurface hostilities toward them:

> It concerns Petey Ravanno, who tries to commit suicide for love of Gracie Montez, and who wins her in marriage by that desperate strategy. What makes him desperate is her elusiveness: Gracie is always running away, and though men sometimes catch her, they cannot "get close to her"; she always seems to withhold "something nice" from them. This elusiveness has another strange effect on desperate admirers: "It made you want to choke her and pet her at the same time. It made you want to cut her open and get that thing that was inside of her." (64)

It seems apparent, in this light, that Steinbeck's troubling women characters—Curley's straying wife, the deceptive Jelka, the exploitative Cathy Ames—are all like the elusive Gracie Montez: they are all subject to dreamlike or subsurface expressions of the male need for violent and vengeful possession; they are

3. "Of George and Lennie and Curley's Wife: Sweet Violence in Steinbeck's Eden," 59–60. Further page references will be given in the text.

all defined as characters—not by their own needs and natures—but by their resistance to male control. In his early fiction Steinbeck seems trapped by such extreme forms of frustrated and decidedly dreamlike desires for possession and control: he is unable to take us beyond the adolescent "perplexities of sexual rage." Yet the rich tensions of this poignant perplex are often, as I said, honestly and powerfully presented.

I concluded that essay, as I will now conclude this one, with the following comments on such perplexities from *Tortilla Flat,* and with some further comments on Steinbeck's partial resolution of them in *East of Eden:*

> Pilon complained. "It is not a good story. There are too many meanings and too many lessons in it. Some of these lessons are opposite. There is not a story to take into your head. It proves nothing."
>
> "I like it," said Pablo. "I like it because it hasn't any meaning you can see, and still it does seem to mean something, I can't tell what."[4]

Steinbeck himself liked simple stories well enough to write straight allegories such as *The Pearl.* But chiefly he liked the puzzling kind. In *Tortilla Flat,* an otherwise comic novel, he shows, for instance, how Danny tires of the chivalric life and reverts to the "sweet violence" of outlawry. "Sweet violence" means something more here than the joys of boyish rebellion: it means delight in pulling the house down on one's own and other people's heads, which is what Danny does when the friendship dream proves insubstantial, and he pays with his life—and later, with his friends' help, with his house—for the pleasure of destroying it. Lennie too pays with his life for the pleasure of destructive rages; but he serves in this respect as an extension of his friend's desires: he is George Milton's idiot Samson, his blind avenger for the distastefulness of aggressive sexuality. Which may be why their friendship dream seems impossible from the first, why the pathos of their dream, and of its inevitable defeat, seems less important than the turbulence it rouses. Once more, "sweet violence" is the force that moves these characters, and us, to contemplate their puzzling fate.

By *East of Eden* Steinbeck would learn that rages generally follow from rejected love, that parental coldness or aloofness breeds violence in youthful hearts; and he would come also to accept sexuality as a vulnerable condition, a blind helplessness by which men and women may be "tricked and trapped and enslaved and tortured," but without which they would not be human. Oddly, he would create in Cathy Ames a monstrous projection of his old hostility toward women as exploiters of the sex impulse; and he would impose on her his own

4. *Tortilla Flat,* 122.

preternatural alertness to its selfish uses and his own fear of being absorbed and blinded by it in his youth. But by accepting sex now as a human need, he would redeem his Lennies and Dannies from outlawry and animality, and he would finally repair the ravages of sweet violence.

The Murder

by John Steinbeck

This happened a number of years ago in Monterey County, in central California. The Cañon del Castillo is one of those valleys in the Santa Lucia range which lie between its many spurs and ridges. From the main Cañon del Castillo a number of little arroyos cut back into the mountains, oak-wooded canyons, heavily brushed with poison oak and sage. At the head of the canyon there stands a tremendous stone castle, buttressed and towered like those strongholds the Crusaders put up in the path of their conquests. Only a close visit to the castle shows it to be a strange accident of time and water and erosion working on soft, stratified sandstone. In the distance the ruined battlements, the gates, the towers, even the arrow slits, require little imagination to make out.

Below the castle, on the nearly level floor of the canyon, stand the old ranch house, a weathered and mossy barn and a warped feeding-shed for cattle. The house is deserted; the doors, swinging on rusted hinges, squeal and bang on nights when the wind courses down from the castle. Not many people visit the house. Sometimes a crowd of boys tramp through the rooms, peering into empty closets and loudly defying the ghosts they deny.

Jim Moore, who owns the land, does not like to have people about the house. He rides up from his new house, farther down the valley, and chases the boys away. He has put "No Trespassing" signs on his fences to keep curious and morbid people out. Sometimes he thinks of burning the old house down, but then a strange and powerful relation with the swinging doors, the blind and desolate windows, forbids the destruction. If he should burn the house he would destroy a great and important piece of his life. He knows that when he goes to town with his plump and still pretty wife, people turn and look at his retreating back with awe and some admiration.

Jim Moore was born in the old house and grew up in it. He knew every grained and weathered board of the barn, every smooth, worn manger-rack. His mother and father were both dead when he was thirty. He celebrated his majority by raising a beard. He sold the pigs and decided never to have any more. At last he bought a fine Guernsey bull to improve his stock, and he began to go to Monterey on Saturday nights, to get drunk and to talk with the noisy girls of the Three Star.

Within a year Jim Moore married Jelka Sepic, a Jugo-Slav girl, daughter of a heavy and patient farmer of Pine Canyon. Jim was not proud of her foreign family, of her many brothers and sisters and cousins, but he delighted in her beauty. Jelka had eyes as large and questioning as a doe's eyes. Her nose was thin and sharply faceted, and her lips were deep and soft. Jelka's skin always startled Jim, for between night and night he forgot how beautiful it was. She was so smooth and quiet and gentle, such a good housekeeper, that Jim often thought with disgust of her father's advice on the wedding day. The old man, bleary and bloated with festival beer, elbowed Jim in the ribs and grinned suggestively, so that his little dark eyes almost disappeared behind puffed and wrinkled lids.

"Don't be big fool, now," he said. "Jelka is Slav girl. He's not like American girl. If he is bad, beat him. If he's good too long, beat him too. I beat his mama. Papa beat my mama. Slav girl! He's not like a man that don't beat hell out of him."

"I wouldn't beat Jelka," Jim said.

The father giggled and nudged him again with his elbow, "Don't be big fool," he warned. "Sometime you see." He rolled back to the beer barrel.

Jim found soon enough that Jelka was not like American girls. She was very quiet. She never spoke first, but only answered his questions, and then with soft short replies. She learned her husband as she learned passages of Scripture. After they had been married a while, Jim never wanted for any habitual thing in the house but Jelka had it ready for him before he could ask. She was a fine wife, but there was no companionship in her. She never talked. Her great eyes followed him, and when he smiled, sometimes she smiled too, a distant and covered smile. Her knitting and mending and sewing were interminable. There she sat, watching her wise hands, and she seemed to regard with wonder and pride the little white hands that could do such nice and useful things. She was so much like an animal that sometimes Jim patted her head and neck under the same impulse that made him stroke a horse.

In the house Jelka was remarkable. No matter what time Jim came in from the hot dry range or from the bottom farm land, his dinner was exactly, steamingly ready for him. She watched while he ate, and pushed the dishes close when he needed them, and filled his cup when it was empty.

Early in the marriage he told her things that happened on the farm, but she smiled at him as a foreigner does who wishes to be agreeable even though he doesn't understand.

"The stallion cut himself on the barbed wire," he said.

And she replied, "Yes," with a downward inflection that held neither question nor interest.

He realized before long that he could not get in touch with her in any way. If she had a life apart, it was so remote as to be beyond his reach. The barrier in her eyes was not one that could be removed, for it was neither hostile nor intentional.

At night he stroked her straight black hair and her unbelievably smooth golden shoulders, and she whimpered a little with pleasure. Only in the climax of his embrace did she seem to have a life apart, fierce and passionate. And then immediately she lapsed into the alert and painfully dutiful wife.

"Why don't you ever talk to me?" he demanded. "Don't you want to talk to me?"

"Yes," she said. "What do you want me to say?" She spoke the language of his race out of a mind that was foreign to his race.

When a year had passed, Jim began to crave the company of women, the chattery exchange of small talk, the shrill pleasant insults, the shame-sharpened vulgarity. He began to go again to town, to drink and to play with the noisy girls of the Three Star. They liked him there for his firm, controlled face and for his readiness to laugh.

"Where's your wife?" they demanded.

"Home in the barn," he responded. It was a never-failing joke.

Saturday afternoons he saddled a horse and put a rifle in the scabbard in case he should see a deer. Always he asked, "You don't mind staying alone?"

"No. I don't mind."

At once he asked, "Suppose someone should come?"

Her eyes sharpened for a moment, and then she smiled. "I would send them away," she said.

"I'll be back about noon tomorrow. It's too far to ride in the night." He felt that she knew where he was going, but she never protested nor gave any sign of disapproval. "You should have a baby," he said.

Her face lighted up. "Some time God will be good," she said eagerly.

He was sorry for her loneliness. If only she visited with the other women of the canyon she would be less lonely, but she had no gift for visiting. Once every month or so she put horses to the buckboard and went to spend an afternoon with her mother, and with the brood of brothers and sisters and cousins who lived in her father's house.

"A fine time you'll have," Jim said to her. "You'll gabble your crazy language like ducks for a whole afternoon. You'll giggle with that big grown cousin of yours with the embarrassed face. If I could find any fault with you, I d call you a damn foreigner." He remembered how she blessed the bread with the sign of the cross before she put it in the oven, how she knelt at the bedside every night, how she had a holy picture tacked to the wall in the closet.

One Saturday of a hot dusty June, Jim cut oats in the farm flat. The day was long. It was after six o'clock when the mower tumbled the last band of oats. He drove the clanking machine up into the barnyard and backed it into the implement shed, and there he unhitched the horses and turned them out to graze on the hills over Sunday. When he entered the kitchen Jelka was just putting his dinner on the table. He washed his hands and face and sat down to eat.

"I'm tired," he said, "but I think I'll go to Monterey anyway. There'll be a full moon."

Her soft eyes smiled.

"I'll tell you what I'll do," he said. "If you would like to go, I'll hitch up a rig and take you with me."

She smiled again and shook her head. "No, the stores would be closed. I would rather stay here."

"Well, all right, I'll saddle the horse then. I didn't think I was going. The stock's all turned out. Maybe I can catch a horse easy. Sure you don't want to go?"

"If it was early, and I could go to the stores—but it will be ten o'clock when you get there."

"Oh, no—well, anyway, on horseback I'll make it a little after nine."

Her mouth smiled to itself, but her eyes watched him for the development of a wish. Perhaps because he was tired from the long day's work, he demanded, "What are you thinking about?"

"Thinking about? I remember, you used to ask that nearly every day when we were first married."

"But what are you?" he insisted irritably.

"Oh—I'm thinking about the eggs under the black hen." She got up and went to the big calendar on the wall. "They will hatch tomorrow or maybe Monday."

It was almost dusk when he had finished shaving and putting on his blue serge suit and his new boots. Jelka had the dishes washed and put away. As Jim went through the kitchen he saw that she had taken the lamp to the table near the window, and that she sat beside it knitting a brown wool sock.

"Why do you sit there tonight?" he asked. "You always sit over here. You do funny things sometimes."

Her eyes arose slowly from her flying hands. "The moon," she said quietly. "You said it would be full tonight. I want to see the moon rise."

"But you're silly. You can't see it from that window. I thought you knew direction better than that."

She smiled remotely. "I will look out of the bedroom window, then."

Jim put on his black hat and went out. Walking through the dark empty barn, he took a halter from the rack. On the grassy sidehill he whistled high and shrill. The horses stopped feeding and moved slowly in towards him, and stopped twenty feet away. Carefully he approached his bay gelding and moved his hand from its rump along its side and up and over its neck. The halter-strap clicked in its buckle. Jim turned and led the horse back to the barn. He threw his saddle on and cinched it tight, put his silver-bound bridle over the stiff ears, buckled the throat latch, knotted the tie-rope about the gelding's neck and fastened the neat coil-end to the saddle string. Then he slipped the halter and led the horse to the house. A radiant crown of soft red light lay over the eastern hills. The full moon would rise before the valley had completely lost the daylight.

In the kitchen Jelka still knitted by the window. Jim strode to the corner of the room and took up his 30–30 carbine. As he rammed cartridges into the magazine, he said, "The moon glow is on the hills. If you are going to see it rise, you better go outside now. It's going to be a good red one at rising."

"In a moment," she replied, "when I come to the end here." He went to her and patted her sleek head.

"Good night. I'll probably be back by noon tomorrow." Her dusky black eyes followed him out of the door.

Jim thrust the rifle into his saddle-scabbard, and mounted and swung his horse down the canyon. On his right, from behind the blackening hills, the great red moon slid rapidly up. The double light of the day's last afterglow and the rising moon thickened the outlines of the trees and gave a mysterious new perspective to the hills. The dusty oaks shimmered and glowed, and the shade under them was black as velvet. A huge, long-legged shadow of a horse and half a man rode to the left and slightly ahead of Jim. From the ranches near and distant came the sound of dogs tuning up for a night of song. And the roosters crowed, thinking a new dawn had come too quickly. Jim lifted the gelding to a trot. The spattering hoof-steps echoed back from the castle behind him. He thought of blond May at the Three Star in Monterey. "I'll be late. Maybe someone else'll have her," he thought. The moon was clear of the hills now.

Jim had gone a mile when he heard the hoofbeats of a horse coming towards him. A horseman cantered up and pulled to a stop. "That you, Jim?"

"Yes. Oh, hello, George."

"I was just riding up to your place. I want to tell you—you know the springhead at the upper end of my land?"

"Yes, I know."

"Well, I was up there this afternoon. I found a dead campfire and a calf's head and feet. The skin was in the fire, half burned, but I pulled it out and it had your brand."

"The hell," said Jim. "How old was the fire?"

"The ground was still warm in the ashes. Last night, I guess. Look, Jim, I can't go up with you. I've got to go to town, but I thought I'd tell you, so you could take a look around."

Jim asked quietly, "Any idea how many men?"

"No. I didn't look close."

"Well, I guess I better go up and look. I was going to town too. But if there are thieves working, I don't want to lose any more stock. I'll cut up through your land if you don't mind, George."

"I'd go with you, but I've got to go to town. You got a gun with you?"

"Oh yes, sure. Here under my leg. Thanks for telling me."

"That's all right. Cut through any place you want. Good night." The neighbor turned his horse and cantered back in the direction from which he had come.

For a few moments Jim sat in the moonlight, looking down at his stilted shadow. He pulled his rifle from its scabbard, levered a cartridge into the chamber, and held the gun across the pommel of his saddle. He turned left from the road, went up the little ridge, through the oak grove, over the grassy hogback and down the other side into the next canyon.

In half an hour he had found the deserted camp. He turned over the heavy, leathery calf's head and felt its dusty tongue to judge by the dryness how long it had been dead. He lighted a match and looked at his brand on the half-burned hide. At last he mounted his horse again, rode over the bald grassy hills and crossed into his own land.

A warm summer wind was blowing on the hilltops. The moon, as it quartered up the sky, lost its redness and turned the color of strong tea. Among the hills the coyotes were singing, and the dogs at the ranch houses below joined them with broken-hearted howling. The dark green oaks below and the yellow summer grass showed their colors in the moonlight.

Jim followed the sound of the cowbells to his herd, and found them eating quietly, and a few deer feeding with them. He listened for the sound of hoofbeats or the voices of men on the wind.

It was after eleven when he turned his horse towards home. He rounded the west tower of the sandstone castle, rode through the shadow and out into the moonlight again. Below, the roofs of his barn and house shone dully. The bedroom window cast back a streak of reflection.

The feeding horses lifted their heads as Jim came down through the pasture. Their eyes glinted redly when they turned their heads. Jim had almost reached the corral fence—he heard a horse stamping in the barn. His hand jerked the gelding down. He listened. It came again, the stamping from the barn. Jim lifted his rifle and dismounted silently. He turned his horse loose and crept towards the barn.

In the blackness he could hear the grinding of the horse's teeth as it chewed hay. He moved along the barn until he came to the occupied stall. After a moment of listening he scratched a match on the butt of his rifle. A saddled and bridled horse was tied in the stall. The bit was slipped under the chin and the cinch loosened. The horse stopped eating and turned its head towards the light.

Jim blew out the match and walked quickly out of the barn. He sat on the edge of the horse trough and looked into the water. His thoughts came so slowly that he put them into words and said them under his breath.

"Shall I look through the window? No. My head would throw a shadow in the room."

He regarded the rifle in his hand. Where it had been rubbed and handled, the black gun finish had worn off, leaving the metal silvery.

At last he stood up with decision and moved towards the house. At the steps, an extended foot tried each board tenderly before he put his weight on it. The three ranch dogs came out from under the house and shook themselves, stretched and sniffed, wagged their tails and went back to bed.

The kitchen was dark, but Jim knew where every piece of furniture was. He put out his hand and touched the corner of the table, a chair back, the towel hanger, as he went along. He crossed the room so silently that even he could hear only his breath and the whisper of his trouser legs together, and the beating of his watch in his pocket. The bedroom door stood open and spilled a patch of moonlight on the kitchen floor. Jim reached the door at last and peered through.

The moonlight lay on the white bed. Jim saw Jelka lying on her back, one soft bare arm flung across her forehead and eyes. He could not see who the man was, for his head was turned away. Jim watched, holding his breath. Then Jelka twitched in her sleep and the man rolled his head and sighed—Jelka's cousin, her grown, embarrassed cousin.

Jim turned and quickly stole back across the kitchen and down the back steps. He walked up the yard to the water-trough again, and sat down on the edge of it. The moon was white as chalk, and it swam in the water, and lighted the straws and barley dropped by the horses' mouths. Jim could see the mosquito wigglers, tumbling up and down, end over end, in the water, and he could see a newt lying in the sun moss in the bottom of the trough.

He cried a few dry, hard, smothered sobs, and wondered why, for his thought was of the grassed hilltops and of the lonely summer wind whisking along.

His thought turned to the way his mother used to hold a bucket to catch the throat blood when his father killed a pig. She stood as far away as possible and held the bucket at arms'-length to keep her clothes from getting spattered.

Jim dipped his hand into the trough and stirred the moon to broken, swirling streams of light. He wetted his forehead with his damp hands and stood up. This time he did not move so quietly, but he crossed the kitchen on tiptoe and stood in the bedroom door. Jelka moved her arm and opened her eyes a little. Then the eyes sprang wide, then they glistened with moisture. Jim looked into her eyes; his face was empty of expression. A little drop ran out of Jelka's nose and lodged in the hollow of her upper lip. She stared back at him.

Jim cocked the rifle. The steel click sounded through the house. The man on the bed stirred uneasily in his sleep. Jim's hands were quivering. He raised the gun to his shoulder and held it tightly to keep from shaking. Over the sights he saw the little white square between the man's brows and hair. The front sight wavered a moment and then came to rest.

The gun crash tore the air. Jim, still looking down the barrel, saw the whole bed jolt under the blow. A small, black, bloodless hole was in the man's forehead. But behind, the hollow-point took brain and bone and splashed them on the pillow.

Jelka's cousin gurgled in his throat. His hands came crawling out from under the covers like big white spiders, and they walked for a moment, then shuddered and fell quiet.

Jim looked slowly back at Jelka. Her nose was running. Her eyes had moved from him to the end of the rifle. She whined softly, like a cold puppy.

Jim turned in panic. His boot heels beat on the kitchen floor, but outside, he moved slowly towards the water-trough again. There was a taste of salt in his throat, and his heart heaved painfully. He pulled his hat off and dipped his head into the water. Then he leaned over and vomited on the ground. In the house he could hear Jelka moving about. She whimpered like a puppy. Jim straightened up, weak and dizzy.

He walked tiredly through the corral and into the pasture. His saddled horse came at his whistle. Automatically he tightened the cinch, mounted and rode away, down the road to the valley. The squat black shadow traveled under him. The moon sailed high and white. The uneasy dogs barked monotonously.

At daybreak a buckboard and pair trotted up to the ranch yard, scattering the chickens. A deputy sheriff and a coroner sat in the seat. Jim Moore half reclined against his saddle in the wagon-box. His tired gelding followed behind. The deputy sheriff set the brake and wrapped the lines around it. The men dismounted.

Jim asked, "Do I have to go in? I'm too tired and wrought up to see it now."

The coroner pulled his lip and studied. "Oh, I guess not. We'll tend to things and look around."

Jim sauntered away towards the water-trough. "Say," he called, "kind of clean up a little, will you? You know."

The men went on into the house.

In a few minutes they emerged, carrying the stiffened body between them. It was wrapped up in a comforter. They eased it up into the wagon-box. Jim walked back towards them. "Do I have to go in with you now?"

"Where's your wife, Mr. Moore?" the deputy sheriff demanded.

"I don't know," he said wearily. "She's somewhere around."

"You're sure you didn't kill her too?"

"No. I didn't touch her. I'll find her and bring her in this afternoon. That is, if you don't want me to go in with you now."

"We've got your statement," the coroner said. "And by God, we've got eyes, haven't we, Will? Of course there's a technical charge of murder against you, but it'll be dismissed. Always is in this part of the country. Go kind of light on your wife, Mr. Moore."

"I won't hurt her," said Jim.

He stood and watched the buckboard jolt away. He kicked his feet reluctantly in the dust. The hot June sun showed its face over the hills and flashed viciously on the bedroom window.

Jim went slowly into the house, and brought out a nine-foot, loaded bull whip. He crossed the yard and walked into the barn. And as he climbed the ladder to the hayloft, he heard the high, puppy whimpering start.

When Jim came out of the barn again, he carried Jelka over his shoulder. By the water-trough he set her tenderly on the ground. Her hair was littered with bits of hay. The back of her shirtwaist was streaked with blood.

Jim wetted his bandanna at the pipe and washed her bitten lips, and washed her face and brushed back her hair. Her dusty black eyes followed every move he made.

"You hurt me," she said. "You hurt me bad."

He nodded gravely. "Bad as I could without killing you."

The sun shone hotly on the ground. A few blowflies buzzed about, looking for the blood.

Jelka's thickened lips tried to smile. "Did you have any breakfast at all?"

"No," he said. "None at all."

"Well, then, I'll fry you up some eggs." She struggled painfully to her feet.

"Let me help you," he said. "I'll help you get your shirtwaist off. It's drying stuck to your back. It'll hurt."

"No. I'll do it myself." Her voice had a peculiar resonance in it. Her dark eyes dwelt warmly on him for a moment, and then she turned and limped into the house.

Jim waited, sitting on the edge of the water-trough. He saw the smoke start out of the chimney and sail straight up into the air. In a very few moments Jelka called him from the kitchen door.

"Come, Jim. Your breakfast."

Four fried eggs and four thick slices of bacon lay on a warmed plate for him. "The coffee will be ready in a minute," she said.

"Won't you eat?"

"No. Not now. My mouth's too sore."

He ate his eggs hungrily and then looked up at her. Her black hair was combed smooth. She had on a fresh white shirtwaist. "We're going to town this afternoon," he said. "I'm going to order lumber. We'll build a new house farther down the canyon."

Her eyes darted to the closed bedroom door and then back to him. "Yes," she said. "That will be good." And then, after a moment, "Will you whip me any more—for this?"

"No, not any more, for this."

Her eyes smiled. She sat down on a chair beside him, and Jim put out his hand and stroked her hair and the back of her neck.

Ann Petry's Determinist Dilemma

UNCHOSEN VIOLENCE IN "LIKE A WINDING SHEET"

Ann Petry's early story "Like a Winding Sheet" has been twice celebrated. About a year after its first appearance in *Crisis* in 1945, Martha Foley selected it for her prestigious anthology, *Best American Short Stories.* Again in 1975 Susan Cahill selected it for her feminist anthology, *Women and Fiction: Short Stories by and about Women.* Foley's choice reflects the story's early appeal as a fine postwar example of hard-hitting realism by a black woman writer; Cahill's choice reflects the new concern among feminists of the 1970s with the victimization of women. My own concern is with the powerful ways in which the tale deals with the unsuspected impetus toward domestic violence in a black working-class household, and so anticipates recent treatments of that theme by black women writers.

More specifically, I am concerned with the conflicting claims of racism and sexism among black women writers on domestic violence, and the sympathetic treatment sometimes given in that context to black male batterers. In my brief stint as a co-counselor of educational groups for male batterers, I was quickly made aware of the need to discourage self-pity and sympathy among white and black clients alike—men who saw themselves almost without exception as victims of their female partners, respondents to provocations, batterers only by defensive reaction. The real perpetrators of violence, in their view, or at the very least the equal sharers of blame, were their partners. Indeed, the problem for counselors was how to get these self-styled male victims to accept complete personal accountability for their own violence, and our twenty-one-week program was devoted to accomplishing and reinforcing that total shift in attitude. Meanwhile the need for special attention to the impact of racism on black male batterers was also recognized, and black counselors were assigned to a few experimental groups composed entirely of black batterers. Here the problem of self-pity and sympathy could at least be treated in a common ethnic context.

I might add now that the problem invaded our own dealings with sister organizations offering shelter for battered women, for we were at one point in conflict with them over the aggressive sexual behavior of one of our own black counselors. We raised the charge of racism in our counselor's behalf; our sister organizations, including many black members, understandably denied the charge and insisted on the primary claims of sexism. We ended by apologizing to them for our own sexist behavior.

This episode coincided with the similar clash between the claims of racism and sexism in the exchange between Clarence Thomas and Anita Hill during the Senate hearings on Thomas's candidacy for a Supreme Court post. As with our local controversy, the issue of sexual harassment raised there was seen differently by the black candidate and by his female accuser. In the black community at large, however, men and women alike rallied behind Clarence Thomas, with some dissent, as the victim on a national scale of racist sentiment. Although the Senate's final judgment seemed to confirm that position, the issue of sexual harassment had meanwhile become a nationally recognized problem, and in that sense the primary claims of sexism were tacitly confirmed.

By citing these local and national controversies, I want to indicate my credentials as a concerned American who is neither black nor female but who may be able to shed some light on the fictional equivalents of such conflicts. What interests me, in my chosen instance, is the extent of Ann Petry's apparent sympathy for the protagonist of "Like a Winding Sheet"—a black male batterer, himself the victim of racial prejudice at his workplace and elsewhere. Here the problem of male accountability is also decidedly confounded, or at the least confused and obscured, by the conflicting claims of racism and sexism. It is a confusion that occurs, moreover, as early in African American fiction as Zora Neale Hurston's *Their Eyes Were Watching God* (1937) and as recently as Toni Morrison's *Jazz* (1992). I want accordingly to take a closer look at Petry's fictional world to see if the problem can be clarified by relevant parallels from other stories.

I

Petry's only collection of tales, *Miss Muriel and Other Stories,* offers a few helpful clues. "Like a Winding Sheet" appears there between two relevant stories: "Olaf and His Girl Friend" (1945) and "The Witness" (1971). In the first story, Olaf is a big black dockworker in Bridgetown, Barbados, whose love for a slender native dancer named Belle Rose is thwarted by her socially ambitious aunt, who wants her to marry a teacher like her father. Thus, when the lovers become engaged, the aunt tricks Belle Rose into visiting New York with her and so abandoning Olaf, who then signs up on a merchant ship and tries to track her down. Eventually he locates her in a New York bar, where she now works in a questionable role as a dancer. Olaf's bravery has been similarly questioned by the girl's aunt because he fears his father's fate of death by drowning; but his voyaging is a sign of braveries to come. In a barroom showdown Olaf, knife in hand, confronts his lost fiancée during her devil dance as if meaning to kill her for past desertion and present disgrace. Instead he drops the knife, meets her in a mutual embrace, and walks out of the bar with her on his way back to Barbados. The story closes with the narrator speculating about whether Olaf decided not to kill her because "he remembered that he loved her and that he'd gone through hell to find her," or because Belle Rose was performing an obeah dance—the emotionally swaying dance, that is, of a conjure woman like her grandmother, who apparently meant more to her than her schoolteacher father or her snobbish aunt.

In "The Witness," the question of conscious choice versus unconscious pressure is raised in a different fashion. The protagonist of this story, Charles Woodruff, is a retired professor and a lonely widower who once taught in a black college in Virginia. He has been hired in retirement to teach high school English to white students in Wheeling, New York, as part of the integration movement that began in the late 1960s. Now he quietly enjoys some of the white man's privileges that his new income allows—a new station wagon and a new gray cashmere coat—against which his dead wife would have warned him. Meanwhile he has been asked by the local Congregational minister to help out with a class in religion for seven white delinquents, sophomores from the local high school, who have been assigned there by the juvenile court. The class meets in the church on Sunday nights, and Woodruff quickly realizes that these middle-class delinquents are dangerous.

The main events of the story occur on a snowy Sunday night when the class ends with a small rebellion. The leader of the group asks a trick question about cannibalism, and when the minister calls it a sin the boy points out that the minister eats his own flesh, bites his own fingernails in an act of "self-cannibalism"; then, as the group files out, the boy runs his fingers through the minister's hair and says, "Don't sweat it, Doc." Since the minister is too overwhelmed for their usual after-class discussion, Woodruff soon leaves, only to surprise the boys outside as they force a local girl into their battered old car. At first Woodruff thinks he should leave this "white man's problem" alone and mind his own "black man's business." Then he accosts the boys with "the voice of authority, the male schoolteacher's voice," though painfully aware that he speaks only as "a black man with a white man's voice." They move in on him as he continues, knock off his hat, smash his glasses, pin his new coat around him like a straitjacket, steal the keys to his station wagon, blindfold him, and force him into their own car with the girl as a form of "pro-tec-shun." He will be the black witness to the gang rape that eventually follows; his car will be left for him at the scene of their crime; they will accuse him of the crime if he reports it.

When the gang rape is finished, they force him to place his hand on the girl's thighs and breasts as if to confirm his participatory guilt; then they throw him his empty wallet and his car keys and move off with the badly damaged girl. Burning with fury, shivering and shaking, determined to call the state police, Woodruff gropes around in the snow for the keys, finds them, starts the car, drives home slowly, finds some old glasses—and realizes that the boys have boxed him in, that he can't call the police without exposing himself to their countercharges. The next day he sees a local doctor about signs of angina, uses the doctor's recommendation to take three or four months off as an excuse to resign from school, and drives back to Virginia.

As the story ends he hears a raucous song on the car radio with a "ho-daddy" refrain, which recalls the delighted remark of the delinquent boy who empties his wallet: "We got us a rich ho-daddy." He is acutely aware then of what his wife would have warned him to avoid: being a rich *black* ho-daddy in a white man's world. As the boxed-in victim of unvoiced cultural pressures beyond his control, he unwittingly abets a gang rape he cannot publicly protest, then runs from the scene of his participatory crime. But as his closing self-indictment suggests, he has reached a bitter form of racial self-acceptance: he is now just "another poor scared black bastard who was a witness."

It seems plain that Petry sympathizes with this man's painful dilemma and his chastened choice. In other stories, however, Petry imagines situations in which the decision to overcome such racial pressures is made to seem the braver option. In "The Necessary Knocking on the Door" the very title affirms the author's judgment. Petry's protagonist, while attending a conference in the Berkshires on "Christianity and the Modern World," awakens one night in her Rest House bedroom to the sound of moaning and "heavy, strangled breathing" coming from a nearby room. When she investigates she realizes that the woman within is sick and needs help. But she also sees a neat sign on the door indicating the occupant's name, Mrs. Taylor, and feels overwhelmed by "images of all the things" that now prevent her from knocking.

On the previous day, as the only black in a room full of white women, she had basked in "the warm-hearted acceptance of all the other delegates." But when a woman slipped into the one vacant seat, on her left, and she had turned to include her in the conversation, the woman had jumped up, thrust herself away from the table, and said before leaving, "I've never eaten with a nigger and I'm too old to begin now." Later that day she learned the woman's name (Mrs. Taylor) and origin (Mississippi) and that her room was on the same floor as hers. Now she is unable to knock because she fears the woman will call her "nigger" again, or accuse her of wanting to steal her jewels. She returns to her room, finally falls asleep, and dreams she is running away from the tentacled moonlight, the name card on Mrs. Taylor's door, and the shouted accusation: "Yours is the greater crime." The next morning she learns from the floor maid that Mrs. Taylor had died in the night: "Doctor say if anybody'd known about her havin' a heart attack they coulda saved her."

The protagonist's name is Alice Knight. At one point she calls herself a coward for her failure to act like a knight, and the author apparently agrees. In the next and penultimate story in this collection, "In Darkness and Confusion," Petry turns to an even larger and grimmer situation that calls for overcoming the pressures of racism, this time through brave rebellion. As with the Rodney King uprising in Los Angeles, a black community is outraged, during World War II, when a policeman shoots and kills a black soldier who had tried gallantly to keep him from beating a black woman in a bar. Ultimately we learn that the protagonist's son Sam, a draftee in a training camp in Georgia, was similarly shot by an MP when he refused to go "to the nigger end of the bus." The son had wrested the MP's gun away from him, shot him in the shoulder, and was quickly sentenced for his crime to twenty years at hard labor. When the protagonist tells this story to his two-hundred-pound wife, Pink, after the mob gathers to protest the local barroom killing of the gallant black soldier, she lets out a wail, throws a bottle of cream soda through the nearest plateglass store window, then reaches in for something to throw at the next window.

So the riot and looting begin. As they continue Petry registers the event through the male protagonist's mixed feelings—elated surges of strength and power; anger, guilt, and confusion at the unreality of being swept up by mob compulsions. At the end, however, the protagonist's mob-leading wife dies from exhaustion, and he curses the unnamed "sons of bitches" who have killed her and court-martialed his defiant son.

Late in this powerful and prophetic story the two-hundred-pound wife overtaxes her great strength by pulling down the flexible metal gate that protects a liquor store. Such demonstrations of the defiant strength of black women occur elsewhere in Petry's fiction and anticipate similar acts of defiance by outraged or determined women created by Alice Walker and Toni Morrison. In recent times the higher incidence of reactive resistance to domestic violence among black women has been noted by feminists intent on overcoming the popular image of women as helpless victims.[1] In her prizewinning first novel, *The Street,* Ann

1. See Katherine Dunn, "Truth Abuse." Dunn cites research in the field by Richard Gelles and Murray Straus to the effect that women not only engage in domestic violence as often as men, but initiate it as often. She notes also that black women do so with greater frequency than white

Petry was there long before them. Two scenes of violence will illustrate her prescience.

The novel's protagonist, Lutie Johnson, is a young divorced woman, mother of a small boy, who has moved into a cheap tenement apartment in New York and is looking for a job to support herself and her son, Bub. In the first scene she is returning at night from an audition as a singer at a casino. The superintendent of her tenement has from the first lusted after her, has even handled her clothing—as she later realizes—while she was out of the apartment. Now he has worked himself up to the point where he believes she will not refuse his advances. When she reaches the dark entryway he sees a faint smile on her face, assumes it's for him, blocks her way when she tries to move up the stairs, then pulls her toward the cellar when she resists his excited sweet-talk. She tries frantically to break free, clawing and kicking, but is unable to scream until his dog is loosed from a nearby apartment and leaps on her back. Her screams bring unexpected help:

> A pair of powerful hands gripped her by the shoulders, wrenched her violently out of the Super's arms, flung her back against the wall. She stood there shuddering, her mouth still open, still screaming, unable to stop the sounds that were coming from her throat. The same powerful hands shot out and thrust the Super hard against the cellar door.
>
> "Shut up," Mrs. Hedges ordered. "You want the whole place woke up?"
>
> Lutie's mouth closed. She had never seen Mrs. Hedges outside of her apartment and looked at closely she was awe-inspiring. She was almost as tall as the Super, but where he was thin, gaunt, she was all hard, firm flesh—a mountain of a woman.[2]

Mrs. Hedges runs a prostitution ring out of her first-floor apartment. She is a partner of the white landlord, the former junkman Mr. Junto, and has been badly scarred by a fire that gutted one of his previous tenements. She wears a turban to hide her bald head, and as she stands panting slightly from her exertion, her big white nightgown balloons around her scarred bulky body. For Lutie she has "the appearance of a creature that had strayed from some other planet." Indeed, when she tongue-lashes the Super even his dog slinks away from her voice: "You done lived in basements so long you ain't human no more. You got mould growin' on you. . . . Ever you even look at that girl again, I'll have you locked up. You ought to be locked up anyway" (237–38). Mrs. Hedges then warns the Super that Mr. Junto has marked Lutie for himself. Returning with Lutie to

---

women. She does not take into account, however, the severity of damage caused by such abusive engagement, as compared with that caused by male batterers, white or black; nor does she discuss the telltale absence of shelters for battered men.

2. *The Street,* 236–37. Further page references will be given in the text.

her apartment, she brings her a cup of hot tea to calm her down and ends their friendly conversation by reminding her "about the white gentleman," Mr. Junto, through whom "she can earn a little extra money."

Lutie finds such words ominous enough, but in the second violent scene she will herself emulate the powerful Mrs. Hedges. Lutie's son, Bub, has been tricked by the vengeful Super into robbing mailboxes and bringing him the stolen letters. Bub is caught and threatened with reform school unless Lutie can get money enough to pay a lawyer for his defense. She wants to borrow the money from her black boss at the casino, Boots Smith; but when she goes to his apartment he introduces her to Mr. Junto and tells her privately in his bedroom that she can get the money by being nice to this white man, who just happens to own the casino and the local bar where she first attracted attention by her singing. She shouts loudly, furiously, with "the accumulated hate and the accumulated anger from all the years of seeing the things she wanted slip past her. . . . 'Get him out of here! Get him out of here quick.' " Boots tells the suspicious Junto to leave, but to come back later when he has had a chance to bring Lutie around; but then he rashly decides to amend that plan. Thus when Lutie moves toward the door he blocks her, forces her to kiss him, and says, "Let him get his afterward. I'll have mine first." The angry Lutie calls him a bastard, says he can tell Junto to get his whores from Mrs. Hedges, as can Boots himself. When Boots then slaps her twice and threatens to beat her into submission, she grabs a heavy iron candlestick from the mantelpiece behind her and strikes him again and again, as if he represents "everything she had hated, everything she had fought against, everything that had served to frustrate her":

> A lifetime of pent-up resentment went into the blows. Even after he lay motionless, she kept striking him, not thinking about him, not even seeing him. First she was venting her rage against the dirty, crowded street. She saw the rows of dilapidated old houses; the small dark rooms; the long steep flights of stairs; the narrow dingy hallways; the little lost girls in Mrs. Hedges' apartment; the smashed homes where the women did drudgery because their men had deserted them. She saw all these things and struck at them.
>
> Then the limp figure on the sofa became, in turn, [her divorced husband] Jim and the slender girl she'd found him with; became the insult in the moist-eyed glances of white men on the subway; became the unconcealed hostility in the eyes of white women; became the greasy, lecherous man at the Crosse School for Singers; became the gaunt Super pulling her down, down into the basement.
>
> Finally, and the blows were heavier, faster, now, she was striking at the whole white world which thrust black people into a walled enclosure from which there was no escape; and at the turn-of-events which had forced her to leave Bub alone while she was working so that he now faced reform school, now had a police record. (430)

As this stunning passage shows, Lutie is in the grip of overwhelming anger and resentment, deep-seated, long internalized, brought to the surface now by a series of relentless external pressures, and touched off by the hapless Smith's outrageous sense of male entitlement. Indeed, it is not even Smith she strikes; her symbolic action is a form of reactive violence, unchosen, waiting as it were to possess her as she strikes out against all that has thwarted her in the Harlem ghetto assigned to her kind, where the women keep their children alive through menial jobs the white folks give them, where the men leave because they can't get better-paying jobs from the same white folks to keep their families going, and where the untended children wind up in reform school. She has defeated her own purpose, moreover, in murdering Smith: instead of rescuing her son she will have to abandon him to reform school and save herself. Her conscious choice now, like Woodruff's in "The Witness," is to get out of town. Meanwhile her unconscious and long-smoldering resentment has chosen for her an all too pyrrhic victory, more self-destructive than triumphant, over unjust pressures.

II

Petry's critics speak of the deterministic nature of her world, where free will has only limited sway, and characters such as Lutie are trapped by environmental pressures or relentless circumstances.[3] There is only a moment, in the final murder scene in Boots Smith's apartment, in which Lutie might be said to choose consciously to kill him. After Junto leaves she thinks of turning to her father for helpful ideas about rescuing her son. She feels she "ought to go see him now" but hesitates, then reviews her feelings:

> Why was she standing here holding this glass of liquor that she didn't want and had no intention of drinking? Because you're still angry, she thought, and you haven't any one to vent your anger on and you're halfway hoping Boots will say something or do something that will give you an excuse to blow up in a thousand pieces. (425)

She doesn't move, and a few moments later Boots unwittingly obliges her and becomes the victim of her accumulated resentment and frustration. In Boots's

3. See Hazel Arnett Ervin, *Ann Petry: A Bio-Bibliography,* xix–xxi. Ervin shows how Petry's work was early placed in the Wright school of naturalistic fiction before being considered in later decades as, among other things, a forerunner of the feminist movement. Nellie Y. McKay, in her 1988 introduction to Petry's third novel, *The Narrows* (1953), vii–xx, similarly shows how Petry was placed in the Wright school—largely to her detriment—but went beyond it in both *The Street* and *The Narrows* with her far more complicated sense of class, gender, and character in a patriarchal world.

bedroom it was Junto she wanted to kill, when she realized how he had set her up at his casino and at his tenement as a "pushover" who would have to pay with sex for his services; and she had even forced herself to wait for Junto to leave, after her blowup at his offer, because she knew she would try to kill him if she met him outside. Her apparent choice, then, has been to substitute Boots for Junto, the black offender for the white manipulator, the visibly present lackey for the elusive and seldom seen controller, as the object of her overwhelming need to strike back at an unjust and oppressive world.

Petry's awareness of this moment of choice is important as it relates to questions of accountability for domestic violence. One of the frequent excuses, for example, offered by male batterers for their violent behavior is that of being overwhelmed by passions, of being out of their heads, unable to do anything else except vent their anger through violent action. To break through that self-protective argument counselors are taught to use two techniques. The first is to point out that all such violent assaults involve choices: the use for instance of a flat hand instead of a fist, or of a fist instead of a weapon; the direction of the blow to this or that part of the woman's body; the use of threats rather than actions to establish or reinforce compliance; the choice of furniture breaking or wall pounding over direct assault; or of hostile or demeaning language; or the mixture of all these choices to achieve, retrieve, or insure unchallenged power and control.

The second technique involves a drawing lesson with the Anger Iceberg Chart, the sketching out of a conscious tip of anger above a spreading iceberg of unexpressed feelings below—resentment, jealousy, inadequacy, impotence, shame, guilt, envy, contempt, hatred, and deep at the bottom, old scores to settle, old wounds from many sources and from earlier times and relations. These deeper sources of rage are like grim old friends and allies, waiting to be roused into overwhelming antagonism against convenient surface objects, whereby the iceberg will suddenly become an erupting volcano.

As that last mixed metaphor suggests, we all tend to cultivate such deep reactions, to talk ourselves up into their release rather than talk ourselves down, because we want them to master us, to overcome our conscious reason, our ability to choose otherwise. This is pretty much what happens to Lutie, or what Lutie makes happen, in Petry's powerful and sympathetic dramatization of her largely pressured outbreak, her largely justified reaction to outrageous events. She talks herself into murdering, not her main white oppressor, but her more conveniently present would-be black male sexual assailant. Given the act of provocation, and her right to resist it in self-defense, and her much-exploited, much-depreciated, and largely weaker gender, we can scarcely blame her.

By her third novel, *The Narrows,* Petry had learned how to trap all her characters, white and black, within such determined dilemmas. She belongs in this sense with Richard Wright and the black male naturalists of the 1940s and after who dealt relentlessly with socially trapped characters. But as Petry's recent feminist defenders insist, her protagonists tend to be more sophisticated, more self-conscious and self-determined than Wright's, though similarly victimized by circumstance.[4] In *The Narrows,* moreover, her chief sympathies are focused on a gallant, idealistic, and intellectually talented black male protagonist who is the victim rather than the perpetrator of a monstrous crime. Indeed, he is ultimately murdered through the collusion between his angry white mistress, her protective and vengeful mother, and her ineffectual white husband—an event so painful for Petry to compose that she once confided to an interviewer, "It was like being witness to the murder of a much loved, much admired friend."[5]

In *The Narrows,* as in *The Street,* Petry is again more sophisticated than Wright in the construction of a fateful and inevitable murder, and more adroit in keeping the lines of accountability clear. She is also more admirably aware of the blinding force of passional loyalties and severities in conjugal, sexual, or parental relations. But she is nonetheless like Wright and other black male naturalists in wanting somehow to sympathize with her black protagonists, male or female, as unwitting victims of an oppressive white world. In "Like a Winding Sheet," the impulse to sympathize while constructing a fateful and passional crime becomes entangled, however, with the need to keep accountability clear. The result is a troubling confusion, to my mind, much like that of our several public experiences, in recent years, in dealing with the clashing claims of racism and sexism.

III

The confusion begins with the story's title, "Like a Winding Sheet." It refers to the protagonist's position, on the morning the story opens, as he rolls over in bed in response to the affectionate greeting of his wife, Mae, and her observation of how "the sheet twist[s] around him, outlining his thighs, his chest":

> Mae looked at the twisted sheet and giggled. "Looks like a winding sheet," she said. "A shroud—" Laughter mingled with her words and she had to pause for a moment before she could continue. "You look like a huckleberry—in a winding sheet—"

4. See Ervin, *Ann Petry,* and McKay, "Introduction."
5. Ervin, *Ann Petry,* 103.

> "That's no way to talk. Early in the day like this," he protested.
>
> He looked at his arms silhouetted against the white of the sheets. They were inky black by contrast and he had to smile in spite of himself and he lay there smiling and savoring the sweet sound of Mae's giggling.[6]

She sees him playfully, then, but predictively, as a corpse wrapped for burial in a winding sheet, and a black corpse at that, colored dark blue or black like the huckleberry, the color heightened now by contrast with the white sheet, with its obvious connotations of the white world that will that day enshroud him. He sees her in turn with reactive fondness as she makes him playfully aware of his oddly predictive position. As we shall see, the confusion comes at the story's end when he begins to beat her compulsively, rather like Lutie Johnson when she murders Boots Smith, and at least one reader leaps to the conclusion that it is Mae, and not her husband, who is or soon will be the corpse in question.[7]

Ideally, of course, she *should* be included in her own metaphor for her husband's dilemma, since it is through her that he will take his misplaced revenge against the white world. But the story is told from his point of view from start to finish, and the question of her victimization is never articulated. Nor does Petry include her in any ironic appeal to our attention like that Joyce makes at the end of "Counterparts," through the piteous cries of the son on whom the humiliated father takes his unjust revenge against a punitive urban world: "Oh, pa. . . . Don't beat me, pa. . . . I'll say a *Hail Mary* for you, pa, if you don't beat me." There is no such focus on Mae's responses as a victimized woman, and, as we shall see, the winding sheet metaphor is completed only as it applies to her beleaguered husband. We have good reason, then, to ask why this is so.

One obvious reason is that Johnson, the protagonist, is a man of good intentions who seldom acts on them. As the story begins we learn that he "had planned to get up before Mae did and surprise her by fixing breakfast." Instead he goes back to sleep and wakes only to the sound of Mae running water in the bathroom and to "the sweet smell of [her] talcum powder . . . drifting down the hall and into the bedroom." Later that day we will see other signs of good intentions on which he fails to act; but these are only untested sins of omission, or of unthinking resistance, for which we all pardon ourselves. They linger in our

6. "Like a Winding Sheet," 199/281. Further page references will be given in the text, with the first number referring to the edition listed in the bibliography and the second to the reprinting of the story below.

7. See Ervin's descriptive entry for the tale in "Primary Works": "With continuous references to his hands. Petry introduces main character Mr. Johnson, and foreshadows for him a violent outcome: after a racially motivated incident, the stressed and discontented Mr. Johnson loses his self-control, and, with his hands, murders the one person who has been his longtime companion throughout the story—his wife" (*Ann Petry,* 2).

responses to the tale only as suggestions of better ways to target his frustrations and resentments.

Among these frustrations are several mild problems with his wife. Although she calls him "babe" affectionately as the story opens, she also chides him lightly for staying in bed until four in the afternoon, adding significantly that if he doesn't stir he'll be "late again" for work. When he questions the word "again," she reminds him that he was late "Twice last week. Three times the week before that. And once the week before." He responds with two complaints that further define their slight dispute:

> "I can't get used to sleeping in the daytime," he said fretfully. He pushed his legs out from under the covers experimentally. Some of the ache had gone out of them but they weren't really rested yet. "It's too light for good sleeping. And all that standing beats the hell out of my legs."
>
> "After two years you oughta be used to it," Mae said.
>
> He watched her as she fixed her hair, powdered her face, slipped into a pair of denim overalls. She moved quickly and yet she didn't seem to hurry.
>
> "You look like you'd had plenty of sleep," he said lazily. He had to get up but he kept putting the moment off, not wanting to move, yet he didn't dare let his legs go completely limp because if they did he'd go back to sleep. It was getting later and later but the thought of putting his weight on his legs kept him lying there. (199–200/282)

It seems plain that Mae has become slightly impatient with his difficulty in adjusting to his job. Her competence at her different job, her cheerful efficiency, and her apparent enjoyment of better working conditions help to explain her mild impatience, but they also serve as irrational goads to his own resentments. In his implicit view, his need for sleep and his aching legs are domestic disadvantages that he tends to hold against her. Indeed, later that day he will even blame her for keeping him up late, when he returns from his night shift, by fooling around—"cooking and eating and listening to the radio"—when they could still catch "a few hours of darkness for sleeping." More immediately, he reacts with strange severity to her panic that day about working on Friday the thirteenth:

> "I oughta stay home," she said. "I shouldn't go out of the house."
>
> "Aw, don't be a fool. . . . Today's payday. And payday is a good luck day everywhere, any way you look at it." And as she stood hesitating he said, "Aw, come on."
>
> And he was late for work again because they spent fifteen minutes arguing before he could convince her she ought to go to work just the same. He had to talk persuasively, urging her gently, and it took time. But he couldn't bring himself to talk to her roughly or threaten to strike her like a lot of other men might have done. He wasn't made that way. (200/282)

One puzzling question here is why Johnson feels that his wife's behavior somehow merits the rough or threatening treatment from which he gallantly abstains. Her superstitious panic scarcely calls for it, nor does the fact that she herself can be blamed this time for making him late. What does impress us, I think, is the inappropriate strength of his discarded chauvinistic response, his unthinking appeal to an ugly form of male entitlement and his willingness to take credit for resisting it.

He begins the night shift with a fine idea: if this were his plant he'd figure out a way that most of the "standing-up jobs," including his own, could be done sitting down. Instead of walking ten hours each night, pushing a little cart around, he'd drive one of those little trucks they used around railroad stations, that moved easily and turned on a dime. Similarly he ends the night shift with another good idea: instead of standing in line before the paymaster's window, "He'd have the pay envelopes handed to the people right at their benches," the way they did it at Mae's plant. Between these good ideas, however, his lateness is challenged, he is flayed by a gross racial insult, and he suffers through a major change of mood.

Thus, as he pushes his cart past his white woman boss, whom he can't bring himself to call "the forelady," he notes that she seems angry and tries to avoid her; but she calls to him loudly above the noise of the machines as if amplifying his wife's mild admonishment:

> "You're late again."
>
> "That's right. My legs were bothering me."
>
> The woman's face grew redder, angrier looking. "Half this shift comes in late," she said. "And you're the worst one of all. You're always late. Whatsa matter with ya?"
>
> "It's my legs," he said. "Somehow they don't ever get rested. I don't seem to get used to sleeping days. And I just can't get started."
>
> "Excuses. You guys always got excuses," her anger grew and spread. "Every guy comes in here late always has an excuse. His wife's sick or his grandmother died or somebody in the family had to go to the hospital," she paused, drew a deep breath. "And the niggers is the worse. I don't care what's wrong with your legs. You get in here on time. I'm sick of you niggers—" (202/283)

Here Johnson interrupts softly:

> "You got the right to get mad. . . . You got the right to cuss me four ways to Sunday but I ain't letting nobody call me a nigger."
>
> He stepped closer to her. His fists were doubled. His lips were drawn back in a thin narrow line. A vein in his forehead stood out swollen, thick. (202/283)

Johnson's first reaction is reasoned and fair, in the face of gross racism, and his anger is plainly justified. But the threateningly doubled fist and swollen vein are signs of worse to come. The white woman backs off slowly and makes her scared apology: "Aw, forget it. . . . I didn't mean nothing by it. It slipped out. It was an accident. . . . Go on and get to work."

> He stood motionless for a moment and then turned away from the sight of the red lipstick on her mouth that made him remember that the foreman was a woman. And he couldn't bring himself to hit a woman. He felt a curious tingling in his fingers and he looked down at his hands. They were clenched tight, hard, ready to smash some of those purple veins in her face. (203/284)

For the rest of the night Johnson tries "to swallow his anger, get rid of it," but though he clears his mind for an hour, the tension stays in his hands as they clench the cart handles, and he begins the familiar process of "talking up" his subdued anger instead of talking it down:

> And he thought he should have hit her anyway, smacked her hard in the face, felt the soft flesh of her face give under the hardness of his hands. He tried to make his hands relax by offering them a description of what it would have been like to strike her because he had the queer feeling that his hands were not exactly a part of him anymore—they had developed a separate life of their own over which he had no control. So he dwelt on the pleasure his hands would have felt—both of them cracking at her, first one and then the other. If he had done that his hands would have felt good now—relaxed, rested.
>
> And he decided that even if he'd lost his job for it, he should have let her have it and it would have been a long time, maybe the rest of her life, before she called anybody else a nigger.
>
> The only trouble was he couldn't hit a woman. A woman couldn't hit back the same way a man did. But it would have been a deeply satisfying thing to have cracked her narrow lips wide open with just one blow, beautifully timed and with all his weight in back of it. That way he would have gotten rid of all the energy and tension his anger had created in him. He kept remembering how his heart had stopped pumping blood so fast he had felt it tingle even in the tips of his fingers. (203–4/284)

As the independent life of Johnson's hands suggests, Petry is following two earlier texts: Sherwood Anderson's opening story, "Hands," from *Winesburg, Ohio* and Nathanael West's *The Day of the Locust,* where the protagonists Wing Biddlebaum and Homer Simpson are similarly unable to control their unruly hands, with ultimately disastrous consequences. More important, Petry is also trying to locate a kind of sexist need in Johnson to smash women's faces. It was a need, however, for which her story has no adequate explanation, perhaps because there was little or no discourse on sexism or misogyny in 1945 on which she could rely for direction and support. In its absence, moreover, she finds only a few revealing symptoms: Johnson's fixation with the red lipstick on the forelady's mouth that reminds him of her gender, and his repeated complaint that he "couldn't bring himself to hit a woman." Now, in the factory, he fuels the anger of his independent hands by dwelling on the deep satisfaction of cracking the forelady's lips "wide open" with a single blow; soon he will also imagine the same satisfaction with a white waitress who seems to deny him a cup of coffee because he's black; and ultimately he will aim and release many such blows at his wife's red lips.

Meanwhile Petry partially excuses Johnson's sexist tensions by connecting them with the effects of factory life on men and women alike. As the hours drag by, for instance, Johnson notices how the women workers begin "to snap and snarl at each other" and gesture irritably with their hands; although quitting time is near he also imagines "that the night still stretched ahead of him, composed of endless hours of walking on his aching legs." Like other Petry characters, then, he continues to be seen strongly as the victim of environmental pressures.

In the next episode, moreover, Petry deliberately delays the clear evidence that Johnson is projecting his racial fears on the preoccupied white waitress in an all-night restaurant, when she tosses her hair vainly, then tells him "No more coffee for a while" once he reaches the front of the coffee line. The initial effect, for us as for him, is much like that of the factory insult—justified resentment at gross racism—though again it comes with the same sexist gloss:

> He looked at the girl without saying anything. He felt his hands begin to tingle and the tingling went all the way down to the finger tips so that he glanced down at them. They were clenched tight, hard, into fists. Then he looked at the girl again. What he wanted to do was hit her so hard that the scarlet lipstick on her mouth would smear and spread over her nose, her chin, out toward her cheeks, so hard that she would never toss her head again and refuse a man a cup of coffee because he was black. (207/286)

A moment later the innocent girl begins to make a new pot of coffee. But Johnson has meanwhile walked away without looking back, "raging at himself and whatever it was inside of him that had forced him to stand quiet and still when he wanted to strike out." In other words, he is now the extended victim of his previous bad experience. Petry protects him, as it were, from useful self-knowledge in order to preserve the strength, and possibly even the purity, of the unchosen violence that soon follows.

IV

Although Johnson has to stand on the crowded subway home, for instance, his hands are too tense to grasp the overhead strap. As he moves near the door the roar and rocking of the train make his head ache and throb, the pain in his legs claws up into his groin, and he tells himself that it is all due to "that anger-born energy" piling up inside him, spreading through him "like a poison" from feet and legs to head, and obviously still unused, still seeking an outlet.

As he enters their apartment his wife greets him with another cheerful "Hello, babe," then responds sardonically when his own half-grunted hello fails to match her cheer. Petry stresses her secure feminine vanity, moreover, as she stands before the dresser mirror, admiring her reflection in her yellow housecoat and "chewing gum vigorously." But when she asks a prescient question—"Whatsa matter? . . . You get bawled out by the boss or somep'n?"—Johnson forgoes the chance to air his resentful feelings and to let her share and ease his tensions; he simply responds "Just tired" and then bursts out, "For God's sake, do you have to crack gum like that?" Petry carefully shows how the complacent vanity, the contrasting prescience, and the increasing sharpness of Mae's replies and actions now subliminally work on Johnson as reminders of the innocent waitress's tossing hair and the racist forelady's accusing harshness:

> "You don't have to lissen to me," she said complacently. She patted a curl in place near the side of her head and then lifted her hair away from the back of her neck, ducking her head forward and then back.
>
> He winced away from the gesture. "What you got to be always fooling with your hair for?" he protested.
>
> "Say, what's the matter with you anyway?" She turned away from the mirror to face him, put her hands on her hips. "You ain't been in the house two minutes and you're picking on me." (209/287)

Johnson sees that her eyes are angry and backs off, moving silently and wisely away because "They'd been married too long and got along too well" to quarrel now. But when he sits down on the edge of a bedroom chair over which her denims "were carefully draped," she snaps at him for leaning against the clothes she has to wear again tomorrow and getting them all wrinkled. Johnson reasons silently that he is too tired to move and that in any case "the overalls were already wrinkled and dirty"; then he defiantly leans farther back in the chair. "Come on, get up," she orders. He wearily complies, then notes a significant change in her mood:

> He saw that her sense of humor was struggling with her anger. But her sense of humor won because she giggled.
>
> "Aw, come on and eat," she said. There was a coaxing note in her voice. "You're nothing but an old hungry nigger trying to act tough and—" she paused to giggle and then continued. "You—" (210/288)

Mae's response, her exemplary cheerful way of coping with anger, is the only rose she receives from Petry in this final sequence. As we shall now see with relentless clarity, the thorny catch to that tribute is the unwitting trigger word "nigger" in Mae's fateful reply:

> He had always found her giggling pleasant and deliberately said things that might amuse her and then waited, listening for the delicate sound to emerge from her throat. This time he didn't even hear the giggle. He didn't let her finish what she was saying. She was standing close to him and that funny tingling started in his finger tips, went fast up his arms and sent his fist shooting straight for her face.
>
> There was the smacking sound of soft flesh being struck by a hard object and it wasn't until she screamed that he realized he had hit her in the mouth—so hard that the dark red lipstick had blurred and spread over her full lips, reaching up toward the tip of her nose, down toward her chin, out toward her cheeks.
>
> The knowledge that he had struck her seeped through him slowly and he was appalled but he couldn't drag his hands away from her face. He kept striking her and he thought with horror that something inside him was holding him, binding him to this act, wrapping and twisting about him so that he had to continue it. He had lost all control over his hands. And he groped for a phrase, a word, something to describe what this thing was like that was happening to him and he thought it was like being enmeshed in a winding sheet—that was it—like a winding sheet. And even as the thought formed in his mind, his hands reached for her face again and yet again. (210/288)

I have quoted this concluding passage in full because it demonstrates the total effect of a man acting unconsciously in response to both external and internal pressures, aware only that he is totally controlled by his own inner compulsions, as personified by his unruly, murderous, and apparently sexist hands, appalled by his behavior yet only able to apply to it the metaphorical emblem his wife has given him, of being enmeshed by the white world's winding sheet, its racist and economic exploitations of black urban workers.

This sympathetic portrait of a black male batterer as the victim not only of his misplaced anger at racist insults and bad working conditions but also of his own sexist feelings has been tempered by our shared awareness of sexist symptoms in his makeup, evasions in his own behavior, defensive denials of blame and accountability, and self-pitying indulgence in imagined acts of vengeful violence against real and unreal female opponents. But in the end he is depicted not as the perpetrator of violence against his hapless wife but as the victim himself of the internal and external pressures that drive him to such misplaced revenge. The primary problem of his accountability for beating and possibly murdering his wife has been shunted aside by the secondary problem of the racial and economic injustices he cannot face directly. Indeed, the tale might be read best as a lesson on how *not* to resist such pressures—namely, by taking them out on your wife. We can even say that this was probably Petry's intention: to confront black men with their apparently uncontrollable and all too deadly feelings, and so force them into thinking through ways to control them; but in fact her stress is on the batterer's victimization by his uncontrollable hands and does not reach out to include his doubly victimized wife. Awareness of her suffering, it seems to me, would be crucial to any real self-confrontation by black batterers.

In my introduction I said that the celebration of this story in the 1970s reflected the new concern among feminists with the victimization of women. I was referring there to ways of teaching the story and to motives among young professors and teaching assistants for using it in feminist contexts. But Susan Cahill actually presents the tale in her introduction and elsewhere as an example of the damaging effects of racism on a black marriage.[8] That she was also influenced by the growing concern with the victimization of women was my interpolation of her probable motives for including the tale in the collection *Women and Fiction: Short Stories by and about Women,* where the word *about* helps to justify my selective phrasing of her motives. My complaint, as a participant in this second wave of celebration of the story's great power and prescience, is that the tale ceases to be *about* Mae Johnson at the end because the problem of the husband's accountability for beating her has been subordinated to the problem of his own sense of victimization by external and internal pressures.

We know from other works by Petry that she could have endowed Mae Johnson with the strength to resist her husband's assault—the strength to fight back. We know also that she could have endowed the husband with awareness of his own need to take responsibility for his actions and omissions, as she does with Alice Knight. We know that she could show us failures to act on such awareness, as with Lutie Johnson, or show us courageous actions that directly defy racist or sexist treatment, as with Mrs. Hedges and the protagonists of "In Darkness and Confusion." But in "Like a Winding Sheet" Petry is apparently limited by her concern with instances of unchosen violence, of self-victimization under the pressures of racial, sexual, and economic forces, and by her understandable sympathy with black men who face such pressures.

Her problem, moreover, is one shared by earlier and later women writers, white and black alike, who are subject to the same patriarchal pressures to support the process of male self-entrapment through supposed entitlement that their women characters often face, and who sometimes extenuate male characters they might otherwise more forcefully indict. In this sense, whether from love or sympathy for their erring characters or from the ongoing need to protect

8. *Women and Fiction: Short Stories by and about Women,* xvii, 132.

themselves, these writers may be said to collude with the powerful male establishment they otherwise want to expose and criticize.[9] It is in the context of this larger hazard for women writers that Petry's strikingly effective and provocative example can help us all to understand the common complications of domestic violence in its fictional and actual forms, and the particular complications that attend the clashing claims of racism and sexism.

9. See the first essay, above, where I show that Eliot uses her religious theme of self-sacrifice to weaken the indictment against Janet's battering husband by focusing on *her* need for repentance—not his. Note also the frequent use of male pseudonyms by Eliot and other Victorian women writers as a conscious form of self-protection against automatic patriarchal dismissals of female authors.

Like a Winding Sheet

by Ann Petry

He had planned to get up before Mae did and surprise her by fixing breakfast. Instead he went back to sleep and she got out of bed so quietly he didn't know she wasn't there beside him until he woke up and heard the queer soft gurgle of water running out of the sink in the bathroom.

He knew he ought to get up but instead he put his arms across his forehead to shut the afternoon sunlight out of his eyes, pulled his legs up close to his body, testing them to see if the ache was still in them.

Mae had finished in the bathroom. He could tell because she never closed the door when she was in there and now the sweet smell of talcum powder was drifting down the hall and into the bedroom. Then he heard her coming down the hall.

"Hi, babe," she said affectionately.

"Hum," he grunted, and moved his arms away from his head, opened one eye.

"It's a nice morning."

"Yeah." He rolled over and the sheet twisted around him, outlining his thighs, his chest. "You mean afternoon, don't ya?"

Mae looked at the twisted sheet and giggled. "Looks like a winding sheet," she said. "A shroud—" Laughter tangled with her words and she had to pause for a moment before she could continue. "You look like a huckleberry—in a winding sheet—"

"That's no way to talk. Early in the day like this," he protested.

He looked at his arms silhouetted against the white of the sheets. They were inky black by contrast and he had to smile in spite of himself and he lay there smiling and savoring the sweet sound of Mae's giggling.

"Early?" She pointed a finger at the alarm clock on the table near the bed and giggled again. "It's almost four o'clock. And if you don't spring up out of there, you're going to be late again."

"What do you mean 'again'?"

"Twice last week. Three times the week before. And once the week before and—"

"I can't get used to sleeping in the daytime," he said fretfully. He pushed his legs out from under the covers experimentally. Some of the ache had gone out of them but they weren't really rested yet. "It's too light for good sleeping. And all that standing beats the hell out of my legs."

"After two years you oughta be used to it," Mae said.

He watched her as she fixed her hair, powdered her face, slipped into a pair of blue denim overalls. She moved quickly and yet she didn't seem to hurry.

"You look like you'd had plenty of sleep," he said lazily. He had to get up but he kept putting the moment off, not wanting to move, yet he didn't dare let his legs go completely limp because if he did he'd go back to sleep. It was getting later and later but the thought of putting his weight on his legs kept him lying there.

When he finally got up he had to hurry, and he gulped his breakfast so fast that he wondered if his stomach could possibly use food thrown at it at such a rate of speed. He was still wondering about it as he and Mae were putting their coats on in the hall.

Mae paused to look at the calendar. "It's the thirteenth," she said. Then a faint excitement in her voice, "Why, it's Friday the thirteenth." She had one arm in her coat sleeve and she held it there while she stared at the calendar. "I oughta stay home," she said. "I shouldn't go outa the house."

"Aw, don't be a fool," he said. "Today's payday. And payday is a good luck day everywhere, any way you look at it." And as she stood hesitating he said, "Aw, come on."

And he was late for work again because they spent fifteen minutes arguing before he could convince her she ought to go to work just the same. He had to talk persuasively, urging her gently, and it took time. But he couldn't bring himself to talk to her roughly or threaten to strike her like a lot of men might have done. He wasn't made that way.

So when he reached the plant he was late and he had to wait to punch the time clock because the day-shift workers were streaming out in long lines, in groups and bunches that impeded his progress.

Even now just starting his workday his legs ached. He had to force himself to struggle past the outgoing workers, punch the time clock, and get the little cart he pushed around all night, because he kept toying with the idea of going home and getting back in bed.

He pushed the cart out on the concrete floor, thinking that if this was his plant he'd make a lot of changes in it. There were too many standing-up jobs for one thing. He'd figure out some way most of 'em could be done sitting down and he'd put a lot more benches around. And this job he had—this job that forced him to walk ten hours a night, pushing this little cart, well, he'd turn it into a sitting-down job. One of those little trucks they used around railroad stations would be good for a job like this. Guys sat on a seat and the thing moved easily, taking up little room and turning in hardly any space at all, like on a dime.

He pushed the cart near the foreman. He never could remember to refer to her as the forelady even in his mind. It was funny to have a white woman for a boss in a plant like this one.

She was sore about something. He could tell by the way her face was red and her eyes were half-shut until they were slits. Probably been out late and didn't get enough sleep. He avoided looking at her and hurried a little, head down, as he passed her though he couldn't resist stealing a glance at her out of the corner of his eyes. He saw the edge of the light-colored slacks she wore and the tip end of a big tan shoe.

"Hey, Johnson!" the woman said.

The machines had started full blast. The whirr and the grinding made the building shake, made it impossible to hear conversations. The men and women at the machines talked to each other but looking at them from just a little distance away, they appeared to be simply moving their lips because you couldn't hear what they were saying. Yet the woman's voice cut across the machine sounds—harsh, angry.

He turned his head slowly. "Good evenin', Mrs. Scott," he said, and waited.

"You're late again."

"That's right. My legs were bothering me."

The woman's face grew redder, angrier looking. "Half this shift comes in late," she said. "And you're the worst one of all. You're always late. Whatsa matter with ya?"

"It's my legs," he said. "Somehow they don't ever get rested. I don't seem to get used to sleeping days. And I just can't get started."

"Excuses. You guys always got excuses," her anger grew and spread. "Every guy comes in here late always has an excuse. His wife's sick or his grandmother died or somebody in the family had to go to the hospital," she paused, drew a deep breath. "And the niggers is the worse. I don't care what's wrong with your legs. You get in here on time. I'm sick of you niggers—"

"You got the right to get mad," he interrupted softly. "You got the right to cuss me four ways to Sunday but I ain't letting nobody call me a nigger."

He stepped closer to her. His fists were doubled. His lips were drawn back in a thin narrow line, A vein in his forehead stood out swollen, thick.

And the woman backed away from him, not hurriedly but slowly—two, three steps back.

"Aw, forget it," she said. "I didn't mean nothing by it. It slipped out. It was an accident." The red of her face deepened until the small blood vessels in her cheeks were purple. "Go on and get to work," she urged. And she took three more slow backward steps.

He stood motionless for a moment and then turned away from the sight of the red lipstick on her mouth that made him remember that the foreman was a woman. And he couldn't bring himself to hit a woman. He felt a curious tingling in his fingers and he looked down at his hands. They were clenched tight, hard, ready to smash some of those small purple veins in her face.

He pushed the cart ahead of him, walking slowly. When he turned his head, she was staring in his direction, mopping her forehead with a dark blue handkerchief. Their eyes met and then they both looked away.

He didn't glance in her direction again but moved past the long work benches, carefully collecting the finished parts, going slowly and steadily up and down, back and forth the length of the building, and as he walked he forced himself to swallow his anger, get rid of it.

And he succeeded so that he was able to think about what had happened without getting upset about it. An hour went by but the tension stayed in his hands. They were clenched and knotted on the handles of the cart as though ready to aim a blow.

And he thought he should have hit her anyway, smacked her hard in the face, felt the soft flesh of her face give under the hardness of his hands. He tried to make his hands relax by offering them a description of what it would have been like to strike her because he had the queer feeling that his hands were not exactly a part of him anymore—they had developed a separate life of their own over which he had no control. So he dwelt on the pleasure his hands would have felt—both of them cracking at her, first one and then the other. If he had done that his hands would have felt good now—relaxed, rested.

And he decided that even if he'd lost his job for it, he should have let her have it and it would have been a long time, maybe the rest of her life, before she called anybody else a nigger.

The only trouble was he couldn't hit a woman. A woman couldn't hit back the same way a man did. But it would have been a deeply satisfying thing to have cracked her narrow lips wide open with just one blow, beautifully timed and with all his weight in back of it. That way he would have gotten rid of all the energy and tension his anger had created in him. He kept remembering how his heart had started pumping blood so fast he had felt it tingle even in the tips of his fingers.

With the approach of night, fatigue nibbled at him. The corners of his mouth drooped, the frown between his eyes deepened, his shoulders sagged; but his hands stayed tight and tense. As the hours dragged by he noticed that the women workers had started to snap and snarl at each other. He couldn't hear what they said because of the sound of machines but he could see the quick lip movements that sent words tumbling from the sides of their mouths. They gestured irritably with their hands and scowled as their mouths moved.

Their violent jerky motions told him that it was getting close on to quitting time but somehow he felt that the night still stretched ahead of him, composed of endless hours of steady walking on his aching legs. When the whistle finally blew he went on pushing the cart, unable to believe that it had sounded. The whirring of the machines died away to a murmur and he knew then that he'd really heard the whistle. He stood still for a moment, filled with a relief that made him sigh.

Then he moved briskly, putting the cart in the storeroom, hurrying to take his place in the line forming before the paymaster. That was another thing he'd change, he thought. He'd have the pay envelopes handed to the people right at their benches so there wouldn't be ten or fifteen minutes lost waiting for the pay. He always got home about fifteen minutes late on payday. They did it better in the plant where Mae worked, brought the money right to them at their benches.

He stuck his pay envelope in his pants' pocket and followed the line of workers heading for the subway in a slow-moving stream. He glanced up at the sky. It was a nice night, the sky looked packed full to running over with stars. And he thought if he and Mae would go right to bed when they got home from work they'd catch a few hours of darkness for sleeping. But they never did. They fooled around—cooking and eating and listening to the radio and he always stayed in a big chair in the living room and went almost but not quite to sleep and when they finally got to bed it was five or six in the morning and daylight was already seeping around the edges of the sky.

He walked slowly, putting off the moment when he would have to plunge into the crowd hurrying toward the subway. It was a long ride to Harlem and tonight the thought of it appalled him. He paused outside an all-night restaurant to kill time, so that some of the first rush of workers would be gone when he reached the subway.

The lights in the restaurant were brilliant, enticing. There was life and motion inside. And as he looked through the window he thought that everything within range of his eyes gleamed—the long imitation marble counter, the tall stools, the white porcelain-topped tables and especially the big metal coffee urn right near the window. Steam issued from its top and a gas flame flickered under it—a lively, dancing, blue flame.

A lot of the workers from his shift—men and women—were lining up near the coffee urn. He watched them walk to the porcelain-topped tables carrying steaming cups of coffee and he saw that just the smell of the coffee lessened the fatigue lines in their faces. After the first sip their faces softened, they smiled, they began to talk and laugh.

On a sudden impulse he shoved the door open and joined the line in front of the coffee urn. The line moved slowly. And as he stood there the smell of the coffee, the sound of the laughter and of the voices, helped dull the sharp ache in his legs.

He didn't pay any attention to the white girl who was serving the coffee at the urn. He kept looking at the cups in the hands of the men who had been ahead of him. Each time a man stepped out of the line with one of the thick white cups the fragrant steam got in his nostrils. He saw that they walked carefully so as not to spill a single drop. There was a froth of bubbles at the top of each cup and he thought about how he would let the bubbles break against his lips before he actually took a big deep swallow.

Then it was his turn. "A cup of coffee," he said, just as he had heard the others say.

The white girl looked past him, put her hands up to her head and gently lifted her hair away from the back of her neck, tossing her head back a little. "No more coffee for a while," she said.

He wasn't certain he'd heard her correctly and he said, "What?" blankly.

"No more coffee for a while," she repeated.

There was silence behind him and then uneasy movement. He thought someone would say something, ask why or protest, but there was only silence and then a faint shuffling sound as though the men standing behind him had simultaneously shifted their weight from one foot to the other.

He looked at the girl without saying anything. He felt his hands begin to tingle and the tingling went all the way down to his finger tips so that he glanced down at them. They were clenched tight, hard, into fists. Then he looked at the girl again. What he wanted to do was hit her so hard that the scarlet lipstick on her mouth would smear and spread over her nose, her chin, out toward her cheeks, so hard that she would never toss her head again and refuse a man a cup of coffee because he was black.

He estimated the distance across the counter and reached forward, balancing his weight on the balls of his feet, ready to let the blow go. And then his hands fell back down to his sides because he forced himself to lower them, to unclench them and make them dangle loose. The effort took his breath away because his hands fought against him. But he couldn't hit her. He couldn't even now bring himself to hit a woman, not even this one, who had refused him a cup of coffee with a toss of her head. He kept seeing the gesture with which she had lifted the length of her blond hair from the back of her neck as expressive of her contempt for him.

When he went out the door he didn't look back. If he had he would have seen the flickering blue flame under the shiny coffee urn being extinguished. The line of men who had stood behind him lingered a moment to watch the people drinking coffee at the tables and then they left just as he had without having had the coffee they wanted so badly. The girl behind the counter poured water in the urn and swabbed it out and as she waited for the water to run out, she lifted her hair gently from the back of her neck and tossed her head before she began making a fresh lot of coffee.

But he had walked away without a backward look, his head down, his hands in his pockets, raging at himself and whatever it was inside of him that had forced him to stand quiet and still when he wanted to strike out.

The subway was crowded and he had to stand. He tried grasping an overhead strap and his hands were too tense to grip it. So he moved near the train door and stood there swaying back and forth with the rocking of the train. The roar of the train beat inside his head, making it ache and throb, and the pain in his legs clawed up into his groin so that he seemed to be bursting with pain and he told himself that it was due to all that anger-born energy that had piled up in him and not been used and so it had spread through him like a poison—from his feet and legs all the way up to his head.

Mae was in the house before he was. He knew she was home before he put the key in the door of the apartment. The radio was going. She had it tuned up loud and she was singing along with it.

"Hello, babe," she called out, as soon as he opened the door.

He tried to say "hello" and it came out half grunt and half sigh.

"You sure sound cheerful," she said.

She was in the bedroom and he went and leaned against the doorjamb. The denim overalls she wore to work were carefully draped over the back of a chair by the bed. She was standing in front of the dresser, tying the sash of a yellow housecoat around her waist and chewing gum vigorously as she admired her reflection in the mirror over the dresser.

"Whatsa matter?" she said. "You get bawled out by the boss or somep'n?"

"Just tired," he said slowly. "For God's sake, do you have to crack that gum like that?"

"You don't have to lissen to me," she said complacently. She patted a curl in place near the side of her head and then lifted her hair away from the back of her neck, ducking her head forward and then back.

He winced away from the gesture. "What you got to be always fooling with your hair for?" he protested.

"Say, what's the matter with you anyway?" She turned away from the mirror to face him, put her hands on her hips. "You ain't been in the house two minutes and you're picking on me."

He didn't answer her because her eyes were angry and he didn't want to quarrel with her. They'd been married too long and got along too well and so he walked all the way into the room and sat down in the chair by the bed and stretched his legs out in front of him, putting his weight on the heels of his shoes, leaning way back in the chair, not saying anything.

"Lissen," she said sharply. "I've got to wear those overalls again tomorrow. You're going to get them all wrinkled up leaning against them like that."

He didn't move. He was too tired and his legs were throbbing now that he had sat down. Besides the overalls were already wrinkled and dirty, he thought. They couldn't help but be for she'd worn them all week. He leaned farther back in the chair.

"Come on, get up," she ordered.

"Oh, what the hell," he said wearily, and got up from the chair. "I'd just as soon live in a subway. There'd be just as much place to sit down."

He saw that her sense of humor was struggling with her anger. But her sense of humor won because she giggled.

"Aw, come on and eat," she said. There was a coaxing note in her voice. "You're nothing but an old hungry nigger trying to act tough and—" she paused to giggle and then continued, "You—"

He had always found her giggling pleasant and deliberately said things that might amuse her and then waited, listening for the delicate sound to emerge from her throat. This time he didn't even hear the giggle. He didn't let her finish what she was saying. She was standing close to him and that funny tingling started in his finger tips, went fast up his arms and sent his fist shooting straight for her face.

There was the smacking sound of soft flesh being struck by a hard object and it wasn't until she screamed that he realized he had hit her in the mouth—so hard that the dark red lipstick had blurred and spread over her full lips, reaching up toward the tip of her nose, down toward her chin, out toward her cheeks.

The knowledge that he had struck her seeped through him slowly and he was appalled but he couldn't drag his hands away from her face. He kept striking her and he thought with horror that something inside him was holding him, binding him to this act, wrapping and twisting about him so that he had to continue it. He had lost all control over his hands. And he groped for a phrase, a word, something to describe what this thing was like that was happening to him and he thought it was like being enmeshed in a winding sheet—that was it—like a winding sheet. And even as the thought formed in his mind, his hands reached for her face again and yet again.

Death and the Maiden in John Cheever's "Torch Song"

When ordinary male or female characters are raised by writers to mythic or symbolic status, the elevation inevitably heightens some attitude toward them that the writer wants to stress and preserve, as it were, as a kind of timeless and unchanging attribute. To mythicize is to say, usually in capital letters, this is what X or Y is really like; this archetype will stand for all time as the real resonant truth about X or Y. But sometimes, when a male writer's attitudes toward X or Y are sexist, he converts familiar and limited views about them into falsely mysterious and timeless truths—he moves, that is to say, from familiar stereotypes into bogus archetypes. One such bogus archetype/stereotype conversion is that death is a woman, or that women bring death to men, or that women are somehow deadlier than men, as in that Kipling adage that the female of the species is deadlier than the male.

This may be true of lions, where the lean lioness sometimes hunts for food while the regal male guards the cubs; but statistically speaking it is not true of the human species, where the male breadwinner is more likely to kill the female who guards the cubs than the other way around. But in the 1920s and after male writers especially imagined otherwise. I say especially because of the social and historical pressures on men—their exposure to random slaughter in the major and minor wars of this century, to job layoffs during the Great Depression and in later periods of high unemployment, and to ruthless competition and oppressive job relations even in good times. These distinctly modern conditions often led to a personal sense of insecurity and failure and to embittered domestic relations. But instead of attributing such problems to their external social and economic sources, men often found it easier to blame women for them and to imagine women as inferior yet powerful creatures who somehow created or exacerbated most modern ills.

It is instructive, certainly, to note how often the fathers of modern writers suffered from economic displacements and losses for which their seemingly more sheltered and domineering wives sometimes took them to task. One thinks of D. H. Lawrence's portraits of his warring parents in *Sons and Lovers,* or of Hemingway's suicidal father and his own lifelong view of his stronger mother as the Great American Bitch, or of Joyce's record of his father's steady economic descent through job losses, of subsequent family moves into poorer neighborhoods, and of at least one violent attack on his long-suffering mother. John Cheever's early life reflects a similar pattern of paternal defeat and maternal ascension that may be said to have affected his outlook on women and on domestic relations.

Thus, in her compelling biographical memoir, *Home before Dark,* the author's daughter Susan notes that her paternal grandfather, a relatively affluent gentleman sailor, had owned a shoe factory near Lynn, Massachusetts, had sold it in the 1920s, and had then invested his profits in stocks that became worthless by the time of the stock market crash in 1929. Soon the bank repossessed the family's comfortable home in Wollaston, and like the Joyces, they began moving to less comfortable quarters. Although her grandfather gamely sought employment, he was unable to find it and began drinking heavily. Her father, then in his teens, was, like Joyce before him, forced to leave a good private school, Thayer Academy, and to enroll in a public high school where his grades promptly dropped. Meanwhile his mother had started a small gift shop to help support the family, had moved upward to a larger shop, and had begun running a summer tearoom. Although she soon earned enough to send John back to Thayer Academy, her embittered husband felt humiliated by his displacement as the family breadwinner and by his wife's all too cheery self-reliance. They quarreled often, ignored their children, separated temporarily, and only later reconciled. Meanwhile the young Cheever had developed his lifelong view of his father as "a noble man humiliated by an eccentric and overbearing wife."[1]

It was, of course, the stock market crash, and not his wife's overbearing nature, that had led to his father's humiliation. But like many modern writers, Cheever identified with his father as a threatened and rejected male and would score his greatest successes in depicting that jeopardized condition, sometimes unquestioningly, but more often with saving ambivalence. Indeed, it was his self-critical grace to be aware of shortcomings in his otherwise privileged male victims and to complicate his characters—male or female—with human frailties. There is nonetheless a sexist disposition in his fiction that probably begins with the domineering mother and weak father of his early years, and with his own early resentments and identifications, and that acquires mythic dimensions in those few stories in which he moves toward the extreme ranges of domestic abuse.

1. Susan Cheever, *Home before Dark,* 100. Further page references will be given in the text.

I

This is very much the case with "Torch Song," a story about a long friendship between a man-about-town named Jack Lorey and a convivial woman named Joan Harris, who in Jack's view seems to have buried many husbands. He thinks of her as the Widow since she always wears black "and he was always given the feeling, by a curious disorder in her apartment, that the undertakers had just left."[2] According to the unnamed narrator, there is no malice in this opening impression. Jack is fond of Joan; they are of the same age; they have come from the same city in Ohio, have both arrived in New York in the middle 1930s, and during that first summer "they used to meet after work and drink Martinis in places like the Brevoort and Charles', and have dinner and play checkers at the Lafayette" (89/307). In other words, they are both relatively innocent midwesterners seeking work and sophistication in the big city and enjoying a relatively innocent friendship.

We begin, then, with a fairly realistic account of their early friendship, only mildly tinged by Jack's odd observation about Joan's frequent widowings, presumably in later years; and we continue with a more or less realistic account of their casually crossing urban lives. By such means Cheever moves gradually to a view of the woman as an agent of death, an exclusively female embodiment of what seem to be the inherent consequences of casual affairs and bad marital choices.

From this gradual mixture of mild hints with realistic accretions we learn that Joan Harris is drawn to substance abusers—men with serious problems with drink or drugs—and that she herself seems to thrive on such relationships. Indeed, though we learn very little about Jack's health and appearance, and almost nothing about his own casual affairs, we are informed from the first about Joan's ironically pleasing voice, presence, and pristine innocence: "She was then a big, handsome girl with a wonderful voice, and her face, her whole presence, always seemed infused with a gentle and healthy pleasure at her surroundings, whatever they were. She was innocently and incorrigibly convivial, and would get out of bed and dress at three in the morning if someone called her and asked her to come out for a drink, as Jack often did" (89/307). From this description we might assume a ripening and serious friendship, leading to love. But as the next few lines reveal, these chummy friends begin seeing less and less of each other, and soon stop altogether, apparently when Jack starts living with "a girl

2. "Torch Song," 89/307. Further page references will be given in the text, with the first number referring to the edition listed in the bibliography and the second to the reprinting of the story below.

he had met at a party" and "it never occur[s] to him to wonder what had become of Joan" (89/307).

Jack feels "intensely happy" about his illicit affair with this girl, their shared life in a Village apartment, their weekend visits with friends in the country: all this is "what he had imagined life in New York to be" (89/307). Then one Sunday night when Jack and his girlfriend return from the country, Jack sees Joan in the lighted window of a New York diner, trying to rouse a drunken man whose head rests on their diner table: "It troubled Jack to see in these straits a girl who reminded him of the trees and the lawns of his home town, but there was nothing he could do to help" (90/308).

Later that summer Jack again sees Joan in a New York restaurant. For some unexplained reason he is now with a new girl, one of the "many Southern girls in the city that year." Joan is also with a new companion, but where Jack's friend is never described, we learn much about Joan's: he is a tall man with a monocle who bows stiffly to Jack when Joan introduces him, and whom she delightedly identifies as a Swedish count with his own radio program. That winter Jack also learns, through a mutual friend, that the count sings Swedish folk songs on the radio, that Joan had met him at a party, and that he had moved in with her the following night. Within a week he had revealed his desperate need for morphine and had become "abusive and violent" when he couldn't get it (91/308–9). To help him Joan began to deal with dope peddlers in dubious parts of the city and in short order got pregnant, had an abortion, was abandoned by her abusive lover, found him in a fleabag near Times Square, and—though she continued to buy him narcotics—soon lost him altogether. Jack is so appalled by this tale of "the innocent girl from Ohio [who] lived with a brutal dope addict and traded with criminals" that he phones Joan the next morning and makes a date for dinner:

> He met her at Charles'. When she came into the bar, she seemed as wholesome and calm as ever. Her voice was sweet, and reminded him of elms, of lawns, of those glass arrangements that used to be hung from porch ceilings to tinkle in the summer wind. She told him about the count. She spoke of him charitably and with no trace of bitterness, as if her voice, her disposition, were incapable of registering anything beyond simple affection and pleasure. Her walk, when she moved ahead of him toward their table, was light and graceful. She ate a large dinner and talked enthusiastically about her job. They went to a movie and said goodbye in front of her apartment house. (91/309)

That same winter Jack becomes engaged to still another nondescript girl, receives an invitation to cocktails from Joan when his fiancée is out of town, and meets her latest drunken boyfriend. The mythic hints continue as the bell Jack rings above Joan's mailbox in the vestibule is "answered with a death rattle in the lock," and as Jack receives the impression, while moving through Joan's disordered apartment, that "the place was all wrong, somehow" and "that there had been a death there recently." Meanwhile her new boyfriend, another big courtly man with a red face and pale blue eyes, gets very drunk:

> He began to spill liquor, as if drinking, for him, were a kind of jolly slaughter and he enjoyed the bloodshed and the mess. He spilled whiskey from a bottle. He spilled a drink on his shirt and then tipped over someone else's drink. The party was not quiet, but Hugh's hoarse voice began to dominate the others. He attacked a photographer who was sitting in a corner explaining camera techniques to a homely woman. "What did you come to the party for if all you wanted to do was sit there and stare at your shoes?" Hugh shouted. "What did you come for? Why don't you stay at home?"
>
> The photographer didn't know what to say. He was not staring at his shoes. Joan moved lightly to Hugh's side. "Please don't get into a fight now, darling," she said. "Not this afternoon."
>
> "Shut up," he said. "Let me alone. Mind your own business." He lost his balance, and in struggling to steady himself he tipped over a lamp.
>
> "Oh, your lovely lamp, Joan," a woman sighed.
>
> "Lamps!" Hugh roared. He threw his arms into the air and worked them around his head as if he were bludgeoning himself. "Lamps. Glasses. Cigarette boxes. Dishes. They're killing me. They're killing me, for Christ's sake. Let's all go up to the mountains and hunt and fish and live like men, for Christ's sake." (92/310)

Although Joan now stands at the door, saying good-bye to "her routed friends" with her usual soft voice and "genuinely simple" manner, the raging drunk at her back has just given us our first clue to the frustrated life-urge this cheerful woman rouses in her angry male partners—an urge that will well up again as the story ends, when Jack himself almost becomes one of those violent victims of her deadly cheer—and manfully rebels!

Next on this cheerful maiden's death list is a middle-aged German refugee from the Nazis named Franz Denzel, a man unlike Hugh in that he prizes rather than despises domestic dishware. Jack and his wife meet Franz at a party where five other German guests mount an attack on American as opposed to German culture, then begin conversing among themselves in German. When coffee and ice cream are served a chipped cup catches Franz's attention. He begins to question Joan about it sharply and follows her into the kitchen, from which "the sound of a blow and a cry" are soon heard. When Jack and his disapproving wife escape from this unnerving scene, Jack supposes that he will never see Joan again (94/312).

Their own life improves when his wife has a baby boy and Jack feels "proud and happy." At a wedding party for another Ohio girl, however, he unexpectedly passes Joan again in a dim corridor of the hotel, where she is pressed against the wall by a man intent on breaking her arm (94/312).

Such contrasting parallels begin to seem portentous. Two years later, for instance, Jack's wife divorces him, and when news of this unexplained event reaches Joan, she calls again asking for Jack's help. She has been harassed by her neighbors and by the police; she is now being evicted from her apartment as an immoral woman—a drunk and a prostitute—and has nowhere to go. As Jack listens to her recital of these supposedly fantastic charges and their consequences, he thinks of a torch song, "one of those forlorn and touching ballads" that had been popular in the past, as if bemused by this plaintive twist in Joan's peculiar life. Still, it angers him "to think of this big, splendid girl's being persecuted by her neighbors," and he agrees to help her. In the morning he asks his secretary to find Joan an apartment, and she is soon settled in a slum neighborhood in the West Twenties (95–96/313).

The torch song motif that Cheever raises here is slightly inappropriate. Torch songs were laments against mistreatment by male partners—men who did the blues singers wrong, but whom they nonetheless continued to love—and Joan's lament is against her treatment by her neighbors and by the police: she never complains about her violent partners. It is Jack himself, as Cheever's point-of-view figure, who is recording the sad saga of Joan's mistreatment by drunken and abusive lovers. It is Jack, and not Joan, who "seem[s] to be singing her [relational] wrongs" (96/313). We have license to speculate, then, that Cheever may have some private stake in distorting Joan's lament and raising it to this mythic level. What is he saying at this point about complaining women who paradoxically tend to drunken and abusive partners with unshakable good cheer?

Cheever was himself an alcoholic for most of his adult life. He did not stop drinking until 1975, some seven years before his death, when he spent a month in an alcohol clinic and began to attend AA meetings regularly and soberly. He was then sixty-three years old, a frail and ailing man. According to his daughter, his wife Mary's first impression of him, when they met in 1938, was of a disorderly man who "needed someone to take care of him" (47). She provided such care over the next forty years of seesaw marital bliss and infidelity, rejection and reunion, dinner-table wars and bedroom detentes, and increasing alcoholic debility. A poet herself, she may have expressed one source of the "Torch Song" lament in a published poem about a distressed wife called "Gorgon I," from which her daughter quotes these lines in *Home before Dark:*

> I have sometimes complained, husband,
> that as you feinted, shadowboxed and blindly

> jived to that misty monolithic woman in your mind
> I have been battered, drowned under your blows. (49)

Like Joan Harris, this complaining, emotionally battered woman was also a cheerful, nurturing person drawn to weakness, illness, and suffering. Indeed, this is how her daughter describes her—with more positive intent—through comparison with her husband:

> My father was drawn to strength. My mother is drawn to need and the sweetness of the needy. An injured animal, a waif, a person in trouble—all elicit overwhelming concern from her. She has nursed countless animals back to health, feeding them with eyedroppers, wrapping their shivering bodies in soft covers. A blue jay, a squirrel, our own dogs, all owed their lives to her. Later, when she became a teacher, it was the students who could not succeed in conventional ways who attracted her finest energies. My warmest memories of my mother are from times when I was sick, or in pain, or in some kind of trouble. (76)

We can only conclude that Cheever's Joan Harris is a deliberate reversal of this familiar positive view of life-giving feminine nurture, a perverse and conflictual view of the nurturing woman as one who seeks out the weak and ailing so as to see them to the grave. In that sense we can also place this story as part of Cheever's long-standing quarrel with his wife and mother, the two cheerful Marys in his own vulnerable, ailing experience as a resentful child and as an addictive and perhaps infantile adult dependent on alcoholic.

One further connection between Cheever's wife and this fictional character is worth mentioning here. In midlife Mary Cheever taught creative writing to women students at Briarcliff College. In the midsixties I was introduced first to her, and a bit later to her husband, by one of her colleagues at Briarcliff, my old friend Charles Shapiro. She struck me at the time as an attractive and amiable woman with an odd mode of speech, one I can only describe as an adult modification of baby talk. Perhaps I'm being chauvinistic myself in noting this trait. I'm famous in academic circles for my classroom mumble and can even remember wondering at the time about the effect of *her* distinctive voice in the classroom; so I may indeed be guilty of projection. She seemed, in any event, a capable and cheerful woman, as she moved about in the kitchen, and her voice seemed pleasant and appropriate in a domestic setting. When we came into the room where Cheever himself was sitting alone in a chair, however, he seemed by contrast unable or unwilling to move or even speak much, as if "stoned" or paralyzed by too much midday alcohol and reduced to a kind of stupefied smile. The only relief was a knowing glint in his eye at the absurdity, I presume, of the social or perhaps even the literary situation of three functioning English teachers hovering momentarily around a famous drunken writer.

Some thirty years later, when I came to read his provocative "Torch Song," I was accordingly struck by that passage already cited in which Cheever tells us that Joan Harris's sweet voice recalls those glass arrangements that "tinkle in the wind" on country porches and that she speaks of her latest abusive partner in remarkably charitable tones, "as if her voice, her disposition, were incapable of registering anything beyond simple affection and pleasure" (91/309). That description would also fit the sweet voice and cheerful disposition of Cheever's wife.

In *Home before Dark* Susan Cheever says nothing about her mother's voice. She tells us, however, that Cheever himself spoke with "an unusual accent," a compound derived from his Yankee father, his English mother, and his Boston South Shore childhood; she notes also that he developed a unique way of speaking, "a clipped mumble" combining "swallowed words and low laughter, short *a*'s and broad Yankeeisms" that made him difficult to understand (38). It may be that his unusual voice made him especially aware of peculiar voice properties in others. Since I have already confessed to my own distinctive classroom mumble, I can at least vouch for that peculiar consequence.

It seems to me reasonable to infer, at any rate, from such textual and personal interconnections between voice, character, and family, that we are present in this story at a projective and fictively disguised version of a deep-seated conflict in Cheever's life, a need to mythicize certain defensive attitudes toward the women who cared for him and his own conduct toward them. In other words, the mythical situation in this story seems more nearly a personal than a universal allegory. As such, it moves toward an instructively disturbing view of domestic violence and of its misogynistic sources.

II

At this point in the story, Cheever also tries to relate Joan's torch song with the gathering knowledge of persecution and violence in Nazi Germany and elsewhere that preceded America's entry into World War II. Thus, after listening to Joan's lament, for instance, Jack walks uptown in the hot summer night and sees a parade "in a dark side street off Broadway near Madison Square." Because the neighborhood is unlit he cannot see the marchers' placards urging the United States to enter the war until he reaches a streetlight. Then he notes that "each platoon represented a nation that had been subjugated by the Axis powers," that there is no sound or music as they march, and that only a "few idle people like himself" line the sidewalks. The marchers consist chiefly of elderly men and women—Poles, Norwegians, Danes, Jews, Chinese—and children dressed in national costumes. They proceed, moreover, "with all the self-consciousness of enemy prisoners," and they hobble "through the darkness of the loft neighborhood like a mortified and destroyed people." Fairly obviously, then, their mute political lament has some mysterious connection, not yet explained, with Joan Harris's torch song.

During the following summer Jack leaves a cocktail party to walk up Fifth Avenue and is again accosted by Joan, who calls him over to a sidewalk table to meet her new friend, Pete Bristol, and to celebrate with them Russia's changed position in the war after the invasion by her former ally, Nazi Germany. They drink champagne until dark, drink more champagne at dinner, and hit two or three more bars before parting. Jack wakes with a hangover but agrees to meet Joan for lunch, finding her fresh and untouched by so much drinking and apparently forgetful of the war: she has called him to ask for advice in selling her jewelry—not for the great cause—but to help Pete Bristol open an ad agency. Shortly afterward Jack learns from a doctor friend that the indestructible Joan—who has "been through enough to kill the average mortal" and who "still has the constitution of a virtuous and healthy woman"—has been deserted by Pete Bristol, who took her money and left her for a girl with a convertible (97/315).

What Cheever is driving at, through this clumsily heightened war sequence, now seems evident: he wants us to believe that women like Joan are attracted to the really serious problem of violence abroad—which many others altogether ignore—simply as another occasion for deadly cheerfulness. Indeed, even when America enters the war the attraction of such women is still cheerfully deadly. When Jack is drafted, for instance, and returns to New York on leave from a New Jersey camp, he is accosted on the train by women who "would often press upon him dog-eared copies of *Life* and half-eaten boxes of candy, as though the brown clothes he wore were cerements" (98/315). Apparently they too are excited by the prospect of his certain death abroad.

As if to hammer this dubious war connection home, Cheever now has Jack meet with Joan at night in her slum apartment during an air-raid exercise. As they sit in the dark, waiting for her latest victim to appear, she talks about her departed lovers and their morbid fates: "Nils, the suspect count, was dead. Hugh Bascomb, the drunk, had joined the Merchant Marine and was missing in the North Atlantic. Franz, the German, had taken poison the night the Nazis bombed Warsaw" (98–99/316). When Jack asks about Pete Bristol, she reveals that he was always very sick but refused to go in for checkups. She is then interrupted, but by this time Jack thoroughly understands her deadly disposition. When he returns after the war and attends one of Joan's cocktail parties, he is able to correctly identify her probable current lover from among the crowded guests as the Englishman who coughs recurrently into his handkerchief.

During the war Jack had married and divorced another woman within the space of a single neutral paragraph. Now he takes a better paying job to cover his doubled living costs and his doubled alimony. When the new job suddenly lapses, he is thrown out of work and has no immediate prospects; but his misguided belief in his own perennial youth and promise makes him indifferent. Moving now from one hotel to another, he soon runs out of money and becomes ill. A bad cold turns to fever and he begins to cough blood. The vampirish Joan then reappears, apparently drawn by the blood. She brings money and a drink and obviously wants to nurse him. She has grown a little fatter but is still dressed in black, still soft-voiced and congenial; although Jack greedily takes her offered drink, her mild manner, her torch-song voice, and her mournful attire make him uneasy. He sits up in bed "as if there were some need to defend himself" and asks her why she has come now when she never came to his place before (101/318).

The answer, of course, is that he has now reached the condition of weakness and self-neglect she had long ago suspected. He has always been a potential victim; his nondescript affairs and marriages have brought him inevitably to this point. In that sense, as Joan now says, he is decidedly the oldest friend she has in New York, the one whose sympathy she could always count on. She begins to reminisce at his bedside, hands him another Scotch, and lights a cigarette for him; but the intimacy of this gesture troubles him because it makes it seem "not only as if he were deathly ill but as if he were her lover" (101/319).

He begins to fight back, at first politely, by asking her to leave so he can sleep; then he becomes angry, shouting at her when she can't recall her latest victim, pushing her off the bed, rising shakily, and telling her to get out:

> "You're sick, darling," she said. "I can't leave you alone here."
>
> "Get out," he said again, and when she didn't move, he shouted, "What kind of an obscenity are you that you can smell sickness and death the way you do? . . . Does it make you feel young to watch the dying? . . . Is that the lewdness that keeps you going? Is that why you dress like a crow? Oh, I know there's nothing that I can say that will hurt you. I know there's nothing filthy or corrupt or depraved or brutish or base that the others haven't tried, but this time you're wrong. I'm not ready. My life isn't ending. My life's beginning. There are wonderful years ahead of me . . . wonderful, wonderful years . . . and when they're over, when it's time, then I'll call you. Then, as an old friend, I'll call you and give you whatever dirty pleasure you take in watching the dying, but until then, you and your ugly and misshapen forms will leave me alone." (102/319–20)

Joan's only response is to finish her drink, look at her watch, decide to go to the office, and promise to return. When she leaves Cheever pulls out all the stops for Jack's magnificently rebellious turn toward life—a turn that oddly prefigures his own late triumph over alcohol and, as we shall see, his own belated turn toward that homosexual love he had repressed since childhood. Indeed, this is the personal allegory we must now read back into the final passage:

> Jack emptied the whiskey bottle into the sink. He began to dress. He stuffed his dirty clothes into a bag. He was trembling and crying with sickness and fear. He could see the blue sky from his window, and in his fear it seemed miraculous that the sky should be blue, that the white clouds should remind him of snow, that from the sidewalk he could hear the shrill voices of children shrieking, "I'm the king of the mountain, I'm the king of the mountain, I'm the king of the mountain." He emptied the ashtray containing his nail parings and cigarette butts into the toilet, and swept the floor with a shirt, so that there would be no trace of his life, of his body, when that lewd and searching shape of death came there to find him in the evening. (102/320)

Cheever here achieves two striking effects, one intended, the other unintended. The first is to demonstrate, through Jack's rebellion, that all the previous brutalities inflicted upon Joan Harris by her abusive lovers were perverse forms of the same life-directed rebellion, the same protest against being destroyed by this deadly woman. The second and scarcely intended effect is the prediction, as I have already indicated, of Cheever's belated triumph over alcoholism at the age of sixty-three, his acceptance of his own suppressed homosexual leanings, his discovery of the young homosexual lover who would become the companion of his final years, and his completion of what some say is his finest novel, *Falconer,* about a drug addict who finds homosexual happiness in prison and who later escapes to new life by zipping himself into the body bag of another dead prisoner. Indeed, the prison scenes in *Falconer* are similarly imbued with the ecstatic feelings found in "Torch Song" for the miraculous blue sky, the snowy clouds, and the remembered sounds and scenes of life outside the prison, when the protagonist was, if not exactly "king of the mountain," a much physically freer and more lyrical aspirant for the throne. These points will bear further attention.

III

Cheever's rousing belief in the use of violence to throw off the deadly toils of a destructive woman is one of several similar justifications used by actual batterers, who frequently observe that their partners started it, asked for it, deserved it, or even liked it and wanted it for punishment. It is also their frequent misogynistic view that such women are castrating bitches, out to do them in, to spend all their money, drive them crazy, run them down, and sap or destroy their virility. The fear that their partners may actually want to kill them is, of course, projective, though sometimes based on the reasonable knowledge that battered women may well fear for their own lives and act against them in self-defense.

In *Janet's Repentance,* the alcoholic batterer Robert Dempster shoves his wife outside the house late one night, and soon after has a frightening vision, while suffering through delirium tremens and withdrawal, that his wife has committed suicide by drowning and has now come back to pull him down with her into the cold slimy river. In *The Sun Also Rises,* the mannish heroine Lady Brett Ashley is so well versed in her own destructive propensities that she voluntarily gives up her hold on the young Spanish bullfighter who wants her to let her hair grow long and live with him in the country. The unmanned hero, Jake Barnes, who serves this mannish heroine in her several adulteries, has already received the kind of war wound that probably explains why misogynistic men fear women are out to kill them or castrate them, or rob them of their virility, whether through vagina dentatas or through callous flirtations with other men. It is a familiar psychological observation that homosexuals share this fear in various severe forms that make women seem sexually frightening and distasteful to them, and it is a good bet that some version of that fear may help to explain the mythic demonization of the heroine in Cheever's story.

He is of course not alone in this propensity. Other modern novelists with known homoerotic leanings—Henry James, D. H. Lawrence, Ernest Hemingway, James Joyce—have demonstrated similar fears of being unmanned by women through fictional male characters: Lambert Strether and Hyacinth Robinson, Paul Morel and Rupert Birkin, Jake Barnes and Leopold Bloom. But of course these writers have heterosexual as well as homoerotic leanings, as does Cheever himself. They are bisexual beings, as in some measure we all are, but with more problematic leanings than most of the rest of us. Cheever is the only one among them, however, to have acted out his bisexuality in sequence, and from his careful observations of that change we may be able to learn something about the shared origins, between heterosexual and homosexual males, of a propensity to fear women as deadly or destructive creatures. This may well be a useful exercise, since professional counselors in the field of domestic violence believe that male homophobia—or the fear of becoming a homosexual—is very close to that male contempt for and disgust with women which activates domestic violence. Both feelings may begin, that is to say, with the fear of becoming like a woman.

These troubling convergences may become more plausible if we suppose, for a moment, that the main characters in "Torch Song," Jack Lorey and Joan Harris, are one person, and that the man named Jack is afraid of his own femininity—afraid, that is, of becoming a man/woman named Jack/Joan Lorey. Joan's open attraction to men with illnesses is, in this light, like Jack's suppressed attraction to the "illness" within himself. The "illness" is homosexuality. Joan's various boyfriends are, as it were, secret homosexuals, and Jack is afraid of losing his present sense of virility and becoming one of them, a potential folksinger like the effete Swedish count, or a teacup tyrant like the prissy German refugee, unless—like the manly Hugh Bascomb who declaims, "Let's all go up to the mountains and hunt and fish and live like men"—he begins once more to act like a real man. As we have seen, the nondescript Jack at the end of this story "manfully" rebels. He is not yet ready for his "friend," the deadly Joan Harris, to take him away, or to take over his life, his body, his present sexual disposition. In other words, Cheever was still in the homophobic phase of his journey toward homosexuality when, at some point in the late 1950s, he wrote this projectively personal story; but he had decidedly begun that psychic journey.

Some such allegorical reading might explain why Jack is such a nondescript character, in this story, while Joan is a detailed mythic monster, a cheerful woman who recalls the wholesome impressions of small-town elms, lawns, and porches, whose sweet voice and disposition register only simple affections and pleasures—only pleasant surface feelings—but who is nonetheless deeply drawn toward "unhealthy" men. In *Home before Dark* Susan Cheever makes the nice observation that her father's stories deal always with appearances, surfaces, and never probe or analyze feelings. Let me quote the relevant paragraph, which interestingly follows that brief contrast, already cited, between her father's attraction to strength and her mother's attraction to suffering:

> My father, by the way, would have nothing to do with discussions like this. He never spoke about feelings or allowed himself to speculate on the inner mechanics of the family. "I love you all equally," he would say, or "I adore your mother." People remember my father's candor. . . . He would tell you exactly what he had done to this or that mistress in a room at the St. Regis or in a motel in Iowa, and he would tell you that *The New Yorker* had paid him less than $1,000 for a story, and he would tell you that he took two Valiums and drank a pint of gin every day before noon. That was different, though. He did not like to talk about how these things felt; he did not like to talk about human emotions. He did talk, often eloquently, about human behavior. Are they really the same? I don't think so. My father's intense concentration on what you can see and hear and smell and touch was at the core of his gift as a writer. He focused on the surface and texture of life, not on the emotions and motives underneath. In creative-writing classes, teachers always say that it is important to "show" and not "tell." My father's work describes the way people live, and the way he lived. It never tells. (76–77)

On the other hand, what it never tells is often very telling. His surfaces are often projections of states of mind in his characters that become the substance of his stories. His characters are possessed, as it were, by dreams and obsessions that the stories dramatize through surface descriptions and events. Thus "Torch Song" may be said to be about an open death-lover, a woman who actively seeks out dying victims, and her male observer, a secret death-lover who fears he will be devoured by his more open and active "friend." "The Enormous Radio" is similarly about a woman who becomes obsessed with the inside view of her neighbors' violent quarrels that her oversensitive radio picks up, to the apparent neglect of her own secret failings. In "O Youth and Beauty!" the gender focus switches to a middle-aged man who is so afraid of losing his athletic and sexual prowess that he arranges items of furniture as hurdles, at the fag end of suburban parties, then leaps over them at the sound of a starter's gun, in a futile effort to relive his youthful triumphs in outdoor hurdle races. The middle-aged male protagonist of "The Swimmer" is less a fellow athlete, however, than an estate lover, a man who samples the pleasures of estate life by swimming in other people's pools, and who decides one day to make his way home in this manner, only to arrive at the darkened and ruined estate he has blocked out of his mind—the painful evidence of a failed home and marriage.

As with "Torch Song," all these stories can be shown to rise up from a depth of feeling in the author and are in that sense biographically revealing. "The Enormous Radio" reflects the frequent domestic battles between Cheever and his wife, his running quarrel with her cheerful outlook; like "Torch Song" it is structured to protect the male protagonist, the nondescript husband who actually bought and installed "the enormous radio," by granting him the final cruel exposure and indictment of his wife's hidden failings. In that sense it constitutes a private/public triumph for long-suffering, truth-loving husbands like Cheever. "The Swimmer" is even more deeply revealing. It goes back to the original loss by the Cheever family of their house in Wollaston, during the Depression, and their consequent descent into much less comfortable quarters; it reflects even more obviously the author's subsequent love of living well on other people's estates, as he did for years at Yaddo and when he later brought his family to live with him in a little white house on the Vanderlip estate in Scarborough, New York; and finally it reflects his sense of failure at real family life and marriage, as if his early and sustaining dream of family harmony had been destroyed or undermined by his contradictory desire for provisional rather than permanent arrangements—a desire that continued to flourish even in his final comfortable home in Ossining, New York.

"O Youth and Beauty!" reflects still another of the author's early problems, his family's attitude toward athleticism as a form of manliness, his brother's greater physical abilities in this context, and his own slight build and more moderate abilities. In his first successful novel, *The Wapshot Chronicle,* there is even a contrast between the manly son, Moses, who loves to travel north with his father to fish under spartan circumstances, and the effeminate son, Coverly, who prefers reading cookbooks about preparing fish dinners, and so profanes "the mysterious rites of virility" by which his father lives.[3] Later Coverly walks away from a hootchy-kootchy dance at a fairground show that his father wants him to attend, and so feels he has imperiled the family's entire way of life (63). Indeed, he feels so ashamed that he forces himself to return to the fair the next night with enough money to pay for the dancer's favor and thereby "join the blessed company of men" (65). But when he reaches the fairgrounds, in what seems to be a replay of Joyce's famous story "Araby," the carnival has gone, the fairgrounds are dark and empty, and the chagrined boy can only breathe in the smell of rotted wood and trampled grass. "Oh, what can you do" asks the self-mocking narrator, "with a boy like that?" (65).

In *Home before Dark* Susan Cheever relates all such stories to the three "astonishing contests" of her father's later life—with alcohol, with his wife, and with homosexuality. This last and final contest was, it seemed, the most distressing:

> My father's sexual appetites were one of his major preoccupations, and his lust for men was as distressing to him as his desire for women was self-affirming and ecstatic. The journals contain argument after argument with himself on the subject of homosexuality. Although he loved men, he feared and despised what he defined as the homosexual community; the limp-wristed, lisping men who are sometimes the self-appointed representatives of homosexual love in our culture. Men who run gift shops, sell antiques, strike bargains over porcelain tea sets. He was terrified that his enjoyment of homosexual love would estrange him from the natural world, from the pure and anchoring influence of his family, from the manly pleasures he also loved. He had been brought up in a world and in a religion that rejected homosexuality absolutely. (174)

Terrified or not, Cheever was at least eventually able to confront his own deep feelings about such rigidly rejected love. Here is a telling response from his journal, also cited by his daughter, to a passing reference to Tolstoy's love for men as well as women:

> It is a dangerously eccentric society that intends to regulate sentimental and erotic love. I wish I could speak clearly about these dark matters. I did not respond consciously to the anxiety my parents endured over the possibility that I might be a pervert, but I seem to have responded at some other level. I can't really blame them since they had no way of improvising sexual mores but had they been less anxious, less suspicious about my merry games of grabarse I might have had an easier life. (174–75)

As Susan Cheever points out, at times her father blamed his parents' fear of homosexuality and their rigid separation of sexual roles for his own painful

3. John Cheever, *The Wapshot Chronicle,* 60. Further page references will be given in the text.

ambivalence; at times he blamed his wife's sexual and emotional coldness; and at other times he blamed society's outdated laws, based on the preindustrial requirement of close cooperation between men and women "to raise crops and breed children." Meanwhile he noted longingly those periods in time "when we have enjoyed a forthright robustness that allowed us to feel the depth and beauty of the love men feel for one another" (175).

Such sortings out may reflect confusion, but they also seem to me like the beginning of self-understanding. Still, when in midlife he finally became a furtive homosexual, Cheever felt more confused and self-condemned than ever, and the sexual freedom of the 1960s only made it worse. After spending fifty years "suppressing his homosexual longings and his bawdy obsession with sex in all its forms," he was forced to watch other writers "coming out of the closet," writing robustly about sex while he persevered "in trying to write a novel without a four-letter word" (175–76). The novel was *Bullet Park* (1969), his first serious professional failure. It was followed by a major breakdown from alcoholism in 1974. Then, in 1975, after a month in the Smithers Alcoholism Rehabilitation Unit in New York, he finally won his contest with alcoholism. In 1971 he had volunteered to teach courses in creative writing to the inmates of the Ossining Correction Facility, more popularly known as Sing Sing. Now he began writing the prison novel, *Falconer,* which took him beyond the urban and suburban middle-class conventions of his earlier fiction. His language, his artistic sensibility, was for the first time liberated by the vulgar speech and manners of the imprisoned criminal classes and by his own happy access to fulfilling homosexual love. Such long-standing personal conflicts as his love-hate relations with his stronger older brother and his "noble" but ineffectual father were also brought to dramatic resolution. Indeed, he even became friends again, at this juncture, with his wife, who accepted graciously—and perhaps gladly—the presence in their home of his new young homosexual companion. Almost miraculously, certainly courageously, he had pulled his life, his family, and himself together in his final years.

IV

Cheever's long struggle with homophobic attitudes toward his own homoerotic impulses strikes me as a useful paradigm for further study. His breakthrough in dealing with such attitudes came late in life, after repeated attempts to sort out the problem in his journals and to overcome his long reliance on surface controls. Perhaps the time has come for a similar process of sorting out such attitudes among professionals in the domestic violence field. The problem of talking about homophobia to probational clients, for instance, has proved all but impossible to resolve. It was dealt with only obliquely in the twenty-one-week program for male batterers at Brother to Brother, the Rhode Island agency with which I am most familiar. In the power-ladder lesson for the seventh week we contrasted heterosexuals with gays and lesbians as our gender example of those who possess greater and lesser power in our culture; and in the previous lesson, on male and female attributes and why we prize or despise them, we touched briefly on male fears of being taken for a gay person or a woman. But we nowhere approached the problem head-on, perhaps out of fear of losing the confidence of our clients. Their resistance to this particular issue was adamant, and there was even some backlash talk, outside our meetings, about fairies and fags who designed and ran the program (there were in fact only two homosexuals among more than twenty counselors). Meanwhile the public outcry against gays and lesbians from the political and religious right has further complicated the issue. It seems plain enough, however, that weak and insecure men who seek power and control over their female partners are often strongly homophobic, and that their fear of being identified with "gays" is related to their misogynistic fears about women.

Perhaps Cheever's case can again be useful here. Before his turn toward homosexuality he had been told by several psychiatrists that he hated women. Since he had remained married, with recurrent happiness, to the same woman, had turned to mistresses when the marriage flagged, and decidedly loved his daughter, he resisted that conclusion; and certainly in sentimental tales such as "The Pot of Gold" and morbid tales such as "The Hartleys," where he sides with long-suffering wives against obtuse and controlling husbands, he shows plainly enough that he liked as well as hated women. He was probably right, then, to resist his doctors' bald conclusions.

It would be fairer to say, I think, that he hated or resisted his own feminine impulses. If we are all to some extent bisexual beings, in a culture with rigid gender categories, then such resistance is a common problem, and an especially severe one for men whose masculinity has been shaken by external and internal pressures—men who scapegoat their female partners out of their own projected fears of weakness or failure in their marketplace or barroom struggles with other men or in their domestic struggles with wives and mothers. Since Cheever can be seen, in "Torch Song" and elsewhere, as a writer who sometimes demonized his wife and mother as Angels of Death, archetypal victimizers of weak or dying men, out of homophobic fears about his own deepest feelings, and since he modified and largely overcame those demonic views once he learned how to confront and validate his hidden feelings, he can serve as a useful model of self-correction.

This is not to say that all or even many batterers are latent homosexuals—only that all or most of them are, like Cheever, strongly homophobic. They badly need to confront their own gender complexity, their own unyielding gender rigidities, and their own suppressed capacity for generous and receptive feelings about the abused women and children they often profess to love. This is essentially what Cheever finally learned to accept about himself. This is the lesson from which all kinds of men can profit.

Torch Song

by John Cheever

After Jack Lorey had known Joan Harris in New York for a few years, he began to think of her as the Widow. She always wore black, and he was always given the feeling, by a curious disorder in her apartment, that the undertakers had just left. This impression did not stem from malice on his part, for he was fond of Joan. They came from the same city in Ohio and had reached New York at about the same time in the middle thirties. They were the same age, and during their first summer in the city they used to meet after work and drink Martinis in places like the Brevoort and Charles', and have dinner and play checkers at the Lafayette.

Joan went to a school for models when she settled in the city, but it turned out that she photographed badly, so after spending six weeks learning how to walk with a book on her head she got a job as a hostess in a Longchamps. For the rest of the summer she stood by the hatrack, bathed in an intense pink light and the string music of heartbreak, swinging her mane of dark hair and her black skirt as she moved forward to greet the customers. She was then a big, handsome girl with a wonderful voice, and her face, her whole presence, always seemed infused with a gentle and healthy pleasure at her surroundings, whatever they were. She was innocently and incorrigibly convivial, and would get out of bed and dress at three in the morning if someone called her and asked her to come out for a drink, as Jack often did. In the fall, she got some kind of freshman executive job in a department store. They saw less and less of each other and then for quite a while stopped seeing each other altogether. Jack was living with a girl he had met at a party, and it never occurred to him to wonder what had become of Joan.

Jack's girl had some friends in Pennsylvania, and in the spring and summer of his second year in town he often went there with her for weekends. All of this—the shared apartment in the Village, the illicit relationship, the Friday-night train to a country house—was what he had imagined life in New York to be, and he was intensely happy. He was returning to New York with his girl one Sunday night on the Lehigh line. It was one of those trains that move slowly across the face of New Jersey, bringing back to the city hundreds of people, like the victims of an immense and strenuous picnic, whose faces are blazing and whose muscles are lame. Jack and his girl, like most of the other passengers, were overburdened with vegetables and flowers. When the train stopped in Pennsylvania Station, they moved with the crowd along the platform, toward the escalator. As they were passing the wide, lighted windows of the diner, Jack turned his head and saw Joan. It was the first time he had seen her since Thanksgiving, or since Christmas. He couldn't remember.

Joan was with a man who had obviously passed out. His head was in his arms on the table, and an overturned highball glass was near one of his elbows. Joan was shaking his shoulders gently and speaking to him. She seemed to be vaguely troubled, vaguely amused. The waiters had cleared off all the other tables and were standing around Joan, waiting for her to resurrect her escort. It troubled Jack to see in these straits a girl who reminded him of the trees and the lawns of his home town, but there was nothing he could do to help. Joan continued to shake the man's shoulders, and the crowd pressed Jack past one after another of the diner's windows, past the malodorous kitchen, and up the escalator.

He saw Joan again, later that summer, when he was having dinner in a Village restaurant. He was with a new girl, a Southerner. There were many Southern girls in the city that year. Jack and his belle had wandered into the restaurant because it was convenient, but the food was terrible and the place was lighted with candles. Halfway through dinner, Jack noticed Joan on the other side of the room, and when he had finished eating, he crossed the room and spoke to her. She was with a tall man who was wearing a monocle. He stood, bowed stiffly from the waist, and said to Jack, "We are very pleased to meet you." Then he excused himself and headed for the toilet. "He's a count, he's a Swedish count," Joan said. "He's on the radio, Friday afternoons at four-fifteen. Isn't it exciting?" She seemed to be delighted with the count and the terrible restaurant.

Sometime the next winter, Jack moved from the Village to an apartment in the East Thirties. He was crossing Park Avenue one cold morning on his way to the office when he noticed, in the crowd, a woman he had met a few times at Joan's apartment. He spoke to her and asked about his friend. "Haven't you heard?" she said. She pulled a long face. "Perhaps I'd better tell you. Perhaps you can help." She and Jack had breakfast in a drugstore on Madison Avenue and she unburdened herself of the story.

The count had a program called "The Song of the Fiords," or something like that, and he sang Swedish folk songs. Everyone suspected him of being a fake, but that didn't bother Joan. He had met her at a party and, sensing a soft touch, had moved in with her the following night. About a week later, he complained of pains in his back and said he must have some morphine. Then he needed morphine all the time. If he didn't get morphine, he was abusive and violent. Joan began to deal with those doctors and druggists who peddle dope, and when they wouldn't supply her, she went down to the bottom of the city. Her friends were afraid she would be found some morning stuffed in a drain. She got pregnant. She had an abortion. The count left her and moved to a flea bag near Times Square, but she was so impressed by then with his helplessness, so afraid that he would die without her, that she followed him there and shared his room and continued to buy his narcotics. He abandoned her again, and Joan waited a week for him to return before she went back to her place and her friends in the Village

It shocked Jack to think of the innocent girl from Ohio having lived with a brutal dope addict and traded with criminals, and when he got to his office that morning, he telephoned her and made a date for dinner that night. He met her at Charles'. When she came into the bar, she seemed as wholesome and calm as ever. Her voice was sweet, and reminded him of elms, of lawns, of those glass arrangements that used to be hung from porch ceilings to tinkle in the summer wind. She told him about the count. She spoke of him charitably and with no trace of bitterness, as if her voice, her disposition, were incapable of registering anything beyond simple affection and pleasure. Her walk, when she moved ahead of him toward their table, was light and graceful. She ate a large dinner and talked enthusiastically about her job. They went to a movie and said goodbye in front of her apartment house.

That winter, Jack met a girl he decided to marry. Their engagement was announced in January and they planned to marry in July. In the spring, he received, in his office mail, an invitation to cocktails at Joan's. It was for a Saturday when his fiancée was going to Massachusetts to visit her parents, and when the time came and he had nothing better to do, he took a bus to the Village. Joan had the same apartment. It was a walk-up. You rang the bell above the mailbox in the vestibule and were answered with a death rattle in the lock. Joan lived on the third floor. Her calling card was in a slot in the mailbox, and above her name was written the name Hugh Bascomb.

Jack climbed the two flights of carpeted stairs, and when he reached Joan's apartment, she was standing by the open door in a black dress. After she greeted Jack, she took his arm and guided him across the room. "I want you to meet Hugh, Jack," she said.

Hugh was a big man with a red face and pale-blue eyes. His manner was courtly and his eyes were inflamed with drink. Jack talked with him for a little while and then went over to speak to someone he knew, who was standing by the mantelpiece. He noticed then, for the first time, the indescribable disorder of Joan's apartment. The books were in their shelves and the furniture was reasonably good, but the place was all wrong, somehow. It was as if things had been put in place without thought or real interest, and for the first time, too, he had the impression that there had been a death there recently.

As Jack moved around the room, he felt that he had met the ten or twelve guests at other parties. There was a woman executive with a fancy hat, a man who could imitate Roosevelt, a grim couple whose play was in rehearsal, and a newspaperman who kept turning on the radio for news of the Spanish Civil War. Jack drank Martinis and talked with the woman in the fancy hat. He looked out of the window at the back yards and the ailanthus trees and heard, in the distance, thunder exploding off the cliffs of the Hudson.

Hugh Bascomb got very drunk. He began to spill liquor, as if drinking, for him, were a kind of jolly slaughter and he enjoyed the bloodshed and the mess. He spilled whiskey from a bottle. He spilled a drink on his shirt and then tipped over someone else's drink. The party was not quiet, but Hugh's hoarse voice began to dominate the others. He attacked a photographer who was sitting in a corner explaining camera techniques to a homely woman. "What did you come to the party for if all you wanted to do was to sit there and stare at your shoes?" Hugh shouted. "What did you come for? Why don't you stay at home?"

The photographer didn't know what to say. He was not staring at his shoes. Joan moved lightly to Hugh's side. "Please don't get into a fight now, darling," she said. "Not this afternoon."

"Shut up," he said. "Let me alone. Mind your own business." He lost his balance, and in struggling to steady himself he tipped over a lamp.

"Oh, your lovely lamp, Joan," a woman sighed.

"Lamps!" Hugh roared. He threw his arms into the air and worked them around his head as if he were bludgeoning himself. "Lamps. Glasses. Cigarette boxes. Dishes. They're killing me. They're killing me, for Christ's sake. Let's all go up to the mountains and hunt and fish and live like men, for Christ's sake."

People were scattering as if a rain had begun to fall in the room. It had, as a matter of fact, begun to rain outside. Someone offered Jack a ride uptown, and he jumped at the chance. Joan stood at the door, saying goodbye to her routed friends. Her voice remained soft, and her manner, unlike that of those Christian women who in the face of disaster can summon new and formidable sources of composure, seemed genuinely simple. She appeared to be oblivious of the raging drunk at her back, who was pacing up and down, grinding glass into the rug, and haranguing one of the survivors of the party with a story of how he, Hugh, had once gone without food for three weeks.

In July, Jack was married in an orchard in Duxbury, and he and his wife went to West Chop for a few weeks. When they returned to town, their apartment was cluttered with presents, including a dozen after-dinner coffee cups from Joan. His wife sent her the required note, but they did nothing else.

Late in the summer, Joan telephoned Jack at his office and asked if he wouldn't bring his wife to see her; she named an evening the following week. He felt guilty about not having called her, and accepted the invitation. This made his wife angry. She was an ambitious girl who liked a social life that offered rewards, and she went unwillingly to Joan's Village apartment with him.

Written above Joan's name on the mailbox was the name Franz Denzel. Jack and his wife climbed the stairs and were met by Joan at the open door. They went into her apartment and found themselves among a group of people for whom Jack, at least, was unable to find any bearings.

Franz Denzel was a middle-aged German. His face was pinched with bitterness or illness. He greeted Jack and his wife with that elaborate and clever politeness that is intended to make guests feel that they have come too early or too late. He insisted sharply upon Jack's sitting in the chair in which he himself had been sitting, and then went and sat on a radiator. There were five other Germans sitting around the room, drinking coffee. In a corner was another American couple, who looked uncomfortable. Joan passed Jack and his wife small cups of coffee with whipped cream. "These cups belonged to Franz's mother," she said. "Aren't they lovely? They were the only things he took from Germany when he escaped from the Nazis."

Franz turned to Jack and said, "Perhaps you will give us your opinion on the American educational system. That is what we were discussing when you arrived."

Before Jack could speak, one of the German guests opened an attack on the American educational system. The other Germans joined in, and went on from there to describe every vulgarity that had impressed them in American life and to contrast German and American culture generally. Where, they asked one another passionately, could you find in America anything like the Mitropa dining cars, the Black Forest, the pictures in Munich, the music in Bayreuth? Franz and his friends began speaking in German. Neither Jack nor his wife nor Joan could understand German, and the other American couple had not opened their mouths since they were introduced. Joan went happily around the room, filling everyone's cup with coffee, as if the music of a foreign language were enough to make an evening for her.

Jack drank five cups of coffee. He was desperately uncomfortable. Joan went into the kitchen while the Germans were laughing at their German jokes, and he hoped she would return with some drinks, but when she came back, it was with a tray of ice cream and mulberries.

"Isn't this pleasant?" Franz asked, speaking in English again.

Joan collected the coffee cups, and as she was about to take them back to the kitchen, Franz stopped her.

"Isn't one of those cups chipped?"

"No, darling," Joan said. "I never let the maid touch them. I wash them myself."

"What's that?" he asked, pointing at the rim of one of the cups.

"That's the cup that's always been chipped, darling. It was chipped when you unpacked it. You noticed it then."

"These things were perfect when they arrived in this country," he said.

Joan went into the kitchen and he followed her.

Jack tried to make conversation with the Germans. From the kitchen there was the sound of a blow and a cry. Franz returned and began to eat his mulberries greedily. Joan came back with her dish of ice cream. Her voice was gentle. Her tears, if she had been crying, had dried as quickly as the tears of a child. Jack and his wife finished their ice cream and made their escape. The wasted and unnerving evening enraged Jack's wife, and he supposed that he would never see Joan again.

Jack's wife got pregnant early in the fall, and she seized on all the prerogatives of an expectant mother. She took long naps, ate canned peaches in the middle of the night, and talked about the rudimentary kidney. She chose to see only other couples who were expecting children, and the parties that she and Jack gave were temperate. The baby, a boy, was born in May, and Jack was very proud and happy. The first party he and his wife went to after her convalescence was the wedding of a girl whose family Jack had known in Ohio.

The wedding was at St. James's, and afterward there was a big reception at the River Club. There was an orchestra dressed like Hungarians, and a lot of champagne and Scotch. Toward the end of the afternoon, Jack was walking down a dim corridor when he heard Joan's voice. "Please don't, darling," she was saying. "You'll break my arm. *Please* don't, darling." She was being pressed against the wall by a man who seemed to be twisting her arm. As soon as they saw Jack, the struggle stopped. All three of them were intensely embarrassed. Joan's face was wet and she made an effort to smile through her tears at Jack. He said hello and went on without stopping. When he returned, she and the man had disappeared.

When Jack's son was less than two years old, his wife flew with the baby to Nevada to get a divorce. Jack gave her the apartment and all its furnishings and took a room in a hotel near Grand Central. His wife got her decree in due course, and the story was in the newspapers. Jack had a telephone call from Joan a few days later.

"I'm awfully sorry to hear about your divorce, Jack," she said. "She seemed like *such* a nice girl. But that wasn't what I called you about. I want your help, and I wondered if you could come down to my place tonight around six. It's something I don't want to talk about over the phone."

He went obediently to the Village that night and climbed the stairs. Her apartment was a mess. The pictures and the curtains were down and the books were in boxes. "You moving, Joan?" he asked.

"That's what I wanted to see you about, Jack. First, I'll give you a drink." She made two Old-Fashioneds. "I'm being evicted, Jack," she said. "I'm being evicted because I'm an immoral woman. The couple who have the apartment downstairs—they're charming people, I've always thought—have told the real-estate agent that I'm a drunk and a prostitute and all kinds of things. Isn't that fantastic? This real-estate agent has always been so nice to me that I didn't think he'd believe them, but he's canceled my lease, and if I make any trouble, he's threatened to take the matter up with the store, and I don't want to lose my job. This nice real-estate agent won't even talk with me any more. When I go over to the office, the receptionist leers at me as if I were some kind of dreadful woman. Of course, there have been a lot of men here and we sometimes are noisy, but I can't be expected to go to bed at ten every night. Can I? Well, the agent who manages this building has apparently told all the other agents in the neighborhood that I'm an immoral and drunken woman, and none of them will give me an apartment. I went in to talk with one man—he seemed to be such a nice old gentleman—and he made me an indecent proposal. Isn't it fantastic? I have to be out of here on Thursday and I'm literally being turned out into the street."

Joan seemed as serene and innocent as ever while she described this scourge of agents and neighbors. Jack listened carefully for some sign of indignation or bitterness or even urgency in her recital, but there was none. He was reminded of a torch song, of one of those forlorn and touching ballads that had been sung neither for him nor for her but for their older brothers and sisters by Marion Harris. Joan seemed to be singing her wrongs.

"They've made my life miserable," she went on quietly. "If I keep the radio on after ten o'clock, they telephone the agent in the morning and tell him I had some kind of orgy here. One night when Philip—I don't think you've met Philip; he's in the Royal Air Force; he's gone back to England—one night when Philip and some other people were here, they called the police. The police came bursting in the door and talked to me as if I were I don't know what and then looked in the bedroom. If they think there's a man up here after midnight, they call me on the telephone and say all kinds of disgusting things. Of course, I can put my furniture into storage and go to a hotel, I guess. I guess a hotel will take a woman with my kind of reputation, but I thought perhaps you might know of an apartment. I thought—"

It angered Jack to think of this big, splendid girl's being persecuted by her neighbors, and he said he would do what he could. He asked her to have dinner with him, but she said she was busy.

Having nothing better to do, Jack decided to walk uptown to his hotel. It was a hot night. The sky was overcast. On his way, he saw a parade in a dark side street off Broadway near Madison Square. All the buildings in the neighborhood were dark. It was so dark that he could not see the placards the marchers carried until he came to a street light. Their signs urged the entry of the United States into the war, and each platoon represented a nation that had been subjugated by the Axis powers. They marched up Broadway, as he watched, to no music, to no sound but their own steps on the rough cobbles. It was for the most part an army of elderly men and women—Poles, Norwegians, Danes, Jews, Chinese. A few idle people like himself lined the sidewalks, and the marchers passed between them with all the self-consciousness of enemy prisoners. There were children among them dressed in the costumes in which they had, for the newsreels, presented the Mayor with a package of tea, a petition, a protest, a constitution, a check, or a pair of tickets. They hobbled through the darkness of the loft neighborhood like a mortified and destroyed people, toward Greeley Square.

In the morning, Jack put the problem of finding an apartment for Joan up to his secretary. She started phoning real-estate agents, and by afternoon she had found a couple of available apartments in the West Twenties. Joan called Jack the next day to say that she had taken one of the apartments and to thank him.

Jack didn't see Joan again until the following summer. It was a Sunday evening; he had left a cocktail party in a Washington Square apartment and had decided to walk a few blocks up Fifth Avenue before he took a bus. As he was passing the Brevoort, Joan called to him. She was with a man at one of the tables on the sidewalk. She looked cool and fresh, and the man appeared to be respectable. His name, it turned out, was Pete Bristol. He invited Jack to sit down and join in a celebration. Germany had invaded Russia that weekend, and Joan and Pete were drinking champagne to celebrate Russia's changed position in the war. The three of them drank champagne until it got dark. They had dinner and drank champagne with their dinner. They drank more champagne afterward and then went over to the Lafayette and then to two or three other places. Joan had always been tireless in her gentle way. She hated to see the night end, and it was after three o'clock when Jack stumbled into his apartment. The following morning he woke up haggard and sick, and with no recollection of the last hour or so of the previous evening. His suit was soiled and he had lost his hat. He didn't get to his office until eleven. Joan had already called him twice, and she called him again soon after he got in. There was no hoarseness at all in her voice. She said that she had to see him, and he agreed to meet her for lunch in a seafood restaurant in the Fifties.

He was standing at the bar when she breezed in, looking as though she had taken no part in that calamitous night. The advice she wanted concerned selling her jewelry. Her grandmother had left her some jewelry, and she wanted to raise money on it but didn't know where to go. She took some rings and bracelets out of her purse and showed them to Jack. He said that he didn't know anything about jewelry but that he could lend her some money. "Oh, I couldn't borrow money from you, Jack," she said. "You see, I want to get the money for Pete. I want to help him. He wants to open an advertising agency, and he needs quite a lot to begin with." Jack didn't press her to accept his offer of a loan after that, and the project wasn't mentioned again during lunch.

He next heard about Joan from a young doctor who was a friend of theirs. "Have you seen Joan recently?" the doctor asked Jack one evening when they were having dinner together. He said no. "I gave her a checkup last week," the doctor said, "and while she's been through enough to kill the average mortal—and you'll never know what she's been through—she still has the constitution of a virtuous and healthy woman. Did you hear about the last one? She sold her jewelry to put him into some kind of business, and as soon as he got the money, he left her for another girl, who had a car—a convertible."

Jack was drafted into the Army in the spring of 1942. He was kept at Fort Dix for nearly a month, and during this time he came to New York in the evening whenever he could get permission. Those nights had for him the intense keenness of a reprieve, a sensation that was heightened by the fact that on the train in from Trenton women would often press upon him dog-eared copies of *Life* and half-eaten boxes of candy, as though the brown clothes he wore were surely cerements. He telephoned Joan from Pennsylvania Station one night. "Come right over, Jack," she said. "Come right over. I want you to meet Ralph."

She was living in that place in the West Twenties that Jack had found for her. The neighborhood was a slum. Ash cans stood in front of her house, and an old woman was there picking out bits of refuse and garbage and stuffing them into a perambulator. The house in which Joan's apartment was located was shabby, but the apartment itself seemed familiar. The furniture was the same. Joan was the same big, easygoing girl. "I'm so glad you called me," she said. "It's so good to see you. I'll make you a drink. I was having one myself. Ralph ought to be here by now. He promised to take me to dinner." Jack offered to take her to Cavanagh's, but she said that Ralph might come while she was out. "If he doesn't come by nine, I'm going to make myself a sandwich. I'm not really hungry."

Jack talked about the Army. She talked about the store. She had been working in the same place for—how long was it? He didn't know. He had never seen her at her desk and he couldn't imagine what she did. "I'm terribly sorry Ralph isn't here," she said. "I'm sure you'd like him. He's not a young man. He's a heart specialist who loves to play the viola." She turned on some lights, for the summer sky had got dark. "He has this dreadful wife on Riverside Drive and four ungrateful children. He—"

The noise of an air-raid siren, lugubrious and seeming to spring from pain, as if all the misery and indecision in the city had been given a voice, cut her off. Other sirens, in distant neighborhoods, sounded, until the dark air was full of their noise. "Let me fix you another drink before I have to turn out the lights," Joan said, and took his glass. She brought the drink back to him and snapped off the lights. They went to the windows, and, as children watch a thunderstorm, they watched the city darken. All the lights nearby went out but one. Air-raid wardens had begun to sound their whistles in the street. From a distant yard came a hoarse shriek of anger. "Put out your lights, you Fascists!" a woman screamed. "Put out your lights, you Nazi Fascist Germans. Turn out your lights. Turn out your lights." The last light went off. They went away from the window and sat in the lightless room.

In the darkness, Joan began to talk about her departed lovers, and from what she said Jack gathered that they had all had a hard time. Nils, the suspect count, was dead. Hugh Bascomb, the drunk, had joined the Merchant Marine and was missing in the North Atlantic. Franz, the German, had taken poison the night the Nazis bombed Warsaw. "We listened to the news on the radio," Joan said, "and then he went back to his hotel and took poison. The maid found him dead in the bathroom the next morning." When Jack asked her about the one who was going to open an advertising agency, she seemed at first to have forgotten him. "Oh, Pete," she said after a pause. "Well, he was always very sick, you know. He was supposed to go to Saranac, but he kept putting it off and putting it off and—" She stopped talking when she heard steps on the stairs, hoping, he supposed, that it was Ralph, but whoever it was turned at the landing and continued to the top of the house. "I wish Ralph would come," she said, with a sigh. "I want you to meet him." Jack asked her again to go out, but she refused, and when the all-clear sounded, he said goodbye.

Jack was shipped from Dix to an infantry training camp in the Carolinas and from there to an infantry division stationed in Georgia. He had been in Georgia three months when he married a girl from the Augusta boarding-house aristocracy. A year or so later, he crossed the continent in a day coach and thought sententiously that the last he might see of the country he loved was the desert towns like Barstow, that the last he might hear of it was the ringing of the trolleys on the Bay Bridge. He was sent into the Pacific and returned to the United States twenty months later, uninjured and apparently unchanged. As soon as he received his furlough, he went to Augusta. He presented his wife with the souvenirs he had brought from the islands, quarreled violently with her and all her family, and, after making arrangements for her to get an Arkansas divorce, left for New York.

Jack was discharged from the Army at a camp in the East a few months later. He took a vacation and then went back to the job he had left in 1942. He seemed to have picked up his life at approximately the moment when it had been interrupted by the war. In time, everything came to look and feel the same. He saw most of his old friends. Only two of the men he knew had been killed in the war. He didn't call Joan, but he met her one winter afternoon on a crosstown bus.

Her fresh face, her black clothes, and her soft voice instantly destroyed the sense—if he had ever had such a sense—that anything had changed or intervened since their last meeting, three or four years ago. She asked him up for cocktails and he went to her apartment the next Saturday afternoon. Her room and her guests reminded him of the parties she had given when she had first come to New York. There was a woman with a fancy hat, an elderly doctor, and a man who stayed close to the radio, listening for news from the Balkans. Jack wondered which of the men belonged to Joan and decided on an Englishman who kept coughing into a handkerchief that he pulled out of his sleeve. Jack was right. "Isn't Stephen brilliant?" Joan asked him a little later, when they were alone in a corner. "He knows more about the Polynesians than anyone else in the world."

Jack had returned not only to his old job but to his old salary. Since living costs had doubled and since he was paying alimony to two wives, he had to draw on his savings. He took another job, which promised more money, but it didn't last long and he found himself out of work. This didn't bother him at all. He still had money in the bank, and anyhow it was easy to borrow from friends. His indifference was the consequence not of lassitude or despair but rather of an excess of hope. He had the feeling that he had only recently come to New York from Ohio. The sense that he was very young and that the best years of his life still lay before him was an illusion that he could not seem to escape. There was all the time in the world. He was living in hotels then, moving from one to another every five days.

In the spring, Jack moved to a furnished room in the badlands west of Central Park. He was running out of money. Then, when he began to feel that a job was a desperate necessity, he got sick. At first, he seemed to have only a bad cold, but he was unable to shake it and he began to run a fever and to cough blood.

The fever kept him drowsy most of the time, but he roused himself occasionally and went out to a cafeteria for a meal. He felt sure that none of his friends knew where he was, and he was glad of this. He hadn't counted on Joan.

Late one morning, he heard her speaking in the hall with his landlady. A few moments later, she knocked on his door. He was lying on the bed in a pair of pants and a soiled pajama top, and he didn't answer. She knocked again and walked in. "I've been looking everywhere for you, Jack," she said. She spoke softly. "When I found out that you were in a place like this I thought you must be broke or sick. I stopped at the bank and got some money, in case you're broke. I've brought you some Scotch. I thought a little drink wouldn't do you any harm. Want a little drink?"

Joan's dress was black. Her voice was low and serene. She sat in a chair beside his bed as if she had been coming there every day to nurse him. Her features had coarsened, he thought, but there were still very few lines in her face. She was heavier. She was nearly fat. She was wearing black cotton gloves. She got two glasses and poured Scotch into them. He drank his whiskey greedily. "I didn't get to bed until three last night," she said. Her voice had once before reminded him of a gentle and despairing song, but now, perhaps because he was sick, her mildness, the mourning she wore, her stealthy grace, made him uneasy. "It was one of those nights," she said. "We went to the theatre. Afterward, someone asked us up to his place. I don't know who he was. It was one of those places. They're so strange. There were some meat-eating plants and a collection of Chinese snuff bottles. Why do people collect Chinese snuff bottles? We all autographed a lampshade, as I remember, but I can't remember much."

Jack tried to sit up in bed, as if there were some need to defend himself, and then fell back again, against the pillows. "How did you find me, Joan?" he asked.

"It was simple," she said. "I called that hotel. The one you were staying in. They gave me this address. My secretary got the telephone number. Have another little drink."

"You know, you've never come to a place of mine before—never," he said. "Why did you come now?"

"Why did I come, darling?" she asked. "What a question! I've known you for thirty years. You're the oldest friend I have in New York. Remember that night in the Village when it snowed and we stayed up until morning and drank whiskey sours for breakfast? That doesn't seem like twelve years ago. And that night—"

"I don't like to have you see me in a place like this," he said earnestly. He touched his face and felt his beard.

"And all the people who used to imitate Roosevelt," she said, as if she had not heard him, as if she were deaf. "And that place on Staten Island where we all used to go for dinner when Henry had a car. Poor Henry. He bought a place in Connecticut and went out there by himself one weekend. He fell asleep with a lighted cigarette and the house, the barn, everything burned. Ethel took the children out to California." She poured more Scotch into his glass and handed it to him. She lighted a cigarette and put it between his lips. The intimacy of this gesture, which made it seem not only as if he were deathly ill but as if he were her lover, troubled him.

"As soon as I'm better," he said, "I'll take a room at a good hotel. I'll call you then. It was nice of you to come."

"Oh, don't be ashamed of this room, Jack," she said. "Rooms never bother me. It doesn't seem to matter to me where I am. Stanley had a filthy room in Chelsea. At least, other people told me it was filthy. I never noticed it. Rats used to eat the food I brought him. He used to have to hang the food from the ceiling, from the light chain."

"I'll call you as soon as I'm better," Jack said. "I think I can sleep now if I'm left alone. I seem to need a lot of sleep."

"You really *are* sick, darling," she said. "You must have a fever." She sat on the edge of his bed and put a hand on his forehead.

"How is that Englishman, Joan?" he asked. "Do you still see him?"

"What Englishman?" she said.

"You know. I met him at your house. He kept a handkerchief up his sleeve. He coughed all the time. You know the one I mean."

"You must be thinking of someone else," she said. "I haven't had an Englishman at my place since the war. Of course, I can't remember everyone." She turned and, taking one of his hands, linked her fingers in his.

"He's dead, isn't he?" Jack said. "That Englishman's dead." He pushed her off the bed, and got up himself. "Get out," he said.

"You're sick, darling," she said. "I can't leave you alone here."

"Get out," he said again, and when she didn't move, he shouted, "What kind of an obscenity are you that you can smell sickness and death the way you do?"

"You poor darling."

"Does it make you feel young to watch the dying?" he shouted. "Is that the lewdness that keeps you young? Is that why you dress like a crow? Oh, I know there's nothing I can say that will hurt you. I know there's nothing filthy or corrupt or depraved or brutish or base that the others haven't tried, but this time you're wrong. I'm not ready. My life isn't ending. My life's beginning. There are wonderful years ahead of me. There are, there are wonderful, wonderful, wonderful years ahead of me, and when they're over, when it's time, then I'll call you. Then, as an old friend, I'll call you and give you whatever dirty pleasure you take in watching the dying, but until then, you and your ugly and misshapen forms will leave me alone."

She finished her drink and looked at her watch. "I guess I'd better show up at the office," she said. "I'll see you later. I'll come back tonight. You'll feel better then, you poor darling." She closed the door after her, and he heard her light step on the stairs.

Jack emptied the whiskey bottle into the sink. He began to dress. He stuffed his dirty clothes into a bag. He was trembling and crying with sickness and fear. He could see the blue sky from his window, and in his fear it seemed miraculous that the sky should be blue, that the white clouds should remind him of snow, that from the sidewalk he could hear the shrill voices of children shrieking, "I'm the king of the mountain, I'm the king of the mountain, I'm the king of the mountain." He emptied the ashtray containing his nail parings and cigarette butts into the toilet, and swept the floor with a shirt, so that there would be no trace of his life, of his body, when that lewd and searching shape of death came there to find him in the evening.

Empathy with the Devil

ISAAC BASHEVIS SINGER AND THE DEADLY PLEASURES OF MISOGYNY

"As a matter of fact, all my life I dreamt about running away; this is always my dream. . . . It is this idea that somehow bothers me. One day, I will actually be running away. . . ."

Isaac Bashevis Singer: Conversations

When I used this murky staircase, I was pursued by all the devils, evil spirits, demons, and imps of whom my parents spoke to prove to the older children that there was a God and a future life.

Singer, In My Father's Court

The effects used by John Cheever in "Torch Song"—his demonic approach to his femme fatale, his attention to the abusive response to her by all her victims, and his placement of such odd relations in times of worldwide distress—are shared by Isaac Bashevis Singer in his novels and folktales. For Singer, however, the world-disrupting events are paramount rather than incidental, and his use of folk narratives to convey them is endemic to their importance. He is the chronicler of a lost European culture, of the lost Jewish villages, towns, and urban enclaves in Poland that he too left behind shortly before the Nazis threatened to invade that country and to wipe out its Jewish inhabitants. His treatment of incidents of domestic violence, within this disruptive context, is accordingly worth reviewing not simply as it reflects a traditional European outlook on that domestic problem but also as it subordinates it to larger and more disastrous public events. What remains nonetheless remarkable, within this subordinated context, is his frequent choice of the devil's partner Lilith as the reigning Angel of Death in all abusive domestic relations, and his equally frequent decision to speak for the devil, or play devil's advocate himself, by adopting the narrative persona of either Satan or one of his lesser demons.

What are we to make of these peculiar choices? Is this a case like that of Milton in *Paradise Lost,* or that of Dostoyevsky in "The Legend of the Grand Inquisitor," of creating Satans so attractive that many readers consider them the true heroes of their respective narratives? Or does Singer simply mean to dramatize the enormity of satanic powers to be resisted? If so, can he avoid creating sympathy with the devil in himself and his readers? Isn't that the risk of his empathetic stance, his adoption of the devil's point of view? Or can he risk even that seeming betrayal for moral ends? And what about his obsession with Lilith? Is she a more unredeemable Eve or Grushenka, a sensuous unfaithful siren now wholly lost to death and the devil? Or is she just an object lesson for foolish males, to be avoided at all costs, the whorish and demonic side of otherwise angelic or even mortally lovable creatures? And can he invoke her powers, even so, without sexist intent?

I

The place to begin to answer all such questions is Poland of the early 1930s, when the threat of the Nazi takeover first became evident. Singer, born in 1904 in a small Polish village, was in his mid to late twenties. His family had moved to Warsaw in 1908, and by 1914 he was devouring Dostoyevsky and other gentile writers and experiencing religious doubt. For the next nine years he seesawed back and forth between Warsaw and a distant village, Bilgoray, teaching Hebrew in a "worldly school," reading Spinoza, joining a rabbinical seminary one year and leaving it the next. Then he began to read proof for a Yiddish journal and to write his own stories. In 1929 he fathered a son by a Communist mistress and/or wife, both of whom he would leave behind.[1] In 1933 he published his first novel in serial form, *Satan in Goray,* in his own literary journal. Meanwhile his brother Israel Joshua Singer had scored a great success in America with a Yiddish novel, *Yoshe Kalb* (Yasha the Loon). In 1935 Isaac too emigrated to America at his brother's request and began writing stories in Yiddish for the *Jewish Daily Forward.*[2]

Some fifteen years later he published his first novel to appear in an English translation, *The Family Moskat,* a realistic history of a large urban Jewish clan

1. The marital status of Singer's Communist "wife" is uncertain. Although some biographers refer to her as his mistress, Singer himself calls her his wife in an explanation provided for Irving Buchen's *Isaac Bashevis Singer and the Eternal Past:* "We were never married by a rabbi. She was my wife. We were very progressive in those days" (18). In his recent memoir, *Journey to My Father, Isaac Bashevis Singer,* Singer's son, Israel Zamir, also refers repeatedly to his mother as Singer's first wife. Since neither Singer nor his son mentions a civil ceremony, perhaps "common-law wife" would best explain these discrepancies.

2. See Edward Alexander's account of these years in *Isaac Bashevis Singer: A Study of the Short Fiction,* 131–32.

in Poland, circa 1900–1939. This massive and impressive novel features two lovable renegades, the avuncular Abram Shapiro and his small-town protégé, Asa Heshel Bannet, who marry into the Moskat family. These lovable outsiders seem closest to the author's heart. The boisterous Abram brings warmth and vitality to family celebrations of Jewish holidays, for instance, but he is also an incorrigible philanderer and a posturing free thinker. The modest young Asa is the novel's nominal hero. His arrival in Warsaw at the beginning of chapter 2, after the opening sequence devoted to the aging family patriarch, Meshulam Moskat, marks him as the obvious general successor to the old man and the old ways.

Thus Asa at nineteen is the grandson of a rabbi and a devoted student of the heretical Jewish philosopher Spinoza. These hints of his divided loyalties further mark him as an attractive oscillator between conflicting views. Like Dostoyevsky's paralyzed and irresolute underground man, who found it difficult to become either a hero or an insect, though he aspired to both possibilities, Asa is unable to act resolutely, much less make up his mind, for the length of the novel. In this and other respects he plainly represents the author's view of himself as a young man in prewar Poland. The portrait is self-critical in that Asa ultimately lacks the strength and wisdom to leave Poland before the German invasion in 1939. In that sense he chooses Death as his Messiah, in keeping with the novel's grim conclusive comment on the fate of Polish Jews. But, as we shall see, he also chooses to die with his fellow Jews. It seems evident from such ambivalence, and from the strength and fidelity of its depiction, that Asa offers a useful key to the author's subsequent sense of himself as a similarly Attractive Oscillator—if I may be allowed to capitalize that working hypothesis at this point.

What makes this irresolute young man so attractive? He is in this respect a bit like Dickens's most sentimental character, Little Nell, a relatively blank possibility whom everyone admires and/or desires for no apparent cause, other than the author's say-so. So too Asa often seems more of an effect than a cause, at least in the early chapters. We know a lot about his reading, but not much about his character. Nevertheless, when Abram Shapiro meets him for the first time, at the home of Dr. Shmaryahu Jacobi, the aging secretary of a Warsaw synagogue, he embraces him at once on the strength of his letter of recommendation from the head of the modern Jewish school in Zamosc. Because Singer has already made us privy to that letter, we know that Asa is "one of those high and aspiring spirits which are so few in number," the grandson and "true limb" of a small-town rabbi, a young man whose early discourse has already won him the praise of learned men, and who has already taught himself foreign languages and mastered much of algebra. Now his soul "yearns for philosophy" and for enlightenment beyond what the small town of Zamosc can provide or his mentor can feed him through books on history, natural science, and psychology bought from travelers on market days. His spiritual hunger unsatiated, this remarkable young man seeks the enlightenment of a university education. But as Singer shows us, through Dr. Jacobi, a great many young gentiles also seek such enlightenment, and all educational doors are open only to them, not to aspiring Jews like Asa. In this context, the supposedly cynical Shapiro's sudden interruptive enthusiasm seems baffling:

> "Then there's something to go on living for!" he cried out. "We still have Torah, Jews, sages, enlightenment! And I, idiot that I am, thought that we were through. Come here, young man. You'll not eat your meal at the free kitchen tonight. . . . Tonight you'll eat at my house," he shouted. "I'm Abram Shapiro. Don't worry, it'll be kosher. Even if you want pork you'll get kosher food."[3]

Plainly the cynical Shapiro is a rampant idealist, a lover of learning old and new as the great Jewish gift, the knowledge and wisdom that the People of the Book might bring to the world. This slightly comical Father Abram is the secular sponsor, apparently, for the new Isaac, or his English (if not Yiddish) fictional anagram, Asa,[4] as the Tribe's best hope. The offer of kosher food indicates the same fond attachment to traditional Jewish forms as the basis for further extensions into modern forms of enlightened behavior that the young Asa seems to champion: he will unite and extend the old and new forms of learning and behavior that Abram now envisions as one gift. Actually he remains divided between these possibilities throughout the novel; like Abram himself, he remains a youthful idealist going nowhere, unable to choose between his religious heritage and its possible secular extensions, a small-time teacher of mathematics who never writes the book on philosophy he seems destined to produce. Nor does he ever get that university education he now seeks. The aging Dr. Jacobi is proved right: he doesn't have a chance in the prejudiced Polish world before the holocaust.

Meanwhile everybody loves him, especially women. He doesn't pursue them; they take him over, the brightest, the most beautiful, the most politically committed; they choose him for his promise, his mysteriously unfounded attractiveness as an irrational yeshiva boy who admires the rational Spinoza and likes making love to women. And he leaves one for another, can't choose between them, except as they choose him. At first he seems destined for the lovely Hadassah—until their elopement fails and she is forced into an arranged marriage to the unattractive but orthodox businessman, Fishel Kutner, whom the family patriarch had chosen for her. Then Asa marries the patriarch's new

3. *The Family Moskat,* 34–35. Further page references will be given in the text.

4. I owe this distinction to Professor of Yiddish Janet Hadda of UCLA, who tells me there is no such Yiddish anagram since Asa in that language is *Oyzer* and Isaac is *Yitskhok.*

stepdaughter, the bright but unattractive Adele Landau; or rather she marries him and has his first child—until Hadassah pulls him back for what seems like a delayed predestined romance, and a second child is born into a second marriage. Then the restless Asa is pulled away once more by a pretty young Communist sympathizer, Barbara Fishelsohn, a converted Jew who has the good sense to leave Poland and "keep on fighting" the Nazis when Asa chooses to stay and die.

What is the point of Asa's attractiveness and of Abram's similarly attractive patronage? Why is the comic Abram so much more interesting in his attractiveness than his moody, brooding protégé, who is the novel's apparent hero? Indeed, the novel's most touching moment comes when the dying Abram asks Asa to kiss him and, raising his arms to Asa's shoulders, murmurs, "I believe in God. . . . I die a Jew" (550), as if drawing a blessing for himself from his misplaced belief in his own protégé.

It should be acknowledged that at such moments Singer touches not just the Jewish but the human heart. Irving Buchen seems to me right, in *Isaac Bashevis Singer and the Eternal Past,* to emphasize the tension between secular rebellion and religious seeking as Singer's greatest strength, and the source therefore of such bittersweet moments; but then contradictory tensions like these are the source of every writer's strength. What matters is that the rebellious Abram now shows his protégé how he too must die; for as Buchen argues, this is the way that Asa eventually follows.[5] He abandons the illusions of secular seeking, comes back to Warsaw as the Nazis approach, and accepts Death as his Messiah. In that sense he too dies a Jew. Indeed, in the original Yiddish version, he even finds spiritual comfort from that decision through his return to the old religious forms.[6]

I would like to suggest, however, that the novel is appealing in that it shows us how to live as a Jew, even in the face of cultural disintegration, as well as how to die as one, and that Abram is attractive because, as Asa himself concludes, he was a brave man who "knew how to live and how to die." Indeed, he "still had in him those juices which nourished the people in all the dark hours they had endured. He was a Jew biologically" (562). It also seems to me vital, in this context, that Abram is a happy adulterer, that he loves women without resentment and doesn't blame them for the complications that his own infidelities inevitably entail. Indeed, he brings to his infidelities the same generous enthusiasm he shows for Asa's possibilities, his unearned and ultimately unrealized strengths as the Jewish savior, the young man who goes to Warsaw to leaven "the divine truths" (21) of Torah study with still more secular wisdom.

---

5. *Singer and the Eternal Past,* 5, 12–13, 47.

6. For this distinction, see Max F. Schulz, "The Family Chronicle as Paradigm of History: *The Brothers Ashkenazi* and *The Family Moskat,*" 90.

This biological Jew has a distinct advantage, then, over his aspiring protégé, an anomaly well worth pondering. For not only does the moody Asa seem somewhat lacking in Jewish juices, he also resents the women whom he variously honors or desires; he holds their restrictions on his freedom against them, quarrels often with all of them, and even beats his first and greatest love. Indeed, his ambivalence toward women—a problem that Singer is honest enough to record in full as a kind of novelistic self-criticism—is not unlike his ambivalence toward those "divine truths" that religious learning and secular enlightenment seem to conjoin.

I want to abstract this problem now from its novelistic context and examine it in the light of its intertextual implications, its relation to other works by Singer and to the author's similar problem elsewhere of ambivalence toward his women characters. I want to ask questions about the special privileges the author grants to his youthful embodiment in Asa Hashel Bannet. He makes no bones, for instance, about Asa's bad performance as a husband and a father; but he oddly grants him a kind of exemption from these normally appealing roles. Apparently he is not cut out for domestic servitude; he is given the male privilege of self-definition, or the search for self-definition, which Singer sadly denies to his female characters. They are obliged to find themselves as wives and mothers and are given little or no heroic cast when they decide to define themselves otherwise. As several commentators have noted, the result of female experimentations along these lines is usually disastrous in Singer's tales, as for instance with "Yentl the Yeshiva Boy" and "Zeitl and Rickel." Perhaps Asa's experiments might also be said to end disastrously, but not, I think, if he decides courageously to die like a Jew.

One of the previously remarked privileges Asa enjoys is that of beating his wife, Hadassah, or perhaps I should say that he shares this privilege with his wife: they strike each other during their developing marital quarrels (534). The point is that Singer presents their violent quarrels as a normally shared part of marital conflict. Although Asa is stronger than Hadassah, and although their quarrels obviously stem from his desire to be elsewhere, it is all a matter of even steven, two people struggling against each other in violation of traditional wisdom on marital restraint and mutual respect: the woman is as much to blame as the man. That too is part of traditional wisdom, which generally goes further to suggest that she is even more to blame, or that she should provide the model for male conduct and has conspicuously failed to do so. Indeed, what Singer stresses, through Asa, are Hadassah's expensive ways, her nagging fears of losing Asa, and her incipient madness, which more than match Asa's "sullen rages" and continuing unrest.

This is what is wrong with Irving Buchen's otherwise generous conclusion: "Singer values the traditional subservience of women not because he is a male chauvinist or wishes to perpetuate the evil image of Eve but because that capacity [in women] for dependence and surrender created a model for men."[7] The statement is generous, that is to say, to Singer, and to men, but not to women: they are stuck with the traditional role of moral guide for both sexes and therefore subject to special criticism for abandoning it.

But Hadassah has not altogether abandoned it. Although she has left her first husband, she hasn't left Asa and in fact "depends" on him and "surrenders" to him and to the chores of wifehood and motherhood. So too has the mannish intellectual Adele Landau, Asa's first wife. If anything, she is now more devoted to traditional family ways than Hadassah. These women have kept the marriage covenant, at least with Asa; if they sometimes begrudge his rebellious ways, they accept the male privileges that go with them and continue to love him. Even Asa's neglect of his two children by these wives is largely forgiven: it is their traditional responsibility to raise them, not his. Nor have they better things to do, like study Torah or write books of philosophy or fiction.

Still there is something to be said for Asa's oscillations, whether with women or with learning. My coupling of philosophy and fiction above, for instance, was deliberate. I think they both function as part of Singer's stake in Asa as his privileged younger fictional self. Although he makes no attempt here, like Chaim Potok does in *My Name Is Asher Lev,* to argue for artistry as a rebellious extension of traditional Jewish learning, his case for Asa's philosophical aspirations is a narrative form of such rebellion, and Asa's oscillations between old and new forms of learning are very much like Singer's artistic oscillations between fictional rabbis and rebels, dybbuks and devils, lost and redeemable souls of any gender. The disruptive adoption of gentile ways, styles, fads, fashions, and ideas, and its tragic outcome in Poland, does not altogether discount the ongoing validity of extended learning as the Jews' contribution to the gentile world.

Indeed, *The Family Moskat* itself, as the first of Singer's works to be translated from Yiddish into English, is decidedly one such contribution. Like all the translations that follow, it breaks the illusion of a totally Jewish audience for Singer's fictions and insists on their inherent universality. They have always been aimed at a wider audience, at humanity itself, as Jewish life conveys it, and cannot accordingly be passed off as modern forms of communal fragmentation and traditional disruption—or as assimilationist "poison," as Singer's father once called such modern Yiddish tales.[8] To record social disintegration and decline, as in *The Family Moskat,* is not to create and sustain it, but to demonstrate rather how men and women confront it, and by that same token how they embrace its contradictions and oscillations and learn from them how to live and how to die.

7. *Singer and the Eternal Past,* 128.
8. Ibid., 7, 30.

It must be in that sense that Hadassah's dream of Abram and Asa as "one and the same person" (158) offers a key to the novel's bittersweet affirmations: their related lives and deaths are narrative revelations, as it were, of surviving Jewish values, secular activations of traditional Jewish learning that Singer refuses to discount. It is Singer himself, moreover, as Asa's prototype and survivor, who salvages these transvalued forms of secularism from the novel's larger indictment, its great satiric panorama of social disintegration and increasing communal disruption of Jewish life in the face of the coming holocaust.

At this point I must forgo those similarly bittersweet moments in tales such as "Gimpel the Fool," "The Little Shoemakers," "Sabbath in Portugal," and "The New Year Party" and their seesaw affirmations of old and new values. I must turn from these familiar triumphs of Singer's artistry to the singularities of his gender problematics. More specifically, I must ask about those odd comparisons, in *The Family Moskat,* between happy and unhappy, selfish and unselfish, callous and caring forms of adultery, as exemplified by the three chief sons-in-law, Abram, Asa, and the former family business manager, the unscrupulous Koppel Berman, who seems even less redeemable than his fellow Jewish adulterers and may well function as Singer's test case for judging them. But why has Singer made some of his best stories out of extramarital conundrums? Why are there almost no real love stories in his fictions that are not adulterous?

In one sense, of course, all love stories in our romantic literature are by definition adulterous: these are the terms set long ago by the courtly love tradition itself; and in modern times, these are the terms also of Freud's erotic version of the family romance. Psychology and cultural history support our recurrent interest in eternal triangles. But Singer's personal stake in such triangles is what I'm after now: the familiar mix of guilt and attraction, sensuality and resentment, and, above all, lurking hostility that his own infidelities and desertions have fostered and that become the secret story of the author's stake in his own fictions that here concerns us. We have already asked why Lilith and Satan are, respectively, his favorite literary bedfellow and narrative persona, and now we have an intertextual trail to follow that may help us to find the answer. We begin, then, with a later story about Asa Heshel Bannet in Poland called "The Witch," from the collection called *Passions,* first published in 1975.

II

Strictly speaking, the nominal hero of this story, Mark Meitels, is not another Asa, but an abstraction of some of his traits and experiences, an austerely selective version of the author's youthful self. Thus, like Asa and Isaac, he is a teacher of mathematics and physics at a private school, in this case a girls' gymnasium. Less imaginative than the young Yiddish writer Isaac, he nonetheless supplements his meager income by writing textbooks on the side for Polish schools; like Asa (and Isaac's brother Israel Joshua), he has also served as an officer in the 1920 Polish/Bolshevik war. Now, in Warsaw in the 1930s, he is largely alienated from the surrounding Polish world and like his predecessors lives chiefly in the modern Jewish community. There he excels like Asa in all things intellectual, and all his pupils love him dearly: but unlike the sensual Asa/Isaac, he is saved by his military discipline and his secular asceticism and avoids all sexual indiscretions. Nonetheless he is stuck like Asa in a bad marriage and wants to get out.

The story begins with a critique of his wife's dazzling vanity. It is a familiar critique. Singer has already worked out the terms for it in a story written circa 1950, "The Mirror," in which one of Satan's imps lures a vain woman to her deadly fate by playing on her female vanities. In "The Witch" that imp is replaced by the scarcely unprejudiced Mark Meitels, from whose point of view the whole story unfolds. Thus, in a "culture of pure egotism," his wife, Lena, still seems to him a remarkable narcissist, a bedazzling case of extreme self-love. Like David Copperfield's childish Dora, Lena still looks at thirty-seven like the young girl Mark first knew, and whom he then made the "fatal mistake" of marrying. But however childish, Dora was at least affectionate, while Lena is an altogether self-centered woman, a kind of Old World predecessor of those shallow Jewish princesses satirized by popular American writers. In this popular vein she tells Mark not to disarrange her hairdo or wrinkle her silk nightgown in bed, sees sexual intercourse as "dirty and brutal," and urges him to get it over with quickly and without hurting her.

Again like Dickens's Dora the childless, girlish, self-loving Lena soon dies an unexpected death. But here the urban satire on female egoism takes an equally unexpected folkish turn. Her nominal death by melanoma is actually caused by witchcraft. An infatuated student from her husband's private school has cast a deadly spell upon her, and will now cast an erotic one on Mark. Those mysterious attractions that Mark shares with Asa Heshel Bannet have worked for his blessed release from a sterile marriage! Once more the passive hero is freed from one woman by another woman's magnetic love. But in this later and in some ways wiser tale the magnet is peculiarly erotic and peculiarly revealing of the author's secret self.

Thus the infatuated student, a girl who calls herself Bella, but who is exceptionally ugly, comes from a poor family from the Warsaw ghetto, where orthodox male Jews in beards and ringlets make surreptitious deals while their wives in wigs and bonnets sell rotten fruit. The enlightened Mark, raised by an assimilated father, knows nothing of their orthodox ways; but he is now introduced to an erotic component that tells much about Hasidic joys and terrors. Through the witchlike Bella he is initiated into throes of passion he had never even imagined with Lena. In this sense her ugliness functions like that of the spinster Black Dobbe in "The Spinoza of Market Street," a tall lean woman "as black as a baker's shovel," with a broken nose and a mustache on her upper lip, who wears men's shoes and speaks with a man's hoarse voice. This unlikely seducer brings the ailing and impotent Spinoza disciple, Dr. Fischelson, back to life, marriage, and erotic potency, through what he himself describes as a form of witchcraft. The even homelier Bella, with a head too big for her body, a sunken brow, black bulging calf's eyes, curved nose, large bosom, wide hips, bowed legs, whom the other schoolgirls call Freak, is even more effective in reviving the ascetic Mark Meitels from his depression at his wife's death. Indeed, his thoughts turn to Bella, presumably through her witchcraft, to the exclusion of prettier, abler, and more popular students, and he begins to imagine her stripped naked in her loathsome yet somehow primitively appealing ugliness. He then longs obsessively to see her, as if possessed by a dybbuk, invites her over when she calls to express her sympathy, and is so roused when she confesses that, unlike the sterile Lena, she wants to have children and "would do anything for Teacher," that he commits what may be the most autobiographically revealing act in Singer's fiction:

> "Do you love me that much?"
> "More than anything in the world."
> "More than your parents?"
> "Much more"
> "Why?"
> "Oh, I don't know. Because Teacher is wise and I'm a dumb cow. When Teacher smiles, it's so interesting, and when he is stern he draws up his brows and everything is somehow so—" She didn't finish. Heat emanated from her, the warmth one feels occasionally standing next to a horse.
> Mark asked, "Can I do with you what I want?"
> "Anything."
> "Slit your throat?" he asked, astounded at his own words.
> Bella trembled. "Yes, the blood would gush and I'd kiss the blade . . ."
> He was overcome by a lust such as he hadn't felt in years, perhaps never. "Don't do anything stupid!" an inner voice warned. "Send her straight home!" Aloud he said, "Good, I'm going for the knife."[9]

He goes to the kitchen for a knife as if playing an earnest game, then returns to face "the pagan ecstasy," the frightening eagerness, that exudes from her:

9. "The Witch," in *Passions and Other Stories,* 125. Further page references will be given in the text.

> He said, "Bella, you'll soon be dead. Say what you have to say."
> "I love you."
> "Are you ready to die?"
> "Yes, ready."
> He put the blade to her throat. "Shall I slash?"
> "Yes."
> Mark put the knife down deliberately on the dresser. He recalled the story from the Bible in which God ordered Abraham to slay his son Isaac and the Angel cried out: "Lay not thy hand upon the lad . . ." It was all like a repetition of something that had happened before. (125–26)

As this remarkable signature story indicates, Singer is discovering something about himself, "something that had happened before." The sudden desire to murder this ugly young woman taps into his own hostilities; its conscious expression helps him to release himself from *their* magical hold upon his heart. The Angel that had spared the biblical Isaac from a jealous father's wrath now spares this fictive woman from the writer Isaac's accumulated resentments of rejection at the hands of other prettier women, from the uncleanness that he remarks upon elsewhere as an orthodox rationale for women's servile and secondary role—and from the orthodox fear of women's beauty upon which he altogether fails to remark. Bella is in this sense only the other half of Lena: the visually beautiful but selfish woman who denies love is also the safely ugly but unclean woman with whom love must be consummated. Only now Meitels learns still another lesson about love.

Although Singer is by no means D. H. Lawrence, he affirms here what Lawrence elsewhere affirms, the difference between visual and sensual beauty, between appearance and touch, and the transfigurative power also of tactile sensual love, by which Bella becomes more and more attractive as her primitive and emotional self becomes more evident to her ascetic Teacher's senses. Thus, after she confesses to putting the curse of a rival lover upon his wife, a curse Lena herself half guesses before she dies, and after he insults her and dismisses her, then demands that she become his mistress, they make passionate love until three that morning. As Bella dresses to go home, Mark muses:

> A witch, a witch! Mark said to himself. He wouldn't have believed that this young girl, and a virgin besides, could fall into such a frenzy. She had clawed at his flesh, bitten his shoulders, spoke strange words, and cried in such a wild voice that he was afraid it might rouse his neighbors. He had sworn to marry her. "How could this happen? Have I lost my mind? Can there really be such a thing as black magic?" (129)

As if in answer to that question Mark begins to seesaw. He fears ridicule, thinks he has probably impregnated her, tries to back out, calls her back when she threatens suicide, offers to run off with her, then pulls her back to the bedroom, where they stand together half naked, staring into a mirror as the true answer comes in the final lines:

> He said, "If there is such a thing as black magic, maybe there's a God too."
> He couldn't wait to get to the bedroom and pushed her down onto the rug—a witch drenched in blood and semen, a monster that the rising sun had transformed into a beauty. (132)

Lawrence would have liked that rising sun. The blood and semen are signs, of course, of the unclean woman Mark has now embraced. The approach to God by way of black magic is our clue to Singer's need to empathize with the devil. Finally, that dropped knife back in midscene, like the mirror in this final moment, is a link with still other stories about actual wife killers. To which we now turn.

III

Strictly speaking, Singer himself is the great wife killer. Like George Eliot's Angel of Death, the authorial power that kills off abusive male villains, Singer dispatches vain women with a punishment that seems rather incommensurate with their crimes. In "The Witch" he allows Bella to dispatch Lena, then grants the relieved Mark Meitels only a moment's distress at making love to his vain wife's apparent murderer. In "The Mirror," as already noted, he adopts the persona of the satanic imp behind the mirror who lures the narcissistic heroine, Zirel, to her death and eternal punishment, all for the crime of admiring herself naked at night before an attic mirror and imagining romantic lovers who might rescue her from her rich, indulgent husband.

Needless to say, the imp admires her nakedness too, in that modest sensual detail that Singer introduced into modern Yiddish fiction, and that he too presumably enjoys punishing, if only by way of Lilith and her staff of female demons, who "really enjoy" tormenting Zirel once she arrives in hell.[10] One suspects that Singer arranges such torments, not because he abhors sensual egoism and real or imagined betrayals, but because like one of Steinbeck's paisano characters, Petey Ravanno in *Tortilla Flat,* he is so disturbed by such elusive women that he wants to cut them open to get at that withheld thing inside them.[11] So too with Mark Meitels, his knife ostensibly aimed at Bella's throat, but possibly also at those unclean passageways for blood and semen inside both

10. "The Mirror," in *Gimpel the Witch and Other Stories,* 87.
11. John Steinbeck, *Tortilla Flat,* 119.

Lena and Bella. This is the problem, I take it, that the seventy-year-old Singer finally resolves by gender identification in his late fantastic story, "The Witch."

Let me pause here to insert some helpful information. Singer had been introduced to the idea of the wife killer by his brother Israel Joshua, who had read to him from his first great novel, *Yoshe Kalb,* even before its publication in 1933. That novel opens with a richly ambivalent portrait of a lusty wife killer, Rabbi Melech of Nyesheve, who has lost three wives and now hopes to marry a fourth. Since his daughters have read in popular Yiddish books "that a Jewish daughter must not marry a man who has buried three wives, for he is known as a *Katlan*—a wife-killer,"[12] they believe that their father will never remarry. The rabbi refuses to be ruled by this folk superstition, however. He soon marries a young virgin, his unhappy bride becomes pregnant by his young son-in-law, made even more unhappy by his own forced marriage at fourteen to the rabbi's daughter Serele, and the rabbi's bride dies in childbirth. The twice-stricken son-in-law then becomes the wandering Yoshe Kalb.

As we shall see, Isaac Bashevis Singer would place his own fictional son-in-law, the adulterous foolish philosopher Asa, at one remove from his fictional parents' unhappy forced marriage at fourteen. He would be similarly selective, in following his brother's precedents, in dealing with his own fictional wife killers. He seems quite ambivalent, for instance, about the unkosher ritual slaughterer, Reb Gedaliya, in his first novel, *Satan in Goray,* which was also published in 1933; and about Pelte "The Wife Killer" some twenty-four years later in the story of that name. Thus Reb Gedaliya, a disciple of the false messiah Sabbatai Zevi, performs "wonders" among the townspeople of seventeenth-century Goray, salving birth pains, restoring speech to a frightened child, resolving relational conflicts, saving lost souls, promoting marriages, and even promising an edenic future when polygamy and free love will be possible and the evils of unclean menstruation will cease. He becomes especially popular with women, who note only that he is a widower, and therefore available, not that he has just buried "his fourth wife."[13] He will be instrumental also in burying the village heroine, the visionary epileptic Rechele, who becomes his mistress, is variously invaded by Satan and a vengeful dybbuk, and dies during a long and lewdly detailed exorcism procedure as the novel ends.

Although Gedaliya is then flogged and chained to a post in jail, he escapes to pursue his deceitful work. Meanwhile the author too has given us his own thoroughly mixed message about that work, his own narrative indulgence in the same deceitful attractions to false messianic hopes. This is the first of the

12. *Yoshe Kalb,* 14–15.

13. *Satan in Goray,* 150. Further page references will be given in the text.

Lilith/Satan stories in which Singer adopts that ambivalent point of view, often quite literally through first-person narration by Satan or one of his lesser demons. The little-known tale "The Wife Killer" seems accordingly like a satanic extract transferred into the more comfortably superstitious folktale world. For Pelte too has lost four wives, and Singer treats him also with an odd protective sympathy throughout the tale.

Thus, for what may be the first if not the last time in his fiction, the tale is narrated by a woman, almost as if Singer wanted to deflect its sexist implications from himself. She begins with a mixture of matter-of-fact shrewdness and oddly pious generosity:

> I am from Turbin, and there we had a wife killer. Pelte was his name, Pelte the Wife Killer. He had four wives and, may it not be held against him, he sent them all off to the other side. What women saw in him, I don't know. He was a little man, thickset, gray, with a scraggly beard and bulging bloodshot eyes. Merely to look at him was frightful. And as for his stinginess—you never saw anything like it. Summer and winter he went about in the same padded caftan and rawhide boots. Yet he was rich. He had a sizable brick house, a storeroom full of grain, and property in town. He had an oak chest which I remember to this day. It was covered with leather and bound with copper hoops, for protection in case of fire. To keep it safe from thieves, he had it nailed to the floor. It was said that he kept a fortune in it. All the same, I cannot understand how a woman could go to the bridal canopy with such a man.[14]

From the female narrator's final vivid memory of that oak chest nailed to the floor, back to her oddly pious opening wish that the death of four wives should not be held against this blatant abuser, we have a subtle enough introduction to the powerful appeal, the attractive repulsion, of Pelte's frightfully mixed charms, in all of which he resembles still another folkish character noted for his cruelty to wives and sweethearts, Dostoyevsky's Fyodor Karamazov. Thus Fyodor too is frightfully ugly, well-to-do, and extremely stingy. More telling, his appetite for extremely young women is also one that Pelte shares. As the narrator now indicates, Pelte's first two wives were a poor orphan girl with no dowry and a penniless widow of eighteen. Although we never learn how the first wife dies, the fate of the second may explain it: after falling head over heels in love with her, Pelte is said to have shamed her unmercifully through perverse and buffoonlike behavior, pretending at the synagogue for instance that his beloved wife has chased him out of his own house. As the narrator puts it, "he drove her to the grave with his tantrums" (47/347).

---

14. "The Wife-Killer: A Folk Tale," 45–46/346. Further page references will be given in the text, with the first number referring to the edition listed in the bibliography and the second to the reprinting of the story below.

Apparently he applies the same kind of zany Dostoyevskian spitefulness to his third wife, a rich widow named Finkl. Although she is "the most beautiful woman in town, and of the very best family," he torments her with moods of black melancholy, particularly after she miscarries their first child. Three years later she dies without changing her will, leaving him with her property.

Now the richest man in Turbin, and soon the most ruthless money-grubber, Pelte attracts the attention of a worthy rival, Zlateh the Bitch, a fishmonger's feisty widow, herself a valiant Husband Killer. At this point the folktale may be said to reveal its apparently misogynous or perhaps one should say its traditional gender mission. Pelte has been a nasty husband with his first three wives, but not a violent one; his abuse has been emotional rather than physical, passively rather than actively aggressive, and though many say that such abuse is worse, it leads more magically than convincingly to the reported deaths in this folkish tale, with more in the way of telling than showing. The interesting turn now is the reversal of Pelte's role from persecutor to victim, and Singer's mildly comic collusion in the resultant shift of sympathy.

Thus the entire community concludes that Zlateh the Bitch is worse than Pelte the Wife Killer when it comes to dunning other people for payments and threatening communal welfare: "Then people realized that it isn't wise to wish for a new king" (58/354). Similarly, when Zlateh uses a charm from the witch Cunegunde to win the domestic war with Pelte, the female narrator is so liberal with the graphic details of Zlateh's abuse of Pelte, and so vivid in her description of Pelte's abject surrender, that we are persuaded to consider Zlateh the greater domestic beast and to join the townsfolk in spirit when they look to Pelte for help against her oppressive ways. Ultimately, of course, she is so obsessed with Pelte's power as a wife killer that she dies in her moment of triumph, the ironic victim of her own obsessive fears; and then Pelte interestingly says Kaddish for her and becomes a vegetarian, an idle and apparently embittered loner, indifferent to his wealth, living to the age of one hundred, outliving everything and everybody, and leaving after him only "a heap of dust" (63/356).

By my own count, this parting view of the Wife Killer and his supposedly empty fate contains three or four elements that Singer himself is known to favor: vegetarianism, cultivated pessimism, indifference to wealth, and unobtrusive pieties. These parallels with his known preferences raise some interesting questions. Has Singer quietly redeemed his deadly hero—or, at the least, let him suffer for and outlive, and thereby pay for his marital and economic crimes? Or is all this really in keeping with an empty fate?

Similar and perhaps more helpful questions can be posed by placing "The Wife Killer" back into the context from whence it came. Four other tales from *Gimpel the Fool and Other Stories,* for instance, also involve the powers of

Lilith and her devilish supporters, three of them literally told by devils—"The Gentleman from Cracow," "The Mirror" (on which we have already commented), "From a Diary of One Not Born," and "The Unseen." In all these tales the gleeful agents of Satan and Lilith bring various forms of sexual and emotional discord and destruction into the lives of Jewish villagers; in "The Gentleman from Cracow," as in *Satan in Goray,* a whole town is destroyed by induced sexual frenzy at Lilith's specific instigation. Why, we may ask again, does Singer demonize Lilith? Why does he so often choose to play devil's advocate himself, as the satanic narrator of these related tales, for such deadly sexist pleasures? Does he most enjoy the pleasures or their punishments? Does he ask his readers to join him in such vicarious enjoyments, or to see their own propensities for them by sharing them himself? Let us pause for some considered answers.

IV

There is a familiar view of such matters that seems to apply here. It is customary, in many fictions, first to allow readers to have fun with sinners from a slightly removed vantage point, then to let them enjoy the sinners' comeuppance—as for instance with Edith Wharton's frustrated country lovers in *Ethan Frome,* who get their earthly punishment when they try for a last suicidal sled ride together. These grim but would-be happy adulterers are then placed under the wronged wife's watchful care for the rest of their miserable crippled lives. I've never much liked Edith Wharton for taking us through that painfully sensual sequence, but it is not unlike the perverse sequential enjoyments that Singer arranges for us in these and similar tales. We may take it then as a common artistic process, almost a literary convention; or we may push a little further.

In "The Witch" we have allowed, for instance, for a more positive answer: "If there is such a thing as black magic, maybe there's a God too." We have suggested that this is Singer's backdoor policy for approaching God, the positive thrust of his negative choices: he adopts the devil's point of view, or the witch's, to prove that the world makes religious sense after all, that miraculous irrational forces exist that must have been put there by a God in whom it is otherwise rationally impossible to believe. The energy of his rational heroes—the Spinoza disciples Asa Heshel Bannet in *The Family Moskat* and Dr. Fischelson in "The Spinoza of Market Street"; the gentile Schopenhauer disciple Dr. Yaretzky in "The Shadow of a Crib"—is directed toward rational proofs of a godless or man-centered world. Even the doubting and disillusioned rabbi of "Something Is There" has to accept that commonsense approach to faith implied by the title as wiser than his previous learning. Does God exist? All the energy and weight of rational evidence belong on the negative side of that philosophical question: but the irrational hunches, the black magic, the dybbuk's electrifying presence, and the archly satanic narrations imply that something else is indeed there, behind them all, at least for Singer and persuaded readers. There is a positive stake, then, in Singer's world, in taking us through these perversely negative experiences.

The urgency of pursuing that stake is further dramatized, in Singer's world, by communal breakdown and disaster. Singer's awareness of the imminence of such disaster was evident enough in his first novel, *Satan in Goray.* During his four youthful years in the small village of Bilgoray, the nearby town of Goray had fascinated him as the site in the seventeenth century of a takeover by disciples of the false messiah Sabbatai Zevi. The novel begins, appropriately, with the peasant uprisings of 1648–1658, in which Jews in the Goray region were massacred by the Ukrainian chief Bogdan Chmelnicki and his followers: "They slaughtered on every hand, flayed men alive, murdered small children, violated women and afterwards ripped open their bellies and sewed cats inside" (3). Towns and villages were razed and their scattered inhabitants were elsewhere enslaved or forced to convert to Christianity. Some hundred thousand Jews were said to have died during that bloody decade. Then, sixteen years later, after the deserted towns had been rebuilt, expectations of the imminent coming of the Messiah were raised by cabalistic predictions of "the end of days," based on the biblical notion that the Messiah would appear soon after the Battle of Armageddon.

Singer took the atmosphere of religious hysteria that followed as his fictional métier. He created a fable of the town's conversion by cabalistic swindlers like Reb Gedaliya and his local predecessors into a religious bedlam, and as we have seen, he indulged in a kind of sympathetic identification with the sensual follies of the new messianic dispensation. There is some evidence that, like Asa Heshel Bannet and Reb Gedaliya, he once believed himself in loveless sexual freedom as the only path to "divine truths" like the future banishment of the evils of menstruation.[15] But of course the fable runs to its grim conclusion and allows us to enjoy, as already indicated, the punishments meted out to the foolish believers in the false messiah, the dupes as well of Satan and Lilith. As Singer notes in the italicized preface to the final chapter, this punishment is the exemplary lesson, the curiously modern moral, of his quaintly medieval text, a lesson that history would soon reinforce (219–20).

But whatever its modern reinforcements, this prescient fiction seems to me to betray at every point Singer's personal stake in an admonitory sequence and

15. Buchen, *Singer and the Eternal Past,* 72, 79.

is thus exemplary also of the risks and hazards of his ongoing private struggles. Singer's father had been a cabalist writer, and Singer himself was early drawn to cabalistic studies. In *Satan in Goray* he submitted such inclinations to secular scrutiny and criticized their historical irresponsibilities and appalling social consequences. But at the same time he seems to have found a way to indulge his attraction to those consequences, even while denouncing them. His early rebellion from his father took a more compromising turn than did his brother's more open rebellion and would continue in that seesaw direction.

Satan in Goray was soon followed by Singer's migration to America to join his older brother and shortly thereafter by the holocaust. In 1944, as if in keeping with that larger tragedy, Israel Joshua unexpectedly died. Then in 1945, as if in response to all these related events, Singer began writing *The Family Moskat.* It is hard not to see, in this novel and the tales that followed it, Singer's fictional struggle to cope with his own strong sense of guilt at escaping the holocaust, outliving his beloved brother, and surviving to appropriate their common subject. He had his own fate to work out, along with the fate of the Jewish people in prewar Poland; with his brother's death, he became the chief chronicler of that bygone time and place and, by that same token, the chief resolver of their common quarrel with their father's world.

It seems to me important, in this context, that Singer's brother was in many ways his mystical father's enlightened double. He had moved out of the family home at the age of twenty-one, in dramatic protest against his father's orthodox rigidities, and had established a kind of artist's atelier, which the young Isaac visited as the family go-between. There nude paintings and talkative young girls disturbed Singer's orthodox expectations and contributed to his own passive departure from the family in 1923, when, at the age of nineteen, he decided to stay in Warsaw while his father, mother, older sister, and younger brother moved to a small Polish town.

Shortly before that, however, Singer and his younger brother, Moishe, had gone to live with his mother in Bilgoray, from 1917 to 1921, when she herself left her husband behind, with Israel Joshua's assistance, ostensibly to renew early family connections. Irving Buchen has noted the importance of those four adolescent years to Singer's development, as well as the opposing pulls on his youthful sensibility of his mother's dreamy rationalism and his father's oddly practical mysticism;[16] but no one has noted that Singer and his younger brother were his mother's sole male companions, as if displacing their father during these crucial adolescent years. In *The Family Moskat* Asa's delicately reared father interestingly disappears, in what seems to be a fictional transformation of

16. Ibid., 5, 9.

this real-life episode, leaving Asa to be raised in a fatherless household as his mother's chief male darling. Asa's father too had returned to renew family ties, in this case with his own strong-minded mother, after his own cabalist father died, and had then sent back a bill of divorcement to his nineteen-year-old wife. Their traditionally arranged marriage at fourteen—like that of Israel Joshua Singer's Yoshe Kalb—had ended abruptly after an unhappy run of about five years.

Perhaps too much can be made of Singer's odd arrangement here, for an absent father and an absent God; but there is another pattern worth noting, that of withdrawal, withholding, and eventually walking away. Boys raised alone with their mothers sometimes learn to suppress their affections as a way of resisting too much enforced intimacy, and to become moody and withdrawn partners in later relationships with women—partners like Asa Heshel Bannet, whom Hadassah cannot reach when he pulls away into melancholy moods and sullen rages, and literally cannot reach after he walks away with another woman; or like Pelte the Wife Killer, whose pretended sufferings and black melancholy moods do in his first three wives. Among domestic violence counselors, such withdrawals are considered forms of passive aggression, while the relationship lasts, and are a familiar part of the pattern of emotional and physical abuse in most batterers. The actual battering that Singer records for such heroes is minimal, but the withdrawal pattern is decidedly maximal in both author and texts. How much it bothered Singer can be illustrated by one final example, "The Shadow of a Crib," which in many ways prefigures "The Witch" as a kind of trial run toward an emotional solution to the same set of problems, and which contains—as we shall see—a remarkable tribute to Singer's cabalistic father.

V

In this long tale a thoroughly skeptical Polish doctor decides to settle down in Zamosc, a town with a large Jewish population. Dr. Yaretzky is a gentile bachelor in his thirties; he is also a disciple of Schopenhauer, whose contemptuous view of women as the blind agents of the Will and Idea that control the world has further ensured his ongoing bachelorhood. All women want, he decides, is to get pregnant so the world may continue; all he wants is to exploit their desire, then leave them, and so evade their enslaving power. Thus, when a matchmaker tries to fix him up with a spinsterly maiden from a noble gentile family, something of a man-hater herself, Dr. Yaretzky asks insultingly, "Who sent you? . . . the mother or the daughter?" When the lady then invokes God and Jesus in her responses, he adds a few blasphemies about Jesus being "nothing but a lousy

Jew" and God not existing. When the poor woman asks, "Then what is there?" he tartly replies, "Worms. . . ."[17]

Word of these insults inevitably reaches the spinster, Helena, on her widowed mother's estate. Since her father has already disgraced the family by committing suicide, she feels doubly dishonored by her mother's apparent meddling with the matchmaker. Imagining herself as an avenging knight, she dreams up terrible tortures for Dr. Yaretzky. Then the narrator intrudes with a bit of helpful sexist wisdom:

> Who can understand the feminine soul? Even an angelic woman shelters within herself devils, imps, and goblins. The evil ones act perversely, mock human feelings, profane holiness. . . . It is all part of the perversity so characteristic of the female nature. (67)

Although Singer writes here with tongue in cheek, he half believes his concluding maxim, and now describes a ball at which Helena proves his point through shameful conduct. Thus the normally retiring Helena decides to go to this ball dressed to the nines, as if to show the insulting doctor what he's missing. When she sees the doctor surrounded by admiring maidens, however, her antagonism mysteriously dissolves and she asks to be introduced to him. But when he arrives and offers her his hand, she lifts it to her mouth, kisses it, and laughs strangely. Her mother chokes a scream, all others are struck dumb except the doctor, who quickly relates her perverse action to his own perversities: "If Mohammed does not come to the mountain, the mountain comes to Mohammed. . . . Since I neglected to kiss Lady Helena's hand, the Lady kissed mine"—and he proceeds to kiss her hand three times in turn, "twice on the glove and once on the exposed wrist" (72).

As we shall soon see, Helena's perverse kiss has broken through the doctor's long-held withholding pattern. Her sudden indication of her capacity for passionate devotion, like that of Bella in "The Witch," is the selfless model that errant privileged males must learn to follow. More immediately, Helena and her mother leave the ball as waves of scandalous misrule break out around them:

> Was she insane? Was she madly infatuated with him? Had someone bewitched her? The musicians came to life, as if revived by the indiscretion, and both orchestras began to play with renewed vigor. . . . A debauched mood infected everyone. Couples previously inhibited now danced into the corridors or the courtyard and openly embraced. If Helena could kiss Dr. Yaretzky's hand before everyone, what need was there for decorum? (72–73)

---

17. "The Shadow of a Crib," 65. Further references will be given in the text.

The scene recalls the general frenzy released in Cracow and Goray by Lilith and the devil's agents. Their mad misrule seems to extend to the catcalls that follow the fleeing women's carriage and to invest the mother's admonishment with peculiar force: "Wretched girl, what can you do now but dig a grave and lie down in it?" (73). Yet as Dr. Yaretzky also retreats from the ball to his office, and tries to account for what has happened, we begin to sense that the events of this tale are governed by a different ruling power:

> Obviously, Helena was madly in love with him, but to what end? . . . He had no desire to saddle himself with a wife, to become a father and to raise sons and daughters—to perpetuate all that absurdity. He had his share of money and affairs. . . . Long ago he had concluded that family life was a fraud, a swamp to mire fools—since deceit is as essential to women as violence is to men. It was not likely that Helena would deceive him, but of what use was she to him? (74)

He decides to ignore the incident. But when he tries to go to sleep his bafflement continues. "What is it she sees in me? Why is her love so strong?" he muses, then invokes his Schopenhauerian credo: "It's only that old urge to reproduce" (74). Yet when he decides to get up and take a walk, his feet are guided not by Will and Idea but by his own desire for a fuller and more meaningful life. He decides that the world's Will, like Schopenhauer himself, might also be endowed with intelligence. As if by the prodding of such a Will he arrives at the house of the town's rabbi.

The rabbi has been one of Dr. Yaretzky's patients. Although they have no common language, Yaretzky knows, from what other Jews have told him, that the rabbi is a genius, a man of vast erudition. Now, as Yaretzky looks in at his study window, the old man is "pouring [*sic*] over one of his theological volumes." To Yaretzky he seems "more spiritual than ever now . . . an ancient sage, both saint and philosopher—a Hebrew Socrates or Diogenes":

> "I'd give one hundred rubles to know what the old man is reading!" Yaretzky said to himself. "One thing is certain—he doesn't even know there's a ball tonight. . . . He may not even be aware that this is the Nineteenth Century. Surely he doesn't know that he's in Europe. He exists beyond time and space. . . ." If that were so, perhaps [he] could break through the categories of pure reason and conceive the thing-in-itself, that which is beyond phenomenon? (77)

Arrested by this scene of self-imposed isolation, Yaretzky takes it as characteristic of religious Jews, in their volunteer ghettos. By contrast, the assimilationist Jews, those "who did learn other languages and mingled with the Christians," were "bores" (78). These are the familiar terms, of course, of Singer's seesaw struggle with his cabalistic father, with whom he is about to make his fictional peace. In the same vein, he will also make his peace with the hierarchical system of marriage, which at its best offers mutual satisfaction to men and women who accept their designated roles.

Fittingly, the chapter that follows is called "A Scene of Love." As Yaretzky watches, the rabbi's ancient wife enters the study, picks up the chicken-feather fan from beside the samovar, and fans the coals that warm the rabbi's tea. Although the rabbi keeps his eyes on the book, his face seems to grow gentler as he half concentrates on his reading, half listens to his wife's movements. Yaretzky is stunned by this oriental display of "silent gratitude." He believes he has "witnessed a love-scene, an old, pious, love ritual between husband and wife" (78). Even more avidly, he sees now the possibility that "The thing-in-itself is not blind will, but a seeing will. . . . If this is so," he concludes, "everything has a purpose," his own actions now, Helena's kiss at the ball. He moves hastily away, possessed by a sense of wasted years, determined to change the last fourteen years of life allotted to him, then frightened by doubts and precautions.

Meanwhile his feet have taken him to the widow's estate on which Helena lives. There he pushes inside the gate, as if searching for something behind the house; and in the orchard where her father had committed suicide, he finds Helena lying in a shallow pit, the grave for herself her mother had commanded her to dig. Thrusting a finger safely down her windpipe, Dr. Yaretzky forces her to retch, then rouses the servants, pours milk down her throat, carries her to her bedroom, asks for her hand in marriage, and kisses her burned lips. She in turn kisses his hand for the second time that day.

The upshot of this sad but promising story is that Yaretzky gets cold feet at the prospect of marriage, skips town, and returns fourteen years later as a ghost who haunts the new rabbi's study, his face pressing in at the window. Later he is seen in the fields trying to lift some weight from the ground, and in the orchard behind the new doctor's house.

Behind the doctor's tragic retreat and ghostly reappearance we may posit several events: Israel Joshua Singer's break with his father's world at twenty-one, Isaac's break at nineteen, the Communist wife and son he left behind when he came to America, and his lifelong waverings as an Attractive Oscillator between faith and enlightenment. Behind Isaac's spectacular success as a Nobel Prize winner we may posit his adulterous relation in 1940 with a Jewish woman who left her husband to marry him and his sole repossession, after his brother's death in 1944, of the Polish Jewish past. In reaching America, in surviving the holocaust, in following his brother's leads, he was virtually reborn as a man and an artist. Indeed, he must have felt something like comfort as well as guilt in his survival of those communal and personal disasters—something like the rabbi's silent gratitude in "The Shadow of a Crib." The saving generosity of his finest fictions began then, in the late 1940s, and not before, and his ongoing capacity to work out his personal burdens of guilt and hostility may be attributed to that fortunately mixed heritage of disaster and survival.

VI

It seems to me important, in this light, that there is no question of withdrawal in Mark Meitels's final decision to run off with Bella and to pursue God's existence through black magic. This is more or less what Singer has done, and what he also discovers about himself in this story. This is also what he does, and what he almost discovers, in those several bittersweet moments, already mentioned, that characterize the endings of his greatest tales. In "Gimpel the Fool," for instance, we have the grounds for sexist complaint in his portrait of Gimpel's wife, a woman who continually deceives him with other men, but whom he continues to "believe" in spite of what he secretly knows to be the truth. Only a writer who knows his own capacity for betraying women can grant to this "slut"—as one critic sees her—the possibility of overcoming their common weakness and doing justice to her foolish husband's faith. That kind of saving generosity seems to me to cancel out the nominal sexism here and allow the hero his uplifting movement from faith in a female betrayer who fails him to faith in a God who honors his generous self-delusions and perhaps in that sense—at least in Singer's eyes—transcends the holocaust.

Similarly, in "The Little Shoemakers," the father's unflagging devotion to a bygone craft becomes the means for reuniting the family in America when his assimilated sons adopt his exemplary devotion as a kind of binding value. In "Sabbath in Portugal" the author's haunting re-creation of the tenor of his first great love for a Jewish girl in Poland is generously sustained by the closing line about the holocaust in which she nominally perished—"They never died." Finally, in "The New Year Party," Singer's capacity to see the sustaining love of a shunned survivor of what seems to have been a mildly homoerotic devotion to a vainly selfish and apparently bisexual man strikes me as a tribute to his own sustaining love for his dead elder brother, a much better man, apparently, but one for whom he too sets a kind of belated fictional gravestone with this story.

It was, after all, Israel Joshua Singer who saved Isaac's life by first breaking with the family, then inviting Isaac to follow him to America, then leaving him the imaginative inheritance of their common past. It was Israel Joshua who served as Abraham to his brother's Isaac and spared him for the life ahead. This seems to me the essential source for Mark Meitels's recollection of that Bible story in "The Witch," at the point where Singer himself finally overcomes his hostility and repugnance toward vain and ugly women by recognizing his own vanities and betrayals, his own need to devote himself unselfishly to a loving woman—something he failed to do in private life, by the way, even in his American marriage, according to his son Israel Zamir's recent testimony,[18] but something that he nevertheless succeeds in doing in his finest stories. Indeed, their saving generosity seems to me the great legacy of his fictional oscillations, and remains so, I think, even in the face of his deliberate soft-pedaling, at least in his later years, of the repressive side of patriarchal orthodoxy while at the same time honoring its more commendable restraints.

Unlike Israel Joshua, that is to say, who could conceive of rabbis who were in fact wife killers and proponents of too-early marriages for their own convenience, Isaac created a fair number of decent, wise, sweet-natured rabbis, rather like his studious father—men sometimes baffled like the rest of us, but men who are inconceivably responsible for the controlling violence and subordination of a religious system that finds women unclean, fears their seductive beauty, and perpetuates unchecked fertility in marriage as part of its sharply hierarchical view of married and religious roles. With Isaac, perhaps because of the frightening losses and bafflingly triumphant evils that accompanied his own liberating enlightenment, the memory of saving rabbinical restraints seemed more vital to retain than that of rabbinical repressions. In that light he was able to preserve the best of the lost Euro-Jewish past, to cope over time with his own shortcomings, and to help us all to deal more humanely and insightfully with that other and more troubling religious legacy which—unlike his more radical older brother—he chose to underplay.

What I have been tracing, then, is an imperfect but in many ways an admirable success story, a lifelong struggle to bring together in imperfect union his own attractive oscillations between faith and enlightenment, past and present knowledge and behavior. In working out the passional implications of "The Witch" in 1975, the early and indulgent depicter of cabalistic swindles—the early quarreler with his father's world—had finally justified his confused imitations of the old masters of perverse religious affirmations; he had finally created an arrested moment of transcendent cabalism. Until that moment his affirmations of the similarly arrested affections glimpsed in the rabbi's midnight study in "The Shadow of a Crib" were inadequate; the peace of affection with his father's world was only partial: the old sex-affection split fostered by the hierarchical view of marriage within that world remained unhealed. He would continue his inevitable withholdings and withdrawals as his mystical father's and his rational mother's oscillating son. But once he had faced up to those repressive aspects of the old hierarchical system, once he had worked out the hostilities and the violence and the subjugations that it plainly fostered in himself, he could bring

18. See Zamir's brief memoir, *Journey to My Father,* esp. chap. 10, "The Thief of Love," 84–94.

body and soul together in cabalistic love. The withdrawals from affection and commitment of "The Shadow of a Crib" would never altogether stop, whether in his life or in his fictions; but at least in "The Witch," where unruly male passions are directly confronted, embraced, and satisfied, and where the male need for power, control, and possession through violence is carefully set aside, he could arrest and transcend his lifelong oscillations with exemplary grace. It is that impressive struggle with himself, and with his troubling heritage, that helps the rest of us to deal more humanely and insightfully with the continuing repressions in our time that the old religious legacy set going, along with its saving restrictions—at least in the field of domestic violence.

The Wife Killer

A FOLK TALE

by Isaac Bashevis Singer

I

I am from Turbin, and there we had a wife killer. Pelte was his name, Pelte the Wife Killer. He had four wives and, may it not be held against him, he sent them all off to the other side. What women saw in him, I don't know. He was a little man, thickset, gray, with a scraggly beard and bulging bloodshot eyes. Merely to look at him was frightful. And as for his stinginess—you never saw anything like it. Summer and winter he went about in the same padded caftan and rawhide boots. Yet he was rich. He had a sizable brick house, a storeroom full of grain, and property in town. He had an oak chest which I remember to this day. It was covered with leather and bound with copper hoops, for protection in case of fire. To keep it safe from thieves, he had it nailed to the floor. It was said that he kept a fortune in it. All the same, I cannot understand how a woman could go to the bridal canopy with such a man. The first two wives at least had the excuse that they came from poor homes. The first one—poor soul may you live long—was an orphan, and he took her just as she was, without any dowry. The second one, on the other hand—may she rest in peace—was a widow without a cent to her name. She didn't have even an undershirt, if you'll pardon the expression. Today people talk of love. They think that once upon a time men were angels. Nonsense. Clumsy creature that he was, he fell head over heels in love with her, so that all Turbin snickered. He was already a man in his forties and she was a mere child, eighteen years or even less. In short, kind souls intervened, relatives took a hand in the matter, and things came to a head.

Right after the wedding, the young wife began to complain that he wasn't acting right. Strange tales were told—may God not punish me for my words. He was spiteful all the time. Before he went to pray in the morning, she would ask him, "What do you want for lunch? Soup or borscht?" "Soup," he might say. So she'd make him soup. He'd return later and complain, "Didn't I tell you to make borscht?" She'd argue, "You said yourself that you wanted soup." And he would say, "So now I am a liar!" And before you could turn around he was already in a rage, and would grab a slice of bread and a head of garlic, and run back to the synagogue to eat there. She would run after him and shout, "I'll cook you a borscht! Don't shame me before people!" But he wouldn't even look back. In the synagogue young men sat studying. "What happened that you eat here?" they would ask him. "My wife chased me out," he would say. To make a long story short, he drove her to the grave with his tantrums. When people advised her to divorce him, he threatened to run off and abandon her. Once he did run away and was caught on the Yanov road, near the turnpike. The woman saw that she was lost, so she simply lay down in bed and died. "I am dying because of him," she said. "May it not be held against him." The entire town was aroused. Some butchers and young bloods wanted to teach him a lesson, because she was of their class, but the community would not allow it—after all, he was a well-to-do man. The dead are buried, as people say, and what the earth swallows is soon forgotten.

Some years passed and he didn't remarry. Perhaps he didn't want to, perhaps there was no suitable opportunity; anyway, he remained a widower. Women gloated over this. He became even stingier than before, and so unkempt that it was positively disgusting. He ate a bit of meat only on Saturday: scraps or derma. All week he ate dry food. He baked his own bread of corn and bran. He didn't buy wood. Instead, he went out at night with a sack, to pick up the chips near the bakery. He had two deep pockets and whatever he saw, he put into them: bones, bark, string, shards. He hid all these in his attic. He piled heaps of stuff as high as the roof. "Every little thing comes in handy," he used to say. He was a scholar in the bargain, and could quote Scripture on every occasion, though as a rule he talked little.

Everybody thought he would remain alone the rest of his life. Suddenly the terrible news spread that he was engaged to Reb Falik's Finkl. How should I describe Finkl to you! She was the most beautiful woman in town, and of the very best family. Her father, Reb Falik, was a magnate. It was said that he bound his books in silk. Whenever a bride was led to the *mikveh,* the musicians would stop before his windows and play a tune. Finkl was his only child. There had been seven and she alone survived. Reb Falik married her off to a rich young man from Brod, one in a million, learned and wise, a real aristocrat. I saw him only once as went by, with curly *peios* and a flowered caftan and fine shoes and white socks. Blood and milk. But it was fated otherwise. Right after the Seven Blessings he collapsed. Zishe the Healer was called, and he put leeches on him and bled him, but what can you do against fate? Reb Falik rushed a carriage to Lublin to bring a doctor, but Lublin is far, and before you knew it, it was all over with him. The entire town wept, as on Yom Kippur at Kol Nidre. The old rabbi—may he rest in peace—delivered the eulogy. I am only a sinful woman and I don't know much of learned matters, but I remember to this day what the rabbi said. Everybody memorized the eulogy. "He ordered black and got white . . ." the rabbi began. In the Gemorra this is about a man ordering pigeons, but the rabbi—peace be on him—made it mean wedding garments and burial shrouds. Even enemies mourned. We girls soaked our pillows at night. Finkl, delicate pampered Finkl, lost her speech in her great grief. Her mother was no longer living and Reb Falik, too, didn't survive long. Finkl inherited all his wealth, but what use was money? She refused to hear of anyone.

Suddenly we heard that Finkl was going to marry Pelte. The news came on a wintry Thursday evening, and a chill went through everyone. "The man is of the devil!" my mother cried out. "Such a one should be ridden out of town." We youngsters were petrified. I used to sleep by myself but that night I crawled into bed with my sister. I was in a fever. Later we learned that the match had been arranged by a man who was a bit of this and a bit of that and a general nuisance. It was said that he had borrowed a Gemorra from Pelte and found a hundred-ruble note among its pages. Pelte had a habit of hiding paper money in books. What one thing had to do with the other I didn't know—I was still a child then. But what difference does it make? Finkl consented. When God wants to punish someone He deprives him of reason. People ran to her, they tore their hair trying to dissuade her, but she wouldn't change her mind. The wedding was on the Sabbath after Shevuoth. The canopy was set up before the synagogue, as is the custom when a virgin gets married, but it seemed to all of us that we were attending a funeral. I was in one of the two rows of girls who stand holding candles in their hands. It was a summer evening and the air was still, but when the groom was led past, the flames began to flicker. I shook with fear. The fiddles started to play a wedding tune, but it was a wail, not music that they made. The bass viol mourned. I wouldn't wish anyone ever to hear the like. To tell you the truth, I'd rather not go on with the story. It might give you nightmares, and I myself don't feel up to it. What? You do want to hear more. Very well. You will have to take me home. Tonight I won't walk home alone.

II

Where was I? Yes, Finkl got married. She looked more like a corpse than a bride. The bridesmaids had to support her. Who knows? Maybe she had changed her mind. But was it her fault? It was all from Above. I once heard of a bride who ran away from under the canopy. But not Finkl. She would rather be burned alive than humiliate anyone.

Need I tell you how it all ended? Can't you guess yourselves? May all the enemies of Israel come to such an end. I must say that this time he didn't pull his usual tricks. On the contrary, he tried to comfort her. But he gave off a black melancholy. She tried to lose herself in household duties. And young women came to visit her. There was a constant going back and forth, as with a woman in confinement. They told stories, they knitted, they sewed and asked riddles, anything to distract Finkl. Some even began to hint that perhaps it wasn't such an impossible match. He was rich, and a scholar too. Mightn't he become human living with her? It was reckoned that Finkl would become pregnant and have a baby and get used to her lot. Aren't there many unsuitable marriages in the world! But it wasn't fated that way. Finkl miscarried and had a hemorrhage. They had to bring a doctor from Zamoscz. He advised her to keep herself occupied. She did not become pregnant again, and then her troubles began. He tormented her, everybody knew that. But when she was asked: "What is he doing to you?" she would only say, "Nothing." "If he does nothing to you, why do you have such brown and blue rings around your eyes? And why do you go about like a lost soul?" But she would only say: "I don't know why myself."

How long did this go on? Longer than anyone expected. We all thought she wouldn't last more than a year, but she suffered for three and a half years. She faded like a light. Relatives tried to send her to the hot baths, but she refused to go. Things reached such a pass that people began to pray for her end. One mustn't say it, but death is preferable to such a life. She, too, cursed herself. Before she died, she sent for the rabbi to have him write her will. She probably wanted to leave her wealth for charitable purposes. What else? Leave it to her murderer? But again fate intervened. Some girl suddenly cried "Fire!" and everyone ran to look after his own things. It turned out that there had been no fire. "Why did you cry 'fire'?" the girl was asked. And she explained that it wasn't she who had shouted, but that something inside her had cried out. Meanwhile Finkl died, and Pelte inherited her property. Now he was the richest man in town, but he haggled over the cost of the grave till he got it for half-price.

Until then he hadn't been called Wife Killer. A man is twice widowed—such things happen. But after this he was always called Pelte the Wife Killer. *Cheder* boys pointed at him: "Here comes the Wife Killer." After the Seven Days of Mourning, the rabbi sent for him. "Reb Pelte," he said, "you are now the richest man in Turbin. Half the stores in the market place belong to you. With God's help you have become great. It is time you changed your ways. How long will you live apart from everyone else?" But no words impressed him. Talk of one thing to him, and he answers something entirely different; or he bites his lips and says nothing—you might as well talk to the wall. When the rabbi saw that it was a waste of time, he let him go.

For a time he was silent. He began to bake his own bread again, and to collect chips and cones and dung for fuel. He was shunned like the plague. He seldom came to the synagogue. Everybody was glad not to see him. On Thursdays he went around with his book to collect debts or interest. He had everything written down and never forgot a thing. If a storekeeper said that he hadn't the money to pay him and asked him to come some other time, he wouldn't go but stayed right there, staring with his bulging eyes, till the storekeeper got tired of it and gave him his last cent. The rest of the week he hid away somewhere in his kitchen. At least ten years passed this way, perhaps eleven; I don't remember any more. He must have been in his late fifties, or perhaps in his sixties. Nobody tried to arrange a match for him.

And then something happened, and this is what I want to tell you about. As I live, one could write a book about it; but I will make it short. In Turbin there lived a woman who was called Zlateh the Bitch. Some called her Zlateh the Cossack. From her nicknames you can guess for yourselves what sort of a person she was. It is not right to gossip about the dead, but the truth must be told—she was the lowest and meanest sort. She was a fishwife and her husband had been a fisherman. It's shameful to tell what she did in her youth. She was a slut—everyone knew that. She had a bastard somewhere. Her husband used to work in the poorhouse. There he beat and robbed the sick. How he suddenly got to be a fisherman I don't know, but that makes no difference. Fridays they used to stand in the market place with a basket of fish and curse everyone, whether they bought or not. Curses tumbled from her mouth as from a torn sack. If someone complained that she cheated on the weight, she would grab a fish by the tail and strike out. She tore the wig from the head of more than one woman. Once she was accused of stealing, so she went to the rabbi and falsely swore before black candles and the board on which the dead are washed that she was innocent. Her husband was named Eber, a strange name; he came from far off in Poland. He died and she became a widow. She was so wicked that all through the funeral she howled, "Eber, don't forget to take along all troubles." After the Seven Days of Mourning, she again sold fish in the market place. Since she was a shrew and abused everyone, people taunted her. One woman said to her, "Aren't you going to remarry, Zlateh?" And she answered, "Why not? I'm still a tasty dish." Yet she was already an old hag. "Whom will you marry, Zlateh?" people asked her, and she thought a moment and said, "Pelte."

The women thought she was joking and they laughed. But it was no joke, as you will soon hear.

III

One woman said to her, "But he is a Wife Killer!" And Zlateh answered, "If he is a Wife Killer, I am a worse Husband Killer. Eber wasn't my first husband." Who could tell how many she had before him? She wasn't a native of Turbin—the devil brought her from somewhere on the other side of the Vistula. Nobody paid any attention to what she said, but hardly a week passed before everybody heard that Zlateh hadn't been talking at random. Nobody knew whether she sent a matchmaker or arranged the match herself, but the marriage was going through. The whole town laughed—a fitting pair, falsehood and wickedness. Everybody said the same, "If Finkl were alive and saw who was inheriting her place, she would die of grief." Tailors' apprentices and seamstresses at once began to wager who would outlast whom. The apprentices said that nobody was a match for Pelte the Wife Killer, and the seamstresses argued that Zlateh was younger by some years and that not even Pelte had a chance once she opened her mouth. Anyway, the wedding took place. I wasn't there. You know that when a widower takes a widow, there's little fuss. But others who were there had lots of fun. The bride was all decked out. On Saturday she came to the women's gallery in the synagogue wearing a hat with a feather. She couldn't read. That Saturday I happened to take a new bride to the synagogue, and Zlateh stood right near me. She took Finkl's seat. She talked and jabbered all the time so that I didn't know what to do with myself for shame. And do you know what she said? She abused her husband. "He won't last long with me around," she said; just like that. A bitch—no doubt about it.

For some time nobody talked about them. After all, a whole town can't always bother with such scum. Then suddenly there was an outcry again. Zlateh had hired a maid, a little woman who had been abandoned by her husband. The maid started telling horrible stories. Pelte and Zlateh were at war—not just they, that is, but their stars. All sorts of things happened. Once Zlateh stood in the middle of the room and the chandelier fell down; it missed her by an inch. "The Wife Killer is at his tricks again," she said. "I'll show him something." The next day Pelte was walking in the market place; he slipped and fell into a ditch and nearly broke his neck. Every day something new happened. One time the soot in the chimney caught fire, and the entire house almost burned down; another time the cornice of the wardrobe fell and barely missed Pelte's skull. Everybody could see plainly that one or the other would have to go. It is written somewhere that every man is followed by devils—a thousand on the left and ten thousand on the right. We had a *malamed* in town, a certain Reb Itche the Slaughtered—that's what he was called—a very fine man who knew all about "those" matters. He said that this was a case of war between "them." At first things were fairly quiet; that is, people talked, but the unfortunate couple didn't say a thing. But in the end, Zlateh came running to the rabbi all atremble. "Rabbi," she shouted, "I can't stand it any more. Just think of it: I prepared dough in a trough and covered it with a pillow. I wanted to get up early to bake bread. In the middle of the night I see—the dough is on my bed. It's his work, Rabbi. He's made up his mind to finish me." At that time Reb Eisele Teumim, a true saint, was rabbi in the town. He couldn't believe his own ears. "Why should a man play such tricks?" he asked. "Why; You tell me why!" she answered. "Rabbi, send for him, let him tell it himself." The *shames* was sent and he brought Pelte. Naturally, he denied everything. "She is giving me a bad name," he cried. "She wants to get rid of me and get my money. She cast a spell to make water collect in the cellar. I went down there to get a piece of rope and was nearly drowned. Besides, she brought on a plague of mice." Pelte declared on oath that at night Zlateh whistled in bed, and that as soon as she started whistling there was a squeaking and a rushing of mice from all the holes. He pointed to a scar over his eyebrow and said that a mouse had bitten him there. When the rabbi realized whom he had to deal with, he said, "Take my advice and get divorced. It will be better for both of you." "The rabbi is right," Zlateh said. "I am willing, this very minute, but let him give me a settlement of half the property." "I won't give you the price of a pinch of snuff!" Pelte shouted. "What's more, you will pay me a fine." He grabbed his cane and wanted to strike her. He was held back with difficulty. When the rabbi saw that he would get nowhere in this case he said, "Go your ways and leave me to my studies." So they went away.

From that time on the town had no rest. It was frightening to pass by their house. The shutters were always closed, even in the day time. Zlateh stopped selling fish, and all they did was fight. Zlateh was a giant of a woman. She used to go to the landowners' ponds and help spread the nets. She would get up in the middle of the night in winter, and in the worst frosts she never used a fire-pot. "The devil won't take me," she'd say. "I'm never cold." And now she suddenly aged. Her face blackened and was wrinkled like that of a woman of seventy. She started coming to strangers' houses to ask for advice. Once she came to my mother—peace be on her—and begged to be allowed to stay overnight. My mother looked at her as one demented. "What happened?" she asked. "I'm afraid of him," Zlateh said. "He wants to get rid of me. He makes winds in the house." She said that though the windows were sealed outside with clay and inside with straw, strong winds blew in her bedroom. She also swore that her bed would rise beneath her, and that Pelte spent half the nights in the outhouse—if you'll pardon the expression. "What does he do there so long?" my mother asked. "He has a mistress there," Zlateh said. I happened to be in the alcove and heard all this.

Pelte must have had dealings with the Unclean Ones. My mother shuddered. "Listen to me, Zlateh," she said, "give him the 'dozen lines' and run for your life. If they were to give me my weight in gold, I wouldn't live under the same roof with anyone like that." But a Cossack never changes. "He won't get rid of me just like that," Zlateh said. "Let him give me a settlement." In the end, my mother made up a bed for her on the bench. We didn't shut an eye that night. Before dawn she got up and left. Mother couldn't fall asleep again and lit a taper in the kitchen. "You know," she said to me, "I have a feeling that she won't get out of his hands alive. Well, it won't be a big loss." But Zlateh wasn't Finkl. She didn't give up so easily, as you will soon hear.

IV

What did she do? I don't know. People told all sorts of stories, but you can't believe everything. We had an old peasant woman in town, Cunegunde. She must have been a hundred years old, maybe older. Everybody knew that she was a witch. Her whole face was covered with warts, and she walked almost on all fours. Her hut was at the end of town, on the sand, and it was full of all kinds of animals: rabbits and guinea pigs, cats and dogs, and all kinds of vermin. Birds flew in and out of the windows. The place stank. But Zlateh became a frequent visitor and spent whole days there. The woman knew how to pour wax. If a peasant was sick, he would come to her, and she'd pour molten wax which formed all sorts of strange figures and showed what the sickness came from—though it did little good.

As I was saying, people in town said this Cunegunde taught Zlateh a charm. Anyway, Pelte became a changed man, soft as butter. She wanted him to transfer the house to her name, so he hired a team of horses and went to town to register the transfer. Then she started meddling in his stores. Now it was she who went about on Thursdays with the interest and rent book. She asked for increases right away. The storekeepers cried that they were losing their shirts, so she said, "In that case you can go begging." A meeting was held, and Pelte was called. He was so weak that he could barely walk. He was completely deaf. "There is nothing I can do," he said. "Everything belongs to her. If she wants to, she can drive me out of the house." She would have, too, but he hadn't transferred everything to her yet. He was still bargaining with her. Neighbors said that she was starving him. He used to go into houses and beg for a piece of bread. His hands shook. Everybody saw that Zlateh was having her way. Some were glad—he was being punished for Finkl. Others argued that Zlateh would ruin the town. It's not a small matter when so much property gets into the hands of such a beast. She began to build and to dig. She brought craftsmen from Yanov and they started measuring the streets. She put on a wig, with silver combs, and she carried a purse and a parasol, like a real aristocrat. She burst into homes early in the morning, before the beds were made, and she pounded on tables and shouted, "I'll throw you out with your junk. I'll have you locked up in the Yanov jail! I'll make beggars out of you!" Poor people tried to fawn on her, but she wouldn't even listen. Then people realized that it isn't wise to wish for a new king.

One afternoon the door of the poorhouse opened, and Pelte came in, dressed like a beggar. The man in charge of the poorhouse turned pale as a ghost. "Reb Pelte," he exclaimed, "what are you doing here?" "I came to stay here," Pelte answered. "My wife has thrown me out." To make a long story short, Pelte had transferred all his possessions to Zlateh, everything, down to the last thread, and then she chased him out. "But how does one do a thing like that?" he was asked. "Don't even ask," he answered. "She fixed me! I barely came out alive." The poorhouse was in an uproar. Some cursed Pelte. "As if the rich don't have enough as it is—now they come to eat the food of the poor," they cried. Others pretended sympathy. In short, Pelte was given a bundle of straw to spread in the corner, and he lay down. The whole town came running to see the sight. I, too, was curious and ran to see. He sat on the floor like a mourner and stared at everybody with his bulging eyes. People asked him, "Why do you sit here, Reb Pelte, what happened to all your power?" At first he didn't answer at all, as if they weren't talking to him, and later he said, "She isn't finished with me yet." "What will you do to her?" the beggars jeered. They made a laughing-stock of him. But don't jump at conclusions. You know the old saying: He laughs best who laughs last.

For several weeks Zlateh was a regular demon. She turned the whole town upside down. Right in the middle of the market place, near the stores, she had a pit dug and hired men to mix lime. Logs were brought and heaps of brick were piled up so that no one could pass. Roofs were torn down and a notary came from Yanov to make a list of all her tenants' belongings. Zlateh bought a carriage and a team of fiery horses, and she went riding every afternoon. She started wearing shoes with pointed tips and let her hair grow. She also began to pal around with the *goyim* of the Christian streets. She bought two vicious dogs, regular killers, so that it was dangerous to pass by her house. She stopped selling fish. What did she need it for? But out of habit, she had to have fish around, so she filled bathtubs in her house and stocked them with carp and pike. She even kept a big tub full of *treif* fish, and lobsters and frogs and eels. It was rumored in town that she would become an apostate any day. Some said that on Pesach the priest had come to her house to sprinkle it with holy water. People feared that she might inform on the community—someone like that is capable of anything.

Suddenly, she came running to the rabbi. "Rabbi," she said, "send for Pelte. I want a divorce." "What do you want a divorce for?" the rabbi asked her. "Do you want to remarry?" "I don't know," she said. "Maybe yes and maybe no. But I don't want to be the wife of a Wife Killer. I'm willing to compensate him with something." The rabbi sent for Pelte and he came crawling. Everybody in town stood outside the rabbi's house. Poor Pelte, he consented to everything. His hands shook as in a fever. Reb Moishe the Scribe sat down to write out the divorce. I remember him as if this happened yesterday. He was a small man and had a tic. He ruled the paper with his penknife, and then he wiped the goose quill on his skull cap. The witnesses were instructed how to sign divorce. My husband, peace be on him, was one of the witnesses because he wrote a good hand. Zlateh sat comfortably on a chair and sucked candy. And, yes, I forgot to mention it, she put down two hundred rubles. Pelte recognized them—he had had a habit of marking his money. The rabbi ordered silence, but Zlateh boasted to the women that she was considering marrying a "possessor," but that "as long as the Wife Killer is my husband, I am not sure of staying alive." When she said this she laughed so that everybody outside heard her.

When everything was ready, the rabbi began questioning the couple. I still remember his words. "Hear me, Paltiel, son of Schneour Zalman"—that was the name by which Pelte was called up to the reading of the Torah—"do you want to divorce your wife?" He said something more, from the *Gemorra,* but I can't say it as he did. "Say 'yes,' " he ordered Pelte. "Say 'yes' once, not twice." Pelte said "yes." We could hardly hear him. "Hear me, Zlateh Golde, daughter of Yehuda Treitel, do you want to divorce your husband, Paltiel?" "Yes!" Zlateh shouted, and as she said this she swayed and fell to the floor in a faint. I saw this myself, and I tell you the truth; I felt my brain bursting in my head. I thought I'd collapse too. There was a great outcry and commotion. Everybody rushed to revive her. They poured water on her and stuck pins into her and rubbed her with vinegar and pulled her hair. Azriel the Healer came running and cupped her then and there. She still breathed, but it wasn't the same Zlateh. May God preserve us. Her mouth was twisted to one side and the spittle ran out of it; her eyes were rolled up and her nose was white, like that of a corpse. The women who stood near, heard her mumble, "The Wife Killer! He overcame me!" These were her last words.

At the funeral there was almost a riot. Now Pelte was again on his high horse. Beside his own property he now also had her wealth. Her jewelry alone was worth a fortune. The burial society wanted a big sum, but Pelte wouldn't budge. They shouted, they warned, they abused him. They threatened him with excommunication. Might as well talk to the wall! "I won't give a penny, let her rot," he said. They would have left her lying around, too, but it was summertime and there was a heat wave just then, and people feared an epidemic. In short, some women performed the rites—what other choice was there? The pall-bearers refused to carry her, so a wagon was hired. She was buried right near the fence, among the stillbirths. All the same, Pelte said *kaddish* after her—this he did.

From then on the Wife Killer remained alone. People were so afraid of him, they avoided passing by his house. Mothers of pregnant young women did not allow his name to be mentioned, unless they first put on two aprons. *Cheder* boys fingered their fringes before pronouncing his name. And nothing came of all the construction and remodeling. The bricks were carried off, the lime was stolen. The carriage and its team of horses disappeared—he must have sold them. The water in the bathtubs dried up, and the fish died. There was a cage with a parrot in the house. It squawked, "I'm hungry"—it could talk Yiddish—until at last it starved to death. Pelte had the shutters nailed tight and never opened them again. He didn't even go out to collect the pennies from the storekeepers. All day he lay on his bench and snored, or simply dozed. At night he'd go out to collect chips. Once each week, they sent him two loaves of bread from the bakery, and the baker's wife would buy him some onions, garlic, radishes and, on occasion, a piece of dry cheese. He never ate meat. He never came to the synagogue on Saturdays. There was no broom in his house and the dirt gathered in heaps. Mice ran about even during the day and spider webs hung from the rafters. The roof leaked and wasn't repaired. The walls rotted and caved in. Every few weeks it was rumored that things were not well with the Wife Killer, that he was sick, or dying. The burial society rubbed its hands in anticipation. But nothing happened. He outlived everyone. He lived so long that people in Turbin began to hint that he might live forever. Why not? Maybe he had some special kind of blessing, or the Angel of Death forgot him. Anything can happen.

Rest assured that he was not forgotten by the Angel of Death. But when that happened I was no longer in Turbin. He must have been a hundred years old, maybe older. After the funeral his entire house was turned upside down, but nothing of value was found. The chests had rotted away. The gold and silver were gone. The money and notes turned to dust the minute a breeze touched them. All the digging in the heaps of rubbish was wasted. The Wife Killer had outlived everything: his wives, his enemies, his money, his property, his generation. All that was left after him—may God forgive me for saying so—was a heap of dust.

Translated by Schlomo Katz

Appendix

FOUR PROFESSIONAL TOOLS

Power Ladder

	More Powerful	*Less Powerful*
Gender	Male	Female
Race	White	Black
Sexual Preference	Hetero	Gay
Economic Status	Rich	Poor
Class	Upper/Middle Class	Lower Classes
Religion	Protestant	Catholic/Jew
Law	Rich/White/Male	Poor/Black/Female
Education	College Grads	High Schoolers/Dropouts
Age	Young	Old/Infantile
Physical Ability	Strong/Athletic	Weak/Sedentary
Mental Stability	Sane Men	Hysterical Women
Household Status	Husbands/Fathers	Wives/Mothers/Children

Anger Iceberg Chart

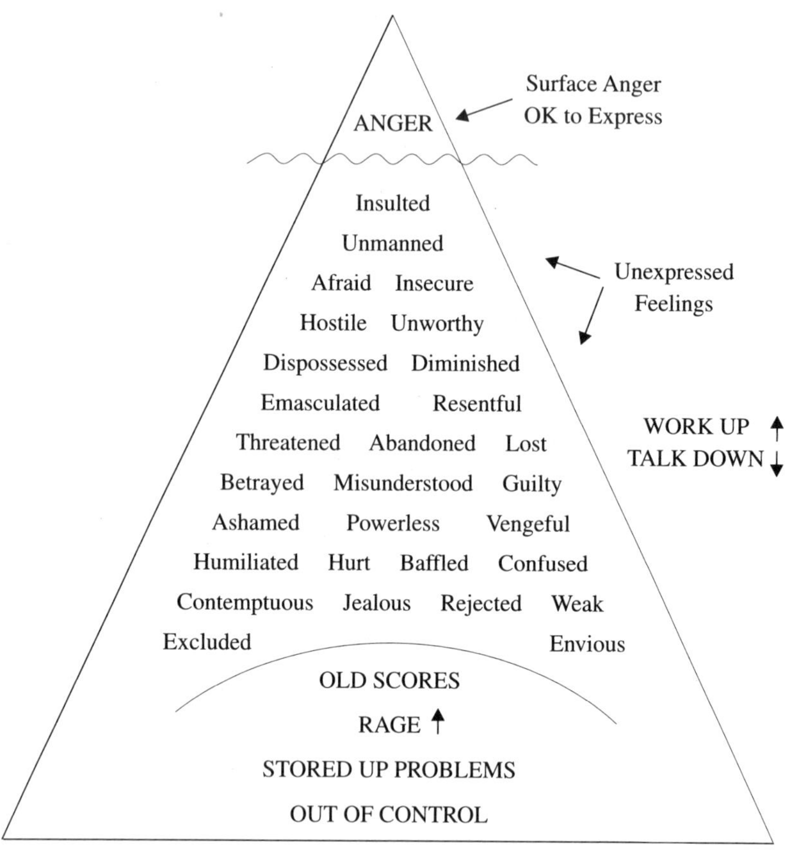

Cycle of Violence

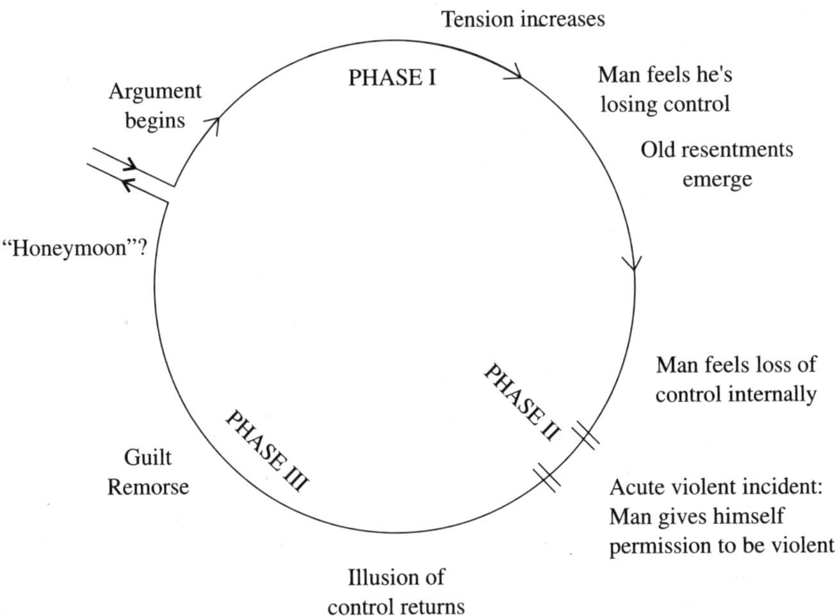

PHASE I: Tension building; woman feels increasingly helpless; man becomes increasingly abusive.

PHASE II: An acute violent incident; man attempts to gain control.

PHASE III: Guilt phase; loss of trust and intimacy; illusion that "good times" will return. They don't and cycle begins again.

Controlling Behavior Checklist

Physical Controls:

_____ hit, grabbed, kicked, choked, pushed, spit at, slapped, restrained, bit
_____ raped, physically forced sexual activity
_____ continued to touch your partner sexually against your partner's wishes
_____ threw things
_____ abused furniture
_____ physically intimidated (for example, stood in the doorway during arguments, made angry gestures)
_____ threatened violence (verbally or nonverbally)
_____ made uninvited visits or calls, followed your partner around, checked up on your partner
_____ didn't leave when asked to
_____ isolated your partner (for example, prevented your partner from seeing or talking to friends or relatives)

Psychological Controls:

_____ criticized (for example, called names, swore, mocked, used put-downs, ridiculed, accused, blamed)
_____ interrupted, changed topics, out-shouted, didn't listen, didn't respond, didn't respect what your partner said
_____ pressured (for example, expected your partner to take care of you emotionally when your partner didn't want to, or rushed your partner by being impatient, or guilt-tripped, sulked, made your partner feel sorry for you, made accusations)
_____ used money to manipulate, controlled other resources (such as the car)
_____ sexually coerced (for example, guilt-tripped your partner into sex, or badgered)
_____ was sexual with others without your partner's consent
_____ claimed "the truth," acted as "the authority," defined your partner's behavior
_____ emotionally withheld (didn't express feelings when appropriate, didn't give praise, attention, information, support, concern, validation, wasn't vulnerable)
_____ didn't take care of self (for example, didn't make own friends, or find own support systems, or care for own health), made your partner feel obligated to you
_____ used other forms of manipulation—please list:

A Domestic Violence Checklist

Ammerman, Robert T., and Michel Hersen, eds. *Assessment of Family Violence: A Clinical and Legal Sourcebook.* New York: Wiley and Sons, 1992.

Bowker, L. H. *Ending the Violence: A Guidebook Based on the Experiences of 1,000 Battered Women.* Holmes Beach, Fla.: Learning Publications, 1986.

Browne, A. *When Battered Women Kill.* New York: Macmillan/Free Press, 1987.

Cantrell, L. *Into the Light: A Guide for Battered Women.* Edmonds, Wash.: Charles Franklin Press, 1986.

Gelles, Richard J., and Murray A. Straus. *Intimate Violence: The Causes and Consequences of Abuse in the American Family.* New York: Touchstone, 1989.

Gondolf, E. W. *Men Who Batter: An Integrated Approach for Stopping Wife Abuse.* Holmes Beach, Fla.: Learning Publications, 1984.

Goolkasian, G. *Confronting Domestic Violence: A Guide for Criminal Justice Agencies.* Washington, D.C.: Office of Justice Programs, National Institute of Justice, 1986.

Hart, Chief William L., et al. *Attorney General's Task Force on Family Violence.* Washington, D.C.: U.S. Department of Justice, 1984.

Horton, A. L., and J. A. Williamson, eds. *Abuse and Religion: When Praying Isn't Enough.* Lexington, Mass.: D. C. Heath, 1988.

Lobel, Kerry, ed. *Naming the Violence: Speaking Out about Lesbian Battering.* Seattle: Seal Press, 1985.

Loseke, Donileen R. *The Battered Woman and Shelters: The Social Construction of Wife Abuse.* Albany: State University of New York Press, 1992.

Martin, D. *Battered Wives.* New York: Pocket Books, 1976.

NiCarthy, Ginny. *Getting Free: A Handbook for Women in Abusive Relationships.* Seattle: Seal Press, 1987.

———. *The Ones Who Got Away: Women Who Left Abusive Partners.* Seattle: Seal Press, 1987.

NiCarthy, Ginny, Karen Merriam, and Sandra Coffman, eds. *Talking It Out: A Guide to Groups for Abused Women.* Seattle: Seal Press, 1984.

Pagelow, M. D. *Family Violence.* New York: Praeger, 1984.

Scarf, Mimi. *Battered Jewish Wives: Case Studies in the Response to Rage.* Ontario: Mellen Press, 1987.

Schechter, S. *Women and Male Violence: The Visions and Struggles of the Battered Women's Movement.* Boston: South End Press, 1982.

Sonkin, D. J., ed. *Domestic Violence on Trial: Psychological and Legal Dimensions of Family Violence.* New York: Springer, 1987.

Sonkin, D., D. Martin, and L. Walker. *The Male Batterer: A Treatment Approach.* New York: Springer, 1985.

Thorne-Finch, Ron. *Ending the Silence: The Origins and Treatment of Male Violence against Women.* Toronto: University of Toronto Press, 1992.

Walker, Lenore E. *The Battered Woman.* New York: Harper and Row, 1979.

———. *The Battered Woman Syndrome.* New York: Springer, 1984.

White, E. *Chain Chain Change: For Black Women Dealing with Physical and Emotional Abuse.* Seattle: Seal Press, 1985.

Yllo, K., and M. Bograd, eds. *Feminist Perspectives on Wife Abuse.* Newbury Park, Calif.: Sage, 1988.

Zambrano, M. *Mejor Sola Que Mal Accompanada: Para La Mujer Golpeada/ For the Latina in an Abusive Relationship.* Seattle: Seal Press, 1985.

Works Cited

George Eliot

Christ, Carol. "Aggression and Providential Death in George Eliot's Fiction." *Novel: A Forum on Fiction* 9 (winter 1976): 130–40.

Eliot, George. *Adam Bede.* 1859. 2 Vols. New York: Collier, n.d.

———. *Amos Barton.* 1858. In *Scenes of Clerical Life,* ed. David Lodge. London: Penguin, 1973; 1985.

———. *Daniel Deronda.* 1874–1876. 3 Vols. New York: Colliers, n.d.

———. *Janet's Repentance.* 1858. In *Scenes of Clerical Life,* ed. Thomas A. Noble. Oxford: Clarendon Press, 1985.

———. *Middlemarch.* 1871–1872. Ed. Gordon S. Haight. Boston: Houghton Mifflin, 1956.

———. *The Mill on the Floss.* 1860. Ed. A. S. Byatt. Harmondsworth: Penguin, 1979.

———. *Mr. Gilfil's Love Story.* 1858. In *Scenes of Clerical Life,* ed. David Lodge. London: Penguin, 1973, 1985.

———. *Silas Marner.* 1861. Ed. Q. D. Leavis. Harmondsworth: Penguin, 1967.

Foucault, Michel. *The History of Sexuality.* Vol. 1. *An Introduction.* New York: Viking, 1980.

Gay, Peter. *The Bourgeois Experience: Victoria to Freud.* 2 Vols. New York: Oxford University Press, 1984, 1986.

Gilbert, Sandra, and Susan Gubar. "George Eliot as the Angel of Destruction." In *The Madwoman in the Attic.* New Haven and London: Yale University Press, 1979.

Haight, Gordon S. *George Eliot: A Biography.* New York: Oxford University Press, 1968.

Hurston, Zora Neale. *I Love Myself When I Am Laughing . . . And Then Again When I Am Looking Mean and Impressive: A Zora Neale Hurston Reader.* Ed. Alice Walker. New York: Feminist Press, 1979.

———. *Their Eyes Were Watching God.* New York: Harper and Row, 1937, 1965.

Kasl, Charlotte Davis. "The Twelve-Step Controversy." *Ms.,* November/December 1990, 30–31.

Lawrence, D. H. "Daughters of the Vicar." In *A Modern Lover and Other Stories,* ed. Julian Moynahan. New York: Ballantine Books, 1969.

———. "The Early Married Life of the Morels." In *Sons and Lovers: Text, Background, Criticism,* ed. Julian Moynahan. New York: Viking Critical Library, 1968.

Lodge, David. "Introduction." In *Scenes of Clerical Life,* by George Eliot. London: Penguin, 1973, 1985.

Morris, Virginia B. *Double Jeopardy: Women Who Kill in Victorian Fiction.* Lexington: University Press of Kentucky, 1990.

Noble, Thomas A. *George Eliot's* Scenes of Clerical Life. New Haven: Yale University Press, 1965.

D. H. Lawrence

Cushman, Keith. *D. H. Lawrence at Work: The Emergence of* The Prussian Officer *Stories.* Charlottesville: University Press of Virginia, 1978.

Harris, Janice Hubbard. *Edwardian Stories of Divorce.* New Brunswick: Rutgers University Press, 1996.

Lawrence, D. H. *The Captain's Doll.* 1921. In *Four Short Novels.* New York: Viking, 1965.

———. *The Fox.* In *Four Short Novels.* New York: Viking, 1965.

———. *Lady Chatterley's Lover.* 1928. New York: Grove Press, 1959.

———. *Phoenix: The Posthumous Papers of D. H. Lawrence.* Ed. Edward D. McDonald. New York: Viking, 1936.

———. *The Plumed Serpent (Quetzalcoatl).* 1926. Ed. L. D. Clark. Cambridge: Cambridge University Press, 1987.

———. *The Prussian Officer and Other Stories.* 1914. Harmondsworth: Penguin, 1990.

———. *Sons and Lovers.* 1913. New York: Viking, 1958.

———. *Studies in Classic American Literature.* Harmondsworth: Penguin, 1977.

———. "The Study of Thomas Hardy." In *Selected Literary Criticism,* ed. Anthony Beale. New York: Viking, 1956. Also in *Phoenix: The Posthumous Papers of D. H. Lawrence,* ed. Edward D. McDonald. New York: Viking, 1936.

———. *The White Peacock.* 1911. New York: Penguin, 1950.

———. "The White Stocking." In *Collected Stories,* intro. Craig Raine. New York: Ballantine Books, 1969.

———. "The Woman Who Rode Away." In *Collected Stories,* intro. Craig Raine. New York: Alfred Knopf, 1994.

Morrison, Toni. *Playing in the Dark: Whiteness and the Literary Imagination.* Cambridge: Harvard University Press, 1992.

Spilka, Mark. "Hemingway and Lawrence as Abusive Husbands." In *Renewing the Normative D. H. Lawrence: A Personal Progress.* Columbia and London: University of Missouri Press, 1992.

———. *The Love Ethic of D. H. Lawrence.* Bloomington: Indiana University Press, 1955.

———. "Repossessing *The Captain's Doll.*" In *Renewing the Normative D.H. Lawrence: A Personal Progress.* Columbia and London: University of Missouri Press, 1992.

Storch, Margaret. *Sons and Adversaries: Women in William Blake and D. H. Lawrence.* Knoxville: University of Tennessee Press, 1990.

Worthen, John. *D. H. Lawrence: The Early Years, 1885–1912.* Cambridge: Cambridge University Press, 1991.

James Joyce

Anonymous. "Part One: Ending Men's Violence." *Brother to Brother* Program Guide, Cranston, R.I., n.d.

Dickens, Charles. *David Copperfield.* 1849–1850. Ed. George Ford. Boston: Riverside, 1958.

———. *Oliver Twist.* 1837–1839. London: Oxford University Press, 1949.

———. *Pickwick Papers.* 1836–1837. London: Oxford University Press, 1947.

Ellmann, Richard. *James Joyce.* New York: Oxford University Press, 1959.

Joyce, James. "The Boarding House." In *Dubliners.* 1914. New York: Modern Library, 1954.

———. "Clay." In *Dubliners.* 1914. New York: Modern Library, 1954.

———. "Counterparts." In *Dubliners.* 1914. New York: Modern Library, 1954.

———. "The Dead." In *Dubliners.* 1914. New York: Modern Library 1954.

———. "Eveline." In *Dubliners.* 1914. New York: Modern Library, 1954.

———. "A Little Cloud." In *Dubliners.* 1914. New York: Modern Library, 1954.

———. *Letters of James Joyce.* Ed. Richard Ellmann. Vol. 2. New York: Viking, 1966.

———. "A Mother." In *Dubliners.* 1914. New York: Modern Library, 1954.

———. "A Painful Case." In *Dubliners.* 1914. New York: Modern Library, 1954.

———. *A Portrait of the Artist as a Young Man.* 1916. New York: Viking, 1964.

———. *Ulysses.* 1922. New York: Modern Library, 1961.

Scholes, Robert, and A. Walton Litz, eds. *Dubliners: Text, Criticism, and Notes.* New York: Viking, 1969.

Ernest Hemingway

Fetterley, Judith. "*A Farewell to Arms:* Hemingway's Resentful Cryptogram." In *The Resisting Reader: A Feminist Approach to American Fiction.* Bloomington: Indiana University Press, 1981.

Hemingway, Ernest. *Death in the Afternoon.* 1932. New York: Scribner's, 1960.

———. *For Whom the Bell Tolls.* 1940. New York: Scribner's, 1968

———. *The Garden of Eden.* New York: Scribner's, 1986

———. *Green Hills of Africa.* 1935. New York: Scribner's, 1963.

———. *Selected Letters, 1917–1961.* Ed. Carlos Baker. New York: Scribner's, 1981.

———. "The Snows of Kilimanjaro." In *The Short Stories of Ernest Hemingway.* New York: Scribner's, 1966.

———. *The Sun Also Rises.* 1926. New York: Scribner's, 1954.

———. *To Have and Have Not.* 1937. New York: Scribner's, 1962.

Joyce, James. "Counterparts." *Dubliners.* 1914. New York: Modern Library, 1954.

Spilka, Mark. "Hemingway and Lawrence as Abusive Husbands." In *Renewing the Normative D. H. Lawrence: A Personal Progress.* Columbia and London: University of Missouri Press, 1992.

———. *Hemingway's Quarrel with Androgyny.* Lincoln: University of Nebraska Press, 1990.

Wilson, Edmund. "Hemingway: Gauge of Morale." In *Eight Essays.* New York: Doubleday Anchor,1954.

John Steinbeck

Spilka, Mark. "Of George and Lennie and Curley's Wife: Sweet Violence in Steinbeck's Eden." In *The Short Novels of John Steinbeck: Critical Essays with a Checklist to Steinbeck Criticism,* ed. Jackson J. Benson. Durham and London: Duke University Press, 1990.

Steinbeck, John. *East of Eden.* New York: Viking, 1952.

———. *The Grapes of Wrath.* New York: Viking, 1939.

———. *Journal of a Novel: The East of Eden Letters.* New York: Viking, 1969.

———. "The Murder." 1934. In *The Long Valley.* New York: Viking, 1948.

———. *Of Mice and Men.* New York: Covici, Friede, 1937.

———. *The Pearl.* New York: Viking, 1947.

———. "The Red Pony." In *The Long Valley.* New York: Viking, 1948.

———. *Steinbeck: A Life in Letters.* Ed. Elaine Steinbeck and Robert Wilson. New York: Viking, 1975.

———. *Tortilla Flat.* New York: Bantam, 1970.

Ann Petry

Anderson, Sherwood. *Winesburg, Ohio.* New York: B. W. Huebsch, 1919.

Cahill, Susan, ed. *Women and Fiction: Short Stories by and about Women.* New York: Mentor, 1975.

Dunn, Katherine. "Truth Abuse." In "Correspondence," *New Republic,* August 1, 1994.

Ervin, Hazel Arnett. *Ann Petry: A Bio-Bibliography.* New York: G. K. Hall, 1993.

Foley, Martha, ed. *Best American Short Stories.* Boston: Houghton Mifflin, 1946.

Hurston, Zora Neale. *Their Eyes Were Watching God.* New York: Harper and Row, 1937, 1965.

Joyce, James. *Dubliners.* New York: Modern Library, 1954.

McKay, Nellie Y. "Introduction." In *The Narrows,* by Ann Petry. Boston: Beacon Press, 1988.

Morrison, Toni. *The Bluest Eye.* New York: Washington Square Press, 1970.

———. *Jazz.* New York: Alfred Knopf, 1992.

Petry, Ann. "In Darkness and Confusion." in *Miss Muriel and Other Stories.* Boston: Beacon Press, 1971.

———. "Like a Winding Sheet." In *Miss Muriel and Other Stories.* Boston: Beacon Press, 1971.

———. *The Narrows.* Boston: Houghton Mifflin, 1953.

———. "The Necessary Knocking on the Door." In *Miss Muriel and Other Stories.* Boston: Beacon Press, 1971.

———. "Olaf and His Girlfriend." In *Miss Muriel and Other Stories.* Boston: Beacon Press, 1971.

———. *The Street.* Boston: Houghton Mifflin, 1946.

———. "The Witness." In *Miss Muriel and Other Stories.* Boston: Beacon Press, 1971.

Walker, Alice. *The Color Purple.* New York: Harcourt Brace Jovanovich, 1982.

West, Nathanael. *The Day of the Locust.* New York: Random House, 1939.

Wright, Richard. *Native Son.* New York: Harper, 1940.

John Cheever

Cheever, John. *Bullet Park.* New York: Alfred Knopf, 1969.

———. "The Enormous Radio." In *The Stories of John Cheever.* New York: Alfred Knopf, 1979.

———. *Falconer.* New York: Alfred Knopf, 1977.

———. "The Hartleys." In *The Stories of John Cheever.* New York: Alfred Knopf, 1979.

———. "O Youth and Beauty." In *The Stories of John Cheever.* New York: Alfred Knopf, 1979.

———. "The Pot of Gold." In *The Stories of John Cheever.* New York: Alfred Knopf, 1979.

———. "The Swimmer." In *The Stories of John Cheever.* New York: Alfred Knopf, 1979.

———. "Torch Song." In *The Stories of John Cheever.* New York: Alfred Knopf, 1979.

———. *The Wapshot Chronicle.* New York: Harper, 1957.

Cheever, Susan. *Home before Dark.* Boston: Houghton Mifflin, 1984.

Eliot, George. *Janet's Repentance.* 1858. In *Scenes of Clerical Life,* ed. David Lodge. London: Penguin, 1973, 1985.

Hemingway, Ernest. *The Sun Also Rises.* New York: Scribner's, 1954.

Joyce, James. "Araby." In *Dubliners.* 1914. New York: Modern Library, 1954.

Lawrence, D. H. *Sons and Lovers.* 1913. New York: Viking, 1958.

Isaac Bashevis Singer

Alexander, Edward. *Isaac Bashevis Singer: A Study of the Short Fiction.* Boston: Twayne, 1990.

Buchen, Irving H. *Isaac Bashevis Singer and the Eternal Past.* New York and London: New York University Press, 1968.

Cheever, John. "Torch Song." In *The Stories of John Cheever.* New York: Alfred Knopf, 1979.

Dickens, Charles. *David Copperfield* (1849–1850).

———. *The Old Curiosity Shop* (1841).

Dostoyevsky, Fyodor. *The Brothers Karamazov* (1879–1880).

———. *Notes from Underground* (1864).

Farrell, Grace, ed. *Isaac Bashevis Singer: Conversations.* Jackson and London: University Press of Mississippi, 1992.

Lawrence, D. H. *Lady Chatterley's Lover* (1928).

Milton, John. *Paradise Lost.* (1667).

Potok, Chaim. *My Name Is Asher Lev.* New York: Fawcett Crest, 1972.

Schopenhauer, Arthur. *The World as Will and Idea* (1819).

Schulz, Max F. "The Family Chronicle as Paradigm of History: *The Brothers Ashkenazi* and *The Family Moskat.*" In *The Achievement of Isaac Bashevis Singer,* ed. Marcia Allentuck. Carbondale: Southern Illinois University Press, 1969.

Singer, Isaac Bashevis. *The Family Moskat.* 1950. New York: Bantam, 1967.

———. *A Friend of Kafka and Other Stories.* New York: Farrar, Straus and Giroux, 1979.

———. "From the Diary of One Not Born." In *Gimpel the Fool and Other Stories.* New York: Noonday Press, 1957.

———. "The Gentleman from Cracow." In *Gimpel the Fool and Other Stories.* New York: Noonday Press, 1957.

———. *Gimpel the Fool and Other Stories.* New York: Noonday Press, 1957.

———. "The Little Shoemakers." In *Gimpel the Fool and Other Stories.* New York: Noonday Press, 1957.

———. "The Mirror." In *Gimpel the Fool and Other Stories.* New York: Noonday Press, 1957.

———. "The New Year Party." In *Passions and Other Stories.* New York: Farrar, Straus and Giroux, 1975.

———. *Satan in Goray.* 1933. New York: Noonday Press, 1955.

———. "The Shadow of a Crib." In *The Spinoza of Market Street.* New York: Noonday Press, 1962.

———. "Something Is There." In *A Friend of Kafka and Other Stories.* New York: Noonday Press, 1970.

———. *The Spinoza of Market Street.* New York: Noonday Press, 1962.

———. "The Unseen." In *Gimpel the Fool and Other Stories.* New York: Noonday Press, 1957.

———. "The Wife-Killer: A Folk Tale." In *Gimpel the Fool and Other Stories.* New York: Noonday Press, 1957.

———. "The Witch." In *Passions and Other Stories.* New York: Noonday Press, 1975.

———. "Yentl the Yeshiva Boy." *Commentary* 34 (September 1962): 213–14.

———. "Zeitl and Rickel." In *The Seance and Other Stories.* New York: Farrar, Straus and Giroux, 1968.

Singer, Israel Joshua. *Yoshe Kalb.* 1933. New York: Lancer Books, 1972.

Steinbeck, John. *Tortilla Flat.* New York: Bantam, 1970.

Wharton, Edith. *Ethan Frome* (1911).

Zamir, Israel. *Journey to My Father, Isaac Bashevis Singer.* Trans. Barbara Harshav. New York: Arcade Publishing, 1995.

Index